The JFK Assassination Facts They Don't Want You To Know

Philippe J. Cassard

The JFK Assassination Facts They Don't Want You To Know

By Philippe J. Cassard

Copyright © 2019 by Philippe J. Cassard

All rights reserved. No part of this book may be used or reproduced in any manner whatsoever without the prior written permission from the publisher, except in the case of brief quotations and excerpts for reviews purposes.

ISBN: 9781092558891

Independently published

Cover page: photo taken by author of Dealey Plaza, Dallas TX. In the foreground, a memorial plaque with excerpt from speech John F. Kennedy would have delivered at the Dallas Trade Mart on November 22, 1963, had he not been assassinated.

"Truth is a tyrant – the only tyrant to whom we can give our allegiance. The service of truth is a matter of heroism "

John F. Kennedy

Sapiens nihil affirmat quod non probet
The wise man asserts nothing that he cannot prove

Latin proverb

CONTENTS

Preface

1. John Kennedy's Political Legacy..................................8
2. The "Lone Nuts" against the "Conspiracy Nuts".........34
3. The Coup d'état and the Cover-up..............................45
4. The Witnesses' Reactions on Dealey Plaza.................93
5. The Fourth Estate under control................................113
6. The Enigmatic Lee Harvey Oswald...........................164
7. The Murky Role of the CIA, the FBI and the anti-Castro...207
8. The Vindictive Mafia...240
9. Jack Ruby's Contract...259
10. The Ballistic Evidence...273
11. The Medical Evidence..298
12. The Photographic Evidence.......................................311
13. The Acoustic Evidence...321
14. Inconvenient Witnesses. Mysterious Disappearances..328
15. Can the Media's Apathy be justified?........................345
16. Yes, we do want to know!..357

Summary Table: Evidence of a Plot to kill JFK and of a Cover-Up.. 372

Main Actors..378

Timeline..383

Appreciations...389

Sources and References..390

Preface

Every year more than four million visitors from all over the world flock to see the grave, high up in Arlington Cemetery, Virginia, of the 35th President of the United States of America, John Fitzgerald Kennedy, murdered in Dallas, Texas, on November 22, 1963.

Who are these visitors? They are not only simply curious tourists but also parents wishing to pass on the memory to the new generation and those who lived through that fateful day. They come to remember the life and the death of the President before the eternal flame, the one his widow, Jackie Kennedy, wanted for her husband's tomb. The flame of the Unknown Soldier's tomb at the Arc de Triomphe had inspired her during the visit of the presidential couple to Paris in 1961 and she decided to use it as a model.

Two thousand miles away from Arlington, in Fort Worth, Texas, a tomb is, on the contrary, forgotten by history. It is the resting place of Lee Harvey Oswald, shot two days after the assassination of the President and allegedly charged with the double murder of John Kennedy and of a local police officer, less than one hour apart. For those who support the official version of a lone madman's act, Oswald rests in infamy. Wasn't he for them just a cold and deranged communist who rejected authority?

Jack Ruby, the enigmatic assassin of Lee Harvey Oswald, rests in an equally ignored grave at the Westlawn cemetery in Norridge, Illinois. He succumbed to a pulmonary embolism following a fast developing cancer, less than four years after the Dallas event, without ever revealing the truth about a conspiracy in which he himself felt threatened.

For half a century, the disappearance of these three men continues to raise countless questions. Too many enigmas remain unsolved. Ambiguities and lack of tangible evidence blurred the lines of investigation and fueled controversy.

What would have been the historical significance of President Kennedy's second term in office, had he not been so cruelly deprived of it? Historians agree that his thousand days of presidency, tragically interrupted in Dallas, when his re-election was practically secured in 1964, were marked by remarkable accomplishments in a period of worldwide perils with many twists and turns. If John Kennedy who kept us away from a nuclear annihilation had remained in the presidential office longer, would the world have enjoyed a period of lasting peace and security without enduring the tragic Vietnam War launched by the succeeding president? Close to the end of his life, his speeches with strong messages of peace are left to us to think so. Convinced that a better world was possible, his exhortation to work relentlessly to achieve this goal was reassuring. However, all his efforts and hopes were aborted by the bullets of assassins. The plural of the word "assassin" is deliberately chosen here: who really still believes that Lee Harvey Oswald acted alone, without an accomplice, to commit the crime?

Living half of my time in the United States, I have had the opportunity to make various trips to Dallas, to participate in many conferences where I met experts, private investigators, writers, lawyers, journalists and American historians who are constantly investigating the facts surrounding this political assassination. Thanks to this geographical proximity, stimulated by the answers that this community of experts has given to my obsessional questions and after reading many books and articles of American authors, I decided to write this book. My goal is to condense not only the aberrations and the voluntary concealment of the facts around this historical drama but also the evidence of a coup d'état.

What more could be written today about John Kennedy's assassination? Who could possibly still be interested in a new book on the case? Has not everything been said and written on the subject already? The New York Times estimates that 40,000 books have been published on JFK. According to the ABC television channel, 2000 books and thousands of articles have been written on the tragedy of his death itself and about a hundred, in 2013, half a century after his passing, thus making it a real industry! For those who support the official version of the lone gunman, the case is closed. They argue that those in search of a different story are only driven by voyeurism and are obsessed by conspiracy. Those who seek another version are chastised by the anti-conspiracy community who keeps throwing them the invective: "Move on, there is nothing more to see!"

Is it important to know, even today, who really killed President Kennedy? This question certainly matters. However, it is much easier to ignore the facts of this crime and to reject the truth outright for fear of being assimilated with those "enlightened" ones who support the conspiracy theory. To elude this question reveals a persistent indifference and an apathy for History.

There is indisputably a growing number of conspiracy theorists (or conspiracy realists as they should be called) who deplore this flagrant denial of truth that is sustained today by the media in the United States. More than half a century after the Dallas crime, these truth fighters are still dedicated to exposing the accurate historical facts surrounding the assassination of John Kennedy. Unfortunately, in so much the mystery of Dallas has thickened over the years, these guardians of the truth on this crime can only advance half-certainties. The fragility and the relatively recent passing of the few witnesses and actors at the time of this historical drama are not conducive to elucidating the case.

Isn't it shocking to see how many books on this assassination are biased? If the facts that mark History are not authenticated, these books can perniciously be rewritten with convincing words and skillful alterations. Whilst most U.S. citizens do not believe in a foreign conspiracy behind the killing of their President (despite the fact that this is what they were told at the very beginning of the investigation), it is difficult for them to understand why the truth about such a major event in history continues to be concealed, a fact that keeps them wondering what more lies they are being fed by governmental agencies.

Fortunately, despite a remaining apathy or indifference for this historical event, there is undeniably a passionate debate. According to a Gallup poll in 2013, two-thirds of Americans are convinced that there was a conspiracy. Around November 22, 2013, the anniversary of the President's death, History Channel poll even gave a higher figure. It concluded that 71 per cent of the American people refuted the Warren Commission's conclusion of the lone gunman (a committee charged by President Lyndon Johnson to investigate the assassination one week after the Dallas event). While the government still wants the Americans to believe that everything has been said and that one man committed the crime, is there a legitimate reason why American citizens should not have the constitutional right to gain access to existing classified JFK assassination files?

The word "history", derived from the Greek, means "an inquiry into the past facts of humanity or of a person". The research on the JFK assassination is indeed a long, infinitely complex, but incomplete investigation of criminology. By obstructing the American public to consult these top-secret documents, it is History that continues to be squashed. It is the risk that the few remaining witnesses of the assassination will disappear forever and that the facts will phase out from the collective memory. Are we going to let History die this way? As the philosopher, George Santayana, said: *"Those who cannot remember the past are doomed to repeat it."* Those who cannot learn the lessons of the past expose themselves to repeating the errors of History...

Will the voice of truth prevail, as uncertain as it may seem today? The title of this book is a reference to President Richard Nixon's ambiguous words. Having been once asked what he knew about the JFK assassination, he replied: *"You don't want to know!"*

What did Nixon mean by his cryptic words? Would we be shocked and outraged to learn the answer, to be exposed to the facts? Or, did Nixon mean that Americans should not have the right to know in total disdain of the Freedom of Information Act? Whatever Nixon's thoughts were (this conversation was recorded in the White House), we are left without answers.

When will we see at last *all* the classified material on the assassination of John Kennedy published, a chance to test American democracy and political power? Unfortunately, on October 26, 2017, (the deadline set by the 1982 JFK Assassination Act for the JFK files to be published with full transparency) and again on April 26, 2018, only a fraction of them was released. Thousands more files, most of them from the CIA and the FBI, are still locked in the safe of the National Archives and the American public will have to wait even longer to have access to them. Let us hope that this governmental promise will be respected and that it will put an end to the procrastination and the repetitive delays that prevented the legal process shedding full light on this crime.

The reader of this book will first be able to measure the consequences of the Dallas event and the weight of the assassination of President Kennedy that continues to affect America today. I will try to echo the large number of Americans who see in this event the genesis of a transformation of their society. This was a crucial turning point with a political and historical ripple effect. Consequential choices were made that have deeply marked the country and the world ever since. The key topic of this book will then be addressed: the surprising manipulation of the facts surrounding the assassination of President Kennedy and the indolence of the American media surprisingly implicated in a strange enterprise of propaganda that continues, alas, today. At the end of the narrative and after having exposed the evidence of the coup d'état and the motive of those who profited from the crime, I will attempt to explain the reasons for the media shortcomings. Mindful of the guidelines that I have set myself, I will try to disentangle the many references to a conspiracy: those that are based on tangible facts (without possibility of error) and those on which it is permissible to raise doubts. "Death-bed confessions" or witnesses' testimonies that are motivated by any interests must remain fragile evidence because they are not able to convince with the same strength that irrefutable, verifiable and verified facts would. I summarize them in the synoptic table at the end of this book.

Writing a compilation about the many rehashed versions of this historical crime or presenting a new wacky theory about the assassination is not my goal. This narrative is based on an analysis of historical facts that can help my readers form their own opinion on this case. Naturally, I do not anticipate that they all will agree after reading the last page of this book. Some may become convinced that it was an odious coup d'état followed by a cover-up which continues in the United States today but others (hopefully a minority) will continue to reject the conspiracy theory.

The websites on the assassination of John Kennedy imply, for the most part, that a plot is likely to have been fomented from the start. It would however be more accurate to refer to a succession of plots. The assassination of President Kennedy in Dallas, as dramatic and ignominious as it was, was not confined to a single conspiracy. Beyond the preparation and the execution of the tragic event, on November 22, 1963, a second plot ensued: an incredible concealment of evidence in the hasty publication of the botched investigation report of the Warren Commission in 1964.

This commission with no independent investigators relied solely upon FBI and CIA enquiries. Another, but less obvious, phase of the conspiracy has also taken place since. A flagrant disinformation of the facts by the American media that started in 1963 persists today. It was particularly noticeable around the 50th anniversary of the JFK assassination. Although these plots can be proven (I will cover them abundantly), the distortion of truth that is still prevalent in the major American media looks like a collusion that is difficult to comprehend.

I have endeavored to make my personal investigation factual. I will quote references, articles, and interviews of those who either validated the "official" version - Oswald acted alone widely promoted by the media today - or opposed it by defending the alternative interpretation of the event - Oswald was a scapegoat in a large conspiracy. Rather than supporting my analysis with rumors, allegations and statements voiced by questionable or fragile witnesses, I will focus on the facts and the circumstances of the assassination with a concern for objectivity and logic.

The detractors of the conspiracy theory, even those who refute the debate five decades after the Dallas crime, often assert that if there had been a conspiracy, it would not have been possible to conceal it for so long and that surely "someone would have talked"! But this is exactly what did happen; many reliable people have spoken! Investigators, historians, close advisers and friends of John and Robert Kennedy, some who are still alive, have expressed their belief in the circumstance of a conspiracy by some "rogue" elements at the highest level of the state and in collusion with the Organized Crime. I will therefore quote, in the next chapters, several poignant revelations of those who have had the courage not to remain silent; some of them are little known to the public. Yes, these witnesses of History, eager to see the truth prevail, have spoken out. If some people still doubt the credibility of their statements incriminating "the dark forces" behind one of the most hateful political crimes, one may wonder what benefits these old wise men, at the end of their lives, could have gained by purely inventing these allegations.

Chapter 1

John F. Kennedy's Legacy

During the thousand days of his presidency, John Kennedy enjoyed high popularity throughout the United States and around the world. The whole world saw him as a statesman with real leadership and undisputed inspiration. His charm, his sharp wit and his intelligence contributed to the optimism of the planet.

President Kennedy would have been easily re-elected for a second term. Despite his popularity in the eyes of the American people and the world, he also aroused hatred among some influential people in the Establishment who despised the American democratic tradition that he embodied. John Kennedy also aroused suspicion for some because he was popular among the poor, the oppressed, the minorities and the underprivileged whom he addressed with compassion and because he was well liked by the intellectuals and artists he admired and encouraged. He knew how to reach out to Martin Luther King and to inspire hope among African-Americans and Chicanos.

I attended the 20th "*JFK Lancer*" conference in Dallas in November 2015, commemorating the 52nd anniversary of President Kennedy's death. I met a young American lecturer and writer, Jacob M. Carter, passionate about history and intrigued by the assassination of the President. He explained to me his mission: to communicate his enthusiasm for history to younger generations, to educate them about its importance and more specifically to tell them about his hero, John F. Kennedy. He leads debates with the American youth on the subject of the JFK assassination so that the crime of Dallas is not forgotten. He explains to them the impact of the disappearance of an exceptional President who, even though these young people did not known him, marked his era and American society until today. After interviewing American journalists, historians, investigators, Carter decided to write a book on the JFK assassination entitled "*Before History Dies*"[1]. With a subtle play on words, the real message he rather wants to convey is "Before HIS story dies", the recognition of his important political mission and achievements.

Why does the assassination of President Kennedy, more than five decades ago, matter so much today? Has it changed the course of American history as many historians assert? What were the forces hostile to Kennedy and why did a brutal and tragic plot put an end to his presidency?

Yes, it is important to know who murdered the leader of the most powerful nation of the Free World. Justice demands it. The crime was not only perpetrated against a man but its consequences could also have dramatically affected the whole world: as a chapter of this book will cover, the perpetrators, by trying to pin the murder on Cuba and the Soviet Union, took the risk of destabilizing and plunging the world into the chaos of an atomic war. The killing of a great head of state such as John Kennedy also affected western democracies that have been weakened ever since and suppressed the ideals of freedom. Yes, the world must know this story. It must remain in the minds of all those who seek truth and justice.

---

[1] Jacob M. Carter – Before History Dies – 2015

Many historians think that John F. Kennedy was an outstanding president. Despite his personal flaws, he was popularly known for his constant passion for America and his quest for a better world. During his short presidency, John Kennedy was not a polarized man on the Cold War contrary to what he might have portrayed but he was rather a man of peace. He endeavored to avoid a global nuclear conflict in 1962 during the Cuban Missile Crisis and, towards the end of his life, made every effort to soften the relationship with the Soviet Union and Cuba. He showed the example of what could be the stature of a true head of state. Not only do we owe him the recognition of the remarkable legacy he has left us, but also the unveiling of the truth about his assassination. To honor his memory, providing final answers to America's greatest murder mystery is a noble enterprise.

During the 2013 Pittsburgh convention "Passing the Torch", on the 50th anniversary of JFK's death, I asked a man sitting next to me what serious books on the JFK assassination he would most recommend. It was obvious that he was knowledgeable having read many books on the subject. Without any hesitation, he suggested that I should read the honest and convincing book "JFK and the Unspeakable" written by James W. Douglass, a long time peace activist.

This book reads like a political thriller and made a very big impact on me. I find that Douglass has grasped, with much conviction, JFK's vision that moved from his initial Cold War stance towards an engagement for peace at the cost of his life. My gratitude and respect for this JFK researcher are reflected in my book with references to his meticulous work.

During John Kennedy's political ascension, America lived in a state of almost permanent war[2]. The implementation of the nuclear threat was the greatest fear of the President. Towards the end of his tragically ended presidency, under the pressure of the

---

[2] Jacob. M. Carter – Before History Dies - 2015, Interview of David Scheim

Washington hawks, Kennedy endeavored to avoid such a scenario by limiting the nuclear arms race with the Soviet Union.

Beyond the Cold War, he advocated a new era of peace: "*The negotiations for a complete Nuclear-Test-Ban Treaty have for too long been a symbol of disagreements between East and West. Perhaps it is time for them to be a symbol that will help regain mutual trust and work together for peace*", he said. Quoting Nikita Khrushchev's words, "*Survivors would envy the fate of the dead*", he recalled the consequences of an atomic war: "*With the weapons we have today, a very large nuclear exchange would take less than 60 minutes and eradicate more than 300 million Americans, Europeans and Russians besides countless other victims elsewhere*".

John Kennedy was alarmed by the horrendous consequences of atomic radiation: "*the number of children and grandchildren with cancer in their bone, with leukemia in their blood or with poison in their lungs... This is not a natural health hazard – and it is not a statistical issue. The loss of even one human life or the malformation of even one baby – who may be born long after we are gone - should be a concern to us all... Our children and grandchildren are not merely statistics toward which we can be indifferent*". Against the Washington hawks, he had these words: "*This treaty is particularly for our children and our grandchildren, and they have no lobby here in Washington*"[3].

Referring to the danger of the hypothetical spread of communist ideology throughout the world, including the Americas, and the renunciation of the use of nuclear weapons, his words, hammered by the Bostonian accent and the phonetic rhyme that he liked to use, were unequivocal : "*I'd rather see my children red than dead*".

On May 6, 1963, John Kennedy drafted a National Security Action Memorandum, NSAM 239, enjoining his close advisers on national security to complete the Nuclear-Test-Ban Treaty and a comprehensive and general disarmament policy[4]. He finally obtained the support of his Joint Chiefs of Staff and the American people with 80% of opinion favorable to the signing of the treaty. On September 24, 1963, the Senate ratified it after a vote that

---

[3] James W. Douglass, JFK and the Unspeakable, Why He Died and Why it Matters, A Touchstone Book, 2008

[4] Ibid

exceeded the required two-thirds. Soon after, the President told his close advisers that this treaty had marked the happiest moment of his term and that no other accomplishment in the White House had given him so much satisfaction[5].

John Kennedy's intentions regarding the Vietnam war, although ambiguous for some historians (16,000 military advisers were sent by his administration), are however well documented and showed us that he had a repulsion against increasing military intervention in Southeast Asia and sending young men to be killed. Some of his close aides had already warned him of the enormous consequences of an American involvement in Vietnam. At the very beginning of 1961, George Ball, his Secretary of State, told him: "*Within five years we'll have three hundred thousand men in the paddies and jungles that we will find no more. That was the French experience. Vietnam is the worst possible terrain both from a physical and political point of view*".

George Ball was right but he had underestimated the number of recruits by two hundred thousand soldiers that Lyndon Johnson decided to send later[6]. John Kennedy wanted to disengage from Vietnam. As early as May 1962, he went to ask his generals to plan a withdrawal of American military personnel from Vietnam. To start with, he wanted to put a concrete option on the table to negotiate. His military leaders were in shock. They felt that Kennedy had already conceded to the Communists of Laos. For the United States, withdrawing from Vietnam was unthinkable.

The President expressed his reluctance to experience another crisis in his presidency with an engagement in Vietnam. Referring to the Bay of Pigs – the Cuban exiles' attempt to invade Cuba militarily - and to the neutrality of Laos, he told his advisers, "*You must understand that I cannot afford to cumulate so many defeats in a year* "[7]. On October 20, 1963, during his last visit to Hyannis Port, the President's residence on the coast of Massachusetts, he confided to his neighbor, Larry Newman: "*This war in Vietnam,*

---

[5] Ibid
[6] Ibid
[7] Ibid

this nightmare never leaves me. It haunts me day and night. The first thing I do when I'm re-elected, I'm going to get the Americans out of Vietnam ... Exactly how am I going to do it, right now, I do not know, but that is my number one priority – get out of South Asia.. I should have listened to MacArthur. I should have listened to De Gaulle ... We are not going to have men ground up in this fashion, this far away from home. I'm going to get these guys out because we're not going to find ourselves in a war it's impossible to win"[8].

His plan, brutally interrupted in Dallas, was to start bringing back 1,000 military personnel to America in December 1963, followed, against an expected controversy, by a complete withdrawal of troops in 1965, once his re-election would give him legitimacy to do it. Speaking in 1963 about the destiny of Vietnam in 1963, Kennedy had this remark summarizing his desire to put an end to the development of a major military conflict and to avoid a quagmire for America in Vietnam: *"Ultimately, it's their war. They must win or lose it. We can help them, we can equip them, we can send men as advisers but it is up to the people of Vietnam to win against the communists"*.

Ten years before he became president, John Kennedy had understood that it was impossible to win a colonial war in Vietnam. In 1951, as a young congressional representative, he visited Vietnam with his brother, Robert. In the presence of Edmund Gullion, a senior official at the U.S. consulate in Saigon, Kennedy listened to the prophecy of his adviser on Vietnam: *"In twenty-years there will be no more colonies. We're going nowhere out here. The French have lost. If we come in here and do the same thing, we will lose, too, for the same reason. There's no will or support for this kind of war back in Paris. The home front is lost. The same thing would happen to us"*[9].

Moreover, Kenneth O'Donnell, President's aide, reported Kennedy's remarks; how much he expected to suffer the wrath of his military advisers who were pressing him for a massive dispatch of fighting troops and a bombing of northern Vietnam: *"In 1965, I'll become the most unpopular president in history. I'll be*

---

[8] Ibid

[9] Ibid

damned everywhere as a communist appeaser. But I don't care. If I try to pull out completely now from Vietnam, we would have another Joe McCarthy red scare on our hands, but I can do it after I'm reelected. So we had better make damned sure that I am reelected! "[10].

On the morning of November 11, 1963, the American Veterans Day, eleven days before his death, the President laid a wreath on the tomb of the Unknown Soldier at Arlington Cemetery. At the ceremony, he was accompanied by General David M. Shoup, the Marine Commander and a member of the Chiefs of Staff whom Kennedy trusted. As he laid the wreath, the President told the general that he was going to withdraw from Vietnam. Two weeks later, General Shoup was walking behind John Kennedy's coffin at his national funeral in the same cemetery...

The day after Veterans Day, the President received Senator Wayne Morse at the White House. John Kennedy changed the meeting agenda in order to speak to him only about Vietnam. He took the decision to take the senator outside, in the White House Rose Garden, to avoid the indiscreet ears or the potential listening devices. Although he respected Morse's opinion, a strong critic of his policy on Vietnam, Kennedy told him that he understood his objections but that he should also understand his will: *"Wayne, I decided to get out ... Definitely!"*[11].

The man who announced John Kennedy's death at a chaotic conference at Dallas Parkland Hospital on the afternoon of November 22 was Assistant Press Secretary Malcolm Kilduff, one of the President's closest aides. Shortly before his own death, four decades later, Malcolm Kilduff was interviewed by author-historian James Douglass. He told him that the day before he left for Dallas on the morning of November 21, the President had received him in the oval office of the White House and had confided to him, in a serious way, about Vietnam: *"I have just been given the list of the most recent casualties of Vietnam. We're losing too damned people over there. It's time for us to get out. Vietnamese aren't fighting for themselves. We are the ones who are doing the fighting.*

---

[10] David Talbot – Brothers, The Hidden History of the Kennedy Years - 2007

[11] James W. Douglass, JFK and the Unspeakable, Why He Died and Why it Matters, A Touchstone Book, 2008

After I return from Texas, that's going to change. There is no reason for us to lose another man over there. Vietnam is not worth another American life"[12].

In addition to the comments of JFK's relatives and his loyal advisers, there is an archived document from the White House that confirms Kennedy's plans for a total withdrawal of American involvement in South Vietnam. On October 11, 1963, the President signed a National Security Action Memorandum, NSAM 263, planning the return of the first 1,000 military advisers towards the end of 1963. JFK gave specific instructions to his close aides: no immediate announcement was to be made publicly on the imminent withdrawal. He knew that his decision would be a threat, thwarting the clandestine agenda of his dangerous enemies, including military intelligence and factions of the U.S. arms industry, who supported the continuity and the strengthening of the involvement in Vietnam in order to wage a financially lucrative war.

After the President's death, Thomas G. Buchanan wrote: *"I believe that the murder of the President was caused mainly by the fear of the domestic and international consequences that the Moscow Pact could create, namely the danger of disarmament that would have disrupted the industries upon which the plotters depended and because of the threat that an international détente would have represented, in their eyes, such as a possible nationalization of their oil investments abroad "*[13].

Kennedy's NSAM 263 would never be ratified; his murder came six weeks later. On the afternoon of November 24, 1963, two days after John Kennedy's assassination, the new President, Lyndon Johnson, told Ambassador Henry Cabot Lodge, who had returned from a mission to Vietnam: *"I will not lose Vietnam. I will not be the President who will see Southeast Asia fall* [into communist hands] *as China did"*[14]. Less than a week after JFK's assassination

---

[12] Ibid

[13] Thomas G. Buchanan, Who Killed Kennedy? 1964

[14] James W. Douglass, JFK and the Unspeakable, Why He Died and Why it Matters, A Touchstone Book, 2008

in Dallas, President Johnson took the opposite stance from Kennedy's initiative to withdraw from Vietnam! He signed a National Security Action Memorandum, NSAM 273, an extensive military involvement in southern Vietnam to fight the "communist conspiracy". The world then learned the consequence of this massive investment in a war that would last twelve years: the lives of more than two million Vietnamese and of 58,000 U.S. soldiers were lost; a tragic and devastating reality that will forever be the responsibility of Presidents Lyndon Johnson and Richard Nixon; a revolting and infamous war that John Kennedy would have avoided if he had not fallen under the bullets of his enemies.

The end of JFK's unique mandate was marked by his eagerness to end the Cold War. As a man of peace, he served not only as a responsible leader but also as a loving father of his two children, aware of the heavy weight of his decisions on the next generation of his country and the world. Like Martin Luther King and Robert Kennedy, he, too, was a lover of peace, and worked for this noble cause that would be too often neglected by the two American presidents who succeeded him.

John Kennedy was an excellent orator. From his speeches, students in history tend to retain his presidential inaugural address, in January 1961, as a subject for study. Personally, I think that one of his last speeches, the one he delivered on June 10, 1963, at the American University graduation, is perhaps the strongest and the most revealing of the man of peace that he was. Here are some highlights: *"I have, therefore, chosen this time and this place to discuss a topic on which ignorance too often abounds and the truth is too rarely perceived--yet it is the most important topic on earth: world peace...*
What kind of peace do I mean? What kind of peace do we seek? Not a Pax Americana enforced on the world by American weapons of war. Not the peace of the grave or the security of the slave. I am talking about genuine peace, the kind of peace that makes life on earth worth living, the kind that enables men and nations to grow and to hope and to build a better life for their children - not merely peace for Americans but peace

for all men and women - not merely peace in our time but peace for all time...

Let us examine our attitude toward peace itself. Too many of us think it is impossible. Too many think it unreal. But that is a dangerous, defeatist belief. It leads to the conclusion that war is inevitable, that mankind is doomed, that we are gripped by forces we cannot control...

No government or social system is so evil that its people must be considered as lacking in virtue. As Americans, we find communism profoundly repugnant as a negation of personal freedom and dignity. But we can still hail the Russian people for their many achievements, in science and space, in economic and industrial growth, in culture and in acts of courage...

In short, both the United States and its allies, and the Soviet Union and its allies, have a mutually deep interest in a just and genuine peace and in halting the arms race. Agreements to this end are in the interests of the Soviet Union as well as ours, and even the most hostile nations can be relied upon to accept and keep those treaty obligations, and only those treaty obligations, which are in their own interest. So, let us not be blind to our differences but let us also direct attention to our common interests and to the means by which those differences can be resolved. And if we cannot end now our differences, at least we can help make the world safe for diversity. For, in the final analysis, our most basic common link is that we all inhabit this small planet. We all breathe the same air. We all cherish our children's future. And we are all mortal".

John Kennedy's peace speech received a mixed reaction in America; the Capitol Hill Republicans found it limp and expressing weakness. On the other hand, Moscow showed a real interest, such that its broadcast in the Soviet Union was allowed to air on the Voice of America and the publication of the entire speech in the Izvestia newspaper. In private, the First Secretary of the Communist Party of the Soviet Union, Nikita Khrushchev, called it "the best speech of a president since Roosevelt"[15].

Interviewed by author-historian David Talbot, former Secretary of Defense under Kennedy, Robert McNamara, judged the historical significance of the speech in these terms: "*The speech of the American University laid the groundwork for Kennedy's real*

---

[15] David Talbot – Brothers, The Hidden History of the Kennedy Years - 2007

intentions. If he had survived, the world would have been very different. Would we have seen détente earlier, I'm not sure but we would have lived in a less dangerous world".

Many people are unaware that during the Cuban Missile Crisis President Kennedy constantly opposed the masters of the US military power in search of a nuclear confrontation with the Soviets. Kennedy knew how to stop their ardor. In August 1961, during the Berlin Crisis, when the wall was erected, in a tussle with his military advisers in favor of muscular interventions against the Soviets, the man of peace that JFK was, had these words: *"A wall is a hell of a lot better than a war".*

In March 1962, the pressure of the military advisers in John Kennedy's administration reached its climax. On March 13, the United States Army Chief of Staff sent a top-secret memorandum to the Secretary of Defense. This memo prompted the Kennedy administration to create "regrettable incidents" through false attacks on U.S. soldiers stationed in Cuba and other Central American countries, Miami and even Washington. This plan, which was finally dismissed, provided for the destruction of an American ship in Guantanamo Bay, the U.S. military base in Cuba, as a pretext for retaliation and a valid reason to invade the island in the face of rising national outrage.[16] In another showdown, when President Kennedy discovered that senior CIA officials had ignored his orders to stop any plot against Fidel Castro, he sent the FBI and local law enforcement to destroy the training camps of the CIA in Florida.

It was the Cuban Missile Crisis in October 1962 nevertheless that marked John Kennedy's determination and ability to keep a cool head. It could have led to a global nuclear destruction without the judgement of the President whose intelligence led to the negotiation of an honorable agreement with the leader of the Soviet Union: to renounce an invasion of Cuba. He had been strongly against the radical scenario of invading the island that

---

[16] Ibid

had been bitterly advocated by his security advisers and had promised instead a non-aggression in exchange for the dismantling and removal of the Soviet missiles. In the afternoon of October 28, when the crisis was finally dismissed, Robert Kennedy went to the White House to have a long talk with his brother. When Robert was about to leave, John Kennedy made a reference to the death of President Abraham Lincoln (murdered during a theatrical performance by a Confederate sympathizer in the Ford Theater in Washington) and had these prophetic words: *"This is the night I should go to the theater ..."*, an analogy to which his brother replied: *"If you go, then I want to go with you"*[17]. The prophecy was to be fulfilled much later with the same fate that had ended Abraham Lincoln's life: the two brothers would also fell brutally under assassins' bullets, five years apart.

A few months later, in 1963, Kennedy concretized his stature as a man of peace. He worked for a voluntary rapprochement and a frequent dialogue not only with Nikita Khrushchev but also with Fidel Castro. His desire for détente provoked strong hatred among the American President's enemies because, for some, the Cold War represented a military machine generating enormous profits.

On September 20, 1963, nearly two months before his death, John Kennedy made a speech at the United Nations. He reiterated his vision expressed during his speech at the American University: to pursue a peace strategy with a specific roadmap. On the same day, he asked the U.S. ambassador to the United Nations, Adlai Stevenson that his assistant, William Attwood, discreetly get in touch with the Cuban leader through the Cuban ambassador to the United Nations. Was Fidel Castro interested in a dialogue with John Kennedy?

A positive response came from Castro, under the influence of Khrushchev who had inspired him to develop a relationship of trust with Kennedy. Despite the precautions taken by the U.S.

---

[17] James W. Douglass, JFK and the Unspeakable, Why He Died and Why it Matters, A Touchstone Book, 2008

President to conceal his initiative of rapprochement with Cuba, leaks occurred unfortunately. Much later, Attwood confided that *"there was no doubt in his mind that if the assassination had not happened, the United States and Cuba would have started negotiations for the purpose of a normalization of relations between the two countries "*[18].

The tentative rapprochement with Fidel Castro came to fruition with the intervention of a member of the President's brother entourage, the journalist Lisa Howard from ABC television. The mission was to meet and interview Castro. On April 21, 1963, she met him at the Riviera Hotel in Havana. Castro accepted the interview in front of cameras. Upon his return to the United States, Howard briefed President Kennedy directly at the White House. She told him what the Cuban dictator had acquiesced. Castro seemed sincere in saying he was eager to open a dialogue with the US President[19].

The journalist then carried the same message to the CIA - a usual and expected step for journalists returning from communist outposts during the Cold War. However, CIA officials were undeniably less enthusiastic than John Kennedy was when Howard's news came out and they quickly acted in short-circuiting the journalist. On May 2, 1963, John Mc Cone, the CIA Director, sent a memorandum, recommending that *"Lisa Howard's report be treated in the most limited and discreet manner possible"* and *"that it was unthinkable now to take active steps for a rapprochement "*. The harsh elements of the presidential administration even went so far as to consider blocking the broadcast of Howard's interview on ABC television: *"the public broadcast of the interview in the United States could only strengthen the arguments of the actors for peace, and those of liberal thinkers, communists and political opponents opportunistic to the current US policy ... and, by the same token, provide Castro with an audience across the country for his 'conciliatory line ' that he would show"*.

---

[18] Ibid

[19] David Talbot – Brothers, The Hidden History of the Kennedy Years - 2007

ABC nevertheless aired the interview on May 10. The fears of the Washington hawks were confirmed: Castro appeared as someone friendly and reasonable in the eyes of the Americans. In praising the U.S. President for his desire *"to take steps for a lasting peace"* and to suppress the raids against his country, Castro said he was in favor of leaving the door open for reconciliation with the United States. However, it was unthinkable that the hawks of the JFK administration could accept such an omen and they endeavored to block any start of peace talks. Howard's JFK peace initiative thus stalled.

In spite of this, in the last days of his life, John Kennedy's usual tenacity was well noted when he sent messages of appeasement to Castro; one of them was expressed on November 18, 1963, in a speech to the Inter-American Press Association in Miami which set the conditions for a sincere, lasting but conditional rapprochement. For the President, the only obstacle to peace between the United States and Cuba was Havana's support for the insurrections of Latin American revolutionaries: *"That's what divides us and nothing else. As long as this support is there, nothing is possible. Without this support, anything is possible"*.

The American diplomat at the United Nations and JFK's friend, William Attwood, was also a courageous architect of the rapprochement that the President wanted with Cuba. He too had been given the mission by the President to talk to Fidel Castro. In the years following Kennedy's death, Attwood felt haunted by the assassination; he wondered about a possible link between JFK's quest for peace with Cuba and the murder in Dallas[20].

Attwood is credited with the creation of the Church Committee, the first senatorial inquiry into the assassination since the Warren Commission. In October 1975, Attwood wrote a letter to Senator Richard Schweiker of Pennsylvania, suggesting that he persuade Senator Frank Church to form a subcommittee to investigate the assassination of John Kennedy. He also confided to him that he had suspicions about the possible complicity of the anti-Castro

---

[20] Ibid

exiles in the assassination. Later, Schweiker announced to the press that he believed *"the Warren Commission was no more than a house of cards about to collapse"*. Schweiker's suspicions grew thicker over time. He started a communication with the community of investigators about a possible conspiracy.

In February 1977, under the administration of President Carter, Attwood undertook a second trip to Havana to meet Fidel Castro and to discuss the JFK assassination. During their long conversation, Castro told Attwood that Kennedy's speech at the American University foresaw *"that he would have been a great president if he had survived."* Referring to Attwood's suspicions, Castro shared his thinking that it was *"a conspiracy of supporters of the American right wing who feared a shift in U.S. policy towards Cuba and Vietnam ... That's why Kennedy was killed"*.

Later, Attwood kept talking to the press about the conspiracy of the assassination: *"We think there was more behind the drama of Dallas than what we have been told"*. Attwood was convinced the CIA had tapped the telephone calls that Lisa Howard and he had made from Howard's apartment in Havana. In January 1986, Attwood confided to Anthony Summers, a former BBC journalist and pillar of research into the conspiracy against Kennedy, and Richard Tomlinson, a British television producer, that he thought suspicions led to believe some protesting agents of the CIA and Cuban anti-Castro exiles were finger pointed. Attwood told them that *"the secret negotiations with Cuba had been, for the plotters, 'the last straw' "* and that *"it was at that moment they decided to kill Kennedy"*[21].

Attwood's provocative remarks were echoed by the local press in New Canaan, his hometown in Connecticut; he implored the American citizens not to forget the crime of the century: *"if we do not go to the bottom of things, if we let the lie continue, then we take part in the cover-up of this crime"*. Shortly after, the former ambassador died of a heart attack at age 69, his fight fading with him ... apart from the lie of the government...

---

[21] Ibid

Still working towards relaxation with Cuba, John Kennedy decided it was the turn of Jean Daniel, the French journalist of international stature, to carry a message to Fidel Castro and to sound out his opinion about a future improvement of the relations between the United States and Cuba. On October 24, 1963, Jean Daniel, before his mission to meet Fidel Castro, interviewed the American President at the White House. Daniel would later write in The New Republic about his exchanges with Kennedy and with Castro.

Daniel reported John Kennedy's surprising words concerning the Cuban leader: *"I believe that there is no country in the world, including all the African regions, including any and all the countries under colonial domination, where economic colonization, humiliation and exploitation were worse than in Cuba, in part owing to my country's policies during the Batista regime... I approved the proclamation which Fidel Castro made in the Sierra Maestra when he justifiably called for justice and especially yearned to rid Cuba of corruption. I will go even further: to some extend it is as though Batista was the incarnation of a number of sins on the part of the United States. Now we shall have to pay for those sins. In the matter of the Batista regime, I am in agreement with the first Cuban revolutionaries. That is perfectly clear"*.

At the end of the interview, Jean Daniel perceived the doubts of the President when he said: *"The world was on the verge of nuclear war in October 1962. The Russians understood this very well, at least after our reaction, but so far as Fidel Castro is concerned, I must say I don't know whether he realizes this or even if he cares about it. You can tell me whether he does when you come back"*[22]. Kennedy would not have the answer; he had less than a month to live to find the way out of the Cuban problem.

Arthur Schlesinger, JFK's loyal adviser, related the event in his memoirs. While Castro was talking with Jean Daniel in his residence of Varadero Beach, on November 22, 1963, the day of Kennedy's assassination, the Cuban leader, stunned by the Dallas news he had just learned on the phone, said: "*This is bad news*".

---

[22] James W. Douglass, JFK and the Unspeakable, Why He Died and Why it Matters, A Touchstone Book, 2008

Referring to President Kennedy's stature, he had just told Jean Daniel: "*In the eyes of history, he still has the possibility of becoming the greatest president of the United States, the leader who may at last understand that there can be coexistence between capitalists and socialists, even in the Americas*". He had even joked before hearing the dramatic news about the possible help he could bring to JFK's re-election in 1964: "*If you see him again, you can tell him that I'm willing to declare Goldwater my friend* [JFK's political rival during the presidential campaign] *if that will guarantee Kennedy's re-election!*" But the Cuban leader's good mood very quickly turned to gloominess when Kennedy's death was confirmed by a NBC News radio bulletin. At that moment, Castro stood up and said, "*Everything is changed. Everything is going to change*". Then, addressing the French journalist and his entourage, he added these premonitory words: "*You will see; I know them, they will want to put the blame on us for that.*" When the American radio spread very quickly the news announcing that the accused murderer, Lee Harvey Oswald, was married to a Russian and that, as a pro-Marxist, he was a Castro sympathizer, the Cuban leader continued: "*You see! What did I tell you? I will be next*".

In September 1963, Associated Press reporter, Daniel Harker gave another interview with Fidel Castro in Havana. What the dictator said sounded like a condemnation; he linked the exiles' plots against Cuba to John Kennedy' benevolence: "*We are prepared to fight them and answer in kind. U.S. leaders should think that if they are aiding terrorist plans to eliminate Cuban leaders, they themselves will not be safe.*" After Kennedy's death, some political observers considered that Castro's remark had represented some kind of threat to murder JFK, although the comment did not seem to elude it when Harker's article was published. This possibility is nevertheless still promoted today. Years later, when Castro appeared before congressional investigators, he said that "*he never thought that his words could be understood as a physical threat against anyone in the United States*" but that "*he had no doubt wished to give the following message to Washington: he was aware of the existence of plots against his life; it would set a very bad precedent such that it could turn against its authors.*" Some historians have nevertheless commented that it would have made no sense for Fidel Castro to plot against JFK's life because it would have provoked a terrible U.S. retaliation, without mercy, against Cuba: an invasion or even its eradication from the world map[23].

We know, especially since the fall of the Soviet Union, that Kennedy and Khrushchev were working together in secret and through the back door to avoid war between their two countries. They did it behind the backs of their respective generals because they knew it was the only way to avoid a military clash. Their negotiating strategy worked remarkably well twice, during the Berlin Crisis in 1961 and the 1962 Missiles in Cuba.[24]

These two heads of state countered their military advisers so that the planet would not fall into a nuclear madness. The leaders of the two best-armed countries in history, on the verge of a total apocalyptic war, decided to join forces against those on both sides who were pressing for an attack.

Khrushchev proposed, under conditions, the immediate withdrawal of his missiles from Cuba. Kennedy, in return, pledged never to invade Cuba and promised - secretly - the future withdrawal of obsolete American missiles from Turkey. Both mutually agreed; an act decided with courage by the two enemies of the Cold War. Ironically, each leader had found more common interest with his opponent than either could have had with his own generals. The President's speech at the American University bore a particular significance with his words resonating eight months after the extreme military tension between the two countries.

In July 1993, in compliance with the Freedom of Information Act, the U.S. State Department responded to the request of a Canadian newspaper by publishing 21 letters written in the greatest secrecy by John Kennedy and Nikita Khrushchev. The private and confidential correspondence between the two leaders of the Cold War began in September 1961 and lasted two years. Khrushchev sent the first letter to Kennedy during the Berlin

---

[23] Lamar Waldron, The Hidden History of the JFK Assassination, Counter Point Berkeley, 2013

[24] James W. Douglass, JFK and the Unspeakable, Why He Died and Why it Matters, A Touchstone Book, 2008

crisis. To maintain total secrecy, the strategy was to conceal the confidential letter in a newspaper and to hand it over to Pierre Salinger, the President's Press Secretary. The exchange took place in a New York hotel room through two reliable Soviet emissaries of the First Secretary of the Communist Party. Khrushchev certainly took risks, but he wanted at all costs that these letters be kept secret without the knowledge of the Soviet military services, senior Kremlin officials and the press.

In a first letter of 26 pages, Khrushchev expressed his regret that a frank and fruitful exchange could not have taken place when he and Kennedy met in Vienna. Even though political rhetoric prevailed in his letter, Khrushchev wanted to explore the alternative to confrontation. He let Kennedy know it by using a Biblical analogy with Noah's Ark: *"Either we live in peace and cooperate so that ' the Ark stays afloat or sinks'"*. Kennedy replied by thanking Khrushchev for initiating this correspondence and by telling him that despite their differences, collaboration for an essential and lasting peace was urgent[25].

A month and a half after the Cuban Missile Crisis, Nikita Khrushchev sent John Kennedy another private letter in which he invited the American President, his enemy of yesterday, to share with him a vision of peace: *"We think you'll get a second term in the next election. As from now, you will be the American President for six years, which will suit us. In the political world of today, six years is a long time. During this period, we believe that we could create good conditions for a peaceful coexistence on earth and this would be highly appreciated by our two peoples as well as by all the peoples of the planet"*[26].

During the spring of 1963, John Kennedy sent Norman Cousins to Russia as peace envoy to Khrushchev. Norman Cousins, the editor of the liberal magazine Saturday Review, had long been known for his peace activism and informal diplomacy with the Vatican, Washington, and Moscow. Pope John XXIII, dying of

---

[25] Ibid
[26] Ibid

cancer, and Norman Cousins sought to find a point of understanding between Khrushchev and Kennedy. Returning from Moscow, Cousins informed President Kennedy of the result of his discussions with Khrushchev in his dacha on the shores of the Black Sea. Khrushchev was ready to open a new chapter in the relations between the U.S.A. and the Soviet Union. He agreed with Kennedy to sign a nuclear test ban treaty: "*You want me to accept President Kennedy's good faith?* Khrushchev exclaimed, "*All right, I accept President Kennedy's good faith ... You want me to set all misunderstandings aside and make a fresh start? All right, I agree to make a fresh start*".

After having listened to Cousins attentively, Kennedy gave his opinion: "*One of the ironic things about this entire situation is that Mr. Khrushchev and I occupy approximately the same political positions inside our governments. He would like to prevent a nuclear war but is under severe pressure from his hardline crowd which interprets every move in that direction as appeasement. I've got similar problems. Meanwhile, the lack of progress in reaching agreements between our two countries gives strength to the hardline in both, with the result that the hard-liners in the Soviet Union and in the United States feed on one another, each using the actions of the other to justify its own position* ".[27].

Despite the altercations on Berlin, Cuba, Vietnam and the other hot spots of the Cold War, the two leaders endeavored to develop a mutual appreciation and to guide their countries away from a nuclear abyss. Khrushchev was deeply affected when he heard the news from Dallas. He was seen crying in the Kremlin ... According to a family member, he failed in his duties for several days as he was struggling to cope with the tragedy, personally. There was no doubt for Khrushchev: he was convinced that Kennedy had been killed by Washington's militarist forces to sabotage the efforts of the two leaders to reach detente. The hard elements of the Kremlin took less than a year after JFK's death to oust the Soviet leader from power. It was much later, during the

---

[27] David Talbot – Brothers, The Hidden History of the Kennedy Years - 2007

last years of his exile, as a recluse in his "cottage" on the banks of the Istra, that Khrushchev undertook his own "glasnost". He listened to the BBC and the Voice of America, denounced the internment of the dissident Soviet writers and harshly criticized the Soviet invasion of Czechoslovakia in 1968. When Moscow was informed that Khrushchev was writing his memoirs, the Politburo asked him to immediately cease his writings and to hand over his notes to the Central Committee. Khrushchev refused. His book "Khrushchev remembers" was published in the West and quickly became a bestseller. In his memoirs, recalling the days of Kennedy, he praised the merits of the American President, "*A true head of state*," and felt that if he had survived, the two men could have contributed together to peace in the world. His son, Sergei, who became an American citizen and senior international affairs associate at Brown University in Providence, Rhode Island, wrote in his memoirs that his father had found common ground with John Kennedy. If their political terms could have been prolonged, they would have ended the Cold War earlier. "*Since he trusted the American President, my father was ready to cooperate with John Kennedy over a long period of time*"[28].

The Washington elite, hostile to Kennedy and in favor of maintaining the Cold War, could not let this power remain in place. They could not forget the stakes that Kennedy, by his political skill and courage, had significantly limited. The steps taken by the President towards the end of his presidency - the end of nuclear tests, the drastic reduction of weapons, the détente with Cuba and the Soviet Union, the withdrawal from Vietnam - became unbearable for the Washington hawks. Some elements of the American government understood that all Kennedy's undertaking in this direction constituted a treachery for America and that he had to pay for it.

Today, many agree that the assassination of John Kennedy was the result of a conspiracy involving forces of different origins,

---

[28] Sergei N. Khrushchev, Nikita Khrushchev and the Creation of a Superpower (University Park, Pennsylvania State University Press, 2000)

driven by the same motive to eliminate the President. Whoever these forces were - CIA rebels, anti-Castro Cuban exiles or Mafia dons - all had one goal: to end the policy of appeasement against the communists of Cuba and the Soviet Union that was being prepared by the President to be ratified during his second term.

Why were the anti-Castro Cuban exiles so hostile to John Kennedy? Since their failed invasion at the Bay of Pigs in Cuba, they saw Kennedy as a traitor for having denied them the support of the U.S. Air Force that contributed to their humiliating defeat. They thought, with Kennedy removed from power, that they would resume their fight and operations against Castro. Since their allies from the CIA and the Mafia would bring support, this synergy could only benefit the Cubans exiles' undertaking.

John Kennedy was not naïve. He showed top generals his mistrust and the first thing he thought of telling his successor would be '*Do not trust the military, even military affairs*'". He knew that his life would be endangered if he continued to oppose the Washington hawks. He often told his relatives that he had a premonition that the end of his presidency would be violent.

The facts would confirm the omen. The military conspiracies that reigned at that time in the capital were such that they inspired writers and filmmakers. In 1962, the publication of the book "Seven Days in May", a fiction about a military coup in the United States, was a bestseller. John Kennedy read the book with fascination. He contacted his friend, Hollywood director John Frankenheimer and encouraged him to make a movie.[29] The President wished to send a strong message to his enemies in Washington. Arthur Schlesinger, JFK's friend and adviser, confided a few years later that "*Kennedy wanted 'Seven Days in May' to be a warning to the generals ...*

John Kennedy also encouraged John Frankenheimer to make his next film, "The Manchurian Candidate"; a fiction in which the premonitory theme focused on the forces of right wing extremists

---

[29] David Talbot – Brothers, The Hidden History of the Kennedy Years - 2007

determined to assassinate a president and eventually dispose of American democracy. *United Artists* hesitated to launch the film for fear of exacerbating the tensions of the Cold War and tried to convince the President to intervene to cancel the film's preparation. However, Kennedy confirmed his recommendation to maintain the project. Once the "Manchurian Candidate" was completed, Kennedy organized a special screening of the movie at the White House. His support for the project showed how much democracy could be threatened.

As for the movie "Seven Days in May", it was released after JFK's death, in February 1964. Several media commentators felt that the movie was too disturbing. A critic of the *Los Angeles Herald-Examiner* questioned the value of having made such a film that *"tarnished the image of America"* and reassured his readers: such a military coup could not happen here in America.

Five decades later, like many people, I was eager to see how JFK's legacy was still perceived and if there was any future action plan to reveal the truth about his passing. I was hoping to find the answers by attending the 2013 Pittsburgh convention "Passing the Torch" on the 50th anniversary of JFK's death.

The conference started with U.S. political commentator, Larry Sabato, who reflected on five major reasons for continuing the study of this historic assassination, a huge task left to the younger generation, students and criminology specialists. First, this crime is not solved, Sabato said. No serious U.S. federal criminal investigation has yet shed light on the mystery of the assassination of President Kennedy. However, the American public demands it: a large percentage of the American population - between two-thirds and three-quarters - do not believe in the Warren Commission's version and do not think a single individual acted alone. All opinion polls prove it: the American people are far from losing interest in the assassination of their president.

The second reason, according to Sabato, is based on the means and tools of investigation in criminology, ballistics and expertise in other sciences available today. Through these means and methods, the most hateful crimes on the planet have been explained. Why cannot we elucidate the Dallas assassination with these same methodologies? For example, the police tapes of the sounds recorded all day on November 22 should be found and examined by experts (a kind of "black box" of the drama that happened that day). This story is alive and we should bring irrefutable evidence of the assassination of JFK.

Sabato saw a third reason to justify a new serious study of the Dallas crime. In addition to the documents the American government still kept secret, perhaps photos, films and diaries might be found, hidden in attics or in drawers, somewhere, that have not yet been discovered because these documents might compromise specific individuals!

The fourth reason for reopening the investigation is the duty to explain the inconceivable fact that John Kennedy's protection was so weak in Dallas, a protection that was limited to 12 Secret Service agents, during the presidential motorcade, thus making the President very vulnerable. After the assassination of President McKinley in 1901 and the numerous assassination attempts against Ted Roosevelt, Herbert Hoover and Franklin Delanoe Roosevelt, the lessons of the past had been soon forgotten.

The fifth reason according to Sabato - and not the least - is the moral and historical obligation to hold government agencies accountable. They lied to the American people about the assassination of President Kennedy with impunity, disguising the evidence or conducting lengthy falsified investigations. It is outrageous that the American taxpayers paid those investigations, which proved to be botched and costly!

Every American president probably faced the same difficulties that President Kennedy did in containing the bellicose zeal of rogue government elements, and some presidents succeeded more than others. The clique of these secret men wanted these commanders-in-chief to understand that the supreme power was no longer in the hands of the presidency itself. Certainly, their presidential term may well have been granted by the American people's will but the power, the political management, came rather from the outside, from forces acting in the shadow. They made it clear to each president that his life and his administration depended on the interests of a clandestine power with political and foreign affairs entrusted to them. This power aspired in particular to the deployment of the Vietnam War because it represented a financial windfall, a project thwarted by President Kennedy who was preparing to withdraw the United States from South-East Asia. This war represented 220 billion dollars of business for the warmongers. They did not even intend to win it, they just wanted to make it last as long as they could in order to run the arms industry at high speed, killing, at the same time, thousands of U.S. soldiers and more than two million Vietnamese civilian casualties.

Kennedy had wisely listened to General Douglas MacArthur who was the architect of the defeat of Japan, ending the Second World War in the Pacific. Having learned the lesson of the Korean War too, the General had advised the President not to get involved further in Southeast Asia and to withdraw at the earliest possible time. President De Gaulle had advised Kennedy to do the same thing. The French had suffered a terrible defeat in Indochina and Ho Chi Minh forced them leave the quagmire of this enduring war. Why did the CIA and the Washington hawks seek to replace the French in Southeast Asia? Certainly, for ideological reasons, but mainly because of the staggering financial stakes of the arms industry during the ten-year funding of this American war.

If the guilt of some senior government officials is ever proven, it will be a duty to rewrite their stories, their biographies to erase the legacy they left behind even after their death and of course the history books. Democracy demands it. Truth, even revealed late, cannot leave future generations indifferent. This murder must be explained to the American people and the world without any ambiguity, in memory of this President whose peace mission could not be fulfilled.

America, known in the past for its constant propensity for entanglements in foreign affairs and for the marginalization of millions of Americans, has not always followed the political guidelines of humanity left by John Kennedy's legacy, especially near the end of his life. Many historians recognize that his presidency, if it began with the vision of an aristocratic Cold War follower, became that of a subtle peacemaker until his death.

John Kennedy never had the opportunity to make his final speech that he was to give at the Dallas Trade Mart, the meeting place for lunch, after the parade in Dallas downtown streets. The text of what was to be an eloquent speech remains with us; it bears witness to the unfinished mission of a head of state who chose the path to peace: "*We in this country, in this generation, are - by destiny rather than choice - the watchmen on the walls of world freedom. We ask, therefore, that we may be worthy of our power and responsibility, that we may exercise our strength with wisdom and restraint, and that we may achieve in our time and for all time the ancient vision of 'peace on earth, good will toward men.' That must always be our goal, and the righteousness of our cause must always underlie our strength...*" Instead of delivering this inspiring speech, John Kennedy was brutally murdered in a sunny street in downtown Dallas, in full view of the world. His quest for peace, civil rights and for the general well-being of the American people was his fatal mistake.

In his book, "*JFK and the Unspeakable*", author-historian James Douglass pays tribute to the peacemaker John Kennedy was, by evoking, with force and emotion, the political legacy of the young president. I quote here Douglass' evocation of Nature - protected from a near-miss global nuclear disaster - around the celebration of the American Thanksgiving holiday: "*I believe it is a providential fact that the anniversary of the President's assassination always falls around Thanksgiving, and periodically on that very day. Thanksgiving is a beautiful time of the year, with autumn leaves falling to create new life. Creation is alive, as the season turns. The earth is alive. It is not a radioactive wasteland. We can give special thanks for that. The fact that we are still living...is reason for gratitude to a peacemaking president and to the unlikely alliance he forged with his enemy, partner in peace, Nikita Khrushchev*" [30].

---

[30] James W. Douglass, JFK and the Unspeakable, Why He Died and Why it Matters, A Touchstone Book, 2008

Chapter 2

The "*Lone Nuts*" against the "*Conspiracy Nuts*"

In the United States, five decades after the assassination of President Kennedy, two clans are opposed more than ever: the "*Lone-Nuts*" (those supporting the theory of a lone assassin) and the "*Conspiracy Nuts*" (the conspiracy theorists). Whatever side is advocated, the name - for short - has of course a derogative connotation. It reflects the immense disdain that one clan has for the fanciful theories expressed by the other, often for the commercial purpose of writing a book and having it published, so much the case of the assassination of President Kennedy arouses passion!

The "Lone Nuts" defend the "official" version; that of the American government at the time of the Dallas drama, still promoted today by the American media. They claim the following: John Kennedy was murdered in Dallas on November 22, 1963, by a lone gunman, Lee Harvey Oswald, acting on his own initiative; a communist "drifter" who made the American society responsible for his failure. Using a 6.5-millimeter Italian Mannlicher Carcano rifle he owned, Oswald fired three gunshots from his "sniper" position on the sixth floor of a schoolbook warehouse, the Texas School Book Depository (TSBD), located on Dealey Plaza, along the path of the presidential limousine. These

"*Lone Nuts*" claim that three gunshots - and only three - were fired at the President's car that had just passed the TSBD window. After firing, Oswald wiped his rifle to eliminate his fingerprints, hid it somewhere opposite his sniper window on the same floor, went down several stairs and calmly entered the lunchroom to buy a soda from a vending machine. After being confronted at the scene by a police officer who pointed a gun at him but decided to let him go, Oswald left the TSBD and walked four blocks to a bus stop that would take him to his landlady's house in another part of the city. As the bus hit a traffic jam, Oswald got off the bus and took a cab towards his rental where he grabbed a jacket and a revolver before going outside.

Still according to the official version, about 45 minutes after firing at the President, Oswald was trying to flee. He allegedly shot a Dallas police officer, JD Tippit, about a mile away from his landlady's house and was arrested by the Dallas police in a nearby movie theater.

Just after the assassination of President Kennedy, a commission of seven key members, the Warren Commission, was appointed by the new President, Lyndon Baines Johnson, to conduct the official investigation. The commission gave the conclusions of its investigation in a 26-volume report during fall of 1964. It found:

"*No evidence of Oswald's involvement with another person or group of individuals in a plot to assassinate the president; no evidence that Oswald was an FBI or CIA agent or informant of any other government agency ... nor any evidence of a direct or indirect connection between Lee Harvey Oswald and Jack Ruby, the Dallas nightclub owner who shot him in the police station, two days after the assassination of the President ... No evidence of conspiracy, subversion or disloyalty on the part of any U.S. government agent whatsoever* "[31]. The Warren Report considered that there was also no evidence of the involvement of Lee Harvey Oswald or Jack Ruby in a foreign conspiracy to assassinate President Kennedy.

---

[31] Report of the President's Commission on the Assassination of President Kennedy – September 24, 1964

Dealey Plaza: The building in the center is the TSBD from where Oswald allegedly fired three gunshots (circled window) according to the official version. The grassy slope (the "Grassy Knoll") and the palisade are hidden by the elm trees that have grown since 1963. The two stars mark the location of the limousine at the time of the gunshots (author's photo)

The "Lone Nuts", who support the Warren Report, adopt the pivotal theory of the investigation; that of the "Single Bullet" or rather the "Magic Bullet" as their detractors ironically like to call it; a single bullet which was supposed to have gone through the President Kennedy's back and throat and then struck Texas Governor John Connally, sitting in front of the President in the limousine, penetrating his chest, and his wrist ending its run in his thigh.

The commission thus incriminated a confused isolated individual, author of the two murders and of seriously wounding John Connally. Moreover, Oswald was a communist, the stereotype of what the Americans despised. After all, we were in the midst of the Cold War. Oswald appeared to be the ideal culprit; he had found a job right where the presidential motorcade was planned; he had left the Texas School Book Depository after the assassination; he was a member of the Fair Play for Cuba Committee, a group of activists supporting the Cuban revolution, and he may well have been guilty of murdering police officer J.D. Tippit too.

The following chapters will provide evidence of the Warren Report's inaccuracies, omissions, and cover-ups. In contrast, medical, ballistic, photographic and acoustic evidence supporting a conspiracy will be largely covered in this book based on the work of scientific, forensic and criminal experts in the five decades that followed the Dallas drama.

Historians and investigators, who refute the Warren Report's results on the JFK assassination, represent a community that has strongly developed overtime. Thousands of individuals, armed with a lot of patience and determination, have brought to light a far more reprehensible machination than the negligence of the Warren Commission. Although some "Lone Nuts" recognized the commission's oversight, they attributed it however to the pressure to submit its report.

Those who criticize the official government version can see an ominous alteration of the facts and a vast camouflage of evidence. They revealed the testimony of the witnesses who were intimidated or threatened by government investigators so as not to make them public. Thanks to their tenacity, documents, kept secret in the National Archives and in American government agencies, were found and published. They fought - and still struggle - against media misinformation and thwarted the interference of the government, which was trying to block their investigations. The supporters of the official version call these skeptics with irony: the "Conspiracy Nuts".

There are always – and always will be - those who promote wacky theories, cleverly developed to profit their books sales. Adding to the confusion, the authors of these crazy theories defend themselves by asserting that so long as they have not been refuted by contradictory evidence, they are therefore viable. I choose here three most revealing examples of this hoax. Jackie Kennedy had her husband killed because of his infidelity and his very libertine life! The driver of the presidential limousine, William Greer, a Secret Service agent, slowed down and braked after the first shot. They say: take a good look at the Zapruder film (an amateur cinematographer who filmed the assassination); the vehicle is almost at a halt and we can see the driver briefly turn his back to glimpse at the president then shoot him. Yes, we really mean it ... we can see his weapon that he points towards Kennedy! In fact, a close look at the film reveals the reflection of the sun on the front passenger's forehead, giving the illusion that the driver pointed a weapon! Even worse, a Secret Service member who was standing in the car that followed the presidential limousine, pulled, by mistake, the trigger of his machine gun that had been left with the safety lock off. Can you believe this sad coincidence, they say seriously? The shot accidentally hit the skull of the President!

These wacky theories, the false testimonies and the circumstances of the assassination that have been totally invented, can only fuel the criticism and ridicule the "Conspiracy Nuts" to the great satisfaction of their detractors. This undertaking does not serve the community of the many serious and credible investigators whose expertise and honesty cannot be doubted.

The word "Conspiracy" is intentionally mocked at by the "Lone Nuts" and especially by the media pointing out an infantile controversy rather than a desire to lead a serious investigation. History must be reminded to these "Lone Nuts": many political leaders have been assassinated and the facts often proved, without the shadow of a doubt, that there was a conspiracy. Those who have been relentlessly investigating for many years should be considered with respect.

There is a tendency to be bogged down in the multitude of details of the investigation. It requires a lot of rigor and patience to explain the inconsistencies of the official government version, to provide tangible evidence of a conspiracy and to answer to an imbroglio of questions that have left people boggled for years. Who fired and where? How many bullets? Was Oswald's only partial fingerprint on the rifle found in the Texas School Depository Building a true set up? Have the photographs of President Kennedy's autopsy been doctored? Choose your side and you will have the opinion of an expert opposed to that of a counter-expert, which will stick to any theory.

Among the experts who criticize the official version, let us respect, among others, the eminent forensic pathologist, Cyril H Wecht, a consultant before the House Select Committee on Assassinations (HSCA); Dr. Gary Aquilar, an authority on factual medical evidence of a cover-up based on the x-rays and the photographs taken during President Kennedy's botched autopsy;

Jefferson Morley, a journalist and editor of the excellent website JFKfacts.org; Robert J. Groden, a photo-optics expert who was a consultant at the HSCA and a contributor to Oliver Stone's movie, "JFK"; Sherry P. Fiester, a crime scene investigator and an expert in ballistic and blood projection analysis.

The opinions of prominent figures believing in a highly probable conspiracy in the JFK assassination have also been well documented. Some have been surprising and unexpected: President Lyndon Johnson and CIA Director John McCone, President Kennedy's personal physician Admiral George Burkley, JFK press officer Pierre Salinger, JFK advisers Ted Sorensen and Arthur Schlesinger Jr., have all expressed doubts about the official version of the assassination. Disbelief was also voiced by Dave Powers and Kenneth O'Donnell, two very close JFK aides, who were themselves eye witnesses of the assassination on Dealey Plaza, and also by Dallas Police Chief Jesse Curry, who maintained that two shooters were involved. In France, it was clear to President De Gaulle that a conspiracy was hatched around the drama in Dallas. When a journalist briefed him on the official position, the theory of the "Lone-Nuts", he expressed his skepticism with irony: *"You're kidding me! Cowboys and Indians!"*[32].

All these people criticized the botched investigation led by the members of the Warren Commission - appropriately renamed the "Warren Omission" by the historian Walt Brown! They deplored the censorship of the testimonies of witnesses, which the commission found embarrassing. These advocates of the truth refuse to be called "conspiracy theorists". They prefer to call themselves "Conspiracy Realists". Dan Hardway[33], one of the investigators of the House Select Committee on Assassinations, recalls that the term "Conspiracy Theorists" originated in a 1967 memorandum that was broadcast to all CIA stations around the world; with arguments to counter the critics of the Warren

---

[32] David Talbot, The Mother of All Cover-Ups,
http://www.salon.com/2004/09/15/warren/

[33] Jacob. M. Carter – Before History Dies - 2015, Interview of Dan Hardway

Commission, (a future chapter will cover this in detail). This disinformation campaign was aimed at the "Conspiracy Nuts" who continued to discredit the "Lone Nuts" community. Despite all sorts of pseudo-scientific presentations aimed at supporting the official version whose credibility could be questioned, this campaign was not very successful. These "Lone Nuts" thought they could play with science to better refute any theory of conspiracy - some examples will be highlighted in the following chapters. However, at a closer look, the "Conspiracy Nuts" win the final argument thanks to the dominant conspiracy evidence they present. They regularly face one of the favorite counter-arguments that skeptics of the conspiracy keep endlessly repeating: "No, there was no conspiracy. For over fifty years, we would surely have heard of it. Someone would have talked..." The "Conspiracy Nuts", for their part, never miss a chance to recall the numerous testimonies and the evidence of a plot. Many witnesses at the time *did* speak but were not heard. The media also carefully ignored the seriousness of their convictions.

The "Lone Nuts" also evoke "a loss of memory" to invalidate the "confused" testimonies of those who believe in the conspiracy. They say that too many years have passed, that memory has faltered and that it is difficult to relive mentally - half a century later - the exact circumstances of the tragedy. Therefore, one should doubt that these witnesses can speak with credibility today, that errors of interpretation are conceivable.

Clint J. Hill, the secret service agent who, just after the final gunshots on Dealey Plaza, ran towards the presidential limousine and climbed on the trunk to provide a late protection for the president and his wife, remains a staunch defender of the Warren Report. He mentions this "confusion of memory" in his book, Five Presidents: *"There were insinuations of suspicious acts and accusations of cover-up. However, there cannot be two persons who can react in the same way to a tragedy of this magnitude or who remember these events in an identical way. Jackie Kennedy did not remember finding herself perched on the trunk of the car as she was undeniably seen in the photographs. Even in the absence of concrete evidence of a conspiracy, we did not want to believe that an individual - a lonely man - could take the life of our dear President"*[34].

How can Hill draw this parallel? He takes the example of a subconscious reaction due to the circumstances of total panic or extreme trauma and then affirms that the memory of credible witnesses might be failing? Whereas the "Lone Nuts" doubt the credibility of the witnesses who claimed gunshots were coming from the front of the presidential limousine on Dealey Plaza, they refrain, however, from making their own self-criticism for the errors of interpretation and for the possible memory loss of witnesses who support the government version!

Sticking to the official version, the government and the American media are careful not to spread the revelations of the "Conspiracy Nuts" but rather ridicule them. It is not unusual nowadays that an investigator, when presenting the evidence of a possible coup d'état against President Kennedy to a journalist, meets with the immediate reaction: *"Oh! You are not really one of those conspiracy theorists, are you?"*.

Today there are some who say that the assassination of John Kennedy was the response of a conspiracy of the Secret Service, the military and the Mafia forces. This position is much better recognized abroad than in America, which is struggling to accept the evidence of an odious coup d'état. But some important figures in American politics are now cautiously voicing their disbelief to the official government position. Just recently, a major official of President Obama's administration had the courage to evoke the high probability of a conspiracy in the assassination of John Kennedy in front of an American television. On November 13, 2013, Secretary of State John Kerry told NBC reporter Tom Brokaw in an interview that *"to date, he had serious doubts that Oswald acted alone"*. He added that he believed that Oswald *"had been persuaded somewhere by something"* and suggested that *"it might have something to do with the time Oswald spent in the Soviet*

---

[34] Clint J. Hill, Five Presidents My Extraordinary Journey with Eisenhower, Kennedy, Johnson, Nixon and Ford, Gallery Nooks, New-York, 2016, p.178

Union and his relations with communist sympathizers". John Kerry thus publicly revealed, on the fiftieth anniversary of JFK's death, that he did not believe that the assassin of the President acted alone, as claimed in the government investigation report. Although his remarks were somewhat cryptic (he eluded the journalist's question asking him to elaborate), Kerry displayed a personal position that made the conspiracy theory about the death of the President credible. John Kerry, one of the most senior politicians, had joined the community of skeptics who openly and publicly claim that there is suspicion about the outcome of the official investigation[35].

Cicero, the Roman statesman and philosopher, said, *"Whoever is ignorant of the past remains a child."* To know the truth about the facts surrounding the assassination of John Kennedy remains a relevant duty today, not least to honor his memory, hence this book. The following chapters will present not only the serious conspiracy facts that have been argued by many reliable and well-verified sources, but above all, much evidence in order to better accept the plot version. For, better than theories, we now hold the evidence that some rebel individuals of the U.S. government fomented a series of plots with the help of the Mafia and the anti-Castro exiles in order to kill JFK.

Why and in what circumstances was this murderous coup d'état followed by a shameful cover-up that the American media has been allowed to maintain for years? Those supporting the government version continue to assert - even nowadays - that there is a "mountain" of overwhelming evidence showing that one single man was behind Kennedy's assassination. Yet, we must climb the mountain and take the time to examine the evidence that was ignored or distorted by the Warren Commission! The CIA's recurrent attitude of deception and violation of the law, their obstruction of congressional investigators in 1978 and their

---

[35] https://www.youtube.com/watch?v=No0JSg7wp0Q

denial of the plethora of medical evidence on the origin of the wounds in Kennedy's head are powerful facts invalidating the single shooter theory. For example, did these "Lone Nuts" take the time to read the documents that have been "declassified" since 1990 that incriminated senior CIA officials aware of Oswald's movements six weeks before the President was killed?

The evidence of the assassination plot and the cover-up will be documented in the next chapters. The documents are sourced from an abundance of investigation results and are very convincing. We will see in detail that:

- Lee Harvey Oswald most likely did not fire at the President nor was even in the "right" place at the "right" time, as the official version claims.
- at least two assassins - and perhaps more - fired at President Kennedy.
- these assassins acted on behalf of the Mafia, with the complicity of some right-wing extremists, Cuban anti-Castro exiles and CIA rebels, all deeply hostile to John Kennedy against whom death threats had been uttered.
- agents of the powerful American intelligence services, who had reason to hate the President, were involved in some way in preparing and perpetrating the plot and no doubt in covering up the evidence of a conspiracy later on.
- Oswald was in close contact not only with the Russian and the U.S. intelligence agencies (probably as a double agent) but also with the Mafia, the Cuban anti-Castro exiles and the right-wing extremists and that he was manipulated for taking the blame of JFK's murder, as he claimed when he was arrested.
- this scheme required a "double Oswald" who was seen, before the assassination, in order to create several false trails and to provide fake evidence to incriminate Oswald later as the criminal.
- Jack Ruby was strongly linked to Organized Crime, the CIA, and Cuban exiles.
- Oswald was silenced by the Mafia who gave Jack Ruby a contract to eliminate him.

- Ruby managed to kill Oswald at the Dallas police station with the help of at least one corrupt police officer.
- since the assassination of John Kennedy, many witnesses providing "inconvenient" evidence have been murdered as they were about to give testimony before the investigation committees.
- investigation committees were constantly stonewalled by the CIA, the FBI or the police.
- obstacles occurred such as lies, intimidation and harassment of witnesses, concealment, retention and destruction of compromising files.
- the American mainstream media have been complacent with the governmental agencies by maintaining the cover-up.

After being exposed to the facts, perhaps the reader, like a jury, will be convinced that a well-planned and executed conspiracy caused the death of President Kennedy. Alternatively, will the reader remain skeptical? No doubt, whatever the opinion reached, a side will be taken; that of the irreducible conspiracy theorists or that of the supporters of the official version claiming a mad, single shooter did it without complicity.

Chapter 3

The Coup d'État and the Cover-Up

Because of his changing position to peace making towards the end of his presidential term, John Kennedy had many enemies. The animosity towards the President and his brother, Robert Kennedy, the Attorney General under his administration, reached unparalleled proportions compared to other U.S. presidencies. Hatred for the President and his brother was palpable on all sides. Wall Street, the magnates of the oil industry, the steel industry and the arms industry, the big publishers of the press, the Pentagon's hawks, the CIA and the Mafia, all cherished the hope of seeing the President ousted. As he entered into the campaign to run for a second term in 1964 (most likely with success according to political observers), it was unimaginable for JFK's enemies to endure four more years under the Kennedy clan. The CIA hard-liners, the extremist military protesters, the masters of the big industrial trusts whose super-profits could be severely cut because of the White House policy, all saw John Kennedy as a traitor of the nation. After the derailed invasion of the Bay of Pigs in early 1961, the resentment against the President culminated two years later when he took the decision to disengage the United States from Vietnam and to reduce military credits. Enough was enough. JFK's opponents saw him as an enemy of big capitalism, a dangerous threat for the military security and the "prestige of the country".

Dwight Eisenhower, the previous president, had warned public opinion when he addressed the American nation for the last time: "Beware of the military-industrial complex!" Eisenhower was even willing to denounce the influence of this group, despite the fact that it had facilitated his election to the presidency. While Eisenhower did not face this threat, Kennedy did with his ancestral Irish boldness. He paid for it with his life.

Many political opponents and enemies of the President were found among elites of the military-industrial complex, government intelligence agencies and Organized Crime. They feared the likelihood that the Kennedy Clan would monopolize the entire political stage for much of the 1960s. John Kennedy was well on his way to win another four-year term in 1964. His enemies were concerned that he would pass the torch to his brother. The popular, Robert Kennedy, might indeed fulfill the continuity of the Kennedy era by winning two cumulative terms, thereafter. Moreover, wouldn't the youngest brother, Teddy, try his luck to run for one or two presidential terms too? After all, the Kennedy dynasty, a visionary for a lasting peace, was so inspiring. The electoral support of the American people, confident in a strong and respected America in the world, could then be granted. It was inconceivable for these opposition elites to tolerate nepotism and the political omnipresence of the Kennedy clan for at least nine more years. The many enemies of John Kennedy had to do everything to eliminate this dreaded scenario. Their reasons were plentiful.

If the question "why was the president assassinated?" has been answered, the relentless question, "who killed President Kennedy?" remains in our minds and has generated a passionate debate for more than five decades without clear answers. Because the botched investigation of the Warren Commission failed to shed full light on this crime, the American people suspect that evidence has been omitted and covered-up over the years and conclude that an obvious complicity took place. The American people and the whole world feel they have been deluded, unconvinced that a young and crazy gunman without any accomplices perpetrated the crime of the century. Without an identified complicity, the concept of a plot would then be dismissed, an argument used by the government. However, without motives, means and opportunity convicting the alleged assassin, a conspiracy and a cover-up could then be argued by those with an opposing view, while at the same time making sure that future inquiries would not be hindered in the name of democracy.

The word "Conspiracy" is not taboo. It is quite appropriate to what exactly happened on November 22, 1963. Merriam-Webster dictionary defines it, as "a secret plan or act made by two or more people to do something that is harmful or illegal". The Latin origin "Conspirare" refers to "an agreement, a plot between two or more individuals or literally 'breathing together'". Two individuals and only two conjuring in secret, without resorting to a larger group of plotters, are a sufficient number for their evil plan to be called a conspiracy, although in the JFK case several of his enemies possibly participated in the plot. As soon as there is controversy and polemic about a major disturbing historical event, in so much as there is a political context attached, the words "conspiracy theory" unfortunately have a derogative connotation in the eyes of those who ridicule its supporters. But conspiracies are not all theories. History is sadly rich in political events, which have caused heavy human losses due to conspiracies. Sinister plots have been hatched in order to either overthrow a statesman (the conspiracy to assassinate President Abraham Lincoln for example is now well established in the United States) or to trigger so-called "necessity" or "retaliation" wars. Ingenious military advisers have indeed deceived the public by presenting fully invented facts. For example, during President Lyndon Johnson's administration, the American intervention in the Indochinese conflict escalated as a result of the controversial attack of two American destroyers in the Gulf of Tonkin in 1964. More recently, the decision by the administration of President George W. Bush to invade Iraq was based on a false "demonstration" to the world that weapons of mass destruction had been found. The "theory" that Thomas Jefferson had an African-American slave mistress, Sally Hemmings, with whom he had an offspring, was considered scandalous and was refuted for a very long time and those conspiracy theorists were highly criticized. Like the critics of the Warren Report's findings who have been chastised, with the connivance of the American mainstream media, in the Jefferson case, Washington academic historians and journalists have ridiculed the "conspiracy theorists" for 175 years. Those who fueled the rumor about Thomas Jefferson's "bewilderment" were seen as pathological peddlers, evil spirits, devoid of patriotic fervor, whose behavior was damaging the American civil life in the eyes of "rational" historians. However, according to the very serious scientific journal "Nature", science was the light of salvation. Indeed, as late as 1998, a search for DNA, among Sally Hemmings' descendants, confirmed, without a shadow of a doubt, that Thomas Jefferson had been the father of her children. This put an end to the rumor that had unfortunately already tarnished the image of one of the most revered founding fathers of the young American nation. All in all, conventional wisdom collapsed and factual data outweighed timely fiction. As with the Jefferson-Hemmings case, it is to be hoped that modern criminal investigation science will also shed full light on the assassination of John Kennedy!

So conspiracy is a reality in history. With reference to the assassination of JFK, why would serious investigators then be blamed when they have the courage to bring the overwhelming evidence of a conspiracy? More than a conspiracy, it was a coup d'état. Here again how does Merriam-Webster dictionary define it? "A sudden attempt by a small group of people to take over the government usually through violence". What happened in Dallas on 22nd November 1963 matches well this definition. In order to understand this state crime, the basic question is not so much "What happened?" but rather "Why did this coup d'état take place"? "How did it unfold?", and "what were the consequences?"

How did government investigators address this political crime over five decades? The Warren Report was published in 1964 to put an end to doubts about a possible conspiracy and to calm the American public. But since then, the investigation into the JFK assassination has not stopped. It has been conducted by five governmental or independent groups: the *Garrison Investigation* leading to the 1969 trial of Clay Shaw, presumed guilty in the conspiracy but cleared; the *Rockefeller Commission* in 1975 (the commission under President Gerald Ford to examine the activities of the CIA in the United States); the *Church Committee* (the Senate Select Committee on Intelligence Activities) also in 1975 and the *House Select Committee on Assassinations* (HSCA) in 1977. Much later, *the President John F. Kennedy Assassination Records Act* (or JFK Records Act) was also drawn-up by the U.S. Congress in 1992 following the public response over the release of Oliver Stone's movie "JFK". Many revelations about the Kennedy assassination became known and some 4.5 million pages of records were published. An independent agency, the *Assassination Records Review Board* (ARRB) was appointed in 1992 by President Bill Clinton to identify the remaining secret files about the assassination of JFK and to publish them. In November 1998, 400,000 pages of documents were published by the National Archives, those that had been compiled over four years by the ARRB. We must also not forget the *Freedom of Information Act* of 1966, a federal law. The legal framework of this law however does not specifically cover political assassinations. It is addressed to the U.S. government executive branch agencies which must respond to any U.S. citizen's request for the publication of information or documents under the control of the U.S. government, in part or in whole.

It was during the post-Watergate period (1970s) that this political scandal undermined American confidence in their own government. We were perhaps at this time the closest to solving the mystery of John Kennedy' assassination, especially due to the revelations about the CIA's activities to carry out anti-Castro operations. The agency had deliberately hidden these revelations from the Warren Commission. As a result, the Warren Report conclusions were first reviewed by the Church Committee and afterwards by the House Select Committee on Assassinations. Following this, these committees then uncovered new evidence of conspiracy and, by making their findings public, called into question the possible role played by government agencies in the covering up or even the involvement of some CIA rebel elements in the execution of assassination plots.

But, in the end, these commissions faced frustration as internal and external political pressure limited their investigations. Their efforts were doomed to failure because of the real lack of cooperation from the CIA and the FBI. These deeply secretive agencies had openly deceived the Warren Commission in the past and their obstruction of Congressional investigations in the 1970s proved equally effective.

One of the members of the Church Committee, the tenacious senator from Pennsylvania, Richard Schweiker, believed that the CIA had been involved in the cover-up of the JFK assassination, and that some rebel agents of the agency might even have participated in the plot, at least in support of the Organized Crime. The senator also favored the concept of a conspiracy initially organized by the Mafia in retaliation for the attacks of the Kennedy brothers against its corruption, which they wanted, eradicated in America.

The Church Committee did not succeed: it ran out of time to complete its investigation and lacked political support. The obstructions of the CIA members, who appeared before the commission and resorted to perjury plus the absence of subpoena of key Mafia witnesses such as Johnny Roselli and Sam Giancana, forced the commission to suspend its investigation[36].

The last U.S. governmental investigation into the assassination of President Kennedy was the House Select Committee on Assassinations (HSCA) in 1977. After two and a half years of investigation, at a cost of US$ 5.4 million, the findings of the commission were astounding but tempered by cautious language: it concluded that JFK was probably murdered as a result of a conspiracy but that the commission could neither

---

[36] David Talbot – Brothers, The Hidden History of the Kennedy Years - 2007

identify the second gunman nor the extent of the conspiracy. The commission dismissed the complicity of the Cuban and Soviet governments, the Secret Service, as well as of the FBI and the CIA. However, it did not exclude the possible involvement of individuals linked to Organized Crime or to anti-Castro groups.

The conclusions of the HSCA were based on the results of acoustic studies on Dealey Plaza, more specifically on the emission of sound pulses from a police motorcycle behind the presidential limousine who had accidentally left his microphone turned on. The acoustics experts identified four gunshots and located one of them at the "Grassy Knoll", the small grassy hill near a pergola on Dealey Plaza, which overlooked the progression of the limousine. However, counter-experts challenged this acoustic evidence. Although the HSCA criticized the failings of the Warren Commission's investigation, including its negligence for not considering a possible conspiracy, this failure was explained by the fact that the Warren Commission was unable to present relevant information in time because government agencies and departments had retained documents. Clearly, there was obstruction from these agencies.

View of the retaining wall of the " Grassy Knoll" , near the pergola on Elm Street. An ideal cover for firing at the incoming presidential limousine (author's photo)

Richard A Sprague head of the HSCA appointed Robert Tanenbaum, as Deputy Chief Counsel, the legendary and successful prosecutor of the New York Homicide Bureau. In December 1976, Tanenbaum went to Richard Schweiker's Senate office for the handover of the Church Committee's files and to ask the senator for advice. Schweiker wanted to share his opinion from his experience at the Church Committee. He told Tanenbaum that he "should expect the new commission to be obstructed" and that "in his opinion, the CIA was involved in the murder of the President". Tanenbaum remembered that those words "gave him goose bumps". *It was a senator from the United States who was telling me that*! he said.

The new HSCA investigators were resolved to ask particular CIA officials aggressive questions about the assassination of President Kennedy and immediately began to subpoena them. Tanenbaum came to the same conclusion as Richard Schweiker did during the hearings: "*The more we were digging into the case, the more productive our investigation became with respect to the CIA's involvement. Some of their officials had cooperated with the anti-Castro Cubans*". But, the HSCA investigation faltered and soon became the target of the press. A New-York Times article violently criticized the committee's "McCarthy era" tactics. Congressional funds began to dwindle and committee members were no longer paid. Sprague and Tanenbaum resigned.

During the Pittsburgh Conference "Passing the Torch" in 2015, I had the opportunity to appreciate Robert Tanenbaum's fascinating presentation. Tanenbaum spoke quite eloquently about the frustrations of his team whose investigation had been stonewalled by the CIA, 38 years earlier.

G. Robert Blakey, an expert lawyer on Organized Crime, replaced Richard Sprague at the head of the HSCA. Blakey made the decision to voluntarily limit attacks against the CIA in his investigation (unlike his predecessors who had relentlessly directed them) and to follow a strategy of cooperation with the intelligence agency.

Two HSCA investigators, appointed by Blakey, Dan Hardway and Eddie Lopez, endured the same CIA obstructions. In 2014, at the AARC conference on the 50th anniversary of the Warren

Report publication, I heard Blakey, Hardway and Lopez speaking with emotion about their misfortune. At the CIA Headquarters, as soon as they were about to discover compromising and tangible documents, the two HSCA attorneys, Hardway and Lopez, faced obstruction and intimidation[37]. A striking example of the CIA resistance was revealed in April 2001: the Miami New Times published an article by the journalist Jefferson Morley about the actions of George Joannides, the CIA agent whom Hardway and Lopez had accused of obstructing their investigation. The article revealed that Joannides, who was based in Miami in the early sixties, was running a Cuban-funded group of Cuban exiled students who were trying to get Oswald to act as a Castro pawn, before and after the JFK assassination. We know today that Joannides, who died in 1990, played a key role in Oswald's mysterious involvement and that he was able to cover up his actions before the HSCA investigators. The CIA not only manipulated the Warren Commission but also deluded the HSCA, obstructing the investigation 14 years later. The obstruction did not however prevent the HSCA from ending its investigation with the conclusion that President Kennedy "was probably murdered as a result of a conspiracy" and that the Mafia and some Cuban exiles could have fomented it.

Under President Jimmy Carter's administration, attempts were made to continue investigating the JFK assassination. However, the movement wore itself out and when President Reagan became president in 1981, the grip of the Washington Secret Service intensified. The media then took over, but instead of trying to find answers to the many unanswered questions, they started to castigate the conspiracy theorists and embraced the single murderer's version. The investigation of the House Select Committee on Assassinations had left far too many unresolved issues and when the Department of Justice took over the case, it took no action and preferred to ignore it. By doing so, the acoustic tests could not be completed and the witnesses of the autopsy,

---

[37] David Talbot – Brothers, The Hidden History of the Kennedy Years - 2007

who could prove the President's evident injuries, were unable to testify. No more disturbing questions were asked about the lack of evidence or the anomalies in the Warren Report. However, all the polls since 1963, without exception, still showed that a large majority of Americans (50 to 80 percent depending on when the survey was conducted) did not believe in the official version of the assassination and considered the Warren Report had duped the nation.

On November 22, 1963, in Dallas, John Kennedy was ambushed by his enemies, those who feared his foreign policy, his weakness to fight against communism and who saw the President as a threat to the United States. Many documents confirm that John Kennedy wanted to disengage from Vietnam, to drastically reduce the threat of nuclear weapons, and to work for détente with the Soviet Union, Cuba and the Eastern bloc[38]. Despite his efforts, his enemies opposed his instructions by continuing to practice secret operations against Cuba behind his back.

Cuba might well be the core of the mystery about the JFK assassination. With the help of the Mafia, the many CIA and anti-Castro conspiracies aimed at eliminating Fidel Castro were all unsuccessful. It is still amazing today that the Cuban dictator was able to escape all assassination attempts.

John Kennedy was killed because of his opposition to maintaining the hostile relations between the United States and Cuba and because of the repeated failures to destabilize Fidel Castro. The co-conspirators therefore decided to change their target: their enemy became JFK. Their strategy was to direct the conspiracies against Kennedy such that the Cubans would be blamed for the assassination of the President, giving them a pretext to invade the island. Since it was unthinkable that such a sinister scenario could be unveiled, a cover-up operation was agreed on and implemented by the government agencies and the

---

[38] James W. Douglass. JFK and the Unspeakable: Why he died and why it matters. Touchstone 2010.

national security services immediately after the death of the President.

Fabian Escalante, head of counterintelligence at the State Security Department in Cuba in 1960, (the Cuban service equivalent to the CIA), was certainly apt for interpreting intelligence during the difficult and very tense relationship between the United States and Fidel Castro. Much later, in 1993, as head of the Cuban Security Studies Center, he gave the following analysis of the coup against JFK: *"The 'hawks'* [of Washington] *did not understand and disagreed deeply with his* [JFK] *strategy. Everything that was not in favor of an invasion of Cuba was reprehensible. The hawks felt betrayed. Two strategies were opposed: that of the Kennedy administration and that of the CIA, Cuban exiles and the Mafia. As a result, they made every effort to assassinate Kennedy because he was in deep disagreement over the question of invasion"*[39].

According to a memo kept confidential for ten years by the lawyers of the Warren Commission, the motive of the anti-Castro exiles was to involve Oswald so that he could be arrested as a sympathizer of Castro after the murder of JFK. The memo also revealed that such a scheme would cause condemnation of the Castro regime by the American public and authorities, horrified by such a tragedy, and would result in the overthrow of the Cuban regime by force[40]. Robert Morrow, a former CIA agent, himself active in many anti-Castro operations, summed up it all: *"the assassination of President Kennedy was, to put it simply, an anti-Castro provocation, an act aimed at blaming Castro in order to lead an American invasion of Cuba in retaliation. Such an act would not only have benefited the Mafia bosses who had lost their grip on the gambling industry in Havana following the Castro putsch but also some CIA agents who had lost their credibility with Cuban exile fighters after the fiasco of the Bay of Pigs invasion"*[41].

---

[39] Fabian Escalante. Cuban Officials and JFK Historians Conference. 7 December 1995

[40] Lamar Waldron & Thom Hartmann. Ultimate Sacrifice (New York: Carroll & Graf, 2005)

[41] Robert D. Morrow. First Hand Knowledge: How I Participated in the CIA-Mafia Murder of President Kennedy (S.P.I. Books: 1992)

Despite his status as President of the United States, John Kennedy was at war, in his own administration, against the White House hawks, his military and national security advisers, who constantly kept him under pressure. On July 20, 1961, the President was enraged at a major meeting of his National Security Council. He was appalled at being asked by the Joint Chiefs of Staff, General Lemnitzer, and Allen Dulles, the CIA director, to approve a plan for a nuclear attack against the Soviet Union. As he was leaving the meeting room, the President yelled to his Secretary of State *"And we call ourselves the human race!"* [42] [43] As soon as he left the meeting, the Chiefs of Staff of the Armed Forces, who had stayed in the meeting room, began to utter insanities against the President by calling him a "wimp". How do we know this? Under the administrations of Presidents Kennedy, Johnson and Nixon, it was usual for the White House discussions, especially during the National Security Council meetings, to be recorded. During the crisis that marked his presidential term, Kennedy secretly recorded his meetings at the White House and with his military advisers. For Kennedy, it was a way to protect the American people from the potential evil designs of its leaders. The tapes were later declassified and the transcript published in the late 1990s. They are kept in the National Archives[44].

Curtis LeMay, the Air Force Chief of Staff, was arguably the most hostile military "advisor" to the President. In response to the installation of Soviet missiles in Cuba, LeMay wanted an immediate and full-deployed military action. He vehemently made disrespectful remarks against the President present in the room: *"If we leave them there, the Communist bloc would wield a blackmail threat against not only us but the other South American countries"*. He then added that if the President's response to the Soviet challenge was weak, there would be political repercussions overseas and the U.S. government's position would be perceived as too soft. *"And I'm sure a lot of our own citizens would feel that way*

---

[42] David Talbot – Brothers, The Hidden History of the Kennedy Years - 2007
[43] McGeorge Bundy, Danger and Survival, 354; Dean Rusk, As I Saw It 246-247
[44] Ted Widner. JFK's Secret White House Recordings Unveiled" September 5, 2012

too... In other words, you're in a pretty bad fix at the present time" he said. Kennedy could not let the sarcasm pass. Annoyed, he replied, *"What did you say?"* LeMay repeated: *"You're in a pretty bad fix."* The President replied sharply, *"You're in there with me"* and added with a mocking laugh: *"Personally."*[45] Still challenging the President, LeMay was heard saying that the blockade of Cuba was almost as bad as the Munich appeasement in 1938: *"I just don't see any other solution except direct military intervention, right now"*[46].

John Kennedy endeavored to contain these ominous forces. With his team of loyal advisers, he shared his views for developing a consensus for peace. He was determined to do it rapidly especially because the White House "hawks" were strongly opposed to his peace policy; losing hope, that reason could prevail on his side. He was heard to say, *"They all want war"*[47].

The lobbying in favor of the Cold War was then very aggressive. Right-wing activists and even retired military leaders were vocal about the dismissal of the President and Liberals such as Earl Warren, the Chief Justice of the Supreme Court. A retired Marine colonel even proposed that Earl Warren be hanged. A retired Marine general suggested a coup d'état if no vote could be obtained against these "traitors".

Kennedy's exasperation peaked in October 1961 when the Dallas Morning News' reactionary publisher, Ted Dealey, confronted him at a meeting in the White House, which the President was holding with a group of newspaper publishers in Texas. Dealey harangued the President in these terms: *"We can annihilate Russia and should make that clear to the Soviet government... The general opinion of the grassroots thinking in this country is that you and your administration are weak sisters. We need a man on horseback to lead this nation and many people in Texas and the Southwest think you are riding Carolina's tricycle* [JFK's

---

[45] David Talbot – Brothers, The Hidden History of the Kennedy Years - 2007

[46] James W. Douglass, JFK and the Unspeakable, Why He Died and Why it Matters, A Touchstone Book, 2008

[47] Jesse Ventura – They Killed Our President – 2013. Skyhorse Publishing, Inc.

daughter]". Visibly troubled but with a piercing glance at Dealey, the President shot back: *"The difference between you and me, Mr. Dealey, is that I was elected president of this country and you were not. I have the responsibility for the lives of 180 million Americans, which you have not... Wars are easier to talk about than they are to fight. I'm just as tough as you are and I didn't get elected president by arriving at soft judgments.* "[48].

Jefferson Morley[49], journalist and moderator of the website JFKfacts.org, believes that the reason for supporting the conspiracy theory lies more in the circumstances of the crime itself than in the suspicions of a plot against John Kennedy. It was once we saw and learned what had happened in Dallas during that fateful day that we quickly concluded that it was impossible for one person to have committed the crime. The many articles and books on the conspiracy theory might have influenced our opinion but the facts of the Dallas event have certainly challenged us and left us to doubt more than ever about the conclusions of the Warren Report.

Even the opinion of some members of the Warren Commission evolved at the end of their investigation. Doubt gained ground. They criticized the investigation many years after the publication of their report. Two major events contributed to undermine the findings of the Warren Report: the discovery of President Kennedy's back wound, positioned much lower than his throat injury, and Oswald's possible involvement with the FBI and the CIA. Allan Dulles, former CIA director, after being dismissed by Kennedy became, by irony of fate, a very active member of the Warren Commission and endeavored to hide Oswald's connection with the agency from the eyes of the public. Some members of the commission said they did not believe in the conclusions - especially on the ballistic evidence. Earl Warren even said: *"never in our life will we know the full truth about what happened in Dallas"*. Congressman Hale Boggs, although he

---

[48] David Talbot – Brothers, The Hidden History of the Kennedy Years - 2007
[49] Interview of Jefferson Morley by Jacob M. Carter – 2015 – Before History Dies.

accepted the "Single Bullet" version initially, thought that there was no real satisfactory answer to this question. Senator John Sherman Cooper had the same reservations. Richard Russell did not believe Oswald's guilt who, he said, was incapable of planning or executing the murder on his own. Thanks to the White House tapes published in recent years, we now know that Lyndon Johnson himself did not believe in the conclusions of the Warren Commission. On September 18, 1964, the last day of the commission's session, Richard Russell telephoned Johnson to tell him that he did not believe in the single bullet theory. Johnson then replied "*Nor do I*"[50].

From the very beginning, Russell had been dragging his feet when President Johnson put pressure on him to accept serving on the Warren Commission. Based on the phone recordings at the White House, Russell resisted though: "*Now, Mr. President, I don't have to tell you of my devotion to you, but I just can't serve on that commission. I'm highly honored you'd think about me in connection with it. But I couldn't serve on it with Chief Justice Warren. I don't like that man*". Johnson, in a condescending manner, replied, "*Dick, it has already been announced. And you can serve with anybody for the good of America. And this is a question that has a good many more ramifications than on the surface. And we've got to take this out of the arena where they're testifying that Khrushchev and Castro did this and did that and kicking us into a war that can kill forty million Americans in an hour ... The Secretary of State came over this afternoon. He's deeply concerned, Dick, about the idea that they're spreading throughout the Communist world that Khrushchev killed Kennedy. Now he didn't. He didn't have a damned thing to do with it*". Approving him on this last point, Russell finally yielded under Johnson's coercion: "*I don't think he did directly. I know Khrushchev didn't because he thought he'd get along better with Kennedy* "[51].

Other members of the Warren Commission, however, maintained their position. John McCloy remained a fierce

---

[50] David Talbot, The Mother of All Cover-Ups, http://www.salon.com/2004/09/15/warren/

[51] James W. Douglass, JFK and the Unspeakable, Why He Died and Why it Matters, A Touchstone Book, 2008

supporter of the "Single Bullet" - a theory developed by its staunch defender, Arlen Specter, the deputy commissioner of the commission. He denied any existence of a conspiracy to kill President Kennedy.

Gerald Ford, the future President of the United States, well known for his many blunders, openly disclosed parts of a document - that the commission had classified "top secret" - in his book on the assassination of Kennedy, "Portrait of the Assassin"! He later declared that he had not been aware of his goof. The government went as far as absolving him in order to make the document accessible! And Ford did it again! Edgar Hoover, the FBI director, had agreed with Gerald Ford that everything the latter was going to report on the activities of the Warren Commission, had to remain confidential, between the director and him. Five days after the discussion with Hoover, Ford broke his promise. He revealed to an FBI contact that "*two members of the commission were not convinced yet that the President had been shot from the sixth floor window of the TSBD*"[52]. According to Daniel Schorr, the CBS reporter on the CIA activities investigated by the Rockefeller Commission, Gerald Ford also told New York Times publishers at a luncheon in the White House, that he should choose the members of the Rockefeller Commission with great care because "*there was a danger that the commission would stumble on much more sensitive matters than on matters of domestic surveillance*". One of the Times editors asked: "*What matters are we talking about*? Ford replied: "*Between us and confidentially ... of assassinations ...*" [53].

Leon Jaworski, the special adviser to the Warren commission, investigated Oswald's contacts with the CIA and the FBI in Texas. He told the commission that there was no evidence on the allegations that Oswald might have worked for U.S. intelligence.

The commission's chief counsel, J. Lee Rankin, acting as a liaison with the FBI and the CIA, rejected the criticism of its members by

---

[52] Lamar Waldron, The Hidden History of the JFK Assassination, Counter Point Berkeley, 2013
[53] Robert J. Groden and Harrison Edward Livingstone. High Treason: The assassination of JFK. What really happened? The Conservatory Press, 1989

expediting the report; *"We're done with memoranda. The report must be published"*[54].

Ten days before the final drafting of the investigation report, Richard Russell, urged the commission to include a clause in the report stating that the likelihood that Oswald might have had co-conspirators could not be categorically rejected[55]. Behind his back, Lee Rankin, redacted the clause of the report himself to avoid disagreements within the commission. However, Russell refused to sign the report's conclusion[56]. In mid-January 1970, a year before Richard Russell's death, the Washington Post relayed his words on Oswald: *"I think someone else had cooperated with him ... There are too many things... some of his trips to Mexico City and several discrepancies in the facts such as his means of transportation, details on his luggage or the person who might have travelled with him ... all that challenges me and makes me doubt that he could have acted alone "*[57].

The conviction as it was expressed by some members of the Warren Commission that there might have been a conspiracy in the assassination of President Kennedy, is generally ignored by Americans and forgotten by mainstream media today. Lee Harvey Oswald's involvement not only with the U.S. intelligence services but also with the Mafia will be widely developed in a future chapter.

The true purpose of the Warren Commission was not to find the truth but to bury it ... In addition to facts, testimonies and to lack of an alibi, any serious investigation can lead to a verdict of guilt incriminating an alleged criminal so long as three basic pillars of the investigation are proven: the motive, the opportunities and the means. In the case of the Warren Commission, a shameless method of investigation was pursued. The commission worked backwards, immediately finger pointing the culprit (Lee Harvey Oswald) and then becoming entangled in an "ingenious" enterprise to try to match the clues and evidence with a

---

[54] Robert J. Groden, The Killing of a President, Vicking Studio Books, 1993
[55] http://22november1963.org.uk/richard-russell-warren-report
[56] David Talbot – Brothers, The Hidden History of the Kennedy Years - 2007
[57] Washington Post, January 19, 1970.

preconceived conclusion! While it was aware of Jack Ruby's acquaintance with Lee Harvey Oswald, what did the Warren Commission do? It totally eluded the question! It was also aware that Oswald had links to U.S. intelligence but concealed the evidence. It knew very well that Oswald could not have fired all the gunshots from the Texas School Book Depository but preferred to painstakingly compose extravagant reflections about it!

Later, when President Nixon was asked about what he thought of the Warren Commission, he replied: "*It was the greatest hoax that has ever been perpetuated* "[58]. A top Republican official once asked Nixon what he knew about the JFK assassination. In his reply, "*You don't want to know!*"[59] was Nixon's remark rather a reminder of how dangerous that knowledge would be for those learning the truth about the JFK assassination? Was there a bit of humor in Nixon's reply, a casual reference to threat, that was not really meant to be taken seriously, like someone engaged in highly confidential research would crack the joke: "If I were to tell you that secret, I'll have to kill you !".

Historians have commented about Robert Kennedy's uncertain opinion about the murder of his brother and his troubling apathy when he was Attorney General and even much later during his political life, while he was expected to do his utmost to identify those behind the crime. However, as soon as he heard that his brother had been assassinated in Dallas, he immediately suspected a conspiracy.

The President's brother was certainly one of the earliest skeptics as was JFK's immediate entourage who shared with him the strong belief that something sinister had happened in Dallas. But what surprised many was that, in public, Robert Kennedy, and to some extent the Kennedy family, seemed resigned. He gave the impression of being beaten by the "reason of state" when he publicly endorsed the theory of the lone murderer. He thus

---

[58] Kevin Anderson. "Revelations and gaps on Nixon tapes" March 1, 2002.BBC News.
[59] David Talbot – Brothers, The Hidden History of the Kennedy Years - 2007

remained silent, fearing to create a huge chaotic crisis in a country in shock and showed in public an attitude of fatalism, even an apparent support of the official version. When he heard of his brother's death in his home in Hickory Hill, Virginia, he told Edwin Guthman of the Justice Department's press service, who had joined him at his home: "*I thought they would get one of us, but Jack, after all he'd been through, never worried about it... I thought they would get me instead of the President* "[60].

Privately though, Robert Kennedy confided to his relatives. He rejected the Warren Report based on the theory of the lone gunman and believed an internal plot had been fomented by the forces in the shadow of the American government. He was prepared to undertake his own investigation to understand the assassination of his brother.

There was no doubt for Bobby Kennedy: behind the elimination of his brother, he did not see a solitary mad shooter but he was referring to several plotters. On November 29, 1963, just one week after the Dallas assassination, Bobby Kennedy sent Bill Walton, Kennedy family's intimate friend, to the Soviet Union with a secret message from Bobby and Jackie Kennedy to Georgi Bolshakov, a Soviet agent. While stationed in Washington under the JFK administration, Bolshakov had been chosen by the President to follow the secret communication of rapprochement between him and Khrushchev after the period of extreme tension between the two countries and especially during the Cuban Missile Crisis. What Walton revealed to Bolshakov during a dinner in Moscow had an unforgettable impact on the Soviet. Walton confided that Bobby and Jackie believed that President Kennedy had been killed by the perpetrators of a large political conspiracy; "*Perhaps there was only one assassin but he did not act alone ... There were others behind Lee Harvey Oswald's gun ...*" The Kennedys did not think however that the act could have been committed on foreign orders. They were convinced that JFK had been the victim of U.S. opponents. Walton also discussed with the Soviet the plans for the future of Robert Kennedy; a possible race

---

[60] Ibid

to the U.S. presidency and that if he were confirmed at this supreme position, he would pursue his brother's quest for a détente with the Soviet Union[61].

The remarkable meeting between Walton and Bolshakov was covered in a 1997 book, "One Hell of a Gamble," written by Timothy Naftali about the Cuban Missile Crisis. The dean of journalism in Washington, Evan Thomas of Newsweek, ignored, in his critique of Naftali's book, Bobby Kennedy's message that Walton had conveyed during his mission to Moscow. Instead of mentioning Bobby Kennedy's opinion about the assassination of his brother, Thomas rather castigated Bobby Kennedy for his *"irresponsible and mischievous act of backdoor diplomacy"*, for his anti-Johnson sentiments and political ambitions. Bobby Kennedy's astonishing secret message to Moscow, one of the most revealing testimonies we have today about what he thought about his brother's assassination, would thus be forgotten as soon as it was made public.

Robert Kennedy faced a terrible internal political dilemma. The new President, Lyndon B. Johnson, was the arch-nemesis of Robert Kennedy. Both entertained mutual hatred for each other. J. Edgar Hoover, although his subordinate, also hated Bobby Kennedy viscerally, to the extent that he rejected his phone calls after the assassination of his brother. Hoover knew well how to exploit the Dallas drama in the face of a distressed Robert Kennedy who was quickly losing his authority as Attorney General. He saw his power disintegrate and was quickly isolated. The Deputy Minister of Justice, Nicholas Katzenbach, remembered the words of his depressed and defeated boss who was not seeing the usefulness of a thorough investigation: *"What difference can it make? He's gone "*.

But, although he felt resigned, Robert Kennedy was biding his time. When he ran for the presidential campaign in 1968, he thought that if elected President he would then have an opportunity to shed full light on the assassination of his brother. Despite his family obligations (he was the father of 11 children)

---

[61] Ibid

and the pleading from both his sister-in-law, Jacqueline, and his brother, Ted, not to run in the election campaign because of the danger he would face, Robert Kennedy however made that choice. He told his entourage privately that he was going to reopen the investigation. In order to achieve this goal, he asked for the help of trustworthy men such as Walter Sheridan, a former FBI investigator and Frank Mankiewicz, his press secretary, to secretly follow the tracks of a conspiracy. Robert Kennedy was about to reopen the case when he was murdered in Los Angeles in 1968 during the presidential primaries.

Bobby Kennedy was certainly ready to take that risk. In the midst of the election campaign, he went for a break in Malibu, California, at the home of his friend John Frankenheimer, a Hollywood director, in the company of his friends and supporters from the entertainment world. Among them, the French novelist, Romain Gary, said aloud to Bobby: *"You know, don't you, that somebody's going to try to kill you?"* Robert Kennedy, staring blank into space, replied: *"That's a chance I have to take"* then continued: *"Take De Gaulle. How many attempts on his life has he survived exactly?* Gary replied: *"Six or seven, I think"*. Bobby then said with a slight smile: *"I told you, you can't make it without that good old bitch, luck"*[62].

In January 1964, while the American press was hastily closing the file on the assassination of President Kennedy, Menachem Arnoni, the editor of the provocative monthly magazine, *The Minority of One*, wrote an article on the assassination entitled *"Who killed Whom and Why? Black Thoughts about Dark Events "*. In the article, Arnoni spoke of the chilling possibility that Kennedy's assassination might have resulted from a machination organized by some officials at top government level coveting a change of political power. What he wrote would somehow clarify Bobby Kennedy's apparent paralyzed and wretched condition after receiving the news from Dallas, and his lack of immediate decision to publicly launch an investigation into his brother's

---

[62] Ibid

death. "*The possibility can by no means be dismissed that important men in Washington do know the identity of the conspirators, or at least some of them, and that these conspirators are so powerful that prudence dictates that they not be identified in public ... Let us make the fantastic assumption that President Lyndon Johnson and Attorney General Robert Kennedy know or believe that the murder was planned by a group of high-ranking officers who would stop at nothing to end American-Soviet negotiations. However strong their desire to avenge John Kennedy, what course would be open to them? To move against such formidable conspirators might start a disastrous chain of events. It could lead to American troops shooting at other American troops. It could lead to a direct take-over by a military clique. To avert such catastrophes, it might well be considered prudent to pretend utter ignorance, in the hope that the conspirators might be removed from power discreetly, at a later date, one by one*".

There was nothing unreasonable or inconsistent in Arnoni's article. Robert Kennedy undoubtedly made this painful choice, in a state of distress. He told an old friend of the family, "*If the American people knew the truth about Dallas, there would be blood in the streets*"[63].

Dick Goodwin was one of Bobby Kennedy's band of friends. Early on, he was the one with whom Bobby shared his doubts about his brother's assassination. Goodwin shared his opinion on the phone when the author David Talbot contacted him: "*We know the CIA was involved and the Mafia. We all know that. But how do you link those to the assassination? I don't know*". For four decades, Goodwin suspected there was a plot but did not initiate any investigation to elucidate the Dallas crime. He was waiting for Bobby Kennedy to do it. He was convinced that he would have done so had he become President: "*Whatever way he went about it, he would have tried to find out if there was more there, once he had the power to actually get information. That was always my assumption*"[64].

---

[63] Ibid
[64] Ibid

The defenders of the Warren Report of course exploited Robert Kennedy's silence: if the president's own brother (the country's most powerful lawyer at the time) did nothing to follow the case, surely there was then nothing! They therefore concluded that Bobby Kennedy indirectly supported the Warren Report and, for the same reason, confirmed its validity.

Robert Kennedy's enemies actually conducted the investigation of the assassination, including Edgar Hoover, the FBI director and Allen Dulles. Dulles, the former CIA director, was appointed by Lyndon Johnson to play a leading role in the Warren Commission's investigation. According to Talbot, Allen Dulles, who had been dismissed by President Kennedy after the Bay of Pigs fiasco, could have been an influential member of the group plotting against the President, possibly by involving some CIA agents, those in his entourage who had remained loyal to the deposed director. For them, John Kennedy had disrupted the order of this elitist power at the CIA and he had to pay for it with his life.

The final investigating commission, the House Select Committee on Assassinations, became very close to reaching the truth. Unfortunately, politicians put enormous time pressure on the commission to write its report. The Committee believed that: *"On the basis of the evidence available to it, President John F Kennedy was probably assassinated as a result of a conspiracy. The committee is unable to identify the other gunman or the extent of the conspiracy"*[65].

While unable to provide answers to important leads of its research received at the last minute, the House Select Committee on Assassinations left future researchers and historians to explore these unanswered questions. The committee was however convinced that Oswald had had accomplices and had been manipulated to become a patsy.

---

[65] Findings of the Select Committee on Assassinations in the Assassination of President John F. Kennedy in Dallas, Tex., November 22, 1963, Section C

Today there are hundreds of thousands classified documents related to John Kennedy's assassination that are concealed from the American people by the government. What is the CIA hiding? What does it fear that the American people might discover? Why this relentlessness to maintain secrecy half a century later?

Jacob Carter interviewed Dan Hardway, a member of the House Select Committee on Assassinations who ran the investigation at the CIA premises. Hardway believes it is due time that U.S. citizens demand that the seal of secrecy on President Kennedy's assassination be broken and that the CIA admit its accountability. *"There is no place for something like that in a free and open democratic society. It is totally incompatible with what we are as a country"*[66].

What is most disturbing is that the U.S. government is unwilling - or not interested - to use today state-of-the-art technologies to help solve this crime. It would rather maintain the secret in documents about the JFK assassination that are still hidden from the public in the vaults of the National Archives. We can understand that, in the 1960s or 1970s, investigative work on the assassination could only be limited to the technology available at the time. But five decades later, the means, the scientific resources and the state of the art scientific technology in forensic criminology using medical, photographic, acoustic or ballistic expertise are such that the U.S. government ought to shed light on this case.

Who benefited from the crime? We are not short of motives as far as John Kennedy's enemies are concerned. The CIA, the Mafia, the Anti-Castro, the tycoons of the oil industry, the steel industry, the arms industry, and U.S. military forces, all cherished the hope to remove the President from office. Jesse Ventura, former independent governor of Minnesota, believes that some members of the military forces were involved in the conspiracy by providing false information on Lee Harvey Oswald, by

---

[66] Jacob. M. Carter – Before History Dies - 2015, Interview of Dan Hardway

manipulating him, by pinning the President's assassination upon him and making him a scapegoat[67].

As for the anti-Castro operation conducted jointly by some members of the CIA and the Mafia, their goal was to recruit Cuban militants hostile to Fidel Castro and exiled in the USA in order to give support to the removal of Kennedy. They operated in several places including Miami where the cell JM / WAVE, the largest CIA station in the world, was based. However, these Cubans anti-Castro did not mastermind the conspiracy operation itself against John Kennedy. The CIA probably provided it with the necessary means.

While some rebel CIA and Pentagon members were planning to foment an invasion of Cuba and bring a massive military involvement in South Vietnam to fight communism, a change of policy towards a détente with America enemies was clearly announced by John Kennedy in 1963. The President's policy shift to work towards peace took the opposite view of the military-industrial complex. Kennedy went to war against his own national security advisers whenever a crisis affected his presidency: the invasion of the Bay of Pigs, the Berlin Crisis in 1961 and the Cuban Missiles Crisis in October 1962. He had to fight constantly against the CIA and some of its National Security advisers to avoid a permanent state of war.

Some researchers and historians have advanced the possible complicity of the anti-communist tycoons of the oil industry who were very hostile to Kennedy. They might have provided the financial means to carry out the plot against him by "buying" the executors of his assassination. The District Attorney of New Orleans, Jim Garrison, who investigated the JFK assassination and charged alleged perpetrators, said on September 21, 1967, *"President Kennedy's assassination was sponsored and funded by a handful of wealthy millionaires in the oil industry "*[68]. The most hostile of these Texas oil moguls was H. L. Hunt, the richest man in the world at the time. Through his research, the author Dick Russell

---

[67] Jesse Ventura – They Killed Our President – 2013. Skyhorse Publishing, Inc.
[68] Joachin Joesten. How Kennedy Was Killed (Dawnay, Tandem; 1968)

established a link between Hunt, George de Mohrenschildt (a pseudo CIA agent who befriended Lee Harvey Oswald) and Jack Ruby.[69] Hunt also had connections with the Organized Crime, including Eugene Hale Brading. Brading was arrested - and released - by the Dallas police as he was taking an elevator to the basement of the Dal-Tex Building near the Texas School Book Depository just after the shooting on Dealey Plaza[70]. Shortly before the day of the assassination, Johnny Roselli and Chuck Nicoletti, two prominent members of the Organized Crime, were also seen at the Cabana Motor Hotel in Dallas, where Lee Harvey Oswald, Brading and Jack Ruby had also been spotted.[71]

John Kennedy's fate was decided. His opponents gave him no chance of survival. His life was just hanging by a thread by the end of 1963 and it was at that time that real threats to his life started to be identified by the U.S. Secret Service. But because the press did not talk about it, many Americans remained in the dark.

Hardly anyone today knows that the tragic death of President Kennedy in Dallas was actually the *third* attempt on his life. There were two previous attempts, one in Chicago and one in Tampa. What is shameful is that the Secret Service had evidence of the two previous attempts and thus could possibly have prevented the third one. The conspiracy to assassinate John Kennedy was very real in both cities and the Secret Service knew it.

Palamara in his book *Survivor's Guilt*[72] and Waldron and Hartmann in *Ultimate Sacrifice*[73] have described in great details how these two foiled attacks were planned and put in place just a few days before the fatal crime in Dallas.

The methods of the Chicago and Tampa assassination plots were virtually identical to those used in Dallas. All three followed

---

[69] Dick Russell. The Man Who Knew Too Much.
[70] Michael T. Griffith: Suspects in the JFK Assassination. December 9, 2002
[71] William Kelly. "November 21, 1963. The Cabana Motor Hotel, Dallas, Texas". October 27, 1998
[72] Vince Palamara, Survivor's Guilt
[73] Waldrom Lanar and Hartmann, Thom – Ultimate Sacrifice – (New York: Carroll & Graf, 2005)

the same *modus operandi:* an ambush at a sharp curve in the motorcade route that forced the presidential limousine to slow down; multiple gunshots fired from a long-range telescopic rifle, and the presence of a lone gunman posted at the window of a tall building.

Both gunmen in the Chicago and Tampa plots were selected because they were embittered military or pro-Castro individuals. Each was skillfully manipulated to take the blame as a scapegoat.

The White House canceled the President's trip to Chicago at the last minute. On November 2, 1963, two hours before Air Force was to touch down at Chicago airport, the police, informed of the assassination plot by the Secret Service and the FBI, arrested Thomas Arthur Vallee who was armed with an M-1 rifle and 3,000 rounds of ammunition. Apart from Vallee, the intended scapegoat, the sniper team also included three other shooters, two of whom were Cuban exiles who, heavily armed on the roof of a tall building, were preparing to launch the attack.

During his arrest, Vallee, a former deranged Marine, said he was framed by someone who was very familiar with his military career and with the fact of *"his assignment by the CIA to train exiles to kill Castro"*. Like Oswald, Vallee had recently found a job in a warehouse overlooking the route of the presidential motorcade in Chicago. Knowing that the other potential conspiracy killers were still at large, John and Robert Kennedy decided to cancel the trip.

If the President had been murdered in Chicago on November 2, 1963 instead of in Dallas 20 days later, Lee Harvey Oswald would be totally unknown to us today. Thomas Arthur Vallee would most likely have become the alleged assassin of the President in a scenario very similar to the one in Dallas. Vallee would have played the same role of a scapegoat that Oswald did three weeks later.

According to Waldron and Hartman, the U.S. Congress was informed about these threats: A Secret Service agent informed the Congress *"there was a real threat against the President represented by a group of individuals"*. The words used by the Secret service Agent, *"by a group of individuals"*, is the perfect legal definition of a conspiracy!

John Kennedy insisted that nothing be said in the press about the threat he was facing. There was, however, just one small article published on the day of the President's assassination in Dallas but this leak was soon neutralized.

Later, while the government was careful not to mention the threats of attacks prior to the Dallas assassination, Abraham Bolden, chosen by President Kennedy as the first black agent of the Secret Service, was arrested because he had spoken to the Warren Commission about the attempted assassination in Chicago. Bolden was one of the Secret Service agents stationed in Chicago at the time of the planned assassination. He voluntarily left the White House Secret Service in protest against the low security level provided to the President in Chicago. After the thwarted shooting in Chicago and the fatal crime in Dallas, Bolden spoke openly with his colleagues about the obvious links between the attacks in the two cities. This quickly provoked the wrath of his superiors who strove to hide the similarities between the two plots. On May 17, 1964, Bolden decided to testify before the Warren Commission. However, his superiors had anticipated his approach by watching him closely. Upon his return to Chicago, he was arrested and charged with obstruction of justice and conspiracy for "selling Secret Service data". Despite a series of lawsuits and unsuccessful appeals, he was convicted and sentenced to nearly four years in a federal prison[74]. Released by the end of 1969, Bolden retired in 2001 and decided to write his autobiography. Today, at eighty years old, he is still struggling for recognition, more than fifty years after the Dallas crime!

On November 18, shortly after the failed Chicago assassination attempt and just four days before the President went to Dallas, the authorities discovered another serious threat during Kennedy's planned visit to Tampa. The police in charge of protecting the President was duly informed. Kennedy himself learned about the threat but decided that he could not afford to cancel his trip. It was important for him to address the Cuban

---

[74] James W. Douglass, JFK and the Unspeakable, Why He Died and Why it Matters, A Touchstone Book, 2008

exile community in Florida, an event to which he remained firmly committed[75]. However, he was reported to be noticeably tense during his trip that day.

Once back in Washington, he said he felt relieved that he had survived the trip. He told one of his closest aides, David Powers, *"Thank God nobody wanted to kill me today!"* Eerily, he then prophesied with a certain resignation that there would be another assassination against him. He said the assassination *"would be tried by someone with a high-power rifle and a telescopic sight during a downtown motorcade when there would be so much noise and confetti that nobody would even be able to point and say, 'It came from that window'"*[76].

The assassination attempts in Chicago and Tampa and the third successful attack in Dallas all had one thing in common: framing someone as a scapegoat. The similarity of the plots in these three cities is astonishing, particularly when comparing Tampa and Dallas.

The Police in each city were tracking a man in his twenties who had recent connections with the pro-Castro group, the Fair Play for Cuba Committee. In Dallas, Lee Harvey Oswald certainly fit this profile. In Tampa, the gunman was Gilberto Policarpo Lopez who, like Oswald, was a defector.

The investigators, Waldron and Harmann, found no less than 18 similarities between Oswald and Lopez. As with Oswald, Gilberto Lopez was under scrutiny by Navy intelligence. He made a mysterious trip to Mexico City in the autumn of 1963 to try to reach Cuba. Lopez crossed the Mexican border at the same point Oswald had chosen, by car, probably with help from someone else, as neither had a car nor a driving license.

Declassified documents from the CIA and the Warren Commission confirmed that Lopez was in charge of a U.S. mission involving Cuba[77]. U.S. citizens were not told by the

---

[75] Lamar Waldron, The Hidden History of the JFK Assassination, Counter Point Berkeley, 2013

[76] ibid

[77] Waldrom Lanar and Hartmann, Thom – Ultimate Sacrifice – (New York: Carroll & Graf, 2005)

Warren Commission of the existence and nature of the Tampa plot because the Commission itself had not received the information![78] The attempt to assassinate President Kennedy in Tampa was concealed from the Warren Commission and subsequently from other government investigative committees. This information was made public much later. On November 14, 1994, the author Lamar Waldron asked the JFK Assassination Records Review Board for an explanation as to why it had been withheld. According to the final report of the Review Board, published two months later, the Secret Service had indicated that it had destroyed notes on the President's protection and on some of his movements in the fall of 1963, notably in Tampa. The Secret Service informed the Review Board a week after destroying the archives when the request for information on the protection of the President was expressly made. This destruction was completely illegal. Congress had passed the 1992 JFK Act by which agencies were required to preserve all relevant records[79].

John Kennedy was thus tracked down methodically in the last weeks of his life. Unfortunately he had little chance of surviving the Dallas shooting since his protection was so inadequate. In the Texan city, the security measures were totally inadequate as we will see.

During his presidency, John Kennedy often referred to the likelihood of an attempt on his life. He was particularly concerned about this risk after the failed assassination attempt in Tampa, so close to his trip to Texas. On the danger of being murdered, when his aides and family tried to reason with him not to leave for Texas, a hostile territory for democrats, he told his friend Larry Newman: "*If this is the way life is, if this is the way it's going to end, this is the way it's going to end*".

Yet, the President had moments of anxiety as he contemplated his trip to Dallas. He admitted his apprehensions with Senator

---

[78] Walt Brown, Ph. D. – The Warren Omission.
[79] Lamar Waldron, The Hidden History of the JFK Assassination, Counter Point Berkeley, 2013

George Smathers: *"God, I hate to go out to Texas. I just hate to go. I have a terrible feeling about going. I wish I could get out of it"*[80].

On the morning of November 22, 1963, after reading the Dallas Morning News, which severely reprimanded him and accused him of complacency towards communism, the President told his wife: *"We're heading into nut country today"*. Then he had these premonitory words: "*But, Jackie, if somebody wants to shoot me from a window with a rifle, nobody can stop it; so why worry about it?*" [81]

As she would report later, Jackie Kennedy felt her husband's fatalist sense of resignation during the first days of the Texas trip. "*You know,*" he said, "*last night would have been a hell of a night to assassinate a president ... I mean it. There was the rain and the night, and we were all getting jostled. Suppose a man had a pistol in a briefcase.*" (Kennedy pointed his right hand, finger extended like a gun at the wall and using his thumb like the trigger of a pistol) "*Then he could have dropped the gun and the briefcase and melted away in the crowd*" [82].

For any presidential motorcade, the Secret Service, in charge of the protection of John Kennedy, stuck to a very strict protocol. The formation of police officers on motorbikes around the presidential limousine was particularly supervised. However, in Dallas, this protocol was significantly modified. The official motorcycle formation with nine bikers - three at the front, one on each side and four at the rear of the presidential limousine - should have been used, as was the case during the President's visit to any foreign country and even to Tampa, a few days before Dallas. The formation was however modified in Dallas. It was decided that only four bikers would escort the President into the streets of Dallas and be positioned at the rear of the limousine while five other bikers would escort ahead of the first lead car at

---

[80] James W. Douglass, JFK and the Unspeakable, Why He Died and Why it Matters, A Touchstone Book, 2008

[81] David Talbot – Brothers, The Hidden History of the Kennedy Years - 2007

[82] James W. Douglass, JFK and the Unspeakable, Why He Died and Why it Matters, A Touchstone Book, 2008

the start of the motorcade just before John Kennedy's limousine[83]. This unusual modified formation thus represented a huge loophole in the protection of the President, who was no longer protected from snipers either from the front or from the sides of his car.

In the morning of November 22, 1963, since the weather in Dallas was sunny, the Secret Service had decided to remove the "bubble top", the plastic dome of the limousine (although it was not bullet proof) because the President preferred to see and to be seen better. Curiously, the press photographers' car, which usually preceded the presidential limousine, was moved back to the eighth position in the motorcade, making it difficult to photograph the President. The ambush could thus occur out of the view of the media!

Admiral George B. Burkley, JFK's personal physician, was among the members of the Security Service and the President's delegation. In the event of having to rescue JFK, his doctor should have been assured of a position not far from his limousine but he was relegated to the very end of the motorcade and unable to provide first aid assistance to the President.

After the Dallas assassination, as they felt compelled to explain the irregularities from the security protocol, the Secret Service criticized the victim! They pretended the President had insisted on this modified motorcycle formation to be set up in Dallas since it was a trip for his re-election campaign and because he wanted to be well seen in order to better communicate with the public. This explanation was absurd and shameful: to blame the victim who is no longer able to contradict the statement! It took the honesty of a Secret Service official to disavow this pretense by testifying before the Warren Commission: *"no president can dictate to the Secret Service what they should or should not do."* They are the ones who decide about a president's protection[84].

---

[83] Jesse Ventura – They Killed Our President – 2013. Skyhorse Publishing, Inc.

[84] Carrier, The United States Secret Service: conspiracy to assassinate a President, Palamara, Survivor's Guilt.

So why was the protection procedure for the presidential motorcade changed? This question was at first eluded. Then a vague answer came from the House Select Committee on Assassinations: *"The modification by the Secret Service of the police motorcycle formation in Dallas, as it was originally planned, created an obstruction to the precautionary procedure for maximum safety. It seems that these maximum-security measures were however well implemented during motorcades of motorcycles during the same trip to Texas, especially the day before the presidential visit to Dallas. This fact illustrates that the motorcycles formation as decided in Dallas by the Secret Service presented unique conditions of insecurity"* [85].

Other irregularities in the measures to protect the President in Dallas contributed to the unfolding of the operation to eliminate him[86]. John Kennedy's limousine was not only inefficiently protected by the police motorcycles as required for any presidential motorcade, but the Secret Service agents in charge of his protection - and that of the First Lady – were prevented from covering them as bodyguards because they were ordered to move away from the running boards of the presidential limousine. A video on the internet shows the incredible decision.[87] Less than an hour before being murdered, upon the arrival of Air Force One at Dallas Lovefield Airport, the President and his wife got in the limousine. As two Secret Service bodyguards were starting to position themselves on the running board on either side of the slow moving vehicle, their superior, Emory Roberts, ordered them to step off the limousine and let the car go. On the video, the body language of one of the two agents, Don Lawton, is eloquent: he questions the order he had just received and, as a sign of frustration, gestures with his open hand palms up in the air, three times, as if to say, *"Hey, what's going on?"* He is confused and does not understand why he is being prevented from performing his role of protecting the President on the rear side platforms of the limousine.

---

[85] Vince Palamara: kennedydetailkennedydetailkennedy. blogspot.com/2012/08/updated-jfk-did-not-order-agents-off.html
[86] Jesse Ventura – They Killed Our President – 2013. Skyhorse Publishing, Inc.
[87] https://www.youtube.com/watch?v=XY02Qkuc_f8

No visible bodyguard was covering the car during the motorcade through the streets of downtown Dallas. It took precious seconds for a Secret Service agent to react after JFK was fatally wounded and slumped in his seat. This unfortunately late gesture came from Secret Service agent Clint Hill, also in charge of protecting the First Lady, who decided to run towards the limousine and to position himself on the rear-riding platform. As Jackie Kennedy was perching herself on the trunk - trying to pick up a piece of her husband's brain or skull– it was reported that Hill pushed her back towards the back seat.

After the attempted attacks in Chicago and Tampa, the threat of another attack in Texas was very real and tension was at its highest. But the Secret Service did not deem appropriate to protect the President by positioning their bodyguards on the limousine platforms or letting them run near the vehicle as the protocol required. Strange ... Furthermore nine agents of the White House Secret Service, even those who were expected to ensure the protection of the President, had been partying, the night before, in Forth-Worth cabarets. One of them even remained there until five o'clock in the morning. They were still well intoxicated when they returned to duty the next morning! Their physical and mental condition could have explained their lack of responsiveness[88]. Senator Young brought these scandalous facts to the attention of Congress on December 3, 1963. He voiced his indignation requesting that the security officers, who had spent the night drinking, in flagrant violation of the regulations, be arrested. But nothing was done.

Was the Texas School Book Depository chosen by the sniper(s) as a location because it was already known that the presidential motorcade would drive past it? Who was responsible for deciding the route? Did Lee Harvey Oswald really know well in advance that the motorcade would be passing by his workplace? If so, did

---

[88] Robert J. Groden and Harrison Edward Livingstone. High Treason: The assassination of JFK. What really happened? The Conservatory Press, 1989

he get the information early enough to take his rifle to work and decide to commit the crime?

Because of the decision to divert the motorcade route in order to pass under the windows of the Texas School Book Depository, some conspiracy supporters interpret this as another flaw in the security protocol in Dallas. But, in my opinion, this is a theory that is not fully supported by the facts. According to the conspiracy advocates, the route of the presidential motorcade had been modified shortly before John Kennedy's visit to Dallas. Earl Cabell, the mayor of Dallas whose brother, General Charles Cabell, Deputy Director of the CIA and in charge of covert operations, had been fired by President Kennedy, decided the change. Others blamed George L. Lumpkin, a colonel from military intelligence, assistant to the head of the Dallas police[89]. According to James Douglass, the Secret Service planned the final route and approved the passing in front of the Texas Book Depository Building. Winston G. Lawson of the Secret Service organized a rehearsal on November 18, with Forrest V. Sorrels, the Dallas Special Agent in Charge, to finalize the path of the presidential motorcade[90]. The diversion of the motorcade route into an unsecured area was published in the Times Herald newspaper in Dallas on November 19, three days before President Kennedy's arrival to Dallas.

If Oswald had known about this diversion passing by his work place, he might have had time to ruminate over his murderous project. Instead of exiting Dallas downtown, heading straight down Main Street to the Dallas Trade Mart where JFK was to give a speech, the motorcade made a right turn into Houston Street and then a zigzag on Elm Street. This maneuver forced the long limousine to considerably reduce its speed to 5 mph before continuing into the crossfire ambush area on Elm Street. According to the conspiracy supporters, this decision was a terrible violation of the Secret Service procedure, which should

---

[89] Vincent Palmara. Survivor's Guilt, The United States Secret Service: conspiracy to assassinate a President, Carrier

[90] James W. Douglass, JFK and the Unspeakable, Why He Died and Why it Matters, A Touchstone Book, 2008

have excluded any risky areas along the route because of the multiple hiding places and buildings with roofs and windows to be secured. Based on my personal research, I was unable to find credible sources from the conspiracy defenders community that proved there was a deliberate attempt by the city of Dallas or the Secret Service to divert the presidential limousine into an ambush area. I also investigated the conspiracy skeptics to know how they refuted the assertion of those who saw a conspiracy act in the choice of a detour of the presidential motorcade. Objectively, the choice of the route was certainly not a sensible decision for security reasons, but nothing proves that there was a change of itinerary at the last minute decided by anyone for the malicious purpose of setting up an ambush. As John McAdams[91], a debunker of the conspiracy regarding the JFK assassination, remarks: in order to get onto Stemmons freeway towards the Trade Mart, approaching Dealey Plaza from Main Street, you have to turn into Houston Street and then Elm Street - the hairpin in question. If you continue straight on Main Street without making the right turn, it is impossible to merge off a ramp to the right to reach Stemmons freeway because a small road concrete separation prevents this manoeuver. Driving over the small chicane would have been illegal and impractical for all vehicles and press buses of the presidential motorcade. McAdams's observation is therefore fair and can be checked by visualizing Dealey Plaza and the photo history on Google Earth (the then Trade Mart is today called Dallas World Trade Center). Going back in time, Google Earth's aerial photo history is limited to 1995, so we cannot know if the concrete road bump existed in 1963. All in all, it does not change things much: the motorcade could have been diverted before reaching Dealey Plaza, higher up on Market Street directly onto Elm Street, without making the hairpin turn. The limousine would have continued straight on Elm Street passing the Texas School Book Depository at a faster speed, instead of making a turn into Houston Street then Elm Street, which forced the driver to significantly reduce the speed.

---

[91] http://mcadams.posc.mu.edu/route.htm

The motorcade route through Dealey Plaza was not unusual. Such an itinerary had previously been chosen for visits to Dallas by Franklin D. Roosevelt and even during John Kennedy's presidential campaign in 1960. However, these motorcades had followed a different approach to Dealey Plaza without taking the hairpin bend[92].

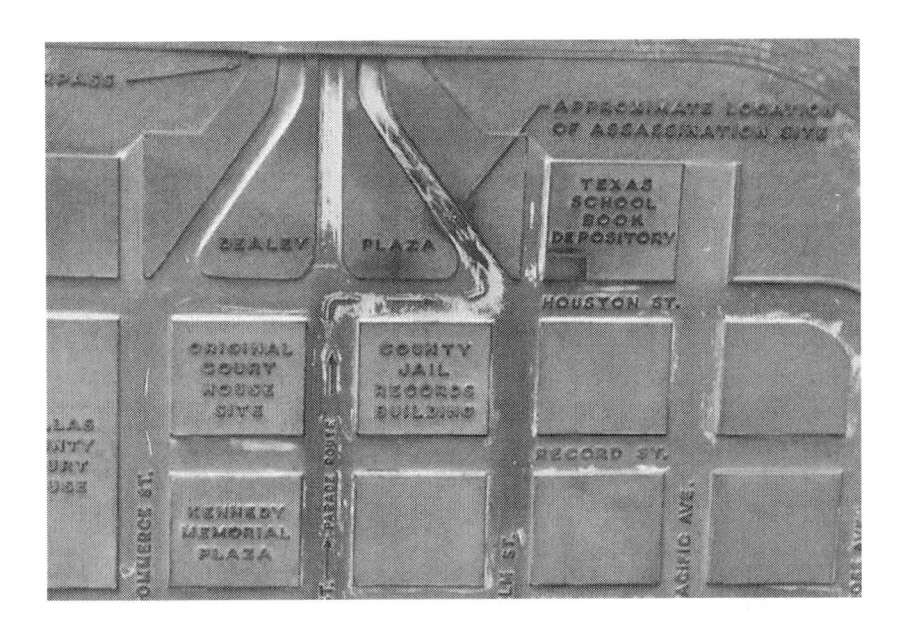

Motorcade diversion taking the President into the ambush area (author's photo)

---

[92] Lamar Waldron, The Hidden History of the JFK Assassination, Counter Point Berkeley, 2013

The Dealey Plaza elms probably obstructed the view when the first shot was fired at the presidential limousine (cross) from the sniper's window (circle). Firing at the car approaching the TSBD on Houston Street, would have been an easier shot for the assassin (author's photos).

During my first visit to Dallas, standing in Dealey Plaza, the inconsistencies of the Warren Commission's version seemed obvious to me: the perimeter of the crime scene is actually narrower than it appears on the historical photographs. One is immediately very aware of the existence of the wooden palisade on the "Grassy Knoll" which could have served as an ideal place for an ambush. As soon as one stands behind this fence, one is struck by the fact that this is a perfect hiding place for a sniper. A frontal, low-trajectory shot, without obstacle, would have been easy to reach the motorcade driving slowing along Elm Street on November 22, 1963. On the other hand, if on the sixth floor of the Texas School Book Depository (the current location of the Sixth Floor Museum where Oswald allegedly posted himself) it is easy to see the constraints of a sniper shooting from the corner window. From this vantage point, the vision range to reach a moving target on Elm Street could have been partially hampered by the elms foliage, although back in 1963 the trees were smaller than they are today.

The photos I recently took of Dealey Plaza may help to convey to the reader the feelings during my visits. The many shocking images of that fateful day are still in our minds; time seems to be suspended, as if the tragedy had just happened yesterday. Although the downtown ultra-modern business center is close, it is unexpected and striking to see that, over the decades, property developers have not been permitted to erect new high-rise buildings on Dealey Plaza, which would have to some extent "erased" the shame and the infamy of the city of Dallas. But strangely everything about Dealey Plaza has been saved, the crime scene remains frozen in time; the Texas School Book Depository, the "Grassy Knoll", the pedestal where Abraham Zapruder stood with his camera filming the crime scene, the white cement pergola nearby, the parking behind the wooden picket fence and the configuration of the streets leading to Elm Street. We understand so well how the reenactment of the JFK assassination in many films and TV series has been done so easily and with remarkable fidelity in the smallest of details.

Pedestal where Zapruder stood to film the scene of the assassination on Elm Street (author's photos)

How did Oswald get his job at the Texas School Book Depository? In October 1963, he applied for a recruitment position that Ruth Paine, his wife's friend, had found for him. He got the job and started to work at the book depository the next day. Yet, another employer had offered Oswald a much better salary, again through a recruiting office in contact with Ruth Paine. Whether the message about the better job had been passed on to Oswald or if he decided not to take it is unknown.

The route of the presidential motorcade through Dallas with its detour under the windows of the Texas School Book Depository was published on November 19. A lone assassin would not prepare a complex plan in advance if it could be hindered by the slightest mishap or simply by an effective surveillance of the local police and Service Secret. The Texas School Book Depository's manager, Roy Truly, should have been ordered by the police to prevent anyone being by the windows on the upper floors of the building. But Truly received no instructions to that effect. During the presidential motorcade, according to eyewitnesses, people were seen not only at the windows of the sixth floor where Oswald was supposedly posted, but also on the floor below.

Professor James Fetzer sums up the many security gaps in the President's trip to Dallas: *"More than a dozen security measures by the Secret Service during the Dallas motorcade were violated: lack of military protection; unsecured windows of buildings; motorcycles riding near the rear of the car, no agents positioned on the limousine platforms; motorcade cars in the wrong order; itinerary change allowing a curve greater than 90 degrees; speed reduction of the car almost coming to a halt on Elm Street; vehicle stopped at the time of the first gunshots* [The brief brightness of the limousine taillights can be seen just before the fatal shot on a video]; *no immediate response from agents; limousine cleaned of the President's blood and brain tissue in front of Parkland Hospital even before his death was confirmed (thus eliminating investigation leads); limousine dismantled and rebuilt immediately, on Monday, November 24, the day of JFK funeral; windshield replaced* [Traces of a lost bullet can be seen on photos of the assassination. The bullet could have hit the chrome frame and its fragment cracked the limousine windshield] "[93].

The total preservation of the crime scene is the basic rule in any criminal investigation. The limousine in which the President was assassinated was itself a crime scene that should have been totally preserved and kept for forensic examination. Reality had fallen far short of these basic precautions: the limousine was shipped to the Ford factory in Detroit, less than three days after the assassination, under President Johnson's order. The precise conditions of how President Kennedy had been killed in the vehicle were missing forever, in total violation of standard procedures. Nobody questioned nor opposed this decision. Once in Detroit, the limousine was dismantled, its interior stripped and replaced and the windshield with bullet marks removed[94]. The evidence of ballistic trajectory and blood spatter had disappeared forever and most likely intentionally...

---

[93] Fetzer Ph.D. "Smoking Guns" in the Death of JFK et "Murder in Dealey Plaza"

[94] Douglas P. Horne, referencing Doug Weldon. "Photographic Evidence of Bullet Hole in JFK Limousine Windshield Hiding in Plain Sight. June 2012

The supporters of a lone gunman recently criticized the conspiracy theorists, especially around the 50th anniversary of the JFK assassination, for making accusations against the U.S. Secret Service's failure to guarantee maximum protection. They qualified as "inventions" the conspiracy theorists' opinion about a possible participation of the Secret Service in the assassination plot. The advocates of the conspiracy corrected: because the protection of the President in Dallas had been neglected, it was not the Secret Service agency they had charged with conspiracy, but it was rather this loophole that had been an additional factor contributing to the assassination. They also rectified the Secret Service's assertion that the President himself had taken the initiative for a change of security protocol. Some Secret Service superiors had in fact, deliberately decided the slack presidential protection. Hence, they had directly or indirectly contributed to the brutal removal of the 35th President of the United States from office. The flaws in the security protocol in Dallas were all the more unacceptable and questionable, as the Chicago and Tampa assassination attempts had been well known to them.

Prior to John Kennedy's arrival in Dallas, the police reported an unusual incident. Despite the fact that police officers had detected the presence of potential shooters on Dealey Plaza, the FBI did not deem it necessary to notify the Warren Commission. On the morning of November 20, two patrol officers on Dealey Plaza noticed several men standing behind the wooden fence on the "Grassy Knoll" overlooking Dealey Plaza. These men seemed to be busy in shooting exercises. Their guns were pointed over the palisade towards Dealey Plaza. The two police officers immediately rushed to the scene but by the time they reached the fence, the suspects had already fled into a car parked in the adjacent parking lot. The two police officers did not pay much attention to this incident at the time but after the assassination of the President, they reported it to the FBI who wrote an assessment report six days later. For unknown reasons, the FBI report was never mentioned in their investigation into the assassination. It even disappeared until it resurfaced in 1978[95].

Fence dividing the "Grassy Knoll" and the parking lot (author's photo)

Ideal sniper's hideout behind the palisade overlooking Elm Street (author's photo)

The "Grassy Knoll" picket fence still shows bystanders' feelings (author's photos)

If a conspiracy can be fomented with only two individuals, it might have involved more than two in the case of the JFK assassination given the number of gunshots reported on that day. For key witnesses, it seemed certain: several enemies of the President had participated in the plot. This is what the President's widow alluded to just after the assassination. Aboard Air Force One returning to Washington with her husband's coffin and the new President's entourage, Jackie Kennedy still had not deigned to change her clothes when she was asked do so because her Chanel suit was still stained with her husband's blood: *"I want*

---

[95] Lamar Waldron, The Hidden History of the JFK Assassination, Counter Point Berkeley, 2013

them to see what they did to my husband! " she said. For her, there was no doubt: "them" and "they" are plural and imply that several killers had murdered her husband. Her use of "they" was quite judicious... When one of the bullets that started flying in the limousine hit John Connally, he shouted: "*My God, they are going to kill us all!*" In both their minds, the scenario of a single shooter was inconceivable.

To better understand the circumstances of the assassination and the likelihood of a conspiracy, several visits to Dealey Plaza are necessary. During my visits, my impression has always been the same. This historic place arouses emotion. One cannot help but think that the itinerary of the presidential motorcade was very complicated and misguided: a right angle turn on Houston Street then a sharp and difficult maneuver for the long limousine on Elm Street where the crowd had already thinned off downtown. Today, any observer on Dealey Plaza can easily understands that this hairpin turn had caused the presidential car to enter an ambush area, behind the Texas School Book Depository, in front of the picket fence and the railroad underpass, two ideal locations for crossfire.

Today, on Dealey Plaza, the Six Floor Museum is very popular because it commemorates the tragic events of November 22-24, 1963. It is located in the Texas School Book Depository itself, on the same sixth floor from where the alleged assassin, Lee Harvey Oswald, fired the gunshots. During my visit, it seemed obvious to me that this museum had been cooperative in endorsing the Warren Report and the theory of a lone killer. My impression is also widely shared by many investigators who have been to the museum. They have since been vocal for a public boycott of the museum for this reason. Although is briefly mentioned, at the end of the exhibition, that Oswald may have had an accomplice, the exhibition is mainly focused on the single crazy gunman, Lee Harvey Oswald.

Is it an illusion, a bias of those who criticize the official version? Surprisingly, a retired CIA member, Charles Briggs, offered his consulting services to the museum's organizers and could have influenced the creation of the museum[96]. In a 1988 documentary by the British TV channel ITV, Gary Mack, a former American television news producer supported the conspiracy theory by endorsing photographic snapshots showing a hypothetical sniper posted on the "Grassy Knoll". Some years later, he was appointed curator of the Sixth Floor Museum and remained in this position until his recent death. Despite having been a fervent defender of the conspiracy plot, Gary Mack, then became a defender of the theory of the lone assassin "Oswald did it". It is of course permissible for anyone to take a flip-flop position for a cause that was defended in the past and to then take the opposite side.

I also noted, as have many visitors to the exhibition, that the Six Floor Museum store virtually sells all the books on the JFK assassination that endorse the governmental version. These books are well displayed; those of Bill O'Reilly, Vincent Bugliosi or Gerald Posner. It is almost impossible to see books criticizing the Warren Report or advocating the conspiracy theory. I dread to think that "protesting" books are censored... On the brochure of the exhibition I was given at the entrance of the museum, it was written: "An event that shook history of America took place on the other side of the street where the museum is located. A young President of the United States was shot dead by a sniper". Here again, no reference to a possible second shooter. The official version is ratified...

The museum visitors cannot approach the sixth-floor southeast corner window from which the gunshots were reported to have been fired. The access to the area is barred by an imposing glass cabin. It is however still possible to get nearer to the other windows in order to see the corner of Houston Street and Elm Street. That is enough to make you realize how illogical the sniper's decision was. Why did the gunman not choose the easiest shooting position, aiming at the President as his car came straight into Houston Street in front of the Texas School Book Depository southeast corner window before making a hairpin turn? While he

---

[96] Jefferson Morley – Charles Briggs, retired CIA officer who assisted JFK museum, was accused of deception by a federal judge - JFKfacts.org, 7 November 2015.

could have enjoyed a perfect viewing angle, without anything to block his view, Oswald, according to the official version, waited for the car to make a very wide angle turn into Elm Street and then to distance itself from his position before he fired. Firing constraints such as the windowsill or the Texas Elm trees in Elm Street must have then hindered his visual field. Illogical decision…unless it was all planned! The plot was to wait for the President's car to drive into an ambush in the middle of crossfire down Elm Street. This absurdity was noted by the Warren Commission, which asked FBI director J. Edgar Hoover if he had an opinion about it. He answered with a misinterpretation of the facts: *"The reason for that, in my opinion, is the fact that there were trees obstructing the presidential car facing the window of the sixth floor when it crossed the park* [Dealey Plaza on the Houston Street side]"[97]. There were certainly no trees in 1963 that could have hindered the sight of the assassin when the presidential limousine came up in front of the building on Houston Street before turning into Elm Street.

More than two thousand books have been published on the JFK assassination, a hundred just around the 50th anniversary of his death. Most of these books and the thousands of articles also published on the crime of Dallas reach the same conclusion: there was a conspiracy to kill Kennedy. Assuming Oswald was involved in the plot, there is poor evidence that he fired one single shot and, if he did, his shot might not have been the one that hit the President's head because the medical evidence - as we will see in a following chapter - proved that John Kennedy was hit with a fatal shot which came from the front.

About two-thirds of Americans are today convinced of a plot and are demanding more than the evidence in articles and books supporting the conspiracy. To be totally convinced, they are demanding the confession of their government. The American people want to understand why there was a cover-up of evidence and why the media have endorsed it.

---

[97] Robert J. Groden, The Killing of a President, Vicking Studio Books, 1993

John Kennedy condemned everything about secrecy. As head of state, he remained of course accountable for ensuring the national security of his country and for this reason, he had to deal with state secrets to protect all the institutions. However, two of his speeches can tell us a lot about his aversion to the cult of secrecy. On April 27, 1961, he had these words to say before the American Newspaper Publishers Association in the Waldorf-Astoria Hotel in New-York City : *"The very word 'secrecy' is repugnant in a free and open society; and we are as a people inherently and historically opposed to secret societies, to secret oaths and to secret proceedings."* On June 11, 1962, at Yale University, he warned of the danger represented by deception: *"the great enemy of the truth is very often not the lie — deliberate, contrived, and dishonest — but the myth persistent, persuasive, and unrealistic."*

The murder of John Kennedy was not a trivial event. The Dallas assassination remains the most important unresolved murder of the century. Those responsible for the crime are the suspected elites who had a great financial or political interest in eliminating the President. Many of John Kennedy's enemies had the motive, the opportunity and the means to commit this crime. They then exercised a massive concealment of the facts of the assassination over half a century and provided the means of controlling four government investigations. In the next chapters of this book, I will focus on the motive, the means and the opportunity for each of the investigation leads condemning the forces behind the plot. Guilt is usually admitted once this trilogy of decisive elements is established. There may be a great deal of evidence of a conspiracy but it must be supported by irrefutable facts. Forensic evidence is crucial because it does not involve personal opinions but rather scientific, logical and rational observations. As an appendix to this essay, a summary table will highlight the facts of the evidence in the Dallas conspiracy case. I will oppose tangible, objectified, and indisputable sources, crosschecked by a large number of experts against fragile or baseless sources from mere rumors or from questionable witnesses. This table should help the reader to make his or her own opinion and draw his or her own conclusion.

On November 22, 1963, there were many onlookers on Dealey Plaza along the presidential motorcade. Many of these witnesses immediately ran, just after the last gunshots, to the "Grassy Knoll", the small incline with a long picket fence, from where they thought the gunshots had come. The historical photos and video films show this massive public reaction. More than 50 witnesses (many have disappeared under bizarre circumstances, as we will see later in this book) reported having heard gunshots and having seen smoke in the "Grassy Knoll" area. The precise testimonies of these onlookers reveal a consensus that greatly contributed to the private investigations concluding that at least a second gunman had positioned himself in front of the presidential limousine. The next chapter will cover the testimonies of those who were convinced that gunshots came from another direction than from the Texas School Book Depository hence endorsing the highly probable mark of a plot.

Chapter 4

Witnesses' Reactions on Dealey Plaza

The Warren Commission knew the names of at least 266 people present at the scene of the assassination. Out of 90 people questioned about the origin of the gunshots, 58 claimed that they came from the "Grassy Knoll". Photos and amateur films taken on Dealey Plaza just after the last shot and as the presidential motorcade rushed to the triple underpass on its way to Parkland hospital, show that dozens of witnesses, ran to the "Grassy Knoll" and the wooden fence area, which separates the parking lot and the railway depot. These witnesses reacted instinctively because it was from this place, facing the presidential limousine, that they heard the gunshots. Among those who were almost certain that the gunshots came from that direction, there were 21 police officers within 150 feet from JFK when the gunshots rang out. Their senses, stimulated by the experience of dealing with gunfire, did not betray them. On the other hand, could they have been wrong, as the Warren Commission said? Ignoring or downplaying these reactions, the commission preferred to focus on selected witnesses who, in turn, testified that the gunshots did NOT come from the "Grassy Knoll".

Clyde Haygood, a police officer on a motorbike who was riding at the rear of the presidential limousine, is one of the witnesses who rushed to the "Grassy Knoll". During his testimony, he indicated that he wanted to check "*the scene where the gunshots had* been fired ... and after having seen some people lying on the grass pointing towards the parking lot of the railway depot".[98]

A police officer, *Bobby Hargis*, whose windshield and clothes had been splashed by the President's blood, when the fatal shot to the head was fired, parked his motorcycle and ran straight towards the "Grassy Knoll" near the overpass. He said he heard two gunshots. He located the origin of the gunshots at the level of the railway on the triple underpass[99].

Dallas County Sheriff *Bill Decker* was in the lead car of the motorcade. When he heard shots, he immediately picked up his radio microphone to give the following order: "*Make sure that all available men leave their offices and go to the parking lot of the railway depot. We need to know what happened and to secure the area until the arrival of the criminal police section and investigators*"[100].

A major eyewitness, *James Tague*, was standing by one of the railway triple underpass pillars where three lanes converge from Dealey Plaza. He was slightly injured on the cheek by a chip from the sidewalk, which was hit by a bullet that missed the limousine. He pointed out that there was more attention paid towards the "Grassy Knoll" than to the Texas School Book Depository area, and that "*no real actions could be seen around the Texas School Book Depository for at least seven minutes after the gunshots* "[101].

In 1988, a British television documentary was made by ITV showing with conviction two events: the presence of a gunman on the "Grassy Knoll" and the fact that Jack Ruby knew Lee Harvey Oswald. *Beverly Oliver*, a cabaret singer at the downtown Dallas Colony Club, near Ruby's strip club, the Carousel, said she

---

[98] Haygood, Clyde "Testimony of Clyde A. Haygood to the President's Commission (Warren Commission) 9 April 1964.
Jfkassassination.net/russ/testimony/haygood.htm

[99] Sherry P. Fiester – Enemy of the Truth, Myths, Forensics and the Kennedy Assassination – JFK Lancer Productions & Publications, Inc. 2012

[100] Galanor, Stewart, "The Art and Science of Misrepresenting Evidence: How the Warren Commission and the House Select Committee on Assassinations manipulated evidence to dismiss witness accounts of the assassination," retrieved 14 April 2013:historymatters.com/analysis/Witness/artScience.htm

[101] James Tague, "Eyewitness Statement of James Tague,"retrieved 14 April 2013:karws.gso.uri.edu/jfk/History/Thedeed/Sneed/Tague.html

knew Jack Ruby well. Known as the "Babushka Lady" (because she was seen on Zapruder's film wearing a scarf on her head) Beverly Oliver was standing on Dealey Plaza watching the presidential limousine go by. She was seen taking a film of the motorcade on the southern corner of Elm Street at the very moment the President's head was fatally hit by a bullet. Her film – to be confiscated later – might have taken symmetrical images of the drama to those caught by Zapruder who was standing on the other side of the street. Her film would not necessarily have shown much of what was happening in the limousine at the time of the gunshots but it might instead have revealed some background details of the "Grassy Knoll" and the Texas School Book Depository areas. She said she filmed the whole assassination scene and even the extreme agitation on Dealey Plaza shortly after the shooting. The following Monday, at her workplace, she was stopped by two FBI agents who ordered her to hand over the film she had taken with her camera. She acquiesced. The agents promised to give her back a few days later but her film was confiscated forever. Still alive, Beverly Oliver remains convinced that her film might have revealed something troubling behind the palisade on the "Grassy Knoll". She said she might have had the best photo of the whole assassination scene and was probably the only one with a very good view of the "Grassy Knoll". For fear of suffering the same fate as those who had made testimonies and "knew too much" discrediting the official version, and who had consequently disappeared, she refrained from testifying for several years. Finally, in her 1997 interview with Sherry Fiester, she gave details of the event. Oliver said she saw the back of the President's head come off at the precise moment she noted someone firing, a shot flash and a puff of smoke from the "Grassy Knoll" which made her flinch. "*I didn't realize I had heard a gunshot. The sound wasn't familiar. I only knew it was a gunshot when I saw the President's head. I don't know how many gunshots were fired, but I know one came from the picket fence area. There was someone there and smoke there. I am convinced the man who shot the President was in that area. Somebody killed my President before my very eyes and they got away with it. After the assassination, I always felt threatened. Lot of folks who testified are no longer around. After all, if they can kill the President of the United States, they can kill me*"[102]. U.S. Senator Ralph Yarborough, also interviewed on the British television program, further confirmed Oliver's observation. He was two cars behind the presidential limousine.

Beverly Oliver also made shocking revelations: two weeks before JFK's assassination, she went to Jack Ruby's Carousel Club, during her singing performance break. Ruby invited her to join him and one of his employees, Janet Adams Conforto, aka "Jada", for a drink. Ruby also introduced her to a man sitting at the same table: *"Beverly, here's my friend, Lee"* he said. It was when she saw Lee Harvey Oswald on television after he was arrested that she realized he was the same man that had been introduced to her in Ruby's club.

Oliver decided not to tell to anyone about her brief meeting with Ruby and Oswald. She kept it quiet for a long time. "Jada", on the contrary, had told reporters the day after the assassination that Ruby knew Oswald. Some people believed that "Jada"'s fate had been sealed as another "embarrassing" eyewitness. She was killed in a motorcycle accident under mysterious circumstances[103].

Should we believe Beverly Oliver? She is still alive and very active on Alan Dale and Debra Conway's team, hosting the "JFK Lancer" conference, which has been successfully held every year since 1996 in Dallas. In addition to her performances as a professional singer, she is also a lecturer and writes books. I had the opportunity to see Beverly Oliver in Dallas in 2015 at the 20th "JFK Lancer" conference when she participated in the commemoration of the 52nd anniversary of John Kennedy's assassination on Dealey Plaza. For the occasion, she sang "Amazing Grace".

The same ITV program described the poignant testimony of *Gordon L. Arnold*, a 22-year-old soldier on leave, whose remarks were also echoed by Robert J. Groden and Harrison Edward

---

[102] Sherry P. Fiester – Enemy of the Truth, Myths, Forensics and the Kennedy Assassination – JFK Lancer Productions & Publications, Inc. 2012

[103] Robert J. Groden and Harrison Edward Livingstone. High Treason: The assassination of JFK. What really happened? The Conservatory Press, 1989

Livingstone in their book "*High Treason: The assassination of JFK. What really happened?* ". The video is available on the Internet.

Arnold wanted to film the presidential motorcade with his camera on Dealey Plaza. He positioned himself first in the parking lot behind the wooden picket fence. A man wearing a suit, carrying a firearm, approached him. He showed him a FBI badge and ordered him to leave the place: "*I am with the Secret Service. I don't want anyone to come here* "he said. Arnold obeyed and this time went to stand and film on the other side of the palisade, at the top of the steps on the "Grassy Knoll", facing Elm Street. He sensed that the man was following him and heard him say, "*I told you to leave the place.*"

Another onlooker, Mary Moorman, who took a Polaroid snapshot a fraction of second after the fatal shot hit JFK, confirms Arnold's testimony. She was standing on the other side of Elm Street, facing the "Grassy Knoll", a few feet away from the presidential limousine. On Moorman's enlarged photo, two silhouettes can be seen: that of Arnold standing on the Grassy Knoll and that of an individual behind Arnold, in the position of a sniper. Arnold recalled that after having heard a shot whistling by his left ear, he immediately fell to the ground in a reflex of self-protection. Then a second shot passed over his head. When he got up, after the last gunshots, Arnold faced an armed individual, in a police uniform, without his cap. A second police officer appeared. He was shaking and appeared to be crying. He had a long rifle in his hand, which he was swinging nervously towards Arnold. The two men asked him if he had filmed anything. Arnold felt intimidated and admitted that indeed he had. One of the men grabbed Arnold's camera, confiscated the film and threw the camera back at Arnold.

On a very large enlargement of Mary Moorman's photo, experts saw a blurred human-like shape of what appeared to be a gunman in a shooting position, possibly a police officer's silhouette because of an epaulette and a badge, which are just detectable. The photo also shows, near the "police officer", a man standing near the railroad depot behind the picket fence, in what seems to be a railroad worker's uniform with perhaps a hard hat.

Gordon Arnold was very terrified by his experience. He decided to resume his military service without talking to the authorities. Well aware of the mysterious deaths of some of the less fortunate eyewitnesses on Dealey Plaza who had talked, he kept a low profile for several years until 1988 when he testified before ITV.

Mary Moorman was standing facing the "Grassy Knoll" (cross) when she took a Polaroid photo, a fraction of second after the fatal shot which hit JFK (author's photo).

Shortly after the shooting, three "tramps" were arrested by the police near the railroad tracks and were escorted across Dealey Plaza. This is widely documented on the internet with photos. The way these men were arrested has intrigued many investigators. Contrary to the usual arrest procedure, the "tramps" were not handcuffed and the police officers seemed to escort them in a casual manner, walking relatively far from the hobos. When one looks closer at the photos, they do not seem to be vagabonds: they wore elegant shoes and had well-cut hair.

Many fancy theories were advanced about the "tramps" episode and some private investigators concluded they might have been accomplices in the assassination.

Another important eyewitness took part in the ITV program in 1988. The then 27 year-old, *Ed Hoffman*, a deaf-mute, was standing near the highway, near Dealey Plaza, about an hour before the JFK assassination to watch the presidential motorcade. From his vantage position, he had a bird's eye view of the parking lot near the railroad depot behind the lattice fence of the "Grassy Knoll". Hoffman's testimony was ignored at the time by the FBI investigators because he was deaf-mute but thanks to an interpreter, British television understood what he had to "say". Hoffman claimed that the FBI agents had offered to pay him to prevent him from "telling" anything. Thanks to his highly developed visual sense given his handicap, he "told" his interpreter that he saw two men behind the fence on the parking lot at the time of the shooting. He saw one of them, in a suit, with a rifle, firing at the presidential limousine. Then, after throwing the weapon at his accomplice, he discreetly walked away. The other man, possibly in railroad worker's clothes, dismantled the rifle and placed it in what seemed to be for Hoffman a long toolbox. The man then walked towards the railroad depot[104]. A police officer quickly arrived on the scene near the palisade, drew his weapon and stopped the man wearing a suit. The latter showed the police officer his empty hands as to indicate that he had no weapon. He produced something, which looked like an ID from his jacket. The police officer re-holstered his weapon and departed. The man in the suit then walked to a green Rambler station wagon and sat in the passenger seat. The vehicle drove away. Ed Hoffman confirmed that it was the same vehicle he had spotted in the parking lot one hour before[105].

---

[104] Robert J. Groden and Harrison Edward Livingstone. High Treason: The assassination of JFK. What really happened? The Conservatory Press, 1989

[105] James W. Douglass, JFK and the Unspeakable, Why He Died and Why it Matters A Touchstone Book, 2008

On the morning of John Kennedy's assassination, around eleven o'clock, *Julia Ann Mercer* was driving down Elm Street. Before the triple underpass, her car was caught in a gridlock, exactly at the spot where, an hour and a half later, the President was heading into a crossfire area. As her car stopped, she looked to her right and saw a green Ford pick-up parked in the traffic lane along the sidewalk, just at the bottom of the "Grassy Knoll". She noticed the inscription "Air Conditioning" on the truck. On the rear deck of the pick-up, she saw what seemed to be toolboxes. A man got out of the pick-up, took a gun-like object from the deck, wrapped in paper, moved away from the truck and headed up the "Grassy Knoll". On the railroad overpass, overlooking the lane traffic where Mercer's car was blocked, three police officers were talking near a motorcycle. They were not paying attention to what was going on. They made no attempt to clear the traffic partly obstructed by the illegally parked pick-up or to question its driver about the "rifle" case. Finally, the traffic moved, Mercer slowly advanced and when her car came parallel to the pick-up, the man at the wheel turned in her direction, staring straight into her eyes. She noticed that he had a chubby face. The man looked away then stared at her again.

Two days later, Mercer recognized Jack Ruby on television, the murderer of Oswald. There was no doubt in her mind, that it was Ruby who was the driver of the pickup[106]. On the same day, Mercer decided to go to the Dallas police to report the incident with a precise description of "the pick-up man with the toolbox".

Much later, the Warren Commission recorded Mercer's statement in its investigation files but did not find it useful to retain her as an official eyewitness. Mercer's name was not even mentioned in the Warren Report.

---

[106] Ibid

View of Elm Street from the triple underpass where Julia Ann Mercer, in a gridlock, witnessed the pickup episode (author's photo)

J.C. Price was watching the presidential motorcade on Dealey Plaza. He stated to the police that after the shooting he saw a young man running towards the vehicles parked near the railroad tracks holding something in his hand. The Warren Commission ignored Price's name and his comment in its report.

The railroad worker, *S.M. Holland*, was watching the motorcade from the viaduct. He testified that he heard a rifle shot and saw smoke behind the picket fence at the top of the "Grassy Knoll". As the presidential limousine headed straight for the viaduct when gunshots were fired, Holland immediately turned his eyes to his left. He saw a small puff of smoke about six feet above the ground in the trees of the "Grassy Knoll". In his testimony the same day, he claimed to have heard four gunshots on Dealey Plaza.

Although these eyewitnesses said they heard more than three gunshots and saw smoke coming from the "Grassy Knoll", the Warren Commission attributed these gunshots to an echo phenomenon and ignored the description of the smoke.

Other eyewitnesses claimed that the gunshots came from the front of the presidential limousine and that the fatal blow to John

Kennedy's head had been fired from the triple underpass near the railroad. *Delores Kounas,* an employee of the Texas School Book Depository, was standing at the southern corner of Elm Street near the intersection of Houston Street. She told the FBI that she had heard three gunshots and that it seemed to her they came from the triple underpass.

Virgie Baker, who was standing in front of the Texas School Book Depository, made the same statement about the origin of the gunshots.

Ochus Campbell, vice president of the Texas School Book Depository, was also standing in front of the building. It seemed to him that the shooting came from close to the railroad tracks on the viaduct.

Wesley Frazier, also a TSBD employee, was standing on the steps of the depository. He testified before the Warren Commission that he heard three gunshots. When asked about the origin of the gunshots, he said, *"Well, to be honest with you, I thought it came from below, you know, where the triple underpass is."*

David Powers, one of the President's aides, was in the Secret Service car just behind the presidential limousine. He said, *"My first impression was that the gunshots came from the right and from the top. I also thought that the noise could come from the front, in the area of the triple underpass".*

Bill and Gayle Newman and their two young sons were standing on Elm Street at the bottom of the "Grassy Knoll". They were probably the closest onlookers to the presidential limousine at the time of the gunshots. They were so near that as soon as they heard the gunshots they immediately laid down on the ground in order to protect themselves and their children. They can be seen very clearly on the historic photographs and films. Just after the assassination, the couple testified on Dallas television. Sherry Fiester, an investigator and criminology expert, also interviewed both later. When the limousine passed less than fifty feet from them, Bill Newman declared that when the first shot was fired he saw blood on Kennedy and Connally. Then, when the car drove even closer, about ten feet from him, Bill Newman was looking directly at the President, when the fatal shot hit the President's head and he saw the side of his skull ripped off by the bullet and blood on his face. The 313th frame of the Zapruder's film, at the precise moment of JFK's head explosion, confirmed exactly Newman's testimony[107].

Author *Stewart Galanor* claims that 52 witnesses heard one or more gunshots fired from the front of the presidential limousine. Richard Charnin, a mathematician, reports the comments of 88 witnesses who located the origin of one of the gunshots from the "Grassy Knoll". Even the fervent anti-conspiracy researcher, John McAdams, accepts the testimony of at least 33 witnesses who said they heard a gunshot from the side of the presidential limousine, and not from the rear[108].

The witnesses, who could only trust their auditory senses, were certainly less reliable than eyewitnesses: an important distinction for police and legal authorities. In all, at least 21 police officers and secret service agents were interviewed. Their experience of investigating crime scenes and their proximity to the President - about 150 feet – gave credibility to the seriousness of their testimony. They were posted, moreover, in different places, which could account for potential differences in interpretation like the illusion of gunshots created by echoes on Dealey Plaza, which are frequent sources of fragile testimonies. However, this was not the case. Instinctively, these 21 police officers immediately headed for the "Grassy Knoll". They had undeniably heard gun gunshots coming from beyond the wooden fence, from the parking lot near the railroad depot.

The *Warren Commission* however decided to ignore these eyewitnesses' testimonies, despite the fact they came from police officers. The commission merely said that there was no evidence of gunshots fired in front of the limousine, but that they only came from the Texas School Book Depository.

---

[107] Sherry P. Fiester – Enemy of the Truth, Myths, Forensics and the Kennedy Assassination – JFK Lancer Productions & Publications, Inc. 2012

[108] JFKfacts.org

Among these 21 witnesses was Secret Service Agent *Paul E. Landis*, who was standing on the platform of the third car of the presidential motorcade. He said: "*My first impression was that it was impossible for the President to survive this salvo of gunshots. I still don't know which direction the second shot came from but I thought it could come from somewhere in front and on the right of the road.*"

Another secret service agent, *Forrest Sorrels*, was in the leading car of the motorcade when he heard gunshots. He said "*to have turned his back to look at the 'Grassy Knoll' because the sound seemed to come from this direction*". He confirmed to the Warren Commission that "*the sounds of gunfire seemed to come from the 'Grassy Knoll'. It was so strong that I thought immediately that someone might have been posted there. That's why I looked towards that direction.*"

Chief of Police *Jesse Curry* was in the car immediately preceding Kennedy's limousine. He was convinced that a gunman had fired from the "Grassy Knoll". In his statement, in April 1964, he said: "*I heard a sharp noise. We were near the railway and at that moment I did not know exactly where the noise came from.*" He remembered having spoken on his radio ordering his men to go to the railway yard, behind the "Grassy Knoll", to check the scene and report. His testimony was confirmed by the radio communications obtained from the Dallas police: "*Send a man up the railway bridge and see what happened.*" He located the spot in front of the path of the presidential limousine.[109]

Another police officer, Deputy Sheriff *Roger Craig*, ran straight to the pergola overlooking Elm Street and the railway depot as soon as he heard the first shot at 12:30pm. At this very spot, Craig distinctly heard two more gunshots. While he questioned witnesses during the next ten minutes, his gaze turned to the south side of Elm Street. He heard someone whistle loudly across the street and saw a white Caucasian man, of about twenty years old. Craig asserted in front of the Warren Commission, to the despair of its members, that it was Lee Harvey Oswald whom he

---

[109] Curry, Jesse E., Retired Dallas Police Chief, Jesse Curry, reveals his personal JFK Assassination File (self-published 1969)

saw coming down the "Grassy Knoll" from the Texas School Book Depository. At that moment, a pale green Rambler station wagon was slowly driving down from west Elm Street. The driver, with a Latin look and black wavy hair, was watching the man who was running in his direction down the "Grassy Knoll". The driver parked along the sidewalk and the other man stepped inside the car. Craig tried to cross the street to stop the car but could not reach it as it headed west towards Elm Street. Craig found the behavior of the two individuals suspicious and decided to report to the security forces surrounding the area. He found a man in a gray suit on the entrance steps to the Texas School Book Depository who introduced himself as a Secret Service agent. Although he did not seem to pay much attention to Craig's account about the Rambler station wagon, he wrote it down in his notebook.

Craig later learned that the pale green Rambler station wagon could have been the car owned by Ruth Paine, Marina Oswald's friend[110]. This however was later rejected because the FBI reported that Ruth Paine did not own a Rambler station wagon but rather a 1955 Chevrolet station wagon.[111] Later in the afternoon, Craig (having heard of the arrest of Lee Harvey Oswald suspected of killing the President), called Captain Will Fritz, head of the police homicide section. The latter accepted that Craig come to the police station to check if the man of the Rambler station wagon was Oswald, the suspect detained by the police. When Craig entered Fritz's office, where Oswald was being held for questioning, Craig recognized Oswald as the same man he had seen hurtling down the "Grassy Knoll" towards the station wagon. When Fritz turned to Oswald and said, "*This man saw you leave* [the TSBD]," Oswald retorted, "*I told you. Yes, I left*". Then Fritz asked Oswald "*What about the car*?" Oswald got up, leaned forward, both hands on Fritz's desk and said, "*This **station wagon** belongs to Mrs. Paine. Don't try to drag her into this*" Then he sat

---

[110] James W. Douglass, JFK and the Unspeakable, Why He Died and Why it Matters A Touchstone Book, 2008

[111] http://mcadams.posc.mu.edu/rambler.txt

down and, aware that he had perhaps said too much, spoke in a low voice. *"Everybody will know who I am now "*. He said these words as if his cover had just been blown or that he felt betrayed by the fact that neither Fritz nor Craig had told him that the car they were referring to was a station wagon. Fritz was then urgently called by Sheriff Decker, a block away from his office, ending the conversion with Oswald.

Ed Hoffman, whose testimony is described above, confirmed Sheriff Roger Craig's observations, a few years later. Hoffman had seen the "man in a suit" ride in a same light-colored Rambler station wagon that he had seen leaving the parking lot near the schoolbook warehouse after the shooting[112].

Two other passers-by watching the motorcade gave the same testimony as Craig and Hoffman about the Rambler station wagon. *James Richard Worrell Jr.,* 20 years old, was standing one yard from the Texas School Book Depository. Just after the presidential limousine drove past, Worrell heard a shot. He immediately looked up at the building above him. He saw the barrel of a gun coming out of a window on the fifth or sixth floor, pointing towards the limousine. Worrell noticed at that moment that the President had slumped into his seat. When he heard two more gunshots followed by a fourth, he ran around the Texas School Book Depository. He then saw a man wearing a sport jacket coming out from the back of the building and running away.

Richard Randolph Carr, another eyewitness, confirmed the association of the man in the sport jacket with the Rambler station wagon. Carr was climbing the stairs of the new courthouse under construction near the Texas School Book Depository. He stopped on the sixth floor to catch his breath. As he glanced at the TSBD, he noticed a man looking through the second window on the top floor at the southwestern corner of the schoolbook depository. Carr identified the man as corpulent, wearing a hat, a beige sport

---

[112] James W. Douglass, JFK and the Unspeakable, Why He Died and Why it Matters A Touchstone Book, 2008

jacket and glasses. A minute later, Carr heard a gunshot and then two other very close gunshots. Carr decided to walk down and out of the building under construction to see what was happening on the street. In Houston Street, he was surprised to see the same man in the sport jacket he had seen at the window of the Texas School Book Depository. The man walked quickly towards Carr and looked behind him over his shoulder. He raced to a street corner and climbed into a 1961 or 1962 Rambler station wagon parked in Record Street. The driver of the car was a young black man. The station wagon drove for two blocks and then made a left turn into Elm Street. It was at this same place that Carr saw, like the other witnesses, the station wagon stop suddenly in front of the Texas School Depository Building.

Like Roger Craig, *Helen Forrest* witnessed the same scene but on the opposite side of the street, on the slope of the "Grassy Knoll". She saw a man suddenly walking out of the rear of the Texas School Depository Building, hurtling down the hill and climbing into a Rambler station wagon. She claimed that it was not Oswald but someone who looked a lot like him, someone who could have been his twin. Another witness, *James Pennington*, would confirm Forrest's testimony.

Two drivers, Marvin C. Robinson and Roy Copper also corroborated Craig, Carr, Forrest, and Pennington's observations of the Rambler station wagon. Right after the final gunshots, *Marvin Robinson* had to break hard because a pale green Rambler station wagon had abruptly stopped along the sidewalk of Elm Street in order to pick up a man who was running down the "Grassy Knoll" away from the Texas School Book Depository Building. *Roy Cooper*, who was driving just behind Robinson, told the FBI that he had witnessed a close fender bender between the two cars and seen a man wave to the Rambler driver to get him to in jump quickly. The Warren Commission rejected all these witnesses' testimonies of the association of the man in the sport jacket with the Rambler station wagon because it had already concluded that Oswald had left the Texas School Depository Building to take a bus. It also ignored Craig's testimony that he had seen Oswald in Captain Will Fritz's office, the latter having denied Craig's presence[113].

Other police statements about the origin of the gunshots, briefly summarized below, are troubling: *Harold Elkins* said, "*I immediately ran to the spot where it seemed the gunshots came from, in the area between the railway and the Texas School Book Depository*".

Four other police officers, *Lummie Lewis, A.D. McCurley, Luke Mooney* and *W.W. Mabra* heard gunshots from the same location and made their way to the "Grassy Knoll" and the freight station[114]. Deputy Scheriff *J.L. Oxford* rushed towards the railway overpass as soon as he heard the gunshots. At the same time, *L.C. Smith* stepped over the picket fence where it joins the bridge in order to control the parking lot just behind the "Grassy Knoll". *Todd* ran toward the railways tracks. *Ralph Walters* and *Jack Watson* did the same. *Harry Weatherford* gave an identical statement: as soon as he heard the sound of a gunshot, he knew what it was: "*I thought to myself that it might have been a rifle. I headed for the 'Grassy Knoll' when I heard the third shot. It was at that moment that I rushed to the railway yard from where the gunshots seemed to have come* ".

Deputy Scheriff, *Buddy Walthers,* was riding his motorcycle just behind Kennedy's limousine. He testified on the day of the assassination and again in July 1964 before the Warren Commission in Washington. He claimed having heard three gunshots. He remembered rushing across Dealey Plaza to the parking lot: "*Something in my head made me think that the gunshots could come from the railway bridge because of the blood splatter I had received from where I was that is a little behind and to the left of Mrs. Kennedy.*"

Clyde Haygood, can be seen on the historic photos trying to climb the northern corner of Elm Street with his motorbike but he gave up and laid it aside the street then rushed to the "Grassy Knoll".

Joe Marshall Smith had his back turned to the Texas School Book Depository Building on Elm Street when the gunshots were fired.

---

[113] Ibid
[114] JFKfacts.org

"I did not know where the gunshots came from ... but I decided to run to the place immediately behind the cement pergola. There I checked the shrubs and all the cars in the parking lot behind the 'Grassy Knoll' ".

Edgar Leon Smith was standing east on the sidewalk of Houston Street about fifty yards from the Texas School Book Depository Building. He thought at first that the two gunshots he heard were firecrackers but on the third shot, he drew his pistol and ran down Elm Street. A lawyer from the Warren Commission asked him to specify the location on a map and if he thought the shot came from the small concrete structure near the pergola. Smith answered in the affirmative.

The railroad employee, Lee Bowers, was the most "inconvenient" witness for the authorities as he made a testimony about multiple gunshots on Dealey Plaza. What he described was very accurate and very detailed. He had an ideal vantage point from the railway depot control tower where he could see gunmen in action behind the picket fence.

Control tower from where the railway man, Lee Bowers, noticed a gunshot flash and smoke behind the picket fence (left, off the photo) (author's photo)

On November 22, 1963, shortly before 12:30 pm when the first gunshots were fired on Dealey Plaza, Bowers had a clear view on what was happening right behind the wooden fence. Since the police had blocked the roads traffic at 10.00 am, Bowers noted the lack of cars movement in the parking lot. Despite this at around 11:55 am, he noticed a 1959 Oldsmobile station wagon which entered the parking lot of the railway depot behind the "Grassy Koll". The car was all smudged with reddish mud and did not have any particular mark that could have identified it as a police car. His driver, a white man with partially gray-hair, was driving slowly, as if to explore the area, then left the parking lot. At around 12:15 pm, a 1957 black Ford arrived on the scene, driven by a white man aged 25-35 years. The driver seemed to be talking in a microphone or a walkie-talkie. He made a large tour of the parking lot and then left. Shortly after, at around 12:20 pm, Bowers spotted a white 1961 Chevrolet Impala, with dirty windows. The driver, a white or blond-haired man, 25-35 year old, left the parking lot around 12:25pm.

Parking lot where Bowers noticed two men near the picket fence when gunshots were fired (author's photo)

At 12:28 pm, immediately before the gunshots, Bowers noticed two men near the picket fence who were not railway men he knew. One of the men, in his mid-twenties, was wearing a plaid shirt or jacket.[115] At the moment the gunshots were fired, at 12.30 pm, Bowers saw a flash of light or smoke near the fence, where the two men were positioned. One of the men was standing on the bumper of a car whose rear was touching the wooden palisade.[116] Just after the shooting, Bowers saw police officers and many witnesses climb the steps of the "Grassy Knoll" leading to the parking lot behind the fence - as shown by several photographs and video films. Several footprints were found in the mud on the spot and, according to an unofficial testimony, an empty cartridge from a rifle as well. The Warren Commission questioned Bowers, intimidated him, told him he was wrong and did not allow him say any more of what he had seen. The investigators quickly moved on to something else.

Dozens of witnesses climbed the steps of the "Grassy Knoll" after the shooting (author's photo)

Picket fence on top of the "Grassy Knoll" and the parking lot behind (author's photo)

The main testimony that "incriminated" Oswald was that of *Howard L. Brennan*. He was the only one to 'have seen Oswald' at the sixth-floor window of the Texas School Book Depository, aiming before firing his last shot. He gave the police the description of the sniper: a thin man, 5'10", about 30 years old, weighing about 160 pounds. At the police station, in a line-up, Brennan was unable to formally recognize Oswald. He told the Warren Commission that the sniper was *standing* just behind the window. In this building, only the lower part of the sash windows

---

[115] Lamar Waldron, The Hidden History of the JFK Assassination, Counter Point Berkeley, 2013
[116] Ibid

could be opened. The official photos show some of the windows open including that of the sixth floor. In order to be standing, the individual would have to break the glass of the upper part of the window to be able to shoot. The most likely gunman's position was kneeling or seating. If he was kneeling, how could Brennan have estimated the height of the man at 5'10''?

Another onlooker, *Eric Walther*, told the FBI that he saw two men at the sixth floor window and the barrel of a rifle pointing downwards. It was also the same testimony that Arnold Rowland had given: a second person in addition to the alleged sniper, Lee Harvey Oswald, was on the same floor.

All in all, it would be foolish to refute the testimony of so many witnesses who had rushed to the "Grassy Knoll", from where, they were convinced, the gunshots had been fired. These witnesses' reactions on Dealey Plaza alone contribute to providing overwhelming evidence that a crossfire was set up by at least two assassins to kill the President.

However, the detractors of the conspiracy supporters remain on their guard. They say everything about a conspiracy is nonsense, that Oswald is the only shooter, that the so-called evidence invalidating the Warren Report's version is therefore unfounded.

Since 1963, the mainstream media stand behind this official position, defended by the American government. The fact that this media advocacy is visible even today is very shameful. What dominant role has the American media played in this terrible undertaking of misinformation, censorship and cover-up? How has this media collusion been able to take place for half a century and why? It is important to understand why the mainstream media have failed, voluntarily or not, in their key role of ensuring unbiased investigative journalism.

Chapter 5

The Fourth Estate under Control

In the United States, many investigators have spent most of their lives trying to unravel the assassination of President Kennedy. For most of them, revealing the evidence of a plot has become an obsession. The results of their investigations and the seriousness of their expertise are impressive. Their discoveries have undeniably puzzled a large population both in the United States and around the world.

Despite their fervor and tenacity, not all has been reported and the mystery around the JFK assassination endures. It persists by lack of key witnesses from that period, because either they have passed away or because they still feel under threat should they reveal inconvenient truth. It also persists because of apathy and obscurantism.

Most American citizens remain unaware of the true perpetrators behind the conspiracy and of the reasons as to why the assassination has given way to a cover-up. However, as said before, 60 to 80 percent of Americans, depending on the time of the polls, do not believe in the "official" government investigation concluding that a single assassin committed the murder of JFK. On the contrary, they suspect a conspiracy behind the elimination of their president who they believe was one of the greatest heads-of-state since the birth of the American nation.

Many questions fuel the debate. Why has the outrageous version of the Dallas murder been constantly maintained by the American government? Why is there a controversy over the President's injuries? How many gunmen were involved on Dealey Plaza? If only one man fired three gunshots (and not a single one more) as the Warren Report asserted, how could one explain that there were so many injuries inflicted on two of the occupants in the presidential limousine? Why were the CIA and the FBI so reluctant to cooperate with the many investigators and eyewitnesses? Why have thousands of documents directly related to the assassination remained classified and hidden by the government for more than half a century? Did Lee Harvey Oswald act upon orders to kill the President and was he framed to be a scapegoat? Did Jack Ruby eliminate Oswald to prevent him from finally talking and revealing the existence of a plot and if so who was behind?

Spending time in America has enabled me (through sheer geographic proximity) to attend the annual conferences about this historical drama and to get to know the researchers' community. I was curious to know how much it could still provoke interest in the United States. Attending these conventions has helped me to campaign to find the truth about the assassination and to write this book.

In November 2013, I participated in the three-day conference *"Passing the Torch"* at Duquesne University, in Pittsburgh, Pennsylvania. About 400 participants attended this convention, dedicated to the 50th anniversary of the assassination of John Kennedy. Its mission was to inform and educate students, professionals and the public about one of the major events in 20th century American history. The evidence of a coup against JFK was widely exposed and debated during high-quality lectures by prominent investigators, historians, authors, scientists and legal experts. Oliver Stone, who directed the movie "JFK", took an active part, notably during a discussion panel about the determination of the mainstream media over years to endorse the official version of the Warren Commission despite the manifest lack of credibility in its report. Even today, Oliver Stone's opinion about the JFK assassination remains unchanged and his arguments are still convincing.

I learned that over the years more and more documents had been declassified, thanks in particular to the *Assassination Records Review Board*, the independent agency appointed by President Clinton, in the 1990s. These documents helped investigators to reveal their own findings, that Kennedy had been assassinated by the National Security State that opposed the fundamentally different direction taken by JFK for America towards détente with the Soviet Union and rapprochement with Cuba.

I was curious to see what the American mainstream media had to say about the 50th anniversary of the JFK assassination. Would the American media continue to promote the government's version, that is, the conclusions of the Warren Commission's report showing Oswald as the sole murderer?

On my return from Pittsburgh, I was eager to hear and read about this commemoration. I decided to follow the debates on the American television channels and to browse the articles in the national press. More specifically, I wanted to know, 50 years on, if the mainstream media had duly covered the historic anniversary and had presented the two theories (single shooter or wider plot) with transparency, lucidity and impartiality. It was inconceivable for me that they could fail in their true journalistic duty.

Although the Pittsburgh convention was an enriching experience, the lack of media coverage of the anniversary left me perplexed and frustrated. Unfortunately and to my dismay, not only was the media coverage negligible or totally ignored, but the very few references to the motives of the Dallas crime also lacked objectivity. All the television stations presented the same litany: "Oswald did it! Don't look for anything else. It was the isolated act of a mad man."

The quality programs and documentaries about a probable conspiracy, those available on YouTube for example, which should have been broadcast on national television channels, were remarkably absent. On the other hand, the hugely publicized release on the big screen of the movie, *Parkland*, co-produced by Tom Hanks, with the scenario written by Vincent Bugliosi, was perfectly timed for the commemoration. Bugliosi, who died recently, was a strong advocate for the Warren Commission's report. He wrote a 1,600-page saga book with the pompous title *"Reclaiming History"* on the assassination of President Kennedy. Known for his active fight against the "conspiracy nuts", the right to "reclaim history" was his livelihood, despite the researchers' assessment proving a highly probable conspiracy!

There was no media coverage, either, of Dr. Robert McClelland's remarkable live video interview, during the Pittsburgh conference. A 34-year-old doctor in 1963, Dr. McClelland had been called to the trauma room at Dallas Parkland Hospital to which John Kennedy had been rushed after the shooting. In Pittsburgh, 50 years later, he described, with absolute lucidity, the wounds inflicted on the President and confirmed his conviction. What he had observed while he stood behind the President's head for 18 minutes was undoubtedly a bullet exit wound; a wide hole from which he saw the cerebellum fall onto the stretcher when Kennedy's body was moved. He also explained that in 1980 during a visit to Washington, he had been able to examine the autopsy photographs of the President showing the back of his head intact). These "official" photographs did not match what he had seen at Parkland Hospital (this forgery will be covered in details in a next chapter). Dr. McClelland's position was also corroborated by other doctors who confirmed that the fatal shot had been fired from a spot facing the presidential limousine; hence the presence of at least two shooters proving there had been a conspiracy. Fifty years later, he clearly no longer feared government pressures at the time on the Parkland Hospital doctors who had opposed the findings of the Warren Report concerning JFK's head wounds.

Did such a testimony, the "scoop" of the conference, make the national press headline or a proper coverage on TV? No, absolutely nothing. You have to go on the internet to see Dr. McClelland's presentation.

In Dallas, a cursed city finger-pointed for a long time by the American people for not having provided a suitable protection for their President, what form did the commemoration of the 50th anniversary of the assassination take? The city gave a moving tribute to John Kennedy on Dealey Plaza but the organizers insisted in advance that no protests nor forums of discussion against the official position concerning the assassination would be tolerated. So it became instead more like a celebration of the denial of truth!

Quite to the contrary, however, once back in Europe, I watched a TV replay of the coverage of the 50th anniversary of the JFK assassination and some less recent programs that had been broadcast again for the special occasion. It was obvious the probable conspiracy on the assassination had been addressed, in the old world, without sensationalism but with conviction. For example, the Arte TV program *"A particular day"* addressed different scenarios: the likely origin of the gunshots to have been from the front of the JFK limousine path, that Lee Harvey Oswald could have been just a patsy and the existence of falsified photographs and fake x-rays of John Kennedy's autopsy.

The American mainstream media have shown us recent examples of apathy for opening the debate on the Dallas conspiracy theory. There has been censorship of some people's opinions, of embarrassing positions or "inconvenient" testimonies that were in opposition to the official version of the U.S. government. On January 11, 2013, in front of a large audience in Dallas, John Kennedy's nephew, Robert Kennedy Jr., interviewed by Charlie Rose, told the talk show host that his father, Bobby Kennedy, then Attorney General, believed, in private, that the *"Warren Commission was a shoddy piece of craftsmanship"* and that *"although he publicly supported the Warren Commission report, he privately was dismissive of it."* His son then added his own opinion: "*The evidence at this point, I think, is very, very convincing that it was not a lone gunman.*" Robert Kennedy Jr. also said that his father had asked the Department of Justice investigators to probe the assertions on which the alleged killer, Lee Harvey Oswald, had received help from the Mafia and the

CIA. He further pointed out that his father's colleagues had obtained lists of Jack Ruby's phone calls that revealed the direct connection between Jack Ruby and Lee Harvey Oswald with certain Organized Crime individuals, they themselves being linked to the CIA. These discoveries had convinced his father that there was something real about these assertions[117].

This program should have been a big media event because 50 years after the Dallas drama it was probably the first time a close relative of the Kennedy family had publicly expressed serious doubts about the official version of the government. The television program however was not broadcast on a mainstream television channel! [118] Charlie Rose's interview was recorded in front of cameras in a public meeting place in Dallas, the Winspear Opera House, with the Mayor of Dallas and Robert Kennedy Jr.'s sister, Rory Kennedy, attending. The whole interview transcript is on Jim DiEugenio's website, *Citizens for Truth about the Kennedy Assassination*[119]. This program, though scheduled well ahead of time, was certainly "inconvenient". Robert Kennedy Jr's embarrassing words had obviously surprised and had better be forgotten. The television channels shunned the program. The editorial in the Dallas Morning News decided to truncate the embarrassing part of Robert Kennedy Jr.'s remarks, the reference to the Oswald-Ruby connection. The less disturbing part such as the " *Warren Commission was a shoddy piece of craftsmanship*" was left in the article.

What a disgrace to the American people and especially to John Kennedy's memory! It was not one of those "Conspiracy Nuts" interviewed but a respectable representative of the Kennedy family, the President's nephew.

---

[117] Elizabeth Woodworth, "JFK, MLK, RFK, 50 Years of Suppressed History: New Evidence on Assassination of John F. Kennedy, Martin Luther King and Robert F. Kennedy" April 5, 2013

[118] Jesse Ventura – They Killed Our President – 2013. Skyhorse Publishing, Inc.

[119] Citizens for Truth about the Kennedy Assassination, "The MSM and RFK Jr: only 45 Years Late this Time" February 3, 2013: ctka.net/2013/The_MSM_and_RFKJr.html

A local newspaper however covered the interview. The Pittsburgh Tribune asked Cyril Wecht, an internationally renowned forensic pathologist, what he thought of Robert F. Kennedy Jr's revelations. Wecht said he was delighted that Bobby Kennedy's son had spoken so openly about his father's doubts concerning the official version of his uncle's assassination. When Wecht was asked why, in public, Bobby Kennedy had been so silent about the case at the time, he explained that so long as Lyndon Johnson and FBI Director J. Edgar Hoover were in power (probably two men who hated Robert Kennedy the most) it would have been foolish for him to publicly criticize the conclusions of the Warren Commission at the risk of "*running into a stone wall*"[120].

In March 2014, on the CNN website, referring to the TV show "The Sixties", there was a little reminder to the public, which was far from being innocent: "*Five things you may not know about JFK assassination. This year marks the 51st anniversary of the assassination of John F. Kennedy in Dallas on November 22, 1963. Whether you were born at that time or not, you probably know that Lee Harvey Oswald killed the president.*"[121] So, CNN presented the act of the *alleged* murderer as a *fait accompli*, an axiom in a way, regardless of the controversy that is still under debate in the United States today.

The state or national press was no more present at the other two conferences that I attended: the *Assassinations Archives Research Center* in Bethesda, Maryland in September 2014, and *JFK Lancer* in November 2015 in Dallas. The Bethesda conference brought together no less than forty-four renowned lecturers: forensic scientists, lawyers, criminal police experts and investigative journalists. New revelations about the assassination of John Kennedy were developed and inconsistencies were highlighted in the conclusions of the Warren Commission report, which was handed over to President Lyndon Johnson on September 24, 1964.

---

[120] http://triblive.com/opinion/qanda/3292514-74/commission-kennedy-warren#ixzz2MjNJAkPy

[121] http://us.cnn.com/2013/11/14/us/jfk-assassination-5-things/index.html

In Bethesda, there were no journalists at the convention and no coverage of the event in the national press. This was particularly surprising given the proximity of the conference venue to Washington D.C., in the Beltway area, the universe of the federal government, Washington politicians and the most influential reporters.

But, I must be realistic; the whole Dallas event goes back a long time for the American people especially for the young generation. When I began my 7th grade at junior high school, the assassination perpetrated in Sarajevo against Archduke Franz Ferdinand of the Austro-Hungarian Empire had occurred 50 years before. The publication of the Warren Report about the JFK assassination in 1964 took place as far back in time for a young 7th grade student in 2014! I do not remember feeling, at that age, a keen interest to know all the details about the June 1914 attack on the Austro-Hungarian archduke or about the real murderer's motive. I was not particularly eager to learn more about the whole drama other than what my history book covered. All I needed to remember was that the event had triggered the First World War. Like the absence of curiosity for the murder of Sarajevo at my young age, the young American generation showing ignorance or lack of interest for the assassination of John Kennedy is easily understood and this is not surprising considering the endless imbroglio connected to the Dallas event. This attitude however brings up the issue that a powerful democracy such as America is not yet ready to face the truth of this historical event.

On May 3, 2016, media distortion of the facts surrounding the assassination of John Kennedy resurfaced during the U.S. primaries campaign for the presidential election. While my wife and I were in the CBP line at Newark airport, that day, TV monitors were frantically broadcasting CNN's "Breaking News" about candidate Donald Trump's accusation of his rival Ted Cruz. Trump was publicly exploiting the accusations of a tabloid, the *National Enquirer*, which reported that Ted Cruz's father - an anti-Castro – was associated with Lee Harvey Oswald, shortly before the assassination of John Kennedy.

The news was detailed once we arrived at our American home. The headlines of major news channels and the news on the internet claimed that "*Trump accuses Ted Cruz's father of helping JFK's assassin, Lee Harvey Oswald*" showing a 1963 photo on which both men could be seen side by side in New Orleans. The media, CNN, Fox, ABC, the New York Times, USA Today and even the respectable BBC News, relayed the sensational allegation of candidate, Donald Trump. The headlines of these news channels - "*the association and help of Lee Harvey Oswald, the assassin of JFK*" - were posted as an indisputable fact carved in stone! It gave evidence of an unbearable distortion of facts.

These media channels continue to deceive the American people with their perennial reminder of "*the isolated act of a lone assassin*". There is never the slightest reference to Lee Harvey Oswald's presumption of innocence. Totally lost in oblivion are also the findings of the House Select Committee on Assassinations whose investigation revealed a probable plot. Forgotten are the words "alleged", underlined by someone on the historic plaque riveted to the Texas School Book Depository wall (a reference to Lee Harvey Oswald who supposedly shot at the President from the sixth floor of this building)!

The CNN commentator added even more confusion during the interview with Donald Trump who was asked the ambiguous question: "*Isn't it once again the conspiracy theory coming back?*" Was the commentator referring to a conspiracy related to the National Enquirer's allegations against an opponent candidate? Or was he alluding to the JFK assassination conspiracy that contradicted the official version of the lone gunman, Lee Harvey Oswald? Was the journalist eluding the fact that accomplices who might have helped Oswald was something disturbing?

Reference to Oswald's alleged act (word underlined by skeptics!) on the historic plaque affixed on the Texas School Book Depository (author's photo)

The major American media, as a whole, seem to be losing interest in this historic event. It is not only recent but recurrent since 1963. This is the opinion of many investigators who are determined to shed light on the conspiracy of the assassination and the cover-up that followed. Their analysis, available on the internet and in their books, tend to denounce the behavior of the media that have turned a blind eye to the new revelations of a plot, confirmed by factual, well supported and tangible evidence. In contrast, the media has accepted and publicly supported investigations "demonstrating" that the official government version of the assassination is the one to be remembered.

There are however some brave, independent and dissident journalists who decide to fight apathy. They choose to regain their freedom by refusing the servitude imposed by the corporate hierarchy of the major media. David Talbot, journalist-historian, is one of them[122]. Everything he writes is heavily referenced and documented throughout the interviews he gives. His access to official government records on the assassination of President John

---

[122] Jacob. M. Carter – Before History Dies - 2015, Interview of David Talbot

Kennedy, thanks to the "JFK Records Act", the public law passed by the U.S. Congress in 1992, also makes him credible. According to Talbot, the collusion of the Fourth Estate, under the influence of its masters, is evident. Power kills the truth. In the assassination of President Kennedy, Talbot sees a contempt for the truth, a machination orchestrated by the U.S. intelligence structure, at least by some dissident members of these agencies responsible for the cover-up.

We have evidence of this practice of misinformation. James Jesus Angleton, a CIA spy hunter, who engaged in lies and false leads in an attempt to confuse the American people, coordinated it. Talbot believes the American people display a certain naivety in this respect whereas Europeans - from experience of an old history or by lucidity - seem to be aware of the errors of their government.

Talbot sees that the United States operates at two levels. On the one hand, there is the elected government, designated democratically by the people, but on the other hand, "dark forces" behind the presidential power are in control of the country. It is an old story that repeats itself in the United States. When whistleblowers (Wikileaks, Edward Snowden) reveal the listening of secret conversations in this country, there is immediate panic among those powerful individuals who actually control the country. Talbot asserts, *"Those who say that all the conspiracy theorists are nuts are just naive by believing in fairy tales."* Admittedly, conspiracy theories, if not well documented, cannot be credible and must be invalidated and rejected. However, when serious investigators refer to official documents and irrefutable facts (research work that 99.9% of U.S. media do not perform) their findings are credible and worthy of consideration.

Talbot is not the only historian to show his frustration at the naivety or disinterest of some Americans in the eyes of history. Russ Baker, an American investigative journalist and founder of the WhoWhatWhy website, defends evidence of a coup against John Kennedy and is proud to be a "Conspiracy Realist". During a discussion panel at the Pittsburgh conference, he admitted to *"getting along better with foreign journalists than with those of his own country when he tackles the cover-up on the JFK assassination"*. For

Baker, the American people are brainwashed, indoctrinated by the media. *"Censorship is in the thinking of the country. The media make fun of "Conspiracy Nuts" but what can we expect from journalists, 90% of whom have not even read the books on the JFK assassination?"*

Censorship may seem like a strong word for the great American democracy. What does Freedom House say about media freedom in the U.S.A.? The appreciation of this respectable organization for the American press is that it is "free" because of the protection of the first amendment of the U.S. constitution. However, Freedom House notes that the coverage of news communicated by major television channels is strongly polarized in the U.S. since their interpretation of events is politicized, taking a constantly biased position to the right or to the left. Whether the trend is "Liberal" or "Conservative", it is particularly noticeable with Fox News, MSNBC and CNN, the country's leading 24-hour coverage news channels. The Justice Department has also been heavily criticized for possible recourse to trials, a threat to force journalists to reveal sources of information they intend to keep secret. President Obama and his Attorney General, however, pledged that these journalists would not be incarcerated if they were not willing to identify their sources.[123]

Among those supporting the official version of the single gunman, there are those who remain faithful to or steady on their position since 1963. There are also those who had criticized it in the past but have strangely flip-flopped since. They now adhere to the official position of "Oswald did it". Around the 50th anniversary of the JFK assassination, I listened to commentator Bill O'Reilly of Fox News and author of a recent book "Killing Kennedy" (a million copies were sold in four months) in which he supports the single gunman version.

During a show presenting his book and the eponymous film that I had just seen on television, O'Reilly defied the conspirators.

---

[123] https://freedomhouse.org/report/freedom-press/2015/united-states

What he did not say in the 2013 show, but which is still fresh in the investigators' memory, is that while he had expressed an opposite position in the 1990s, he had since flip-flopped. As a young reporter then, he had supported the evidence of a killing plot against the President. O'Reilly's comments backing the conspiracy theory are recalled by investigative journalist Russ Baker on his website Whowhatwhy.org:[124] *"Living in Dallas, Oswald was befriended by Russian-born George de Mohrenschildt. Investigators determined he was a contract agent for the CIA in Central America and the Caribbean. In 1977, moments before he was to be interviewed by House* [House Select Committee on Assassinations] *investigators, de Mohrenschildt blew his brains out with a 20-gauge shotgun. House investigators believe he was a crucial link between the CIA and Lee Harvey Oswald. There is no question that the sealed JFK Files are extremely embarrassing for the CIA. House investigators have told Inside Edition that the Agency did not fully cooperate in their investigation and that the CIA had final say in the final report that the House Assassinations Committee made public. Thus, the public report makes no mention of the CIA's links with Lee Harvey Oswald. But, the secret documents are another story. ...House investigators uncovered evidence that the CIA planted nine agents inside the Garrison investigation to feed him false information and to report back to Langley what Garrison was finding out."*

In the same 2013 program, when he referred to the motive of Jack Ruby (Oswald's assassin in the Dallas police headquarters), two days after JFK was killed, Bill O'Reilly, argued that Ruby had acted only on mere impulse and patriotism. Ruby's act, he said, was a moment of madness and nothing more: he wanted to bring down the "disgusting" man who had killed the President; it was not a premeditated act, dictated by anyone as the "Conspiracy Nuts" assert.

We know that a few minutes before Ruby entered the Dallas police headquarters to kill Oswald, Ruby parked his car nearby. He left his favorite dog, Sheba, in the car and went to the Western Union office, near the police station, to send money to one of his

---

[124] http://whowhatwhy.org/2012/02/23/the-jfk-factor-bill-oreilly-on-the-assassination-then-and-now/

employees. For O'Reilly, this was evidence that Ruby's gesture was not premeditated (under pressure from the Mafia, as it has been said) "*since he had momentarily left his dog in his car*". If he had planned to go to kill Oswald, would Ruby have left his dog unattended? Would he not have left it at home or would he not have found someone to take care of it? These questions, however, remain the same whether the act was committed on the spur of the moment or premeditated. Whatever may have been his motive, Ruby knew it would be unlikely that after firing at Oswald, he would be able to leave the police premises to return to find his dog. There was a strong risk he would be arrested, kept in custody until imprisonment. Bill O'Reilly's argument, now a fierce defender of the Warren Commission Report, is trivial. This anecdote illustrates well the "Lone Nuts" superficial arguments. In the end, if Ruby had acted under impulse, was he necessarily exempted from complicity? Had it no help from the Mafia nor financial compensation for the contract?

Russ Baker and Milicent Cranor refer to many examples that highlight the support of the "Lone Nuts" version by the media. Here is an example of the ambiguous position of the U.S. media today: the authors recall the words of the liberal channel MSNBC commentator, Chris Matthews, who promoted the "Lone Nuts" version on the 50th anniversary of the President's death. In his show, "Hardball"[125], he offensively opposed his version to that of David Talbot. Matthews's words were unequivocal: "*It was not a conspiracy. It was a crime of opportunity*! "[126] On *Access Hollywood*, Matthews made his point by supporting the findings in Bill O'Reilly's book: No Conspiracy. "*It's a leftist who killed Kennedy.*" He added, "*It was easy for Oswald to shoot from the Texas School Book Depository window, you do not have to be an experienced shooter*".[127]

---

[125] http://www.nbcnews.com/id/18941406/ns/msnbc-hardball_with_chris_matthews/t/hardball-chris-matthews-may/#.Vk-9ifmrTlV

[126] Russ Baker & Milicent Cranor – The Mystery of the Constant Flow of JFK Disinformation – November 24, 2013

[127] http://www.accesshollywood.com/videos/chris-matthews-talks-jfk-assassination-conspiracies-44633/

Yet, as we will see in a next chapter of this book, ballistic evidence and Oswald's whereabouts carefully timed by investigators in the Texas School Book Depository negate Matthews' claim. In the Los Angeles Times interview, Chris Matthews also said he did not think *"dark forces"* were behind the conspiracy. *"We know what happened that day. No one has yet come forward with evidence supporting an alternative theory"*.[128]

No evidence? This book will widely expose them!

I myself wanted to see most of the programs broadcast on the 50th anniversary of John Kennedy's assassination. For the most part, reports by PBS, National Geographic, The Discovery Channel, The Military Channel, The Smithsonian, Reelz or Fox News - were frustrating. They repeated endlessly the same "Lone Nuts" arguments of the past.

Some programs, such as the one on the Discovery Channel, strove to support the official "Single Bullet" explanation by which the same bullet would have passed through the bodies of John Kennedy and Governor Connally. They claimed that the President was sitting in the limousine seat, leaning slightly forward, with his jacket and shirt pulled up at the back of his neck. But a close analysis of the Zapruder's film showed that this could not be the case. The bulge on the back of the jacket was minor. The wound sketched by the doctors during the autopsy was perfectly aligned with the bullet holes in the shirt and the jacket, about 6 inches below the top of the collar. For the television program supporting the "Single Bullet" theory, the computer animation of the President's neck and shoulders was so distorted that it showed a physically impossible posture! In the Discovery Channel program's reenactment of the shooting scene, the bullet that was supposed to exit John Kennedy's throat, after hitting him in his back, should have exited at the level of his heart and not below his Adam's apple. Discovery Channel did not correctly address the trajectory and did not use any current techniques of

---

[128] http://articles.latimes.com/2013/nov/22/entertainment/la-et-st-chris-matthews-jfk-50-years-assassination-20131122

investigation performed by forensic experts. In reality, this TV channel invented the "evidence" and manipulated their "experts" to guarantee a preconceived result. The reenactment of the actual trajectory of the gunshots which hit the President's throat and his head were based on the incomplete measurements performed by the FBI. However, back in April 1964, the Warren Commission had considered the Dealey Plaza overpass as the possible origin for one shot. On May 24, 1964, the commission asked the FBI to include the overpass in their reenactment tests to determine the trajectory angle of any bullet that could have been fired at Kennedy by a sniper from this position but the FBI ignored the commission's request[129].

For the 50th anniversary of the assassination, Mediaite.com, announcing upcoming television programs, wrote: "*According to four government investigations, Lee Harvey Oswald was the sniper who assassinated the President.*" Nothing more was said. The American people are constantly being reminded of the Warren Report's version of events that fateful day, but there is never any mention of the most recent survey done by the House Select Committee on Assassinations which had concluded that a conspiracy was probable[130].

The deplorable denial of truth still goes on today and is not something new. It goes back several decades. Less than a month after the assassination, on December 19, 1963, a New York lawyer, Marc Lane, was the first American to refute the indictment of a single gunman by the government. He chose the weekly leftist newspaper, the Guardian, to publish his doubts about the official version of the crime. The results of his investigation became the keystone of conspiracy research in the decades that followed. How could Oswald have been the only shooter posted at the top of a building *behind* the path of the presidential limousine, while

---

[129] Sherry P. Fiester – Enemy of the Truth, Myths, Forensics and the Kennedy Assassination – JFK Lancer Productions & Publications, Inc. 2012

[130] http://www.mediaite.com/tv/a-guide-to-all-the-jfk-specials-that-will-air-on-tv-this-month/

Dallas Parkland Hospital doctors were adamant that one of the bullets that hit the President's throat had been fired from the front? How could a gunman with an old fashioned rudimentary weapon (purchased by mail for $12.78) fire three gunshots towards a moving target in less than six seconds - a performance that even a sharpshooter of the National Rifle Association could not match? For what reasons would Oswald, marked as a communist, kill a president who sought to improve U.S. relations with the Soviet Union and Cuba - a man Fidel Castro believed "*could be the greatest president of the United States*"?

Mark Lane's comments were rejected by many American publications: Life, Look, the Saturday Evening Post, Nation and Fact. His article however caused a sensation abroad, especially in European newspapers. On January 14, 1964, Mark Lane accepted Marguerite Oswald's request to posthumously represent her son for his defense. She had insisted, before the Warren Commission, that her son was a U.S. intelligence agent and that he had been framed[131].

James Carter, the young American speaker and writer I met at the "JFK Lancer" conference in Dallas in November 2015, interviewed David Talbot and asked him the following question: "*Could you describe the CIA tactics of misinformation concerning the assassination of John Kennedy and do you think they continue today?*" Talbot confirmed. Thanks to the "Freedom of Information Act", a 1967 federal law designed to clarify and protect the right of the American public to access information, certain documents can be revealed. One of these documents from the 1970s revealed that the CIA had sent memos to complacent journalists, hundreds of reporters whom the agency considered "valuable". Some were even paid by the CIA in return for their work of disinformation or, as the CIA put it, for their "patriotic duty". Some actors in the mainstream American press, the New York Times and the Washington Post, led this campaign of misinformation. The CIA counter-espionage department even sent instructions to the

---

[131] David Talbot – Brothers, The Hidden History of the Kennedy Years - 2007

media on how to systematically interfere with investigators who favored the conspiracy theory.[132] This revelation was mentioned too by Andrew Kreig, an investigative journalist and lawyer, during a discussion panel at the "Assassination Archives and Research Center" conference in Bethesda when he spoke about the background of press editors, many of whom had been trained at the CIA.

At the very beginning of the Cold War (late 1940s), the CIA implemented a secret program called "Operation Mockingbird". The plan was to recruit U.S. news organizations and journalists as spies to penetrate and influence the biggest U.S. media by paying its reporters and hence achieve the CIA's propaganda goal. Frank Wisner, Allen Dulles, Richard Helms and Philip Graham (himself editor of the Washington Post) headed this department to control the "Operation Mockingbird" program[133].

In 1977, after leaving the Washington Post, Carl Bernstein, the journalist well known for having revealed the Watergate scandal with the help of Bob Woodward at the Washington Post, studied the CIA's relationship with the press during the Cold War.[134] According to declassified CIA documents, 400 American journalists performed their "CIA duties" for 25 years, with the management consent of the major media outlets. Many signed confidentiality agreements, pledging to reveal nothing about their actions with the agency.[135] Some of them even signed employment contracts with the CIA to ensure their protection. CIA officials would agree in return not to disclose the names of the journalists who cooperated with the agency. Among the press, the New York Times offered by far the most valuable cooperation.

At the "Assassination Archives and Research Center" conference in Bethesda, Mal Hyman, a professor of sociology,

---

[132] Jacob. M. Carter – Before History Dies - 2015, Interview of David Talbot
[133] Mary Louise. "Operation Mockingbird: CIA Media Manipulation". 2003
[134] http://www.carlbernstein.com/magazine_cia_and_media.php
[135] http://www.justice-integrity.
org/index.php?option=com_content&view=article&id=636:investigative-reporter-implicates- wikipedia-in- smear-campaign&catid=21&Itemid=114%20%20%20

recalled the astonishing behavior of Washington Post's legendary editor-in-chief, Benjamin Bradlee. When based in Paris, after having contributed to the U.S. government's propaganda during "Operation Mockingbird", Bradlee continued to develop relations with the CIA, particularly with Cord Meyer, who was considered to be the leader of the clandestine propaganda department in this program. Despite having been John Kennedy's close friend for a long time, after the President's death, he surprised people by not covering the assassination. When interviewed in 1975 by Robert B. Kaiser, a journalist for Rolling Stone, he had these harsh condescending words for the conspiracy investigators' community: *"I've been up to my ass in lunatics ... unless you can find someone who wants to devote his life to [the case], forget it!"*[136]

This attitude, this lack of journalistic curiosity about the tragic end of his exceptional friend, was all the more strange because it was Bradlee who, from inside the Washington Post, had brought down the Nixon presidency by exposing the Watergate scandal!

The interaction of American intelligence with the media is also well documented by the Congress. It was expressed in 1976 in these terms: *"The CIA is currently maintaining a network of several hundred people around the world who provide the agency information and are trying to influence public opinion by using hidden propaganda. These individuals provide access, to benefit the CIA, to several newspapers and magazines, press services, radio and television stations, commercial book publishers and even to foreign media ... The Committee is concerned that the practice of using U.S. journalists and media corporates for covert operations poses a threat to the integrity of the press*[137].

A senior CIA official even told Carl Bernstein: *"A journalist is worth twenty agents. He has the access and the power to ask questions without arousing suspicion"*[138]. A recent case illustrates this trend:

---

[136] David Talbot – Brothers, The Hidden History of the Kennedy Years - 2007
[137] United States Senate. Final Report, Select Committee to Study Governmental Operations with Respect to Intelligence Activities. April 1976.
[138] Carl Bernstein, The CIA and the Media

by the end of 2014, CNN star reporter Anderson Cooper admitted to having been trained by the CIA and having had connections with the agency before choosing a journalistic career[139].

Two American authors, Robert Hennelly and Jerry Policoff, while they felt that the European media had very quickly rejected the official U.S. government version shortly after the assassination, have painted an edifying picture of the U.S. media collusion with intelligence agencies. Both authors in particular indicated the complicity of the New York Times, Time-Life and television channels such as CBS.

This misinformation and support of the government version by the media began in the first hours after the assassination. It was however the release of Oliver Stone's "JFK" movie in 1991, that precisely revealed the complicity, despite being ridiculed by this same media.

Although the New York Times and CBS polls reported that 67% of Americans rejected the Warren Report's findings, the media was quick to point out that the official version should prevail nevertheless to explain what happened in Dallas. Among this media, the Village Voice, however showed skepticism... After an investigation of hundreds of documents directly related to the media coverage of the assassination, this liberal newspaper demonstrated there was a clear collusion. The New-York Times, Time-Life, CBS and NBC considered there was no serious evidence shown of a conspiracy in the assassination and so made every effort to suppress the "inconvenient" information. They favored the allegations supporting the single assassin theory instead.

Two weeks after the assassination, the FBI boasted that it had obtained NBC's commitment to reject coverage of anything that would not directly be related to the FBI's "official" communication to the American people. On December 11, 1963, J. Edgar Hoover, the FBI director, received a note from the FBI office in New York City reassuring him that NBC had committed to broadcasting

---

[139] https://www.youtube.com/watch?v=kwMCIe2AGW8

information only in accordance with the FBI reports on the assassination[140].

In reference to the promotion of the official government version by the media, I do not think that the term "collusion" is overstated. This outrageous misinformation fits the definition of "collusion" well: *"a secret understanding between two or more persons to gain something illegally"*.

There are other enlightening examples: NBC News was the first media to start crusading against Jim Garrison, the New Orleans District Attorney, who, in 1969, sued businessman Clay Shaw, an alleged accomplice in the assassination of John Kennedy. Walter Sheridan, the NBC producer, supervised a four-year "investigation" to discredit Garrison. Sheridan had previously worked for the CIA and the FBI in key positions[141]. In 1992, John Barbour, author of the documentary "The American Media - The 2nd Assassination of President John F. Kennedy" was the only individual to have covered a detailed video-interview of Jim Garrison since he lost his trial in 1969. In a 2015 documentary, Barbour pursued Garrison's story and centered it on a dirty trick from a NBC producer who, unbeknownst to Barbour, had tampered with his interview of Garrison in 1992. The NBC producer had ridiculed the former District of Attorney by falsely reporting that Garrison *"thought there were thirty gunmen posted on Dealey Plaza!"*[142]

Here is another example illustrating the embarrassment that some journalists felt about the collusion of NBC management. Veteran TV journalist Peter Noyes was told by several NBC News reporters who had covered the events in Dallas, *"that they were convinced that their supervisors were trying to suppress some evidence at Washington's request"*[143].

---

[140] Robert Hennelly and Jerry Policoff - JFK: how the media assassinated the real story.2002. http://www.assassinationresearch.com/v1n2/mediaassassination.html

[141] http://www.justice-integrity.org/faq/896-beware-of-wrong-conclusions-from-new-cia-disclosure-on-Oswald

[142] The American Media – The 2nd Assassination of President John F. Kennedy

[143] Lamar Waldron, The Hidden History of the JFK Assassination, Counter Point Berkeley, 2013

Jerry Policoff, lawyer and activist, treasurer of the Citizens Against Political Assassinations, summarized the collusion and the lack of curiosity of the press: "*The press showed no curiosity when a 7.65 caliber German rifle* [the weapon model identified first by the police at the sixth floor of the Texas Book Depository Building] *was substituted to a 6.5 caliber Italian Mannlicher-Carcano rifle. No inquisitive media when an entry wound in the President's throat became an exit wound or when a 6-inch injury below the President's shoulder was corrected to a neck injury* [in the Warren report]. The press was slowly weaving its way in order to consolidate unconditional support to official conclusions"[144].

The following is critical to understand the misinformation role of the U.S. media about the JFK assassination. Just two days after the assassination of the President, on the day of his national funeral, Nicholas Katzenbach, then in charge at the Department of Justice under the administration of the new President Lyndon Johnson, sent a memo to top aide Bill Moyers telling him what communication strategy should prevail. This is probably the most obvious public and compromising document of the cover-up that may exist today. Here are some excerpts of Katzenbach's memo that can be consulted on the excellent website of Mary Ferrell, the most exhaustive database on the assassination of President Kennedy.[145]

> "*It is important that all of the facts surrounding President Kennedy's Assassination be made public in a way which will satisfy people in the United States and abroad that all the facts have been told and that a statement to this effect be made now.*
> *1. The public must be satisfied that Oswald was the assassin; that he did not have confederates who are still at large; and that the evidence was such that he would have been convicted at trial.*
> *2. Speculation about Oswald's motivation ought to be cut off, and we should have some basis for rebutting thought that this was a Communist conspiracy or (as the Iron Curtain press is saying) a right-wing conspiracy to blame it on the Communists. Unfortunately, the facts on*

---

[144] Jerry Policoff. "The Media and the Murder of John Kennedy". August 8, 1975
[145] https://www.maryferrell.org/showDoc.html?docId=62268#relPageId=29&tab=page

Oswald seem about too pat — too obvious (Marxist, Cuba, Russian wife, etc.). The Dallas police have put out statements on the Communist conspiracy theory, and it was they who were in charge when he was shot and thus silenced.
3. The matter has been handled thus far with neither dignity nor conviction. Facts have been mixed with rumor and speculation. We can scarcely let the world see us totally in the image of the Dallas police when our President is murdered...
...I think, however, that a statement that all the facts will be made public property in an orderly and responsible way should be made now. We need something to head off public speculation or Congressional hearings of the wrong sort."

Katzenbach's memo was undoubtedly a directive to the national press from the new administration seeking to hide the truth. It preceded what the Warren Report would publish a year later! The facts announced in Katzenbach's memo were never made public in their entirety.

According to Hennelly and Policoff, a few days after the assassination, the Washington Post requested an independent investigation. A FBI memo revealed a cautionary statement from Nicholas Katzenback to the Washington Post publisher, Russell Wiggins, signaling that the Department of Justice was seriously hoping that his newspaper would not encourage public disclosure of the Dallas facts, which *"would create confusion and hysteria."* FBI director J. Edgar Hoover wrote in a triumphal memorandum that he himself had called Walter Jenkins, Lyndon Johnson's adviser in the White House, to let Jenkins know that he had "killed" the editorial intended by the newspaper.

On May 24, 1964, Clifton Daniel of the New York Times wrote to Warren Commission Chief Advisor, J. Lee Rankin, congratulating the President of the Supreme Court, Earl Warren, for facilitating the release of his commission's report. Two months later, the newspaper co-authored a book "The Witnesses", but took good care to ignore any testimony deviating from the official theory. The Times wrote that Oswald had been seen at the window on the sixth floor of the Texas Book Depository Building, while expurgating the testimony of an observer who had seen two men on the same floor firing towards Dealey Plaza. Other deletions included the reference to gun firing from the car park near the railway depot, facing the presidential limousine, as well as the sightings of three Secret Service agents present at the President's autopsy who contradicted the official autopsy report. There was no doubt in the book "The Witnesses" that Oswald was posed as the only assassin and without any presumption of innocence. Three months before the Warren Report publication, in September 1964, the same newspaper prepared an exclusive page entitled "*A panel* [of the Warren Commission] *rejects theories of a plot to assassinate Kennedy*".

On June 1, 1964, Anthony Lewis of the New York Times presented the official version in a one-page article. According to Lewis, "*the* [Warren] *Commission analyzed every detail almost with an archaeologist's precision*".[146] For many years, he maintained his attacks against the critics of the Warren Report and especially against Oliver Stone, the moviemaker of "JFK". Oliver Stone nevertheless had a strong ally: Frank Mankiewicz, Robert Kennedy's friend also in charge of his presidential campaign. Mankiewicz was a staunch supporter of the hugely successful "JFK" movie, a box-office blockbuster about Jim Garrison, the New Orleans District Attorney, who was convinced that John Kennedy had been killed by a cabal of the United States National Security in order to lead the country into war. When defending Oliver Stone against the bashing from the Establishment media, Mankiewicz had these few words to say: "*He kicked down a door that was closed for too long*". In January 1992, in front of the National Press Club in Washington, Oliver Stone quoted Mankiewicz as saying, "*How could highly-paid media wise men such as Tom Wicker, Dan Rather, and Anthony Lewis despise the idea of conspiracy so much? They did not deign to get out of their apathy to investigate this dark possibility while they worked in a capital where many examples of*

---

[146] Ventura and Russell. American Conspiracies.

conspiracies swarmed; from Watergate to Iran Contra or the 'October Surprise'during Reagan's 1980 presidential campaign"[147]. Mankiewicz referred to Ronald Reagan's alleged conspiracy against opposition candidate Jimmy Carter during the 1980 presidential campaign. On the day of Reagan's inauguration, the Islamic Republic of Iran released 52 American hostages held prisoners. The perfect timing provoked allegations of a conspiracy agreed by the Reagan team with Iran in order to delay the release of the hostages after the election and thus prevent President Carter from claiming success.

In their investigation, Hennelly and Policoff found even more blatant evidence of the misinformation operated by the American press. Just four hours after the assassination of President Kennedy, Life Magazine was in Dallas to purchase the proofs of the camera film shot by Abraham Zapruder, the Dallas tailor who became famous for filming the crime scene on Dealey Plaza. It is the best of four films taken by onlookers during the presidential motorcade. In their first issue covering the crime of Dallas, Life lied to millions of readers by giving a false interpretation of the photo shots with captions intentionally redacted to support the Warren Report. The magazine was instrumental in eliminating "visible" evidence of the assassination facts.

The publisher of Life, C.D. Jackson, a fierce anti-communist, purchased the film for 150,000 USD, a small fortune at the time (estimation today would be 16 million dollars)[148]. A copy of the film was kept for the Warren Commission investigators. Since the original had been "stolen", the legal value of evidence had been lost and it was conducive to compromising the investigation. The acquisition of Zapruder's film, and, more to the point, the sequestration by Life magazine that lasted twelve years, allowed

---

[147] David Talbot – Brothers, The Hidden History of the Kennedy Years - 2007
[148] Edward Kosner, The Curse of the Zapruders, The Wall Street Journal, November 12-13, 2016

the magazine to manipulate the film frames. It was only in 1975 that the Zapruder film was made public.

The Dallas Parkland Hospital doctors, who had attended John Kennedy to try to give him emergency care, said they had observed an "apparent" *entry* bullet wound in the President's neck. Since Oswald was allegedly in the Texas School Book Depository, behind the limousine's progress on Elm Street when a bullet hit the President's throat, suspicions began to arise. On December 6th, 1963, Life published an edition under a sensational title: "*Let's put an end to persistent rumors. The Critical Six Seconds*" and claimed that Oswald had been successful in hitting his target. Life gave an incredible explanation of Zapruder's film: "*The 8mm film shows that the President turned himself clearly to the right to waive to the crowd. His throat was then exposed towards the sniper just before his hands reached his neck.*" What an ingenious way to elude the suspicions about a conspiracy that were already being heard and to dispel the inconsistencies of the lone gunman version! Life's description of Zapruder's film was very incoherent since it was impossible for the President to have turned 180 degrees in his seat in order to face the Texas School Book Depository since the limousine had already passed the six floor window of the building. The film shows clearly that JFK's body was turned towards the front of the limousine when he was hit in the throat. The film did not show any frame showing John Kennedy in the ridiculous posture as asserted by Life.[149]

Life Magazine was again the author of another disturbing manipulation of the facts. According to Hennelly and Policoff, in order to prepare for its special issue of October 2, 1964 about the Warren Report's revelations, the magazine took time to rectify its proofing prints twice in order to better match the official report. Life made two major and expensive prints in order to be totally credible with the official report before selling their special issue! Basically, this issue was intended to show 8 frames of Zapruder's

---

[149] Ventura and Russell. American Conspiracy, p 38

film with respective captions. The captions of the photographs showing the fatal blow to Kennedy's head were distinctly rectified. For caption number 6, Life first wrote: "*The assassin's shot hit the right side of the President's skull causing a major injury and the explosion of one side of his head.*" This caption corresponded to frame 323 that showed the President sinking into his seat and leaning to his left just after being hit by the fatal bullet. It was evident that the shot came from the front either from the parking lot close to the triple underpass or from the "Grassy Knoll". Life however corrected this version by replacing frame 323 by frame 313, which showed the shocking explosion of the President's head. In doing so, the halo created by the blood projections "conveniently" masked much of the photographic details. The same caption was however kept. In a third version, frame 313 (frame 323 was no longer considered by Life) was preserved with the following corrected caption: "*The gunshots trajectory was calculated using this frame taken at the very moment when the <u>back</u> of the President's head was hit by a bullet that passed through, causing the explosion of a piece of the <u>front</u> of his skull*"!

But a different message would go out to the world: it was the back of the President's head that exploded proving an exit bullet wound. According to the physical laws of ballistics, a human body injury caused by an entrance bullet is sharper and generally smaller in diameter than an exit wound. Jackie Kennedy's reaction to climb out onto the trunk of the limousine where she attempted to retrieve a piece of her husband's brain or skull unequivocally confirmed the trajectory came from the front.

Life magazine had thus taken the liberty to conceal the most obvious evidence from the Zapruder film by first sequestering the original and then presenting to the public a false interpretation of the origin of the gunshots. The irony was that Zapruder himself declared to the same magazine: "*My first impression was that the gunshots came from behind me*", that is from the "Grassy Knoll" according to his position on the pedestal, near the pergola, from where he filmed.

After the public outcry against Life that was accused of having withheld the Zapruder film for so long, the magazine justified itself. It claimed that there was strong competition to acquire the original film and that it was essential to Life that they got it first!

Surprisingly Life Magazine correspondents then began writing articles calling for a new investigation. In its editorial of November 25, 1966, it raised questions that had given way to doubts. "Did Oswald act alone?" A few months later, one of Life correspondents was admonished by his superior: *"It is not Life's mission to investigate Kennedy's assassination"*, he was told. Life even sued Josiah Thompson, a former journalist and private investigator, for what he had written in his book "Six Seconds in Dallas". Thompson had presented the results of his investigation: the trajectory of the fatal bullet to the President's head seemed to have come from the front. Based on the photographs of the Zapruder film, Thompson had reproduced the crime scene but using only artist's drawings. Life, the owner of the film, lost the legal case since there was no evidence that the film reproduction rights had been violated by Thompson.

According to Hennelly and Policoff, another famous news magazine, Time, was trying to fight European rumors already circulating about the likelihood of a conspiracy to kill John Kennedy. Time article of 12 June 1964 accused leftists of speculating that there was a conspiracy of the right behind the assassination. That same year, Thomas Buchanan, a Paris-based American journalist, wrote in the French magazine L'Express that President Kennedy had been the victim of a plot by the far right. Based on his articles in L'Express, he then revealed his critics of the Warren Report in a book titled "Who Killed Kennedy?" published by a British editor in May 1964. It was one of the very first books to touch the probable conspiracy. Buchanan's articles were part of a wave of the European press coverage that challenged readers to question the "assertions" presented by the official version.[150]

Buchanan's book claimed that Oswald was a low-level CIA agent who had received help from other individuals to commit

---

[150] David Talbot – Brothers, The Hidden History of the Kennedy Years - 2007

the crime. The book also addressed the likelihood that Jack Ruby was an accomplice and that he knew Oswald. It further focused on the motive for murdering John Kennedy: to break his efforts to create a détente between Washington and Moscow which was a threat to the arms industry on which the plotters depended.

Whereas the American press rallied to Washington's contentment by supporting the official version, European publications announced that something sinister had occurred in Dallas. As a matter of fact, the first speculations about a conspiracy against President Kennedy were born in Europe which had immediately recognized, in the crime of Dallas, the mark of conjurations, having lived through its own political assassinations, coups d'état and conspiracies. As Raymond Cartier said in Paris-Match at the time: "*Europe rejects almost in its entirety*" the official version of the crime. "*Europeans are convinced that the tragedy of Dallas hides a mystery that, if unveiled, would bring disgrace to the United States and shake its foundations.*"

Of course, Time magazine reacted and declared that Buchanan's book was written by a member of the Communist Party in 1948, which consequently cost him his job at the Washington Star[151].

Despite the growing weight of the evidence presented by the House Select Committee on Assassinations (HSCA), Time ignored them. The magazine did not address the acoustic evidence provided by the Dictabelt analysis of the sound of the gunshots on Dealey Plaza recorded by a microphone left turned on by a Dallas police motorcycle riding next to the presidential limousine. On September 25, 1978, the magazine wrote: "*There will always be people who will always think that a fourth shot was fired. But at the present juncture of the HSCA hearings on Kennedy's assassination, the overwhelming weight of their evidence leads to the same conclusion held by the Warren Commission: Oswald acted alone to kill Kennedy.*" [152]

---

[151] Robert Hennelly and Jerry Policoff - JFK: how the media assassinated the real story.2002.

[152] Robert J. Groden and Harrison Edward Livingstone. High Treason: The assassination of JFK. What really happened? The Conservatory Press, 1989

To illustrate the U.S. media apathy, Jerry Policoff recalled the fate of Earl Golz, a Dallas Morning News reporter, who proposed to the newspaper an article about some leads revealing a probable plot to assassinate Kennedy and also Oswald's alibi. These revelations came from six eyewitnesses who claimed to have seen three individuals on the sixth floor of the Texas School Book Depository shortly before the shooting. Another lead came from a key eyewitness who had met Oswald in the second floor lunchroom, two minutes after the last gunshots were fired on Dealey Plaza. This confrontation was far from furtive because Oswald took the time to ask the eyewitness for change to get a soda from the vending machine. Golz's manager told him not to follow up on his draft article and instead to leave it "on the back burner". Golz ignored his manager's orders and was fired from the newspaper.

In 1966, Americans started to voice their demand for a reexamination of the Warren Report's conclusions. Among them, Arthur Schlesinger Jr, Richard Goodwin, the Saturday Evening Post, the Vatican newspaper L'osservatore, Cardinal Cushing, journalist William Buckley, and the American Academy of Forensic Sciences were the most vocal. In turn, the [New York] Times seemed to flip-flop. The paper planned an independent investigation and the publication of an editorial in November 1966 entitled "Questions without answers". This reversal unfortunately lasted less than a month. A Times reporter admitted, in an interview with Rolling Stone magazine, that there was too much to follow in their investigation and that they preferred not to proceed.

In September 1964, at CBS, legendary reporter Walter Cronkite hosted a special CBS News program that aired 85 minutes before the Warren Report was released. Without a doubt, this program fully supported the Warren Commission's version. The TV news channel seemed to have received leaks and benefited from an exclusivity: the early communication of the Warren Report's findings helped the channel to be well prepared in broadcasting its CBS News Special and therefore avoiding any distortion to the version that would become official[153].

The Zapruder film also caused problems at CBS. Dan Rather, the chief correspondent of the CBS office in New Orleans at the time, was allowed to preview the film before it was secured in a safe. Rather said that he saw the *"President being pushed forward with considerable force."* CBS then found a frivolous excuse saying that Dan Rather had had very little time to see the film and in addition had only seen it with a manual viewer. The American public had to wait 12 years to have the opportunity to interpret the film in their own way and to come to the conclusion that, in fact, John Kennedy had been violently thrown backwards and to the left.

Still loyal to the "Lone Nuts" clan, Dan Rather pursued with great zeal his support of the official version in his CBS broadcasts. One day, however, he conceded to Robert Tannenbaum, the Deputy Chief Counsel of the House Select Committee on Assassinations that *"we really messed up on the case of Kennedy's assassination"*.[154]

While doubts arose in the mid-1960s about the government's version, CBS TV executives, who had personal connections with some members of the Warren Commission, remained strong advocates of the conclusions of its report. On the website, consortiumnews.com, the author-historian, James DiEugenio, describes the attitude and action of CBS through the channel newsletters which supported the cover-up. We know this thanks to CBS dissident assistant director, Roger Feinman, who compiled internal documents.

In 1966, doubts about the Warren Report's findings had reached the ranks of CBS News. Gordon Manning, vice-president of CBS News, felt the need to prepare a series of documentaries lasting

---

[153] Gary Fannin, The Innocence of Oswald, 2015
[154] David Talbot, The Mother of All Cover-Ups, http://www.salon.com/2004/09/15/warren/

several hours with a fair and critical look at the methodology of the Warren Commission investigation and at its conclusions. He suggested "The trial of Lee Harvey Oswald" as the title of the show. It was to be prepared with the cooperation of a panel of law schools deans and experts who would screen all the evidence against Lee Harvey Oswald and all the Warren Commission omissions. The idea of the program was to reconstruct a fictitious trial in order to reach a conclusion of either Oswald's guilt or his exoneration for his crime. Manning associated Les Midgley, the director of CBS News Prime-Time, with this project who wanted to change the title of the show to "The Warren Report brought to justice" in order to give a more critical impact and create skepticism to the Warren Commission's conclusions. A series lasting three hour-broadcast over three nights was planned: one hour devoted to the defenders of the Commission, another to the testimonies that had been neglected or suppressed by the Commission and the last hour to the verdict of the fictitious lawsuit presented by lawyers.

When Manning and Midgley presented the project to their boss, Richard Salant, the latter hesitated to adopt the concept of a mock trial. He preferred sending his associates to California first to take the legal advice of two lawyers on the project.

The legal advisers recommended stopping the project because it would not "*go in the direction of the national interest*", that it would cause too many "political consequences" and that the criticisms of the Warren Commission should be ignored. Manning understood that he had to comply and be forced to present the program in accordance with the wishes of his management. He reluctantly retitled the program "*In defense of the Warren Report*" in order to better reflect the right course of action imposed by his boss. "*The rejection of the absurd, irresponsible and wacky criticisms formulated by Mark Lane and other henchmen of this band*" was the company's conclusion.

During the fall of 1966, CBS presented another series of documentaries on the assassination. Could Oswald have fired the three gunshots on Dealey Plaza as the Warren Report asserted? The TV channel based its program on the firing tests performed at a shooting range. Based on the Zapruder film, the Warren Commission claimed that Oswald fired three shots in 5.6 seconds. CBS recruited 11 snipers instructed to shoot 37 runs – 3 shots per run - on a moving target.

Seventeen of the 37 runs of shots were disqualified due to rifle problems. Faced with this embarrassment, CBS refrained from detailing the methodology of these tests to their audience. They just claimed that 11 snipers had taken an average of 5.6 seconds to fire the 3 shots but did not mention the 17 failures.

Oswald, a poor shooter whose rifle, a Mannlicher Carcano, was slower to fire than the one chosen for the CBS tests, was supposed to have reached his moving target in 5.6 seconds with 3 shots without training. The Mannlicher Carcano rifle can take a minimum of 2.3 seconds between two successive shots.[155] The rifle had been developed in Italy going into World War II and, later, was ridiculed by some Italians experts "as an instrument of love, not a weapon of war" in so much its performances were bad![156]

As mentioned above, the owners of the CBS television channel had personal connections with some members of the Warren Commission. Very few people were aware of the clandestine connection between CBS News President Richard Salant and John McCloy, a member of the Warren Commission. McCloy was also the father of Ellen McCloy, Salant's administrative assistant.[157] As we will see below, Richard Salant was trying to hide the fact that McCloy was writing him anonymous memos.

The CBS investigator, Roger Feinman, came to the conclusion that McCloy's influence on the CBS program was in itself a violation of the channel's ethics charter, which prohibited any conflict of interest in its TV news coverage. Faced with Feinman's enduring investigation into revealing the secret links between

---

[155] Robert J. Groden and Harrison Edward Livingstone. High Treason: The assassination of JFK. What really happened? The Conservatory Press, 1989
[156] https://whowhatwhy.org/2017/02/16/dr-cyril-wecht-jfks-murder-coup-detat-america/
[157] https://consortiumnews.com/2016/04/22/how-cbs-news-aided-the-jfk-cover-up/

CBS News and John McCloy, Salant wrote to McCloy to let him know that at no point did his daughter ever make a secret communication between her father and CBS News.

It was a deliberate lie that tarnished the reputation of the news channel. In 1992, an article of The Village Voice, exposed Ellen McCloy and Salant who were confronted with memos revealing Salant's lies. Collusion and conflict of interest in the family had been proven: Ellen McCloy had been on the distribution list of almost all the memos about CBS's plans to cover the JFK assassination. She had maintained a secret communication between the CBS management and her father. She moreover, admitted the existence of the secret mail exchange and then, in turn, Salant pleaded guilty, while asserting that this practice should not be seen as unusual![158] Another evidence of McCloy's influence on CBS arose afterwards: he wrote to Salant to suggest that the CBS team should carry out a series of firing tests on Dealey Plaza *"but of a more scientific nature than those ridiculous tests performed by the FBI"*.

In 1977, CBS News President Richard Salant also admitted that CBS's relationship with the CIA had begun in the mid-50s. He explained that these close ties had been forged by his predecessor, William Paley, and that it was customary for CBS correspondents upon return from their media coverage abroad to be debriefed by Allen Dulles, the CIA director. Specifically, in February 1976, CIA Director George Bush, the future President of the United States, made a phone call to Salant and Paley to seek their support in maintaining CIA contacts within CBS. One of CBS's top executives addressed Bush with these cryptic terms: *"We protect ours; you protect yours"*[159].

We must pay tribute to Roger Feinman. Without him, the internal scandal at CBS News about these skewed documentaries would never have been known. Thanks to his tenacity in challenging his management, he revealed the obstructions to the Standards and Practices of the channel. But, this earned him his

---

[158] Robert Hennelly and Jerry Policoff - JFK: how the media assassinated the real story.2002.
[159] Robert J. Groden, The Killing of a President, Vicking Studio Books, 1993

dismissal by CBS for his dissenting position in 1976. He was, however, a CBS union member and thanks to the help in finding the compromising documents that revealed the scandal at CBS, he was able to claim his defense.

It was from the very beginning, right after the assassination, that the misinformation of CBS took shape. Dr. Malcom Perry, a medical doctor and a key eyewitness, had treated the President immediately on his arrival at Dallas Parkland Hospital. According to the transcript of the press conference that Dr. Perry gave on November 22, 1963 found at CBS but oblivious to the Warren Commission, Dr Perry indicated that the wound on the anterior part of John Kennedy's neck had the appearance of an entry wound. He mentioned his observation three times during the conference. For him, there was no doubt. He had to make an incision in the neck wound to perform a tracheotomy and this gave him plenty of time to observe the nature of the President's injury and to understand its origin.

CBS reported his words in a rather confused manner[160]. The channel claimed that Dr. Perry had been harassed with questions at the press conference and that he had been confused in answering questions. But Perry formally asserted that he had not been under any pressure from the journalists who had just asked him about the nature of the injuries. In his own words, he had been able to respond calmly.

Why did CBS distort Dr Perry's remarks? Evidently to reject the fact that another gunman had fired at the President since Oswald could not have shot from two locations at the same time, one behind and one facing the presidential limousine?

In another CBS documentary, the channel covered the testimony of an amateur cameraman, Orville Nix, who was filming a specific angle of the "Grassy Knoll" on Dealey Plaza. Because the film gave evidence that gunshots were fired from that

---

[160] https://consortiumnews.com/2016/04/22/how-cbs-news-aided-the-jfk-cover-up/

spot, CBS altered Nix's comments, repeatedly recalling the Warren Commission's conclusions during its program.

In 1967, CBS News felt it necessary to reassure the American people that there was no conspiracy in the assassination of President Kennedy and that it was just the mere act of a lone gunman. To reach their goal, the channel scheduled a series of documentaries to that effect. Despite the controversy following the broadcast of the documentaries, CBS continued to defend the Warren Commission's findings concerning the nature of the President's injuries, the ballistic tests and the testimonies of those who attended the autopsy. The channel claimed that anyone who thought differently was *"confused, unreasoned and out of touch with reality"*. The CBS presenter even went as far as concluding, at the end of the broadcast, that there would of course always be those who *"believe in conspiracies ... .that Hitler was still alive and that it was anyway impossible to conceal the assassination of a president!"*

The complacency of the media, urged by their "CIA masters" to adhere to the official version of the assassination, was not always flagrant. The very first press coverage launched immediately after the assassination affirmed that the gunshots had come from the front of the limousine. This was in stark opposition to the government version that maintained the gunshots had come from behind. As early as November 22, 1963, the day of the assassination, the Associated Press issued a bulletin describing how the gunshots had been fired from the "Grassy Knoll", from the front of the presidential car! This bulletin was quickly corrected. An announcement followed asserting that they had been fired from the Texas School Book Depository, behind the presidential limousine. Time Magazine announced: *"The evidence against Oswald is described as conclusive"*[161].

Dr. Charles Crenshaw, who was assisting his colleagues in the emergency trauma room of Dallas Parkland Hospital, confirmed

---

[161] Ventura and Russell. American Conspiracy, p 38

that the bullets that hit John Kennedy's throat and head had created *entrance* wounds, in other words, that the gunshots had come from the front of the presidential limousine. Dr Crenshaw was a fierce critic of the government that discredited the Parkland Hospital doctors' testimonies. He qualified their disinformation enterprise *"a conspiracy of secrecy"*. He decided to break his silence in 1992: *"Every doctor who was in Trauma Room 1 had his own reasons for not publicly refuting the 'official line'... I believe there was a common denominator in our silence – a fearful perception that to come forward with what we believed to be the medical truth would be asking for trouble.... Whatever was happening was larger than any of us. I reasoned that anyone who would go so far as to eliminate the President of the United States would surely not hesitate to kill a doctor"*.

Crenshaw decided to talk 30 years later, but his remarks cost him his reputation. His book published in April 1992, *"JFK: Conspiracy of Silence"* revealed what, as a doctor, he had seen and understood concerning the President's injuries that contradicted the Warren Report. Although it became a bestseller on the New York Times list, it was quickly demolished by the FBI director of the Dallas office and a former Warren Commission lawyer. Much to Crenshaw's surprise, his observations were even discredited by the prestigious JAMA, the Journal of the American Medical Association. On May 27, 1992, JAMA published two articles stating that Dr. Crenshaw was not even present in the Parkland Hospital ER where President Kennedy received care. The JAMA publisher even went as far as to promote his critical articles at a press conference in New York City in front of a large audience. In response to JAMA's claims, Dr. Crenshaw sent JAMA a series of letters and articles recalling the testimony of five doctors and nurses before the Warren Commission. For his defense, he called upon what these people had seen in the trauma room where they all attempted to save the President's life, performing the same actions he had just described in his book. All of Crenshaw's efforts to correct JAMA's deception were, however, rejected by the publisher. Crenshaw then decided to file a lawsuit against the newspaper. Finally, after mediation, JAMA agreed to pay damages to Dr. Crenshaw in 1994. Despite this, they did not give up and published a second article attacking Crenshaw.

Fortunately, the impact of his book coincided with the release of the movie "JFK" by Oliver Stone that confirmed Dr. Crenshaw's observations and those by the other doctors in the trauma room[162].

Some people might still argue that there was no evidence of the U.S. media being controlled by the CIA in this specific affair. My response to them would be to suggest that they read an edifying CIA document available on the internet that the political commentator and former governor of Minnesota, Jesse Ventura, got hold of from the National Archives.[163] Here, reproduced in part, is the text of the CIA memorandum, referenced 1035-960, dated January 1967 and stamped "Destroy after Reading". This document was written with the intent to give instructions to the media – especially the New York Times, CBS, NBC and ABC - for corrective actions in the event of any criticism of the Warren report: [164] [165] [166]

"*1. Our Concern. From the day of President Kennedy's assassination on, there has been speculation about the responsibility for his murder. Although this was stemmed for a time by the Warren Commission report, (which appeared at the end of September 1964), various writers have now had time to scan the Commission's published report and documents for new pretexts for questioning, and there has been a new wave of books and articles criticizing the Commission's findings. In most cases, the critics have speculated as to the existence of some kind of conspiracy, and often they have implied that the Commission itself was involved. Presumably as a result of the increasing challenge to the Warren Commission's report, a public opinion poll recently indicated that 46% of the American public did not think that Oswald acted alone, while more than half of those polled thought that the Commission had*

---

[162] James W. Douglass, JFK and the Unspeakable, Why He Died and Why it Matters, A Touchstone Book, 2008

[163] Jesse Ventura – They Killed Our President – 2013. Skyhorse Publishing, Inc.

[164] CIA Document # 1035-960. "RE; Concerning Criticism of the Warren Report". 1 April 1967.

[165] gaylenixjackson.com/Research/CIA-Memo-Warren-Commission.pdf

[166] http://www.jfklancer.com/CIA.html

left some questions unresolved. Doubtless polls abroad would show similar or possibly more adverse results.
2. **This trend of opinion is a matter of concern** *to the U.S. government, including our organization. The members of the Warren Commission were naturally chosen for their integrity, experience and prominence. They represented both major parties, and they and their staff were deliberately drawn from all sections of the country. Just because of the standing of the Commissioners, efforts to impugn their rectitude and wisdom tend to cast doubt on the whole leadership of American society. Moreover, there seems to be an increasing tendency to hint that President Johnson himself, as the one person who might be said to have benefited, was in some way responsible for the assassination. Innuendo of such seriousness affects not only the individual concerned, but also the whole reputation of the American government. Our organization itself is directly involved: among other facts, we contributed information to the investigation. Conspiracy theories have frequently thrown suspicion on our organization, for example by falsely alleging that Lee Harvey Oswald worked for us. The aim of this dispatch is to provide material countering and discrediting the claims of the conspiracy theorists, so as to inhibit the circulation of such claims in other countries. Background information is supplied in a classified section and in a number of unclassified attachments.*
3. **Action. We do not recommend that discussion of the assassination question be initiated where it is not already taking place. Where discussion is active addresses are requested:**
  a. To **discuss the publicity problem with and friendly elite contacts (especially politicians and editors)**, *pointing out that the Warren Commission made as thorough an investigation as humanly possible, that the charges of the critics are without serious foundation, and that further speculative discussion only plays into the hands of the opposition. Point out also that parts of the conspiracy talk appear to be deliberately generated by Communist propagandists. Urge them to use their influence to discourage unfounded and irresponsible speculation.*
  b. To **employ propaganda assets to and refute the attacks of the critics. Book reviews and feature articles are particularly appropriate for this purpose.** *The unclassified attachments to this guidance should provide useful background material for passing to assets. Our ploy should point out, as applicable, that the critics are (I) wedded to theories adopted before the evidence was in, (II) politically*

interested, (III) financially interested, (IV) hasty and inaccurate in their research, or (V) infatuated with their own theories. In the course of discussions of the whole phenomenon of criticism, a useful strategy may be to single out Epstein's theory for attack, using the attached Fletcher article and Spectator piece for background. (Although Mark Lane's book is much less convincing that Epstein's and comes off badly where confronted by knowledgeable critics, it is also much more difficult to answer as a whole, as one becomes lost in a morass of unrelated details.)
[Edward Jay Epstein was one of the first investigative journalists to open a "Pandora's box" on the conspiracy plot to assassinate JFK. The investigating lawyer Mark Lane was the first to blame the role of the CIA]

4. *In private to media discussions not directed at any particular writer, or in attacking publications which may be yet forthcoming,* **the following arguments should be useful**:
a. **No significant new evidence has emerged** *which the Commission did not consider. The assassination is sometimes compared (e.g., by Joachim Joesten and Bertrand Russell) with the Dreyfus case; however, unlike that case, the attack on the Warren Commission have produced no new evidence, no new culprits have been convincingly identified, and there is no agreement among the critics. (A better parallel, though an imperfect one, might be with the Reichstag fire of 1933, which some competent historians (Fritz Tobias, AJ.P. Taylor, D.C. Watt) now believe was set by Vander Lubbe on his own initiative, without acting for either Nazis or Communists; the Nazis tried to pin the blame on the Communists, but the latter have been more successful in convincing the world that the Nazis were to blame.)*
b. *Critics usually overvalue particular items and ignore others. They* **tend to place more emphasis on the recollections of individual witnesses** *(which are less reliable and more divergent and hence offer more hand-holds for criticism) and less on ballistics, autopsy, and photographic evidence. A close examination of the Commission's records will usually show that the conflicting eyewitness accounts are quoted out of context, or were discarded by the Commission for good and sufficient reason.*
c. **Conspiracy on the large scale often suggested would be impossible to conceal** *in the United States, esp. since informants could expect to receive large royalties, etc. Note that Robert Kennedy,*

Attorney General at the time and John F. Kennedy's brother, would be the last man to overlook or conceal any conspiracy. And as one reviewer pointed out, Congressman Gerald R. Ford would hardly have held his tongue for the sake of the Democratic administration, and Senator Russell would have had every political interest in exposing any misdeeds on the part of Chief Justice Warren. [The irony is that Senator Russell was one of the three members of the Warren Commission to be the most critical of the lone gunman theory! He expressed his doubts in a telephone conversation with President Johnson on September 18, 1964, a few hours after the last session of the commission. The transcript of this conversation is available online at http://22november1963.org.uk/richard-russell-warren-report#richard-russell-dissent]

A conspirator moreover would hardly choose a location for a shooting where so much depended on conditions beyond his control: the route, the speed of the cars, the moving target and the risk that the assassin would be discovered. A group of wealthy conspirators could have arranged much more secure conditions.

d. *Critics have often been enticed by a form of intellectual pride:* **they light on some theory and fall in love with it**; *they also scoff at the Commission because it did not always answer every question with a flat decision one way or the other. Actually, the make-up of the Commission and its staff was an excellent safeguard against over-commitment to any one theory, or against the illicit transformation of probabilities into certainties.*

e. **Oswald** *would not have been any sensible person's choice for a co-conspirator. He was a "loner," mixed up, of questionable reliability and* **an unknown quantity to any professional intelligence service.**

f. *As to charges that the Commission's report was a rush job, it emerged three months after the deadline originally set. But to the degree that the Commission tried to speed up its reporting, this was largely due to the pressure of* **irresponsible speculation** *already appearing, in some cases coming from the same critics who, refusing to admit their errors, are now putting out new criticisms.*

g. **Such vague accusations as that "more than ten people have died mysteriously" can always be explained in some natural way** *e.g.: the individuals concerned have for the most part died of natural causes; the Commission staff questioned 418 witnesses (the FBI interviewed far more people, conduction 25,000 interviews and re* *interviews), and in such a large group, a certain number of deaths are to be expected. (When Penn Jones, one of the originators of the "ten mysterious deaths" line, appeared on television, it emerged that two of the deaths on his list were from heart attacks, one from cancer, one was from a head-on collision on a bridge, and one occurred when a driver drifted into a bridge abutment.)*

5. Where possible, counter speculation by encouraging reference to the Commission's Report itself. Open-minded foreign readers should still be impressed by the care, thoroughness, objectivity and speed with which the Commission worked. **Reviewers of other books might be encouraged to add** *to their account the idea* **that, checking back with the report itself, they found it far superior to the work of its critics. "**

With its instructions, the CIA took great care to reject any evidence of conspiracy to better control the media. This is not really the demonstration of a free press in a great democratic country! The CIA statement was later challenged thanks to facts and evidence contradicting the naive and simplistic claims of the agency. The up-coming paragraphs of this book will largely reflect on these facts.

According to American publisher, Katharine Graham, the public does not have to know everything. While speaking to senior CIA officials in 1988, she said, *"We live in a dangerous and sordid world. There are things that the general public does not need to know and should not know"*[167].

Unfortunately, the general American public can only form an opinion on news that the U.S. media, belonging to Big Corporates, want to convey. Corporates' control of the major media has often been a concern in the United States. Holdings of America-based multimedia hyper groups such as AOL, Time Warner, Viacom, Walt Disney Co, News Corp, control television networks, newspapers, magazines, entertainment media and even the Internet. The Free Press presents a chilling statement: Big corporations have centralized their hold on U.S. media so much

---

[167] Mary Louise. "Operation Mockingbird: CIA Media Manipulation". 2003

that about ten of them now control pretty much everything concerning the news that the American people can see on TV and hear on the radio, or read in the newspaper: *"Colossal companies dominate the American media landscape. Through the many historic mergers and acquisitions, they have concentrated their control of what we see, hear and read. In most cases, they are integrated in a vertical control system that ensures full control of news from the initial production phase to the final distribution of the messages"* the Free Press wrote[168].

This control is not only directed towards the press, television channels or radio waves. According to journalist-investigator, lawyer and publisher Andrew Kreig, few new media outlets nowadays belong to independent media companies that rely on commercials. U.S. mega-media groups are gaining more profit through the influence of policies, including government regulation. For example, the Tribune Group and CBS News depend largely on the federal regulations that are favorable to them.

The control also comes from influential e-commerce mega sites. The most striking example was the purchase of the Washington Post in 2013 by Jeffrey Bezos, the founder of Amazon for $ 250 million. Shortly after, Amazon signed a $ 600 million contract with the CIA for the needs of its internet cloud[169]. Although Amazon and the Washington Post are separate entities, their interests converge at the top of their management. The public can hardly measure the extent of these interests although the conflicts of interest that these companies sometimes create are obvious. Nothing stops hyper-mergers, such as that of Comcast Corporation with NBC, Universal and Telemundo.

---

[168] Who Owns the Media? Free Press. www.freepress.net/ownership/chart
[169] http://www.justice-integrity.org/index.php?option=com_content&view=article&id=618:june-news-reports- 2012&catid=93:june-2012&Itemid=10

An American blogger, David Martin, ironically explains in his article "17 Techniques for truth suppression": "*The dwindling number of Americans who profess to believe the official story that Lee Harvey Oswald killed President John F. Kennedy and did it alone may be divided into two basic groups. Those who know next to nothing about the facts of the case and those whose livelihoods depend upon believing it*".[170] According to Martin, "*strong and credible allegations of high-level criminal activity can discredit a government. When the government lacks an effective, fact-based defense, other techniques must be employed. The success of these techniques depends heavily upon a cooperative, compliant press and a mere token opposition party*". Martin mentions the typical stratagems of misinformation and those used by the American media about the controversies of the JFK assassination are not that different: If facts are not reported, if it's not news, it didn't happen.... Be indignant. "How dare you?"... Characterize the charges as "wild rumors." If the public still want to learn about the suspicious facts, it can only be because the people are simply "paranoid" or "hysterical."... Call the skeptics names like "conspiracy theorist," "nutcase"... Carefully avoid fair and open debates... Strongly marginalize the critics by suggesting that they are not interested in the truth but are merely pursuing a partisan political agenda or are out to make money... Dismiss the charges as "old news."... Create the impression of candor and honesty while you admit only to relatively harmless, less-than-criminal "mistakes."...Openly lie. Etc.

While Wikipedia is a useful universal encyclopedia, the site is unfortunately not always reliable because anyone can have free access, edit and informally modify its content. When it comes to a contribution or a distortion of text, the vulnerability or the complacency of Wikipedia - if the site does not react to abusive redactions, tactics of misinformation - is a reality. If the information is unsettling, it can be expunged. We know that

---

[170] http://www.justice-integrity.org/index.php?option=com_content&view=article&id=599:jfk-s-murder-the-cia-8-things-____every-american-should-know&catid=21:myblog&itemid=114

anonymous edits have been made to Wikipedia editorials about politicians or business circles. Specifically on the assassination of John Kennedy, BBC News alerted the public, in July 2014, to the alterations made by the U.S. Congress of a Wikipedia page relating to the murder of President Kennedy. The alteration in question referred to the allegation that Lee Harvey Oswald acted "on behalf of the Fidel Castro regime". This change suggested that the Cuban government had ordered the assassination of John F. Kennedy. BBC news reported that Wikipedia had of course reacted by taking the decision to block the provocative corrections of the U.S. Congress[171].

In a Boiling Frogs Post interview, in January 2014, Andrew Kreig said that the American public is conditioned to think that murderers are solitary lunatics. However, in Oswald's case, the facts are overwhelming: he claimed that he was innocent and a patsy. He had been framed and demanded legal assistance for his defense. Oswald's words are not allegations, they are factual; they were heard and recorded in front of television cameras around the world, at the Dallas police headquarters, on the day of John Kennedy's assassination. They can be heard on internet. But, the mainstream media elude the question about Oswald's possible innocence. They refuse to explore, to draw conclusions and prefer to move to something else after a superficial overview of the case.

When the Washington Post presented an official drawing of the shooting trajectories on Dealey Plaza saying *"here is where Oswald fired the gunshots that killed the President"* the notion of "presumption of innocence" is totally ignored by the paper. It's all carved in stone: *"Oswald did it!"* The collusion between the Washington Post and the CIA is indeed not surprising. The Washington Post publisher had weekly lunches with Frank Wisner, the head of the news control program at the CIA. As it will be explained in a next chapter of this book, it was the same newspaper that aimed at "destroying" an article in which

---

[171] http://www.bbc.com/news/technology-28481876

President Truman declared, on December 22, 1963, that the CIA had become too powerful and needed close control.[172]

We also know that, at an early stage, the Washington Post had enthusiastically supported the results of the Warren Commission. Most recently, articles of the same newspaper self-censored their reviews of 70 new books published in 2013 on the assassination of John Kennedy.[173]

The mainstream press gave a far-fetched explanation about the publication of the results of the acoustic testing of gunshots on Dealey Plaza. These tests had been the cornerstone of the House Select Committee on Assassinations which concluded there was a probable conspiracy in the murder of President Kennedy. With incredible bad faith, in order to contradict the evidence of an apparent high-level conspiracy, the press had this diabolical explanation: two "Lone Nuts", two imbalanced gunmen, had met in the firing zone by mere hazard! Here is what the Washington Post wrote on January 6, 1979. *"...In the process, however, it is worth wondering about this easy resort to the use of the word "conspiracy" - a word that suggests many people acting together in a political plot, with cold and careful calculation. If the committee is right about a fourth shot from the Grassy Knoll, could it have been some other malcontent whom Mr. Oswald met casually? Could not as many as three or four societal outcasts, with no ties to any one organization, have developed in some spontaneous way a common determination to express their alienation in the killing of President Kennedy?"*[174]

In May 2013, both the New York Times and the Washington Post referred to Allen Breed's article in the Associated Press

---

[172] http://www.boilingfrogspost.com/2014/01/10/bfp-exclusive-interview-with-andrew-kreig-the-cia-global-empire-the-u-s- presidency/

[173] http://www.justice-integrity.org/index.php?option=com_content&view=article&id=584:self-censorship-in-jfk-tv-treatments-duplicates-corporate-print-media-s-apathy-cowardice&catid=21&Itemid=114%20

[174] Robert J. Groden and Harrison Edward Livingstone. High Treason: The assassination of JFK. What really happened? The Conservatory Press, 1989

online [175] in which he believed that the FBI and the Dallas police had solved the crime within twenty-four hours of the Dallas murder. Breed wrote that the crime had been perpetrated by a misguided delinquent named Lee Harvey Oswald and that the Warren Commission's investigation had proved it beyond reasonable doubt. The author claimed that irrational people, driven to make money in this affair, *"spread seeds of conspiracy"* in the minds of gullible Americans. He added that the conspiracy theorists blamed anyone except Oswald, a former unhinged Marine who was in the right place, at the right time, with the motive and the opportunity to carry out one of the most heinous crimes in the American history.

The lack of motive, opportunity and means have however been extremely difficult to prove in Oswald's case. The next chapter of this book will cover all this. Breed's article ridiculed the proponents of the conspiracy by inventing the most ludicrous theory that could exist, a conscious choice to prove that they were only "nuts": *"One theory even advanced the notion that the limousine driver had fired at the President in an effort to conceal evidence of an alien invasion!"* Breed believed that it was only the conspiracy theories that fueled the JFK books market, totaling ignoring the fact that also the anti-conspiracy books were selling just as much proving that the American public remain interested in all point of view. He also forgot that Oswald, an "unhinged man" as Breed described him, without any complicity, was in fact well known by the CIA. As a CIA cable proved it in October 2013, senior CIA officials knew everything about Oswald's political orientation and his contacts abroad, 7 weeks before the murder of JFK.

The national press rushed to endorse Gerald Posner's book "Case Closed", in which the author defended the Warren Report. The historian Robert Dallek praised the book in the Boston Globe and found that *"it provided the most convincing explanation of the assassination."*

---

[175] http://ap-gfkpoll.com/featured/five-decades-after-jfks-assassination-the-lucrative-conspiracy-theory-industry-hums-along

While media elites endeavored to fuel public confidence by continually promoting the Warren Report, some political elites, on the other hand, privately said that the report was nothing more than a masquerade and a fairy tale for a wide audience - a paradox that historian David Talbot described as one of the greatest ironies in American history. There have been Presidents, White House advisers, intelligence officials, members of Congress, and even foreign heads of state who all suspected that the U.S. government did not tell the truth about the JFK assassination[176].

More recently, on September 16, 2015, 2,500 daily communiqués from the U.S. presidency, under the Johnson administration, classified top secret by the CIA, were revealed. According to sources from the U.S. intelligence which were reported to President Lyndon B Johnson, 3 days after JFK's assassination, one of the press releases mentioned that Lee Harvey Oswald had visited the Cuban and Soviet embassies in Mexico, six weeks before shooting at the President. False conclusions will be drawn by the press from this document. In September 2015, a reporter from the Washington Times, busy preparing a study for the Republican presidential campaign debate, on the evening of the announcement of the declassified CIA news release, briefly mentioned it. He gave his support however to the Warren Report with a different interpretation of Oswald's revealed actions in Mexico. The journalist recalled that Oswald was a sympathetic communist and had killed the U.S. President for reasons of dissatisfaction with the way the Cold War had been handled. The reporter's short article provoked over a thousand comments from the readers on Facebook; an obvious revelation of the public's constant interest in the crime of the century, fifty years on. [177] But, the Washington Times article failed to mention at least two major pieces of evidence concerning the CIA's direct handling of

---

[176] David Talbot, The Mother of All Cover-Ups, http://www.salon.com/2004/09/15/warren/

[177] http://www.justice-integrity.org/faq/896-beware-of-wrong-conclusions-from-new-cia-disclosure-on-Oswald

Oswald. The first was the existence of photos taken by the CIA showing a bald and corpulent man presenting himself at the Soviet embassy and posing as Oswald. Obviously, this individual could not be Oswald. The second CIA manipulation was admitted by FBI director himself, Edgar Hoover, who according to declassified documents, told President Johnson, two days after the assassination of JFK, that the voice recognition tests carried out by the FBI indicated that, despite the CIA's assertion, it was not Oswald who had called the Mexican embassies to make an appointment.

The distortion of facts by the American mainstream media even today is appalling. Nothing has changed as illustrated by a very recent example. As a forthcoming chapter of this book will outline, witnesses distinctly heard four gunshots fired on Dealey Plaza on November 22, 1963. This fact was confirmed by the acoustic analysis of the radio recording of a police motorcycle riding behind the presidential limousine. These findings led the House Select Committee on Assassinations to conclude that there had probably been a second gunman on Dealey Plaza. For The Wall Street Journal reporter Edward Kosner, it was however all simple: on November 12, 2016, he wrote: *"These four gunshots finally proved to be backfires."*

Later in the article, the journalist gave a preposterous explanation of the reaction of John Kennedy's body to the impact of the fatal bullet to his head: *"On Zapruder's film, it seemed obvious to the critics of the Warren Commission that Kennedy's head and torso had been projected backwards, an evidence that the shot came from the front and not from Oswald's rifle from the Texas School Book Depository behind the limousine progression. This argument will last several years, despite the counter-expertise of physicists and the driver's behavior of the limousine. Indeed, when the bullet impacted JFK's head, it was the Secret Service driver's immediate reaction – by hitting hard on the gas pedal - that had propelled the President backwards"*[178].

---

[178] Edward Kosner, The Curse of the Zapruders, The Wall Street Journal, November 12-13, 2016

Nice try! Yet, one of the video films taken during the parade, just before the fatal shot, shows very clearly that the tail lights of the limousine had lit up briefly, proving that the driver had braked instead, a professional negligence for which he received a rebuke from the Secret Service well after the event[179].

Despite the evidence of the cover-up, it is frustrating to see that no American media, to this day, dare to engage in a complete, critical, objective and thorough synthesis of the assassination of the President Kennedy. Some Americans believe that the murder of Senator Robert Kennedy (who was resolute to shed light on his brother's assassination, once elected President of the United States) and even the Watergate scandal, a few years later, are two historical events directly or indirectly related to the JFK assassination and its cover-up. Although it may seem a far-fetched statement at first sight, we may well discover tangible evidence linking these three events together one day.

The unresponsive or distorted media coverage of the JFK assassination is likely to remain one of their most shameful performances in American history, along the same lines as were their indolent acceptance of government manipulation during the Vietnam and Iraq wars. I hope that by now, the readers of this chapter will have acknowledged the U.S. media's resignation to accept the government version of the assassination. It is my hope that the many examples illustrated above have provided answers to these questions: what was the media coverage about the assassination? In what way was it reported? How did their professionals convey the misinformation?

There remain however more questions that tease the mind: why has this coverage been neglected, ignored or falsified? What are the reasons that the media fail to address unbiased reports about what really happened on November 22, 1963 in Dallas? Why is there such a deliberate intention to conceal the truth?

---

[179] Fetzer Ph.D. "Smoking Guns" in the Death of JFK et "Murder in Dealey Plaza"

The next chapter should provide some answers but, first and foremost, it is as important to recall the facts and to present the evidence of the disturbing plot that led to the assassination of President Kennedy and the subsequent cover-up.

Chapter 6

The Enigmatic Lee Harvey Oswald

What kind of man was Lee Harvey Oswald? How much was he involved in the assassination of President Kennedy? Was he the lone mad shooter on Dealey Plaza or a scapegoat? Was he physically at the 6th floor window of the Texas School Book Depository? Assuming he fired a single shot, did he act alone? What secrets would Oswald have revealed during a trial, if Jack Ruby, close to the Organized Crime, had not silenced him? Although "lost" and no doubt driven by a deep desire to be talked about, Lee Harvey Oswald was not the fool that people claimed he was. He nevertheless remains a very ambiguous person.

Jacob Carter[180], the young American writer, whom I met at the Pittsburgh conference in 2013, recalls in his book the troubling facts about Lee Harvey Oswald's past as reported by the Warren Commission. According to the Warren Report, the young Oswald left the United States Marine Corps in October 1959 and went to the Soviet Union, the sworn enemy of America at that time. Two and a half years later, he returned to the United States with a Russian wife. He ostensibly showed an interest in the Cuban communist leader, Fidel Castro. In August 1963, he was seen in

---

[180] Jacob. M. Carter – Before History Dies - 2015

the streets of New Orleans distributing procommunist leaflets "Hands off Cuba" for the *Fair Play for Cuba Committee*. This propaganda provoked an altercation with an anti-Castro partisan that ended with a short jail period for Oswald's public disturbance.

Oswald's public demonstration of his pro-Communist support is however disputed today. Having talked to him after his arrest, a New Orleans lieutenant swore before the Warren Commission that Oswald *"appeared to have engineered a bogus dispute with the anti-Castro supporter"*. A New Orleans lawyer also testified before the commission that *"Oswald told him that he had been paid to distribute leaflets in the streets of New Orleans."* The FBI also found notes written by Oswald that confirmed his comments. The Warren Commission ignored these testimonies and carried out a ploy: to make Oswald into a devout communist.

This not exactly what Oswald's notes have shown. Oswald wrote that the United States and Russia *"had more to cooperate than to engage in an endless cold war. Both countries had flaws but also had common interests and opportunities"*. Oswald said he continued to hate communism: *"There are probably few Americans born in the USA who have personal reasons for wanting to experience communism. They rather distrust communism and even show hostility"*[181].

According to the Warren Report, Oswald traveled to Mexico City where he tried to obtain a visa for Cuba. On September 26, 1963, he boarded a Continental Trail bus heading south to Texas and Mexico for a 6-day stay. What he did in this city remains a mystery to this day. The photos held by the CIA proving that Oswald stayed in the Mexican capital all vanished[182].

As reported by the Warren Commission, Oswald, back in Dallas, assassinated the leader of the Free World, a few weeks later. Oswald was arrested on the day of the assassination. He denied having committed the crime and constantly claimed his innocence. Surrounded by journalists and police officers, two

---

[181] Lamar Waldron- The Hidden History of the JFK Assassination. 2013. Counterpoint
[182] Anthony Summers. Conspiracy.Who Killed President Kennedy,Gollancz,May 1980

days later, Oswald was gunned down by Jack Ruby, a nightclub manager, in the Dallas Police Headquarters, before being transferred to the nearby county jail.

Thanks to the work of the Assassination Record Review Board, we know more about what the CIA and the FBI knew about Oswald and what they had hidden from the Warren Commission.[183] Several senior U.S. secret service officials knew Oswald well. He was constantly under surveillance during his time in Russia, when he returned to the United States and right up until his death in Dallas. This is not a rumor but a fact reported in no less than 50 files. The State Department, the FBI and the CIA, all tracked Oswald. They intercepted his mother's correspondence. Some would have us believe that Oswald was a "loser", out of nowhere, misunderstood by everyone, unknown to the world until he killed Kennedy but it does not make sense. Assuming that he did shoot the President, Oswald was indisputably an individual whom the CIA knew well before the crime. So the questions remain: was Oswald manipulated? For what reasons did he receive so much attention from those agencies before the assassination?

Journalist David Talbot[184] depicts Oswald as a victim; a smart, self-taught young man and not the ignorant person as he was described by the Warren Commission. He spent a lot of time in libraries and was looking for a better future. Intrigued by the secret world of intelligence, he enlisted in the U.S. Marine Corps. He was sent to Atsugi, the U.S. air base in Japan, home to the top-secret U2 spy planes program that the CIA kept most secret. Oswald held the position of a radar operator there from September 1957 to November 1958. Intelligence agencies started to take interest in him from that time onwards for *"his leftist ideal and his curiosity towards the Soviet Union"*. They saw in him the potential to become a false defector in the Soviet Union where the

---

[183] Interview of Jefferson Morley by Jacob M Carter – Before History Dies. 2015.
[184] Interview of David Talbot by Jacob M Carter – Before History Dies. 2015.

CIA would track him. Two and a half years later, he returned to the USA with a Russian woman. No one troubled him despite the fact that he had just given up his U.S. citizenship by handing his passport to the United States Embassy in the Soviet Union before leaving the country. During the interview at the embassy, he even threatened to provide highly confidential information that he held when he was based in Atsugi. Not only was there no prosecution against Oswald but he was given a financial loan when he returned to the country...the very country that he had betrayed! He was given a new passport, 24 hours after making the application (in the section to be completed as the next destination he mentioned "Soviet Union"). So, Oswald had an easy return home and was welcomed as a free man by U.S. government officials who should have found his marriage to a Russian citizen (whose uncle was a colonel in the Soviet Ministry of Internal Affairs) a reason more to be suspicious.

What could have been the secret of Oswald's immunity from prosecution? He had committed an act of treason against the United States. He had continued to make threats against his country by pledging allegiance to the Soviet Union and Cuba. At the most sensitive moment of the Cold War, it is a curious response to give him preferential treatment through the ultra-fast granting of a passport and financial assistance![185]

Talbot asks us to imagine, in the current context of the war on terrorism, that you travel to the Middle East to join Al Qaeda or other Islamist networks, that you show hatred against America and that you return after a while to the United States with a jihadist woman, and yet you are not stopped at the U.S. border and do not endure a long interrogation by the security agencies. Wouldn't we find this story incredible? But that's what happened to Oswald. He returned to the USA in 1962 and settled in Texas with his wife and their baby daughter, without any trouble. He found a job at Jaggars-Chiles-Stovall Inc., a company specializing in high-level government security. Knowing his past as a

---

[185] James W. Douglass, JFK and the Unspeakable, Why He Died and Why it Matters, A Touchstone Book, 2008

defector, it is incredible that he was able to retrieve his passport so quickly unless he was "employed" by the U.S. government. Once in Texas, he became friendly with Georges de Mohrenschildt, a wealthy high-ranking CIA-related businessman who roamed the world and curiously took him under his protection.

There is much evidence that Oswald's defection in the U.R.S.S. was part of a program organized by the CIA and the Office of Naval Intelligence (ONI). These sources came from two CIA Special Operations agents: Victor Marchetti and William Robert Plumlee (who later warned the U.S. Congress about President George Bush's illegal practices during the Iran-Contra scandal)[186]. In his sworn affidavit, and with his military superiors' support, Plumlee claimed that he had known Oswald at the ONI Center in Nags Head, North Carolina, as early as 1957. Oswald took intensive language courses there and prepared himself for secret international operations. Plumlee also obtained confirmation from his superiors of Oswald's association with the ONI intelligence service. Plumlee saw Oswald again in 1962 in Dallas in a safe house secured by Cuban exiles. According to Plumlee's own investigation about Oswald and to his interview by former Minnesota Governor Jesse Ventura, there was no doubt that *"Oswald was a military intelligence officer. It's not an allegation, it's a fact. I know it thanks to my personal experience and the testimonies given by my superiors"*[187].

Military Intelligence and the CIA submitted Oswald's personal files to the *House Select Committee on Assassinations*, but these were incomplete - 37 documents were missing. These claims were also confirmed by Victor Marchetti, a long-time CIA agent. He explained what the ONI program consisted of: it involved some 40 young men from very modest backgrounds who were portrayed as disillusioned with America and attracted to communism. After training at the ONI Center, they were sent to

---

[186] Jesse Ventura – They Killed Our President – 2013. Skyhorse Publishing
[187] William Robert Plumlee, interview with author Jesse Ventura, 12 June 2006

the U.R.S.S. with the specific purpose of having them enlisted by the Soviets either as double agents - if they were suspected of being American spies - or as agents of the KGB[188]. According to Marchetti, this was the plan reserved for Oswald.

Another testimony - and not the least - was given in 1975 by Richard Schweiker, the senator from Pennsylvania who co-chaired the Senate Sub-Committee to investigate the JFK assassination. The senator summarized Oswald's mysterious past in these terms: *"he had the fingerprints of intelligence all over him"*. Schweiker claimed that Oswald's defection to the Soviet Union in 1959 was "bogus" and that he had participated instead in an intelligence program of posing as a false defector[189].

There was another unsettling point: Oswald had failed a Russian language proficiency test in February 1959. Oddly enough, he was able to speak it fluently, as attested by two people close to him whose mother tongue was Russian: his wife, Marina, and, much later, his protector George de Mohrenschildt. Oswald could not have mastered this difficult language without a total immersion language training at the U.S. Intelligence Center.[190]

The CIA agent's profile was indisputable in Oswald's case. A spy camera was found amongst his personal possessions[191], as well as a notebook with references to firearms and methods of microscopic photographic reproduction used in espionage, and a cryptogram hiding information and telephone numbers, one of which traced back to Jack Ruby[192].

After studying the JFK assassination for years, Colonel Fletcher Prouty, chief liaison officer for covert operations between the U.S. Air Force and the CIA, came to the conclusion that Oswald had been manipulated into a perfect scapegoat and that the JFK assassination had to be pinned on him in order to prevent any

---

[188] Anthony Summers, "Interview with Victor Marchetti" in John Simkin, "Lee Harvey Oswald: Biography, "Spartacus Educational, retrieved 22 April 2013.

[189] David Talbot, Brothers, The Hidden History of the Kennedy Years – 2007 p 381

[190] John Armstrong, Harvey and Lee: How the CIA Framed Oswald (Quasar: 2003)

[191] Judyth Vary Baker "Oswald Framed:Convenient Lies and Cover-Ups"June 29, 2011.

[192] Hoke May. "Simple Enciphering System Used to Encode Oswald Notebook – DA. New Orleans States-Item, 13 May 1967.

embarrassing investigation[193]. Oswald was given a false profile of being a dangerous man and was blamed for being a radical leftist. During his arrest, he quickly understood that he had been manipulated and accused of the JFK assassination by claiming his innocence and declaring he was only a patsy.

Oswald supposedly had money problems. While he was a defector to the Soviet Union, he only had $203 in his bank account but spent about $1,500. The Warren Commission explained that this was money he had from investments.[194] Upon his return to America, Oswald seemed to spend beyond what he was earning. Oswald's tax returns have not been disclosed to the American people until now whereas those of Jack Ruby have been published[195].

Something else has intrigued many investigators: when Oswald was allowed to make a single phone call while in police custody, he repeatedly tried someone's phone number in Raleigh, North Carolina, but failed to get a response. People speculated that it could have been a contact from the Office of Naval Intelligence in North Carolina. According to Victor Marchetti, Oswald attempted to contact the intelligence service that had employed him to ask for legal assistance, a SOS which unfortunately remained unanswered. They wanted nothing to do with him and more importantly, they wished to prevent him from talking with Jack Ruby.

Some speculated that Oswald could have survived the serious injury caused by Jack Ruby's bullet. But it was bad luck for Oswald: before the ambulance arrived, the police took the wounded man to an office, placed him on a table and gave him a CPR. This procedure should have been totally proscribed for Oswald was badly wounded in the left side of his abdomen, the

---

[193] Colonel L. Fletcher Prouty. "The Col. L. Fletcher Prouty Reference Site" retrieved 23 April 2013: prouty.org/

[194] Warren Report, New York Times ed. p 367; p 613-14

[195] Robert J. Groden and Harrison Edward Livingstone. High Treason: The assassination of JFK. What really happened? The Conservatory Press, 1989

bullet having passed through several vital organs. This act actually worsened the internal hemorrhage[196].

The "Lone Nuts" claim that Oswald was not programmed by anyone. For them, Oswald remains a violent, sociopathic, narcissistic being, who, craving for public attention, was also obsessed by gaining political power. He had already been blamed for the failed murder of a retired general, Edwin Walker, a fierce supporter of the far right, causing Oswald to be labelled as a murderous lunatic. This murder attempt has however never been fully understood. According to David Talbot, assuming that Oswald used his rifle to shoot the general, there has to have been another person to assist him that day, for he had no car nor a driver's license. To cover several miles from his home to General Walker's residence in suburban Dallas would have been very difficult for Oswald to conceal his Mannlicher Carcano even dismantled. Eyewitnesses, a taxi driver or bus passengers, would surely have noticed him carrying the weapon.

The Dallas police concluded that the bullet that missed General Walker was a 30.06 steel-jacket bullet. This bullet could not have been fired from the Mannlicher-Carcano rifle that Oswald supposedly used[197]. Moreover, according to an FBI memorandum, Jack Ruby and General Walker knew each other. Jack Ruby had been seen visiting Walker at his residence. He had called him on the phone every month, from December 1962 to March 1963. Walker's assassination attempt occurred shortly after Jack Ruby's last visit to the general's residence.

Several investigative journalists found other inconsistencies in the Warren Commission's version. The Commission endeavored to pin the assassination attempt against Walker on Oswald in order to prove his predisposition for violent acts and homicides. However, eyewitnesses noticed two people at the shooting site and two cars with suspicious activity around Walker's house. None of these eyewitnesses said that these men looked like

---

[196] Ibid
[197] Robert J. Groden, The Killing of a President, Vicking Studio Books, 1993

Oswald. The night watchman at Walker's residence noticed a suspicious 1957 Chevrolet driven by a Cuban[198].

In any honest and thorough criminal investigation, three essential aspects of a crime must be warranted: the motive, the means and the opportunity in order to prove the suspect's guilt.

What could have been Lee Harvey Oswald's *motive*? According to the official government version, Oswald called himself a liberal with a Marxist-communist political opinion[199]. For sure, his character and attitude were ambiguous. He pretended to be a pro-Castro while he maintained direct and constant links with an anti-Castro group! The Warren Commission was never able to establish a solid motive to conclude to Oswald's guilt in their investigation. The very few credible arguments put forward by the Warren Commission showed how much they felt beaten by the lack of facts[200]. At best, they speculated that Oswald hated authority because he was a loser, a bitter and a frustrated man and that, being envious of President Kennedy, he wanted to destroy his charisma and wealth. The official version insisted in depicting Oswald as an admirer of Castro, but nothing transpired from his words or his writings to confirm that he had any particular hatred against John Kennedy. On the contrary, he admired the President. His relatives and friends, Ruth and Michael Paine for example - the couple who gave Oswald's wife, Marina, a roof over her head, when the couple separated - said he loved the President. Oswald's friend, George de Mohrenschildt, said Oswald had a great respect for John Kennedy and that he admired him for his positions on civil rights and that, by his dynamism and youth, the President was to his eyes a hope and a force capable of changing the country. As a leftist, Oswald admired the President's liberal positions.

Is this the language of an assassin about his future victim? Oswald had an admiration for John Kennedy and voiced it to the

---

[198] Lamar Waldron, The Hidden History of the JFK Assassination, Counter Point Berkeley, 2013

[199] Interview de Jefferson Morley par Jacobs M.Carter – Before History Dies – 2015.

[200] Interview de David Talbot par Jacobs M.Carter – Before History Dies – 2015.

police after being arrested: "*My wife and I love the President's family. They are interesting people ... I am not a malcontent: nothing irritated me about the President* "[201]. During a civil rights conversation, a month before the assassination, Oswald had said he thought John Kennedy was doing *"a real fine job, a real good job"*, a statement that his wife, Marina, and George de Mohrenschildt confirmed[202].

Oswald's positions concerning President Kennedy are recalled by the author-historian James Douglass.[203] New Orleans Secret Service revealed a published list of books about John Kennedy that Oswald had obtained at the New Orleans Public Library. According to Douglass, Marina Oswald told McMillan in her book "*Marina and Lee*" that her husband had found an interest in reading about Kennedy's life and his political vision. In July 1963, he took out William Manchester's book "*Portrait of a President*" from the library, then, two weeks later, the book written by John Kennedy, *Profiles in Courage*. When he returned the book, he chose Alan Moorehead's book *The White Nile*, just because William Manchester had mentioned that the President had recently read it. Marina explained her husband had told him that he "*liked and approved the President*" and that he "*believed that, for the United States in 1963, John Kennedy was the best President the country could hope for*". She also said that he used to listen to radio speeches of the President notably the one on the Nuclear Test Ban Treaty. Oswald explained to his wife that the President was trying to find a way out of the Cold War by working for disarmament. He told her: "*Some people blame the President for having lost Cuba while in reality he wants to pursue a better and tolerant policy towards Cuba but he is not free to lead it as he wishes.*"

During his very short time in Dallas jail, police officers interpreted Oswald's attitude as that of an individual "*who knew what he was doing and seemed very confident. He acted like he was in

---

[201] Anthony Lewis- Warren Commission Finds Oswald Guilty and Says Assassin and Ruby Acted Alone. The New York Times 27 September 1964.

[202] Anthony Summers & Robbyn Swann;The Arrogance of Power,Penguin Books 2001

[203] James W. Douglass, JFK and the Unspeakable, Why He Died and Why it Matters, A Touchstone Book, 2008

charge".[204] Jesse Curry, the Dallas police chief, admitted that Oswald "*seemed to have been trained in interrogation techniques as he resisted police questions perfectly and calmly*"[205]. This confidence that Oswald boldly showed could be interpreted as that of a defendant who knew how to protect himself thanks to his connection with the American Secret Service. In between his indictment on Friday afternoon and his assassination on Sunday morning, he had the following comments: "*Call the FBI and tell them you hold Lee Oswald ... Everybody will know who I am now.... I'm waiting for someone to come forward to give me legal assistance ...*" He also wanted to reassure his wife: "*It's a mistake. I am not guilty. There are people who will help me*". Everything seemed to indicate Oswald's links to the FBI: when he was arrested, police found his notes with the home and office telephone numbers and the vehicle registration number of FBI agent James Hosty whom Oswald had accused several times in the past for bothering his wife.[206] He continued to maintain his innocence in the killing of both the President and the police officer Tippit: "*I didn't shoot President John F. Kennedy or Officer J. D. Tippit. . . .If you want me to cop out to hitting or pleading guilty to hitting a cop in the mouth when I was arrested, yeah, I plead guilty to that but I do deny shooting both the President and Tippit*".

Are these words of a madman or rather those of a scapegoat? Journalist, Seth Kantor, precisely heard Oswald say: "*I am only a patsy...I never killed anybody*" (we can also hear it on YouTube). His words were analyzed by modern techniques of voice stress detection. Everything indicates that Oswald was telling the truth. Lloyd H. Hitchcock, a member of the American Association of Polygraphists, conducted the Physiological Stress Assessment (PSA) test on Oswald while in custody. The PSA analysis of the recorded soundtracks very clearly concluded that Oswald was

---

[204] Joe Nick Patoski; 'The Witnesses: What They Saw Then, Who They Are Now". Texas Monthly. November 1998

[205] Jim Marrs – Crossfire: The Plot that Killed Kennedy (Carroll & Graf: 1989), citing Dallas Morning News, Nov. 6, 1969

[206] The Last Words of Lee Harvey Oswald: compiled by Mae Brussell.

telling the truth when he denied killing the President, claiming his innocence and that he was a victim[207].

There have been in history many other murders of politicians. Given the importance of the act committed, very often the suspect appears proud of having perpetrated the crime and expresses no regret and no repentance. If Oswald had murdered the most powerful man of the Free World after the police arrested him and charged him for the crime, it seems rather illogical that he failed to manifest in any way some kind of pleasure or pride for having done the impossible; having committed the crime of the century. If Oswald was a true anarchist or communist and had committed the crime for an ideological reason, he certainly made no claim to it. He had the opportunity of taking the responsibility for his action at a press conference, late on that Friday evening, at the police station, in front of television cameras. He unexpectedly remained calm, under control, repeatedly asking for legal assistance and answering to a journalist's questions concerning the cause of the bruises he had suffered during his arrest.

I share David Talbot's bewilderment: after Oswald's alleged attempt of firing at the retired general, Edwin Walker who was a fanatical supporter of the *far right*, how was he able to flip-flop and kill a *liberal* president? We know that some members of the Warren Commission voiced their skepticism. There is no wonder that the Commission was embarrassed in explaining Oswald's motive!

So no *motive*... Could Oswald have had a real *opportunity* to commit his crime or was he manipulated? Would the conspirators have knowingly placed him in the Texas School Book Depository according to a well-designed plan? How could Oswald have chosen a building employing a hundred people with the deliberate intention of committing a murder in broad daylight?

---

[207] George O'Toole; The Assassination Tapes: An electronic probe into the Murder of John F. Kennedy and the Dallas Cover-up (Penhouse Press, 1975).

Critics of the conspiracy theory raise the question about Ruth Paine, Marina Oswald's friend, who had found a job for Lee at the schoolbook depository: how certain were the conspirators that he would be in the building on that Friday November 22? Oswald did not find his job at the Texas School Book Depository on his own initiative and his hiring took place several weeks before the final choice for the presidential motorcade route. If he did not voluntarily chose the place for the ambush, who did? Did Oswald have a real *opportunity* for being, through his own will, beside the window on the northeast corner of the sixth floor of Texas School Book Depository from where the gunshots were fired, as the government version asserted? No eyewitness could formally identify Oswald at this precise location. Jesse Curry, the Dallas police chief, admitted it himself. He believed that the charges against Oswald were slim and that there was no evidence Oswald had fired the gunshots. *"We have no proof that Oswald fired a rifle. Nobody was able to see him in the building with a rifle in his hands"*[208].

On November 22, during the presidential motorcade on Dealey Plaza, the chronology of facts, as we know it, is very precise and detailed to the slightest minute thanks to numerous testimonies. Many of these testimonies enabled to exonerate Oswald because there was a lack of an *opportunity* to fire a rifle, one of the essential factors to incriminate a suspect in any serious criminal investigation. Let us keep in mind that the first bullet that hit John Kennedy occurred at 12:30 pm precisely on Dealey Plaza. Testimonies account for this precise timing were helped by the fact that a giant Hertz advertising sign on the roof of the school book depository showed the exact time and the temperature on Dealey Plaza.

What happened *before* the gunshots were fired on Dealey Plaza? At 11:40am or 11:45am, Oswald was in the Texas School Book Depository, there is no debate about it. He asked another employee why there was a crowd outside the building. When his

---

[208] Jim Marrs – Crossfire: The Plot that Killed Kennedy (Carroll & Graf: 1989), citing Dallas Morning News, Nov. 6, 1969

colleague told him that President Kennedy's motorcade was on its way, Oswald replied, "*Oh, I see.*" While the employees were out for their lunch break, Oswald remained on the sixth floor at his workstation. Then, around 11:50 am, he went downstairs to the first floor where a foreman saw him on the phone. Around noon, eyewitnesses spotted him in the lunchroom on the second floor.[209] According to the Warren Report and to Oswald's statements, when the police questioned him about his whereabouts in the building at the time of JFK's assassination, Oswald replied that "he was having lunch on the first floor" and that "he then went to the second floor lunch room to get a Coca Cola bottle from a vending machine".

At 12.15pm, Mrs. Carolyn Arnold, a secretary of the Texas School Book Depository, saw Oswald in the lobby, on the first floor, and on the second floor lunchroom. She knew Oswald because he used to go to her office from time to time to ask her for change for the soda vending machine. During her statement to the investigators and journalists, she said she had left the schoolbook depository at 12:15 pm to watch the presidential motorcade due to pass by the building around 12:25 pm – 5 minutes before the first shot hit the President. She was adamant about the time; 12:15 pm or a little later. This was because before leaving the building, she remembered that she had been very thirsty. When she entered the lunchroom to get a glass of water, she saw Oswald: "*I don't exactly remember what he was doing*" she said, "*But I know he was sitting there ... in one of the booth seats on the right-hand side of the room as you go in. He was alone as usual and appeared to be having lunch. I did not speak to him but I recognized him clearly*"[210]. Carolyn Arnold, arguably the most valuable eyewitness to vindicate Oswald, was not called to testify before the Warren Commission.

---

[209] Lamar Waldron, The Hidden History of the JFK Assassination, Counter Point Berkeley, 2013

[210] James W. Douglass, JFK and the Unspeakable, Why He Died and Why it Matters, A Touchstone Book, 2008

According to the investigation of the author-historian, Anthony Summers, as recalled by Jesse Ventura[211], at 12:15 or 12:16 pm, an eyewitness on Dealey Plaza, Howard Brennan, claimed to have seen two individuals at the sixth floor window of the Texas School Book Depository. One of them had a rifle but Brennan could not identify Oswald as one of these individuals during a police lineup. This eyewitness spotted precisely a white Caucasian or a dark-haired Latino man with a telescopic rifle at the sixth-floor window on the west end corner and, opposite, a dark-skinned man in a sniper position, on the east side corner of the same floor. According to this eyewitness, one of the two men wore clothes of a style and color very different from those worn by Oswald that day (a red-brown shirt).

At the same time, 12:15pm, a Texas School Book Depository employee, Bonnie Ray Williams, was having lunch on the sixth floor. He left after leaving the rest of his snack there, which the police later attributed as Oswald's leftovers. Williams testified that he did not see Oswald on the sixth floor. His claim supported Carolyn Arnold's testimony to the fact that she had seen Oswald at 12:15 pm in the lunchroom. The sniper Brennan had seen at the sixth floor window could not have been Oswald.

The President was expected at the Trade Mart lunch to give a speech at 12:30pm. This precise time had been *publicly* announced before JFK's visit to Dallas. This information could have helped the assassin to plan his act accordingly. The presidential motorcade should have then passed by the Texas School Book Depository at 12:25 pm. But it ran late by 5 minutes.

It is paramount to understand that it was impossible for Oswald to have been aware that the presidential motorcade had 5 minutes delay because crossing Dallas downtown had taken longer. Oswald having been spotted at 12:15pm in the lunchroom would have had only ten minutes to get himself prepared and fire.[212] It is therefore difficult to imagine that, only 10 minutes before the

---

[211] Jesse Ventura – They Killed Our President – 2013. Skyhorse Publishing
[212] Anthony Summers – The Kennedy Conspiracy (Sphere Books: 2007), 63

presidential limousine was expected to drive by the school book depository (at 12:25pm according to the publicized schedule), Oswald was first spotted on the lunch room, from where he would have rushed upstairs – with or without the warehouse elevator - to his sniper position by the sixth floor window. Surely, it would have taken him much longer to reach his sniper perch, remove the rifle from a hiding spot, assemble it and aim. According to the FBI calculation, it would have taken Oswald 6 minutes to assemble the Mannlicher-Carcano rifle, and 4 to 9 minutes to move and stack the boxes weighing 50 pounds each in order to create his sniper hiding spot at the 6th floor window. If Oswald had planned the assassination, he would not have gone to the lunchroom at 12:15 pm but would have returned to the sixth-floor in good time before firing from the window.

Where was Oswald spotted just *after* the gunshots (12:30pm)? A photo of the Texas School Book Depository, which was taken 30 seconds after the gunshots, showed an individual's shape at the sixth-floor window. It was impossible that this individual could have been Lee Harvey Oswald since a police officer had seen him in the lunchroom on the second floor, only a few seconds *after* the gunshots.[213] After the last gunshots were fired, police officer, Marrion L. Baker, suddenly stopped his motorcycle in front of the Texas School Book Depository and rushed into the lobby of the building where he met Roy Truly, the Superintendent of the Book Depository. They ran upstairs to the second floor where, 75 to 90 seconds after the shooting, they caught a glimpse of Oswald through the glass door of the lunchroom, standing near a Coca Cola vending machine. Weapon in hand, the police officer ordered Oswald to freeze. Oswald had his back turned towards Baker and was walking in the direction of the vending machine. Oswald complied. Baker would later describe him as a calm man who did not say a single word. Having recognized Oswald, the superintendent Roy Truly told Baker that Oswald was one of his

---

[213] Robert J. Groden and Harrison Edward Livingstone. High Treason: The assassination of JFK. What really happened? The Conservatory Press, 1989

employees working in the Texas School Book Depository. Satisfied by Truly's confirmation, Baker continued his search on the upper floors.[214]

The exact time of this encounter with Oswald was confirmed by another eyewitness, Mrs. Reid, a clerical supervisor of the book depository. Back in her office on the second floor, she saw Oswald holding a Coca-Cola bottle in his hand. She said to investigators *"It did not occur to me that he had anything to do with it* [the shooting] *because he was very calm."* She testified, just like Officer Baker, that Oswald did not seem to be out of breath at that moment.

It would seem very unlikely that 75 to 90 seconds after the last shot, Oswald was able to hurtle down the 72 steps of the stairwell, from his presumed sniper position, on the 6th floor, to the 2nd floor where he had been seen, a Coke in his hand. Unless ...Oswald had used one of the two service elevators! This however was a tricky maneuver since the gate at the elevator door had to be closed at the lower level before it could be called from any floor. The debate remains open: Was Oswald forced to take the stairwell to reach the 2nd floor because none of the elevators had been returned to the 6th floor or did someone answer his request for the elevator to go up? According to Roy Truly's testimony, around 12:31 or 12:32, he and police officer Baker found that the two elevators had remained on the 5th floor when they tried to call one. It would seem that Oswald's request to obtain an elevator on the 6th floor had then failed. In any event, the Warren Commission determined that Oswald had chosen the stairwell to go down to the 2nd floor[215]. The timing for rushing down the stairs was also calculated based on another witness. Victoria Elizabeth Adams was watching the presidential parade from the 4th floor window of the Texas School Book Depository. After the last shot, she rushed down the stairs to the first floor to see what was happening outside. In her testimony, she claimed that she had taken the same stairwell as Oswald did but at that precise moment, she had not heard or met anyone. She estimated that it

---

[214] Anthony Summers- The Kennedy Conspiracy (Sphere Books: 2007), 64
[215] www.dealey.org/updown.pdf

took her at least 15 to 20 seconds to reach the stairwell from the 4th floor and at most 60 seconds to reach the first floor[216] [217].

The Warren Commission reported that, according to police officer Marrion Baker, Oswald had nothing in his hands when he encountered him whereas Baker's handwritten statement explicitly mentioned that he had seen Oswald drinking a Coca-Cola in the lunchroom on the second floor. Although Baker's words "was drinking a Coke" were struck through on the document, his initials could be seen near those words showing that he was the author of this deletion. He nevertheless maintained that his initial statement was the correct one until an FBI agent intimidated him and asked him to strikethrough the words. He was told his memory had failed and that his statement could not have been right as it conflicted with the Warren Report which was already in the print shop due for imminent publication.

For the Warren commission, it was necessary to prove that Lee Harvey Oswald, after firing at the President from the 6th floor, had hid his rifle and rushed down 4 floors, in sufficient time to reach the lunch room before Truly and Baker had arrived. The Warren Commission investigators wangled out of the timing issue by inventing an ingenious and convoluted fraud to better create Oswald's movements in the building: they simply corrected the time when Oswald had been spotted at the beverage-dispensing machine, totally ignoring the official testimony. The investigators compressed Oswald's time when he rushed downstairs to 2 minutes and simply eliminated the exact timing of the vending machine purchase of the Coca-Cola bottle. The commission's decision to delete the Coca-Cola bottle episode from its report enabled to deduct the few extra seconds that Oswald would have taken to make the purchase from the vending machine and to open the bottle. All in all, the final timing

---

[216] Lamar Waldron, The Hidden History of the JFK Assassination, Counter Point Berkeley, 2013
[217] http://www.wnd.com/2013/10/girl-on-the-stairs-refutes-p-c-jfk-narrative/

found by the commission could not have matched the time that Oswald would have taken to reach the 2nd floor.

Moreover, the commission simply eliminated five obstacles that would have impeded Oswald's movements. He had to leave his alleged sniper position by extricating himself from the pile of boxes that barricaded and sheltered him by the sixth-floor window. Then, after shooting, he had to crawl over the piles of boxes at the opposite end of the floor to hide the rifle (conveniently found later between two boxes by the police). Having disposed of the rifle, he had to "untangle" himself from the stack of these boxes and rush to the opposite corner of the building towards the stairwell, hurry down 4 floors to reach the 2nd floor lunch room where he purchased a Coca Cola from the vending machine, just before Agent Baker arrived and noticed him, totally calm and not at all out of breath[218]. Logically, after committing a homicide, it would be hard for any assassin to hide emotions and an agitation in the first few minutes following the act. Here in this case, it was not just a homicide against any person but the crime of the century against the President of the United States of America. Immediately after having committed the act, some emotion and the physical effort for having hurried down four floors – puffing or sweating - would have undoubtedly betrayed the murderer. There was none of this: Oswald was found calm and detached when the police officer ordered him to "freeze" in the lunchroom.

In summary, the discrepancies between the Warren Report and the eyewitnesses' testimonies about the timing of Oswald's movements in the Texas School Book Depository, *before* and *after* the shots on Dealey Plaza, are numerous: *Before* the shooting, after his lunch break at 12:15 pm (several eyewitnesses, including Carolyn Arnold, indeed located Oswald in the lunch room at that time), the commission asserted that Oswald had rushed to the six

---

[218] James W. Douglass, JFK and the Unspeakable, Why He Died and Why it Matters, A Touchstone Book, 2008

floor to position himself at the window and that, hidden by boxes of books, he fired three shots at the presidential car, killing the President and wounding Governor Connally despite the fact that Oswald had not been seen at the sixth-floor window by anyone. The commission then stated that, *after* the shooting, Oswald hid the rifle behind boxes then rushed downstairs to the 2nd floor where he met police officer Marrion Baker and the superintendent Roy Truly.

However, during reenactments, time clock in hand, several investigators calculated the distance they covered from the 6th to the 2nd floor. They could not arrive in the lunchroom in the time frame set by the Warren Commission. They came to the conclusion that it was very difficult, even impossible, to run downstairs in just two minutes. This impossibility was reinforced thanks to the eyewitnesses who said that Oswald was not out of breath when they spotted him in the lunchroom.

This means that the conditions of *opportunity* to commit the crime could not be retained in Oswald's case. These testimonies corroborated with what Oswald had told the police: that he had been seen on the second floor by at least two employees whom he could describe.

Shortly after the last gunshots, several police officers arrived at the Texas School Book Depository. Oswald was no longer at his workstation and could not be found in the building. His absence became suspicious for local and government investigators. He was not however the only employee missing in the Texas School Book Depository after the assassination: out of 75 employees, the management identified 48 employees missing at 12:30 pm and 5 had not returned to work that morning.

We know about Oswald's whereabouts as soon as he left the schoolbook depository thanks to eyewitnesses' testimonies and his own words when under questioning at the police station. On leaving the building, he walked to a bus stop and boarded a bus. He found himself in an intense traffic gridlock because the police had started checking the perimeter around the Texas School Book Depository. He then decided to get off the bus and to walk to the nearby Greyhound bus station where he took a taxi. Next, he headed towards Oak Cliff, a suburb of Dallas, where he was renting a room from Earline Roberts, his landlady. The taxi driver, William Whaley, reported Oswald's unexpected behavior. When he got into the taxi, an old woman outside asked the driver through his window if he could call a taxi for her. The driver remembered that Oswald reacted with gallantry because he opened his passenger door, ready to get out of the cab, and suggested to her that she take the taxi instead. This was a strange behavior for a man who had allegedly shot the President of the United States! The taxi driver testified that Oswald was calm and showed no sign of being tense nor of being in a hurry[219].

Greyhound station where Oswald took a taxi to go to his rented room (author's photo)

So, with no apparent *motive* nor an *opportunity* to kill John Kennedy, could Oswald have had the *means* to act alone? According to the Warren Report, Oswald had brought with him the Mannlicher Carcano rifle that morning of November 22, 1963,

---

[219] Ibid

with which he had presumably fired 3 shots. The rifle as well as the paper that might have been used to wrap the dismantled weapon were found by the police at Oswald's alleged sniper position, the northeastern window of the 6th floor of the Texas School Book Depository. The Warren Commission investigators claimed that Oswald carried the rifle hidden in a parcel in the car of Bull Frazier, his friend and colleague, who drove them both to work at the Texas School Book Depository (Oswald had no car nor a driver's license). The commission stated that Oswald had lied to his colleague when he told him that the parcel he placed on the back seat of the car, contained curtain rods which he had bought for his room at his landlady's.

There are plenty of facts that contradict the Warren Commission's explanation. Bull Frazier and his sister testified that Oswald could not have carried the dismantled rifle to his place of work. While Oswald and Bull Frazier were getting into the car that morning, Frazier's sister watched them from the window of the house next to Ruth Paine's where Oswald had visited his wife the day before. The Mannlicher-Carcano rifle was an outdated weapon that was difficult to completely dismantle. Even when dismantled, the wooden stock and the barrel would remain relatively long. Upon arrival at the Texas School Book Depository, Frazier dropped Oswald before he went to the parking lot and Frazier saw him heading toward the depository entrance. He was adamant that Oswald was carrying the package alongside of his body, one end under his armpit and the other end cupped in his hand. Even for a man taller than Oswald it would have been physically impossible to hold the package this way if it had contained the dismantled rifle because the size of the wooden stock and the barrel would have exceeded the package size and dragged on the ground. Bull Frazier's observation was also confirmed by her sister when she saw Oswald leave with the package from the neighbor's house. Oswald was only average height, and in order to hold one end of the package under his armpit and the other end in the palm of his hand, it would mean the length of the pack could not have exceeded 23 inches while the length of the Mannlicher Carcano rifle, once dismantled, was approximately 35 inches.

Nobody saw Oswald with the rifle in the Texas School Book Depository on November 22. Jack Dougherty, a shipping clerk, saw Oswald enter the depository that morning and testified that he was not carrying a package[220]. One can of course always assume that Oswald could have passed the parcel to someone, an accomplice, who was waiting for him in the building or in the parking lot.

Bull Frazier is still alive. I had the opportunity of seeing and hearing him twice, first at the Pittsburgh 2014 conference and again at the Dallas 2015 conference. He recalled the event with a lot of emotion, trying to explain Oswald's mysterious package. His friendship for Oswald and his fight to claim the innocence of his former colleague had not faded. Assisted by his son, he came to the Dallas conference to present an exact replica of the packing package - as found by the Warren Commission investigators. Frazier's goal was to convince the audience that the measurements of the dismantled rifle and those of the package did not match. If the Mannlicher-Carcano rifle had been wrapped in the parcel, it would have been 12 inches too long!

What else could the package have contained? According to a Mafia informant, the package could have contained a pro-Cuban protest banner. Oswald and an accomplice had maybe decided, that day, to deploy it on Dealey Plaza out of a window of the Texas School Book Depository, to embarrass John Kennedy during his parade beneath the windows. This plan, of course, was not carried out[221].

The mysterious package remains a puzzle, for many including myself. I wanted to know if there was tangible evidence that the package found by the Warren Commission's investigators in the Texas School Book Depository (now at the National Archives) had really contained the dismantled rifle, and if for example, the wrapping paper had been analyzed for traces of grease from the lubricated mechanical parts of the rifle. The FBI claimed that the

---

[220] Lamar Waldron, The Hidden History of the JFK Assassination, Counter Point Berkeley, 2013
[221] Ibid

packaging did not show any traces of rifle oil nor wrinkles in the paper corresponding to the measurements of the dismantled rifle. The "Lone Nuts" never talk about this. On the other hand, if the package had contained curtain rods, as Oswald claimed it, they should have been found somewhere in the Texas School Book Depository during the police search that day. Nothing is ever said about this. The government version suggested that if they had not been found, then Oswald must have lied. Another hypothesis: the curtain rods were found but the evidence of their discovery was removed ... leading to the same conclusion as designed by the Warren Commission: Oswald was guilty.

The Warren Commission believed there was other significant piece of evidence of Oswald's guilt, such as Oswald's fingerprint that was found on the package which allegedly contained the dismantled rifle. It claimed having also found fibers identical to those of the blanket in which Oswald had presumably wrapped his rifle in storage. This blanket was found in Ruth Paine's garage, without the weapon, by FBI investigators. They also identified fibers on the rifle butt that they believed could have come from Oswald's shirt when he was arrested at the Texas Theater. But the shirt he wore was totally different from the one he wore at the time of JFK's assassination because, according to his landlady, once back in his rented room he had changed his shirt before heading to the movie theater where he was arrested.[222]

Oswald's fingerprints as "evidence" of his guilt according to the Warren Commission were apparently found on the Mannlicher-Carcano. In fact, only a partial print was found on the trigger but the match with Oswald's prints was extremely dubious. Legally speaking, depending on jurisdictions, a minimum of 6 to 12 match points from a fingerprint are required to meet the conditions for indictment. The partial print found on Oswald's alleged weapon corresponded only to 3 points of similarity, that is, a very

---

[222] Robert J. Groden and Harrison Edward Livingstone. High Treason: The assassination of JFK. What really happened? The Conservatory Press, 1989

approximate and insufficient correlation for lawyers[223]. The Warren Commission investigators also found another partial print on the rifle corresponding to "the palm of Oswald's hand". The investigators however did not find it on the visible exterior part of the weapon (the way a shooter would have held it) but it was noticeable once they had disassembled the rifle. The FBI found no match with that print either.

This partial handprint was not recorded by the FBI on the very day of the assassination when the rifle had been found in the Texas School Book Depository but a few days later. Ruby killed Oswald two days after JFK was murdered. According to Paul Groody, the director of the funeral home where Oswald's body laid, government officials came and asked to be left alone in the room with the body. After their departure, Groody noticed that Oswald's hands were stained with ink, something that he had not seen before their visit[224]. The Dallas police also admitted having taken additional Oswald's fingerprints after he died. It does not seem unreasonable to think that the fingerprints could have been placed on the weapon *after* the crime.

During his arrest, Oswald was also tested for residual nitrate traces on his right cheek. The paraffin tests were negative, proving that he had not recently fired a rifle. He was tested positively however on the hand which could prove that he had been in contact with a weapon (he had a revolver on him during his arrest at the Texas Theater) but traces of nitrates could just as easily have come from urine, a newspaper he read in the Texas School Book Depository or ink from his fingerprints taken at the police station[225]. According to the chronology of Oswald's whereabouts over a period of 15 minutes between the final gunshots on Dealey Plaza and his confrontation with an eyewitness on the second floor of the depository, it is unlikely that Oswald could have had the time to wipe his fingerprints off the rifle. It is inconceivable that he had had time to dismantle the gun

---

[223] Gary Savage, JFK: The First Day Evidence (The Shoppe Press: 1993) p 105-106

[224] Michael T. Griffith – Was Oswald's Palm Print Planted on the Alleged Murder Weapon? 2012

[225] Jesse Ventura – They Killed Our President – 2013. Skyhorse Publishing

to eliminate his palm print, then reassemble it again and to wash his face to eliminate traces of residual gunpowder. The police officers who tried to assemble the rifle took 6 minutes to do this same operation!

There is another disturbing fact about the lack of means available to Oswald. It again eludes to the weapon that Oswald allegedly used for the crime. The Warren Commission claimed that Oswald was connected with the rifle that killed John Kennedy because the investigators found two photographs of him posing with the weapon, which the commission certified to be exactly the model used for the crime. The two pictures showed Oswald in two different postures, a rifle in his hand, in the same location of his house backyard.

The police showed him one of the two photographs during his detention. Oswald reacted with suspicion and arrogance: *"In time I will be able to show you that this is not my picture, but I don't want to answer any more questions. . . . I will not discuss this photograph....There was another rifle in the building. I have seen it. Warren Caster had two rifles, a 30.06 Mauser and a .22 for his son. . . . That picture is not mine, but the face is mine. The picture has been made by superimposing my face. The other part of the picture is not me at all, and I have never seen this picture before. I understand photography real well, and that, in time, I will be able to show you that is not my picture..."*[226][227] Oswald could certainly have knowledge about photographic montage. He was an employee at Jaggars-Chiles-Stovall Inc., a Dallas firm specialized in graphic art and photographic printing.

These two photos were analyzed by a large number of experts. Everything indicated a forgery and a photographic montage as Oswald had said. The shadows, for example, were not logical: the shadow under Oswald's nose was in a direction totally different from that of the shadow projected by his body. The background

---

[226] The Last Words of Lee Harvey Oswald: compiled by Mae Brussell
[227] http://reopenkennedycase.forumotion.net/t1382-caster-and-the-two-rifles

on both photos was exactly the same although the position of Oswald's body had changed between the two gunshots; a photographic impossibility.

According to government sources, Oswald's wife, Marina, reportedly took the two photos later found in Oswald's belongings by the FBI. On several occasions, they raided Ruth Paine's house, where some of Oswald's possessions had been left during the time Marina Oswald was staying with her friend, having recently separated from her husband. Marina however claimed: *"These are not the photos that I took"*[228]

So let's summarize: absence of motive; lack of evidence of opportunity and insufficient evidence of means to carry out the crime. All this does not make Oswald guilty and the lack of undeniable evidence would certainly have had him acquitted in a trial.

In the wake of Oswald's repeated requests for legal assistance on national television, Mark Lane, a lawyer from New York, endeavored to defend him but his representation was unsuccessful. It was rejected by the authorities and the murder of Oswald sealed of course all attempts of defending him. Mark Lane later became one of the pioneer critics of the Warren Commission's investigation. He struggled with his own investigation that led him to suspect the role of the CIA in the assassination of the President and in the cover-up - just as Robert Kennedy who also raised this probability as soon as he heard about the assassination of his brother. In 1966, Lane published his book *"Rush to Judgment"* one of the most comprehensive criticisms of the findings of the Warren Commission inquiry[229]. During the same period, other books supporting the conspiracy theory were written by Edward Jay Epstein and Josiah Thompson. The latter,

---

[228] Harrisson Edward Livingstone; High Treason 2 (Carroll & Graf: 1992)

[229] Andrew Kreig
http://www.justice-integrity.org/index.php?option=com_content&view=article&id=599:jfk-s-murder-the-cia-8-things-every-american-should-know&catid=21:myblog&itemid=114

a former professor of philosophy at Haverford College, a private investigator and a writer of a book "Six Seconds in Dallas", proved, with a cautious re-enactment of the facts, the presence of three shooters on Dealey Plaza and the firing of at least four bullets.

Much has been written about Oswald's ambiguous role. He might have worked for both the CIA and the FBI. On behalf of the CIA, he could have played the role of a subversive provocative agent: one day he pretended to be a pro-Castro, conveying the image of an activist for the *Fair Play for Cuba Committee*; and another day he showed his support to the cause of the anti-Castro militants. Without knowing he was going to be framed in a secret CIA operation, Oswald might have been involved in the assassination plot against President Kennedy.

Oswald also appeared to have been a FBI informant. Given his distinctly pro-Kennedy stance, some have even supported the surprising theory in which Oswald had attempted to prevent the murder of the President. During a speech Oswald gave on his cousin's invitation at the Jesuit House of Studies, Spring Hill College in Mobile, Alabama, he warned of the danger of a possible government coup[230].

On January 27, 1964, the Warren Commission was informed that Oswald had been an informant. The Commission Attorney General called it "a dirty rumor" and the FBI denied it too. In a top-secret meeting in January 1964, Allen Dulles spoke out to the commission members and gave his opinion on this matter. If Oswald had worked for the FBI and the CIA, the representatives of these agencies would be compelled to lie under oath when questioned.

Some agents ignored Dulles's recommendations. William Walter, an FBI employee who was working in the New Orleans office in 1963, told the House Select Committee on Assassinations that Oswald had been *"an informant in our office."* In addition, the owner of a New Orleans bar, Orest Pena, who was himself an FBI

---

[230] http://22november1963.org.uk/lee-oswald-speech-in-alabama

informant, said that *"he had seen Oswald with FBI agent [Warren] deBrueys several times"*. The latter had threatened Pena physically, warning him to keep quiet, before being subpoenaed by the Warren Commission.[231] Adrian Alba, a friend of Oswald's who managed the car maintenance for the FBI and the Secret Service in a New Orleans garage, testified that one day he had seen Oswald approaching a FBI car that was parked in front of his garage. According to Alba, someone handed a white envelope through the car window to Oswald who hid it under his shirt. Two days later, Alba identified Oswald again, this time speaking briefly with the driver of a car that Alba recognized as that of a "Washington FBI agent" who had travelled to New Orleans. Another event marked Oswald's acquaintance with the FBI. Oswald was arrested by the New-Orleans police and charged for disturbance in the streets of New Orleans for distributing pro-Castro flyers. Once arrested, Oswald asked to make a call to a FBI agent[232].

The "Conspiracy Nuts" keep the mystery about Lee Harvey Oswald very much alive, especially about Oswald look-alike! They believe that the "Oswald double", an impostor acting in parallel to the activities of the real Oswald, was created and "planted" by the U.S. intelligence service in order to create false leads.

Sheer imagination on the part of the "Conspiracy Nuts" on this matter is of course possible, but the fact remains that Oswald's double appearances are puzzling. Oswald could not be in two different locations at the same time, as was often recorded. The investigators concluded that the only viable explanation was that U.S. intelligence had used the "two Oswalds", each one taking part to a covert operation. It was a common practice in espionage, especially during the Cold War[233]. The differences in human size and physical features between the "two Oswalds" were too

---

[231] James W. Douglass, JFK and the Unspeakable, Why He Died and Why it Matters, A Touchstone Book, 2008

[232] Ibid

[233] Jesse Ventura – They Killed Our President – 2013. Skyhorse Publishing

noticeable to ignore the imposture and to doubt the existence of a ubiquitous Oswald. I wish however to put aside all the farfetched fabrications on this matter which have unfortunately over time tarnished the image of the conspiracy supporters. I would like however to examine here the most convincing evidence of an "Oswald double".

Upon Oswald's death, following his assassination by Jack Ruby, funeral director Paul Groody was asked if he had noticed a mastoid scar on the left side of Oswald's neck and scars near his left elbow. In 1945, Oswald had a mastoidectomy at the Harris Hospital in Fort Worth, Texas, and a three inches scar was recorded on his Marine medical record. Moreover, in 1957, Oswald had accidentally shot himself in the arm with a derringer while serving in the Marines. Groody certified that he did not see a bullet scar nor a mastoidectomy scar on Oswald's corpse[234] [235]. Dr. Earl Rose, who performed Oswald's autopsy, made the same remarks as Groody. Twenty-seven color photos were taken of Oswald's body at the morgue. They are currently in the vaults of the National Archives. They show no three-inch scar from the mastoidectomy.

The existence of an "Oswald double" was also reported based on dental records. While the young Oswald had lost a tooth at school, there was no missing tooth or crown on the remains of the "Oswald" who was buried[236].

Several investigators also found another peculiar fact. Very early in Oswald's Marines life, his possible "double" was questioned because his name strangely differs from one file to another: Lee Harvey Oswald, Harvey Oswald Lee, Alek James Hidell. These investigators thought that Hidell was the name Lee Harvey Oswald took as an American or Soviet intelligence agent. Some even claimed that the real Lee Harvey Oswald had been

---

[234] James DiEugenio & Lisa Pease – The Assassinations: Probe Magazine on JFK, MLK, RFK & Malcolm X (Feral House 2003, p 131

[235] John Armstrong – Harvey and Lee: "The Magic Tonsillectomy, Vanishing Scars" mindserpent.com

[236] Richard Belzer & David Wayne, Dead Wrong.

given another identity and had been placed in a witness protection program.[237]

Another disturbing fact: Lee Harvey Oswald was arrested by the police at 1:50 pm on November 22 in the Texas Theater, following the assassination of police officer J.D. Tippit in Oak Cliff. Lee Harvey Oswald was handcuffed and taken by force out of the front door of the movie theater. At 1:53 pm a man looking like Oswald was also arrested in the same cinema but was taken out by the back door!

On the same day, around 3:30 pm, an Oswald look-alike was spotted by Sergeant Robert Vinson of the U.S. Air Force, a passenger on a flight leaving Dallas aboard a C-54 cargo plane. Vinson had been lucky to find a plane leaving Andrews U.S. Air Force Base near Washington D.C. for the U.S. Air Force base in Denver, Colorado, allowing him to reach Colorado Springs where he was based. Apart from two men in the C-54 cockpit, Vinson was the only passenger aboard the huge, empty military plane. Vinson was surprised that the two men never spoke to him during the whole flight and that they did not even ask him to sign boarding papers. At around 12:30 pm, while flying over Nebraska, Vinson heard an emotionless voice, through the cockpit intercom, announcing that President Kennedy had been shot in Dallas. At that moment, the plane changed course abruptly and headed south. The plane landed in Dallas at around 3:30 pm on a makeshift runway that Vinson thought must have been a road under construction along the Trinity River. With the plane engines still running, two men in a jeep drove towards the aircraft. One of the pilots opened the door to let the two men hurry on board. They had no luggage and sat far from Vinson behind the cockpit and did not say a single word to him during the entire flight. One of the men appeared to be Latino, Vinson said, and the other, smaller, and whom having seen Kennedy's "official" killer on television during that fateful weekend, he would identify later as Lee Harvey Oswald's perfect lookalike. The plane took off immediately, flew northwest and landed at a

---

[237] Robert J Groden – The search for Lee Harvey Oswald

U.S. Air Force base in Roswell, New Mexico, just at sunset time. Vinson watched the two men leave in a hurry and stayed alone on board. Late that night Vinson returned by bus from Roswell Military Airport to his base.

The next day, while watching the Dallas events on television with his wife, Vinson yelled out: *"This guy* [Oswald] *looks exactly like the man who boarded my plane!"* His incredulous wife told him that it was impossible because Oswald had already been in custody by the police well before the time the plane landed with the two men in Roswell. But Vinson was formal. He swore the man on the plane was Oswald's perfect double. It was after Oswald's murder by Ruby on November 24 that Vinson realized the risky circumstances surrounding the stowaways aboard the military plane and became frightened. At this point, he made the decision to remain silent for the next thirty years...

Did Vinson fake this encounter with Oswald's "double"? He was truly onboard the CIA plane which had taken off from Andrews' U.S. Air Force base. Vinson's presence was confirmed by an airbase attendant who had registered him as a passenger on that cargo plane. On November 23, 1993, Vinson finally decided to talk about his encounter aboard the flight to a television station in Wichita. Thanks to survey maps, he had been able to locate the aircraft's hasty landing and take-off on the sandy track along the Trinity River. This was in the perimeter of Oak Cliff, a suburb of Dallas, not far from the Texas Theater and where Tippit had been murdered. In 2003, Vinson told his adventure to two co-authors for their book "Flight from Dallas"[238].

Of course, it would be easy to dismiss this whole "Oswald double" story as fake news. But this possibility had already been communicated officially by J. Edgar Hoover, the FBI director himself, three years before the tragic events in Dallas, hence bringing dramatic evidence to the story! In June 1960, Hoover was informed of the existence of an Oswald in the U.S.A. and of

---

[238] James W. Douglass, JFK and the Unspeakable, Why He Died and Why it Matters, A Touchstone Book, 2008

another Oswald in Russia during the same period. Hoover found it useful to inform his associates of the FBI various branches, warning them that an imposter could have impersonated Oswald by using his birth certificate. Although the Warren Report did not mention it, there were many notes in FBI files about a Lee Oswald in the U.S. and a Harvey in Russia (a fact that could explain how easy it had been for the latter to speak Russian so well). The historian John Armstrong had written extensively on this subject and his research can be found either in his book "*Harvey and Lee*" or on the Internet.

Former Minnesota Governor Jesse Ventura believes that there is no doubt that Lee Harvey Oswald was a liaison agent with U.S. intelligence. In a possible scenario, before he was arrested by the police at the *Texas Theater*, in Oak Cliff, for the double murder of John Kennedy and police officer Tippit, Oswald could have had a pre-arranged appointment in the cinema to meet with his intelligence contact or even Jack Ruby who lived nearby. In America, especially during the Cold War, movie theaters were typical rendezvous places for secret agents. Unless he had had a sudden urge to go and see a movie at such a crucial moment in history: "Well, I just killed the President of the United States and a cop but I am in the mood to watch a movie!"

The few spectators who were in the Texas Theater on that afternoon described Oswald's behavior as strange: he constantly changed seats as if he were looking for his contact in the dark room. Was it Jack Ruby who lived in an apartment not far from the scene where Tippit was killed. John Martino, partner of Mafia godfathers, Carlos Marcello and Santo Trafficante, told a friend that "*Oswald was scheduled to meet his contact at the Texas Theater. He had to be met there to arrange his escape out of the country*".[239]

Why would the murderer of the President of the United States have decided to seek refuge in a public place like the movie theater? The logical reaction of a killer would have been to leave

---

[239] Lamar Waldron, The Hidden History of the JFK Assassination, Counter Point Berkeley, 2013

the crime scene, to flee far away, and, as quickly and as discreetly as possible, to find a hideout for at least one week in order to avoid being seen in public. But, although he behaved like a solitary assassin, Oswald's plan must have been to reach out an accomplice. This was the most likely reason why he went to the movie theater, a dark place where he would decide his next movements. Without this explanation, Oswald's conditions of arrest in a movie theater are difficult to understand, just one hour after the assassination of the President of the United States, not far from the place where police officer Tippit was shot.

The police search had been based on the mere physical description of the suspect as given by the eyewitnesses on Dealey Plaza. This was a general and approximate search that could have corresponded to the description of thousands of any individuals. The official version concluded that Oswald was the murderer, who had no accomplice and because he had panicked, he had decided to seek refuge in a movie theater to escape the police.

Oswald's only crime, according to the movie theater cashier who called the police, was that he had sneaked into the cinema without paying for a ticket. The cashier's booth was situated at the entrance on the sidewalk. For such a minor offense, how can we explain the disproportionate reaction and the rapid intervention of the police followed by the media? Very shortly after the cashier's call, there were no less than ten police patrol cars and two dozen police officers sent to the theater to arrest Oswald. It would seem somewhat an extreme reaction for the sole reason that Oswald had not bought an entrance ticket! Or, was it because he was already being hunted by those who wanted to pin the double murder on him according to a scenario planned in advance? Some researchers believe the plan was to seal Oswald's fate forever, to kill him in the movie theater while he was trying to escape or fire at the police officers but this scenario failed because Oswald showed no resistance to his arrest.

The Texas Theater where Oswald was arrested by the police (author's photo taken in 1978)

Oswald could not have killed police officer J. D. Tippit, a murder for which he was charged. According to Jesse Ventura, Oswald, in this case too, had neither the motive nor the means nor the opportunity. The police officer was killed in the Oak Cliff suburb of Dallas, 40 minutes after the assassination of the President.

The government version quickly concluded that Oswald had shot Tippit, and later sought refuge in a nearby movie theater. According to the eyewitnesses, Tippit's police car was moving very slowly. As he was approaching a man walking on the sidewalk, Tippit lowered the passenger window in order to talk to him. But instead of being on his guard, of ordering the man to "freeze", the police officer began a brief discussion with the suspect who, at this moment, came towards the car and leaned on the door. The eyewitnesses described the short conversation between the two men as friendly. They concluded that they must have known each other. But then Tippit got out of his car and, as he was about to draw his gun, was shot by the suspect who had by this time hustled past the front of the car. One of the eyewitnesses, Jack Tatum, testified before the House Select Committee on Assassinations that he saw the suspect fire at the police officer twice. Then he deliberately took the time to fire a final shot at close range in the head. The House Select Committee on Assassinations estimated that the murderer had inflicted a real coup de grace, expected only by an experienced killer.

The exact chronology of the Oak Cliff's crime at this point is paramount for proving Oswald's innocence. After the presidential limousine had rushed to Parkland Hospital, Oswald left his work at the Texas School Book Depository and returned to his rented room to collect some belongings. The Warren Commission adhered to his landlady's testimony: Earline Roberts, who was watching the events on television, was formal about the exact time – around 1:00 pm - when she saw Oswald come home. She said that she saw a police car with two police officers in uniform stopping in front of her house while Oswald was in his room. The car hooted twice before leaving. At 1:04pm when he left the house, she saw him go to the bus stop nearby.

According to eyewitnesses, agent Tippit was shot between 1:06 and 1:10pm. It was logistically impossible for Oswald to walk in just 2 to 6 minutes the distance of a mile between his rented room and the scene of Tippit's murder. Even if he had taken a taxi or a bus, the timing would not fit. Some investigators, however, thought that the police car, as seen by Mrs. Roberts in front of her house, might have picked up Oswald, a little further down the road, and that the two hoots on the horn could have been a signal to Oswald[240]. According to Jim Maars, writer and former journalist, the Warren Commission admitted its failure to find a single eyewitness who saw Oswald walk or run between his rented room and the spot where Tippit was shot.

How did the Warren Commission respond to this challenge? It simply changed the chronology of the facts by changing the timing of Tippit's murder, later, to 1:16 pm! [241] In addition, an eyewitness at the crime scene, Acquilla Clemons, was "intimidated" by the Dallas police who decided to ignore her testimony because she had mentioned that Tippit had been assaulted by two men - one of whom was "small and chunky[242].

---

[240] Jim Garrison; On the Trail of the Assassin: My Investigation and Prosecution of the Murder of President Kennedy (Sheridan square 1988).

[241] Richard Belzer & David Wayne, Hit List, MJF Books New York, 2013, p 8

[242] John Simkin; Acquilla Clemons: Biography. Spartacus Educational, 30 Sept 2012

Once again, the incriminating evidence - motive and opportunity - for the murder of the police officer by Oswald did not seem to fit but did he have the means to commit the crime? For government investigators, it was a huge problem to prove that Oswald's weapon was the firearm that killed Tippit. Bullets from two different weapons were found on the crime scene. According to a police sergeant and a former U.S. Marine, an expert in combat weapons, Officer Tippit was killed by three bullets, two of them fired from an automatic weapon. Four gunshots in all had been fired according to the ejected cartridge cases found on the ground. Oswald had a Smith and Wesson Special *revolver* of 0.38 caliber, the one he fetched from his landlady's house before going to the Texas Theater.[243] This important point was confirmed by the famous prosecutor and investigator, Jim Garrison. Revolvers do not eject bullet casings, they are dislodged from the barrel. The police, who arrested Oswald in the movie theater, told the Warren Commission that his gun contained six unused bullets in the barrel.[244] How could Oswald have fired four gunshots with a revolver that remained fully loaded during his arrest…. unless he had extra bullets on him to reload his weapon prior to his arrest by the police?

All in all, the Warren Commission and even the House Select Committee on Assassinations concluded that Oswald had killed Tippit but it seems very unlikely. Oswald did not have enough time to get from his rented room to the crime scene and then to the movie theater. Oswald did not fit the physical descriptions of the Tippit's killer provided by the eyewitnesses. There was no evidence that Oswald's weapon had fired that day. The trap inexorably fell on Oswald and the desire to pin this second murder on him was another nail sealing the lid of his coffin.

CIA agent, John Martino, who had connections with the Mafia and Johnny Roselli, was in charge of clandestine anti-Castro

---

[243] Michael T.Griffith; "Did Oswald Shoot Tippit?" A review of Dale Myer's book "With Malice: Lee Harvey Oswald and the Murder of Officer J.D.Tippit" 2002.
[244] Gary Fannin, The Innocence of Oswald, 2015

operations in Florida. He was aware of the plan reserved for Oswald: to pose him as a pro-Castro agent and to use him as a patsy for the JFK assassination. Near the end of his life, Martino made the following confession: *"The anti-Castro people put Oswald together. Oswald didn't know who he was working for; he was just ignorant of who was really putting him together. Oswald was to meet his contact at the Texas Theater. They were to meet Oswald in the theater, and get him out of the country, then eliminate him. Oswald made a mistake...There was no way we could get to him. They had Ruby kill him."* Before dying, Martino confessed his complicity in the assassination of John Kennedy to his wife: the provision of funds, his role as messenger and other collaborative activities[245].

The plan was that Oswald would not leave the Texas School Book Depository or the Texas Theater alive. But his elimination must have failed in the immediate hours following the murders of John Kennedy and Agent Tippit and his arrest at the Texas Theater. The police ended up with an inconvenient suspect who was likely to prove his innocence if he was granted a defense lawyer. The physiological assessment of stress in Oswald's voice concluded that he was telling the truth when he said he had killed no one. The conspirators had everything to gain by eliminating Oswald before he finger pointed anyone in a plot against the President[246].

Oswald was determined to play a role in U.S. intelligence and found himself strongly involve with the CIA. As the next chapter will cover in details, Oswald was under surveillance by the CIA and the FBI in the fall of 1963 and the run-up to the assassination. Both agencies however concealed what they knew about Oswald prior to the JFK assassination from the Warren Commission. The CIA also concealed from the commission the plots to assassinate Fidel Castro during Kennedy's administration, which the Cuban dictator himself had uncovered.

---

[245] Larry Hancock. Someone Would Have Talked (JFK Lancer 2010), jfkfacts.org. The Mary Ferrell Foundation

[246] Robert J. Groden, The Killing of a President, Vicking Studio Books, 1993

The FBI destroyed the evidence of a note written by Oswald - no doubt a threat - that he had given to the local FBI office in Dallas in early November 1963. The note was intended for FBI agent James Hosty Jr. Two hours after Ruby had shot Oswald, Dallas FBI Chief Gordon Shanklin ordered Hosty to destroy Oswald's note before it fell into the hands of the Warren Commission. Hosty took care of it; he tore it up and flushed it down the toilet.

The nature of Oswald's threat to the FBI and the exact words of the note would not be known for at least the next twelve years. Agent Hosty had kept Oswald and his wife Marina under constant surveillance. Oswald probably wanted to give Hosty a strong message to stop stalking them. In October 1975, an FBI statement more or less confirmed it, three months after a press leak. According to the FBI, Oswald's note said: "*Let it be a warning. I'll blow up the FBI and the Dallas Police Department if you do not stop bothering my wife.*"

It is strange that Oswald's note was kept secret for 12 years. What could have been the reason for the FBI to destroy it once Oswald was eliminated? The FBI explained the note destruction for fear that it would be interpreted as evidence that the Bureau knew of Oswald's threat to the President, ten days before his assassination. Some researchers believe that the FBI's interpretation was wrong; instead, they assume the note could have contained information about Oswald's awareness of a plot to kill the President.[247] Others believe that the order to destroy a secret note of such vital importance came from much higher up the FBI chain of command; probably from the director himself, J. Edgar Hoover, to whom Gordon Shanklin and James Hosty Jr. reported[248].

---

[247] Ibid

[248] James W. Douglass, JFK and the Unspeakable, Why He Died and Why it Matters, A Touchstone Book, 2008

At the Pittsburgh Convention, on the 50th anniversary of JFK assassination, the speaker, Walt Brown, answered a question about Oswald's exact role: was he manipulated by U.S. intelligence? Why did he claim his innocence and strongly believe he was a patsy during his arrest? According to Brown - his theory needs to be crosschecked - those who manipulated Oswald wanted him to believe that the plot against JFK would be a bogus attack and no more than a pretense to fire shots at him with the intention to "miss" the target! The Dallas plan was to then implicate Fidel Castro as being behind the assassination attempt. Having escaped a Cuban assassination plot, John Kennedy would then have had no choice than to invade Cuba and have the Cuban dictator deposed; an act of reprisal that the American government and people would have expected from the President. They convinced Oswald that he was elected to be the one to fire "missed" shots at the President. To make this plan credible, Brown believes that a Mannlicher Carcano rifle was purchased by correspondence under the name of Alex Hidell and background checked to Oswald.

The purchase of a rifle by correspondence was indeed very strange. Oswald could have easily bought a more precise weapon from any Dallas gun store with cash, without any background check and without traces of a purchase receipt. Instead, the mail order left evidence of the purchase from a Chicago firearms seller. The rifle would then be found at the schoolbook depository and easily tracked to Oswald who would then be framed as an anti-Cuban fanatic. All in all, according to this scenario, Oswald would have become a real hero as the man who facilitated the invasion of Cuba and the elimination of Fidel Castro.

Brown thinks Oswald did not believe this bogus plan for long. Whether he fired the "missed" shots himself or not, he must have panicked as soon as he realized that several other shots had been fired at the limousine and that the President was seriously wounded. Fearful for his life, he left the Texas School Book Depository and returned to his rented room in order to fetch his revolver and take refuge in a movie theater.

Hopefully, by now, my readers have reached the conclusion that Oswald could not have been the lone gunman, without an accomplice. What's more, the Secret Service of the Navy had the same opinion: *"Oswald could not be the shooter because he was incapable of being the mastermind of an assassination or of having himself executed it"*.

The scenario of a Mafia complicity, "in bed" with the CIA using Oswald to assassinate JFK, will be covered in a following chapter. The theory of Oswald's recruitment by the Organized Crime to be the sole person to kill the President and its help in getting him out of the country is, however, unconvincing without help from the CIA. After decades of experience in professionally executed crimes, the Mafia would not have recruited someone like Oswald and let such an inexperienced man escape by public transport after a murder of this magnitude...[249]. Unless the CIA and the Mafia wanted Oswald to be the scapegoat and therefore seal his fate.

Lee Harvey Oswald however was not the only scapegoat in this affair. Oswald's trap also had a ripple effect for the Soviet Union. The Soviets were indirectly implicated in a false accusation of having orchestrated the assassination plot. Author, James Douglass, relates the facts[250]. As Khrushchev became Kennedy's secret partner for lasting peace, an odious Cold War propaganda plan was shaped in order to make the Soviet Union into a major scapegoat. U.S. government propaganda conveyed the idea that the Soviet Union had plotted the assassination of President Kennedy with communist Lee Harvey Oswald's help. On November 18, 1963, the Soviet Embassy in Washington received a poorly typed letter full of grammatical errors. It was dated nine days earlier, came from Dallas and was signed "Lee H. Oswald". The letter mentioned Oswald's recent meetings at the Soviet Embassy in Mexico City with Valery Vladimirovirovich Kostikov, the KGB director for political killings in the Western Hemisphere.

---

[249] Lamar Waldron, The Hidden History of the JFK Assassination, Counter Point Berkeley, 2013

[250] James W. Douglass, JFK and the Unspeakable, Why He Died and Why it Matters, A Touchstone Book, 2008

The propaganda set up at the Soviet Embassy in Washington, four days before Kennedy's assassination, had, like a bombshell, immediate repercussions in Dallas.

It took until 1999 for the letter incriminating the Soviet Union for its alleged links with Oswald to be revealed to the American people! As with any mail sent to the Soviet embassy, the FBI intercepted the letter and made a copy. On November 23, 1963, FBI Director J. Edgar Hoover spoke on the phone with the new President, Lyndon Johnson, about the significance of "Oswald's letter". This was the same phone call in which Hoover presented to Johnson the evidence discovered by the FBI: either a possible Russo-Cuban plot with Oswald's complicity in killing the President, or, more likely, the impersonation of Oswald by the CIA to implicate him in the plot. As soon as Lee Harvey Oswald was arrested in Dallas and charged with assassinating the President, senior Soviet officials became aware that "Oswald's letter" that arrived four days earlier, had set a trap. The Soviets sent a response that would be part of the highly confidential documents kept for many decades by the Soviets about the assassination of John Kennedy.

By the end of the twentieth century and indeed after the collapse of the Soviet Union, their response was finally revealed. Against all odds, it was handed over to President Bill Clinton by the very first President of the Russian Federation, Boris Yetsin, during their meeting in Germany. In June 1999, this document revealed the following details. Four days after the JFK assassination, the Soviet ambassador to Washington, Anatoly Dobrynin, sent a top secret and high priority telegram to Moscow in response to the U.S. government's insinuations about the Soviet Union's involvement in the assassination plot with Oswald's complicity. Drobynin wrote to Moscow the following: *"This letter was clearly a provocation: It gives the impression we had close ties with Oswald and were using him for some purposes of our own. It was totally unlike any other letters the embassy had previously received from Oswald. Nor had he ever visited our embassy himself. The suspicion that the letter is a forgery is heightened by the fact that it was typed, whereas the other letters the embassy had received from Oswald before were handwritten....One gets the definite impression that the letter was concocted by those who, judging from everything, are involved in the president's assassination... The competent U.S. authorities are of course aware of this letter since all correspondence arriving at our embassy is under constant surveillance on their part. However, they do not refer to it at this time, nor do they ask for information about Oswald at our embassy. Maybe they are waiting for another time to do it?"*

President Johnson would later decide to reject the CIA's "Mexico proof" of a Soviet conspiracy as well. He was mindful of what the revelation of a communist plot to assassinate President Kennedy would have provoked such as pressures for the U.S. to enter into a war against the Soviet Union. In his phone call with Senator Richard Russell, member of the Warren Commission, Johnson confirmed this : *"We need to take this issue [Kennedy's assassination] out of this context [Mexico] ... They say that Khrushchev and Castro did this or did that but all this will lead to a war that will cost the lives of forty million Americans in one hour"*[251].

There are grounds to believe the CIA was trying to feign that Oswald was linked to a communist country, Cuba or the Soviet Union, in order to accuse their leaders of killing John Kennedy. If such a Machiavellian plan of propaganda existed, one can only suspect (for it cannot be proved without a shadow of a doubt) that the CIA – at least some "rogue" agents - hid their direct complicity in the murder. There are also reasons to believe that other accomplices have helped: the FBI - especially in the cover-up - the anti-Castro exiles, and the Mafia. All saw Kennedy as a traitor since the fiasco of the Bay of Pigs and the U.S. rapprochement with Fidel Castro. They all sought to find a way to remove the obstacle to an invasion of Cuba in order to claim back their assets or interests that had been confiscated by the Cuban dictator.

---

[251] James W. Douglass, JFK and the Unspeakable, Why He Died and Why it Matters, A Touchstone Book, 2008

Chapter 7

The Murky Role of the CIA, the FBI and the Anti-Castro

On December 22, 1963, former President Harry Truman published a carefully written article in the Washington Post warning the American people of the dangers of the CIA including a possible takeover of the government by the Agency. Truman wanted his article to be published in the Washington Post for maximum impact in the capital and for a symbolic purpose, just one month after the assassination of John Kennedy.

Despite the fact that he was the founder of the Agency, Truman did not connect the assassination plot to the CIA but the timing of the publication and of his criticism took an accusatory look at the abuse that the Agency had allowed itself. He wrote this: *"I think it has become necessary to take another look at the purpose and operations of our Central Intelligence Agency – CIA… For some time I have been disturbed by the way the CIA has been diverted from its original assignment. It has become an operational and at times a policy-making arm of the Government. This has led to trouble and may have compounded our difficulties in several explosive areas… This quiet intelligence arm of the President has been so removed from its intended role that it is being interpreted as a symbol of sinister and mysterious foreign intrigue – and a subject for cold war enemy propaganda. We have grown up as a nation, respected for our free institutions and for our ability to maintain a free and open society. There is something about the* way the CIA has been functioning that is casting a shadow over our historic position and I feel that we need to correct it"[252].

Clearly, Truman said "that he had created a 'monster' ", that the timing of the assassination of John Kennedy had exhorted him to ask for the abolition of the CIA or, at least, to the limitation of its role.

This warning fell on deaf ears and met with into total indifference. No other media outlet related Truman's opinion, even during a time when there was exceptional media activity following the assassination of John Kennedy.

The CIA put pressure on Truman and expected him to retract his embarrassing accusation. His article was trivialized and the behavior of its old author was considered to be a moment of senile distraction. Allen Dulles, who had been dismissed by Kennedy as CIA director, became alarmed by the possible ripple effects of Truman's warning. On April 17, 1964, Dulles temporarily suspended his functions at the Warren Commission in order to meet Truman. During the interview, Dulles urged him to revise his position and rethink his critical statement about the CIA.

Dulles manipulated the outcome of the interview to suit his own agenda. On April 21, he sent a confidential memorandum to his long-time CIA colleague, Attorney General Lawrence Houston. Dulles insinuated that Truman had disavowed the article published under his name because it did not reflect his opinion. Dulles went as far as to write that Truman *"seemed quite astonished"* by what the Washington Post had written about his intention to ever make such comments about the CIA. The former chief of the CIA also claimed that Truman had told him that all this was very wrong and that he must have made an unfortunate impression. Dulles revealed his well-known immorality when he said: "*At no time did Mr. Truman express other than complete agreement with the viewpoint I expressed and several times said he would see what he could do about it, to leave it in his hands. He obviously was highly disturbed at the Washington Post article.*"

---

[252] http://jfkfacts.org/tag/washington-post/

But former President Truman's historical writings rehabilitated him. Despite Dulles' lies, Truman's handwritten words were found in a document at the Truman Library in Independence, Missouri, on December 1, 1963, three weeks before the publication of his article in the Washington Post. His note fully justified his criticisms of the CIA; without ambiguity: "*The CIA was intended merely as a center for keeping the President informed on what was going on in the world at large and the United States and its dependencies in particular. It should not be an agency to initiate policy or to act as a spy organization. That was never the intention when it was organized.*"

Truman ignored Dulles' pressure. Six months after the publication of his article in the Washington Post, he continued to assert his critical view of the CIA in a letter that he sent to the editor-in-chief of Look magazine following the publishing of an article about the CIA. "*Thank you for the copy of Look with the article on the Central Intelligence Agency. It is, I regret to say, not true to the facts in many respects. The CIA was set up by me, for the sole purpose of getting all the available information to the President. It was not intended to operate as an international agency engaged in strange activities*" [253].

At the end of the 1940s, Truman had indeed advocated the creation of two agencies, the Centre Intelligence Agency and the National Security Agency. However, as Eisenhower and Kennedy saw it, Truman was discouraged by the vast power of the American intelligence networks that very soon became out of control. These agencies were supposed to assist the presidents, not to threaten the executive or the democratic process[254]. It was a strong and cruel message informing the American people that this hidden power had become very evident and that had influence and dominance over any elected president.

---

[253] James W. Douglass, JFK and the Unspeakable, Why He Died and Why it Matters, A Touchstone Book, 2008

[254] Andrew Kreig.
http://www.justiceintegrity.org/index.php?option=com_content&view=article&id=599:jfk-s-murder-the-cia-8-things-every-american-should-know&catid=21:myblog&itemid=114

Decades went by. The history books – in so far as they cover the fateful events perpetrated by the CIA - are forgotten. The younger generation most likely remains in the dark and ignorant of the facts. What Harry Truman created (the CIA), especially under Allen Dulles' leadership, had turned into a ruthless machine of political assassinations in a world, where American interests prevail. Leaders, politicians, trade unionists, journalists, all those with subversive ideas or actions who fought the U.S. democratic model, were directly or indirectly eliminated, with the involvement of the CIA.

The clandestine methods of the CIA have been well documented by historians and U.S. congressional committees. Although the Agency was careful that it was not caught in the front line, it indirectly gave support to local coups by providing the necessary logistical and financial assistance to the insurgents. To varying degrees, the CIA was involved in no less than thirty-five assassination attempts against foreign heads of state or prominent political leaders. Among the "inconvenient" leaders or rulers hostile to America who were assassinated with the help of the CIA were General Rene Schneider – he was the obstacle in the overthrowing of President Salvador Allende, the democratically elected leader in Chile; Patrice Lumumba in the Belgian Congo - the CIA supported the Belgian military forces; Rafael Trujillo of the Dominican Republic, President Ngo Dinh Diem of South Vietnam and the charismatic revolutionary Che Guevara. The CIA with the help of Cuban exiles also participated in multiple assassination attempts against Fidel Castro. All these attempts failed despite the plotters' ingenuity and creative strategies worthy of James Bond's best exploits. Most certainly it is an irony of history that the Cuban dictator was, according to a Cuban intelligence officer, the object of hundreds of failed assassination attempts and yet his life was spared by providential luck and his demise finally came as he was sleeping in his bed, 60 years after the revolution he had launched in Cuba!

During the second half of the twentieth century, there were many military coups to overthrow democratic governments and to replace them by brutal dictatorships. These coups were fomented by national insurgents and were clandestinely backed by the CIA in order to ensure a wider U.S. supremacy in the world or where U.S. interests were threatened. The list is not exhaustive: Mosaddeq in Iran in 1953, Arbenz in Guatemala in 1954, Velasco and Arosemena in Ecuador in 1961 and 1963, Bosch in the Dominican Republic in 1963, Goulart in Brazil in 1964, Sukarno in Indonesia in 1965, Papandreou in Greece in 1965-67, Allende in Chile in 1973 ... The CIA gave support to dictators such as General Pinochet in Chile, Muhammad Riza Pahlevi, the Shah of Iran; Ferdinand Marcos in the Philippines; "Papa Doc" and "Baby Doc" Duvalier in Haiti; General Noriega in Panama; Mobutu Sese Seko in Zaire and the Greek Junta of the Colonels[255]. These external overthrows encouraged by the CIA took place principally during the administration of Eisenhower and of his vice-president Richard Nixon, and were committed with the apathy of the American people and of Congress preferring to "look the other way"...

John Kennedy chose to oppose this hidden power and vetoed belligerent proposals by his military advisers that urged him to retaliate to the Soviet and Cuban threats. He paid a high price for this.

We can only speculate at this point that the elimination of a President, this time on home soil, would seemingly not be a problem for Allan Dulles encouraged by successful political assassinations abroad. All that he had to do was to order his team of henchmen to terminate Kennedy's presidency and consequentially to avoid his re-election in 1964.

Let us not forget what this terrible and appalling act was: the assassination of a very popular president, in broad daylight, in front of his people; the taking of the life of such a great statesman by blowing his brains out with a well-controlled projectile; the horror in the limousine in which his wife, stained with blood and brain matter, would be forever traumatized. It was an

---

[255] Jesse Ventura – They Killed Our President – 2013. Skyhorse Publishing

unspeakable act of extreme violence, not only for the President, his wife, and his family, but also for the American democracy.

The American journalist, David Talbot, interviewed a large number of friends and relatives of the Kennedy family.[256] After ten years of investigation, Talbot is alarmist: a "secret government", "the Deep State", exists in the United-States. These are groups of people who are not usual elected officials but powerful Wall Street actors or influential mega-corporates members who are found principally in the ranks of the National Security Service in Washington. These individuals maintain their power from one presidential administration to another and are members of the same social clubs and organizations. They are called the "American Elite". By the time this elite became aware of the need to eliminate President Kennedy, Allen Dulles became the pivotal promoter of this hidden power. As a former Wall Street lawyer, he was one of the founders of the modern CIA. His tenure was one of the longest ever in the Agency having "served" under both the Eisenhower and Kennedy administrations. In his book *Brothers*[257], Talbot recalls the CIA's relentless search for potential use of nuclear weapons as a means of resolving endless wars. The world came to the brink of a major nuclear confrontation during the Cold War. Long before the Cuban Missiles Crisis in 1962, Allen Dulles' brother, John Foster Dulles, as Secretary of State under Eisenhower, advocated the use of nuclear weapon against the Vietnamese, while the French were bogged down in their colonial war.

In the first days of his term, in 1961, the young President, still inexperienced, learned that the CIA had fomented, behind his back, a hidden plan to invade Cuba in order to get rid of Fidel Castro; this was the Bay of Pigs invasion. This plan had been prepared by the CIA, prior to John Kennedy's presidential inauguration, under the previous administration of President Eisenhower and his Vice President Richard Nixon. Although he accepted his accountability for this failure, JFK was furious for

---

[256] Interview of David Talbot by Jacob M. Carter – 2015 – Before History Dies.
[257] David Talbot – Brothers, The Hidden History of the Kennedy Years - 2007

having been manipulated and for his lack of lucidity to backtrack before he agreed to the invasion. In the company of Senator Mike Mansfield, he expressed his anger and threatened to *"splinter the CIA into a thousand pieces and scatter it to the winds"*[258].

Allen Dulles was fired by Kennedy shortly after the Bay of Pigs fiasco. Kennedy also sacked General Charles Cabell, the CIA Deputy Director, who had been the main architect of the invasion attempt. The President also implemented a cut in the CIA budget in 1962 and again in 1963 with the objective of achieving a 20% budget cut by 1966. At the time of the Kennedy assassination, the mayor of Dallas, was no less than Charles Cabell's brother, Earl. Some saw his complicity and his vengeance through his lack of control of the Dallas police which possibly facilitated the arrest of the alleged murderer, Lee Harvey Oswald.

Allen Dulles remained powerful after his dismissal. He continued to act, underground, on behalf of the CIA. Some CIA agents - James Angleton in particular - remained loyal to him, notably to ensure the cover-up of the assassination. They met frequently at his home in Georgetown, or in clubs and restaurants in the capital. Allen Dulles' animosity towards the President was known to his family and friends. He once said these scornful words when the assistant editor of the Harper magazine, Willie Morris, met him: *"That little Kennedy ... he thought he was a God"*[259].

When the Warren Commission was created to investigate the assassination of John Kennedy, under the direct orders of President Johnson, Allen Dulles was nominated as one of the seven members of the Commission. He was most committed, hardly ever missing a session. While he completed his career at the head of the CIA in 1962, his political exile was very short lived. No one from the mainstream press commented on the remarkable irony that a bitter CIA director was entrusted with the supervision of the investigation into the assassination of the man who had fired him! Dulles repeatedly violated the oath of

---

[258] Ibid

[259] James W. Douglass, JFK and the Unspeakable, Why He Died and Why it Matters, A Touchstone Book, 2008

confidentiality of the Warren Commission. He would systematically inform the CIA of secret developments, internal to the investigation of the Warren Commission. His service at the Commission was a real comeback. Despite the fact he was no longer on the CIA payroll, he continued to act as a true undercover agent by secretly disclosing information to James Angleton at the CIA[260].

According to Talbot, there was a team of killers on Dealey Plaza under CIA orders. The agency knew how to eliminate "embarrassing" heads of state or political enemies having been for years behind so many sinister plots. The assassination of Kennedy was just another contract...

Some of these plots had nevertheless been aborted, such as the attempted *putsch* against President Charles de Gaulle in 1961. Even without President Kennedy's consent, Allen Dulles and his henchmen supported the far-right French generals in their attempt to overthrow President de Gaulle because of his position on the independence of Algeria and of his policy of distrust towards the United-States. Dulles feared that Algeria, once independent, would fall into the hands of the Communists, thus allowing Soviet bases to be set up in Africa. The CIA was indirectly implicated in a plot against de Gaulle. One of the explanations for the failure was that the coup had been foiled thanks to Kennedy's personal intervention. The American President sent his French-speaking Press Secretary, Pierre Salinger, to Paris to explain to de Gaulle that Kennedy had not been involved in any way in the coup attempt. De Gaulle replied that he understood but asked Salinger to remind Kennedy that his control of his intelligence service was one of his biggest problems. Unlike the French President who survived many assassination attempts in the 1960s, Kennedy was less fortunate. His life was taken by professional killers who staged a very well orchestrated conspiracy against their victim and who made sure they would not miss their target.

---

[260] David Talbot – Brothers, The Hidden History of the Kennedy Years - 2007

David Talbot goes on to explain that the assassination of Kennedy was probably the result of a conspiracy involving elements of the CIA, the Mafia and anti-Kennedy Cuban exiles; the plot was to kill Fidel Castro but was changed from its original purpose to attempt to the U.S. President's life. This was what Robert Kennedy suspected immediately during the afternoon of November 22, 1963.[261] The plotters engineered a bogus scenario: the assassination attempts against Castro would continue... but a real conspiracy against JFK would be engaged. This explains why Robert Kennedy personally felt responsible for the assassination of his brother due to his support of - perhaps with some naiveté - the Cuban exiles' actions against Castro.[262] Bobby Kennedy's first reaction to the announcement of his brother's death was to immediately call CIA Director John McCone. He shouted, "*Did you kill my brother?*"[263] Later on, he confided to Arthur Schlesinger, a historian close to the Kennedys, that he had furiously raised the question in such a way that the director could not lie to him. McCone did not have too many doubts: two shooters were on Dealey Plaza but he did not believe that the U.S. intelligence agency had anything to do with it. Robert Kennedy then called his contact of the anti-Castro group in Florida and said flatly, in perfect control of his emotions: "*One of your guys did it?*"[264]

Robert Kennedy had the stature, the experience and the knowledge to carry out his own investigation into the Dallas assassination: he had served in the Ministry of Justice, had lead a long crusade, with his brother, to dismantle the network of the Organized Crime in America and had closely monitored the actions of the CIA. Aware of the possible immorality of American power, he knew he could find out who was behind the assassination of his brother. He immediately suspected the CIA

---

[261] David Talbot. "Case Closed? A new book about the JFK assassination claims to finally solve the mystery" December 2005.

[262] Debra Conway, "US-Cuba Relations: Castro Assassinations Plots" November 2007

[263] Waldron Lamar & Thom Hartmann. Ultimate Sacrifice

[264] Richard Mahoney. The Kennedy Brothers: The Rise and the Fall of Jack and Bobby (Skyhorse Publishing): 2011

for its anti-Castro operations jointly conducted with the Mafia. Long before John Kennedy's presidential election, President Eisenhower and Allen Dulles were aware of this alliance. These anti-Castro operations remained active under the JFK presidency without his knowledge. The joint CIA / Mafia plan to assassinate Fidel Castro was also hidden from Bobby Kennedy when he was Chief Counsel of the Senate Rackets Committee. The CIA finally unveiled this plan in 1962 and reassured Bobby Kennedy that these actions had been terminated... which was the opposite of what happened.

In early 1964, Robert Kennedy contacted one last time the exiled Cuban intelligence team in Miami who worked for the CIA. At the time of the death of his brother, one of them, Angelo Murgado, had expressed his sadness, his dismay and the frustration of his companions over their failed mission to topple Castro. Murgado told Bobby Kennedy, in graphic language, that it was the group's conviction that the assassination had been carried out by their employee: the CIA. *"When that happened, we sh** in our pants...We sit down and we talked. Who the hell is behind all this? We knew that the plot could come from only one source – the CIA. My God, we've been used like toilet paper. The whole infrastructure, the logistics – it was the CIA. We all believed the same thing. It was a highly sophisticated operation. Look, they were so good at it that, even today, nobody knows exactly what happened. There's only one enterprise that can pull off sh** like that. It was the CIA, but not alone. It was the CIA plus something higher"*[265].

Just before Robert Kennedy's assassination in Los Angeles, during the California primaries in 1968 for the presidential election, he entrusted the journalist, Pete Hamill, with the dilemma that haunted him as to how, if elected, he would treat the CIA: *"I have to decide whether to eliminate the operational arm of the agency or what the hell to do with it? We can't have these cowboys*

---

[265] David Talbot – Brothers, The Hidden History of the Kennedy Years - 2007

wandering around and shooting people and doing all these unauthorized things" [266].

CIA conspiracies, aided by the Mafia, to kill Fidel Castro, had failed but their plan deviated from the original goal turning against John Kennedy. The CIA then concealed the facts surrounding Lee Harvey Oswald, whom the Agency had enlisted four years earlier starting with his deportation to the Soviet Union during the Cold War. The "Lone Nuts" only see allegations for this version but serious testimonies exist as recalled by the former governor of Minnesota, Jesse Ventura [267] and other authors and journalists. According to a declassified cable from the CIA dated October 10, 1963[268] (seven weeks before Kennedy's assassination), at least six senior CIA officials knew everything about Oswald: his political orientation, his travels and his contacts abroad[269].

CIA Director John McCone and Bobby Kennedy feared that the assassination attempts against Fidel Castro that were fomented behind the President's back had turned against him. At a meeting with the new president Lyndon Johnson, McCone gave him a dispatch from the U.S. Embassy in Mexico City, claiming that Castro was behind Kennedy's assassination[270]. Three days later, the CIA head of Mexico City branch, Winston Scott, and FBI attorney general Clark Anderson, put forward with a lot of fuss some wild allegations that Oswald's act had been plotted from within the Cuban embassy. Thanks to his investigation, the District Attorney of New Orleans, Jim Garrison had no doubt in his mind: the assassination of Kennedy was the result of a well-organized plot, fomented in New Orleans by individuals linked to the CIA. After the assassination, the CIA endeavored to hide the plot in order to protect the Agency. According to Garrison, the assassination sponsors were CIA "rogue" employees who were angry at President Kennedy for his hesitant position that

---

[266] Ibid

[267] Jesse Ventura – They Killed Our President – 2013. Skyhorse Publishing

[268] http://www.maryferrell.org/showDoc.html?docId=1565#relPageId=2&tab=page

[269] http://jfkfacts.org/faith-overwhelms-facts-aps-un-journalism-on-jfks-assassination

[270] Scott: The CIA, the Drug Traffic and Oswald in Mexico. 1999.

had resulted in the Bay of Pigs fiasco.[271] Author Donald E. Wilkes Jr. summarized Garrison's conclusions in his book: a New Orleans-based anti-Castro group, supported by the CIA - itself involved in covert operations against Castro - plotted the assassination of President Kennedy with the Agency in the late summer or early fall of 1963. According to Garrison, the plotters included Clay Shaw (an influential businessman in New Orleans also linked to the CIA), David Ferrie (a mysterious paramilitary who was a pilot transporting the anti-Castro and the Mafia during their operations), Lee Harvey Oswald, some Cuban exiles and anti-Castro Americans. Their plot reached its conclusion in Dallas on November 22, 1963. It was Kennedy's decision not to authorize an air raid at the Bay of Pigs and his political position for a détente with Cuba after the Cuban Missile Crisis in 1962 that triggered their motive and action. For Garrison, there was no doubt and he told the press: *"President Kennedy was killed for one reason. Because he was working for reconciliation with the Soviet Union and Castro's Cuba... President Kennedy dies because he wanted peace."* He also declared in 1968: *"In a very real and terrifying sense, our government is the CIA and the Pentagon, with Congress reduced to a debating society. I've learned enough about the machinations of the CIA in the past year to know that this is no longer the dream world America I once believed in...I've always had a kind of knee-jerk trust in my government's basic integrity, whatever political blunders it may make. But I've come to realize that in Washington, deceiving and manipulating the public are viewed by some as the national prerogatives of office. Huey Long* [Governor of Louisiana assassinated in 1935] *once said, 'Fascism will come to America in the name of anti-fascism'. I'm afraid, based on my experience that fascism will come to America in the name of national security"*[272].

It was in 1975, during the U.S. Senate hearings chaired by Senator Frank Church, that senior CIA officials reluctantly admitted to having attempted to assassinate Fidel Castro.

---

[271] Donald E. Wilkes Jr, Professor of Law. "Destiny Betrayed: the CIA, Oswald and the JFK Assassination. December 7, 2005

[272] David Talbot – Brothers, The Hidden History of the Kennedy Years - 2007

Already back in 1960, under the leadership of Dwight Eisenhower, they had tried to assassinate Castro and other foreign leaders like Patrice Lumumba in Congo. The code name of this program was ZR / RIFLE. The CIA contacted highly influential Mafia men such as Sam Giancana, John Rosselli and Santos Trafficante and offered them $150,000 for Castro's head. These gangsters were very happy to "join" the U.S. government as a retribution against Castro for having closed down their casinos and brothels in Cuba. In the spring of 1961, unbeknownst to the new appointed President, the CIA's technical department had concocted a batch of poisoned pills to kill the Cuban leader with Rosselli's cooperation.

But this specific attempt to assassinate Castro, planned before the invasion of the Bay of Pigs, failed. John Kennedy's reaction was immediate: he fired Allen Dulles and the CIA Assistant Director, Richard Bissell, for their involvement in the Bay of Pigs invasion. But despite this, Bissell's successor, Richard Helms, strengthened the capacity to eliminate Fidel Castro and the assassination attempts continued. Helms made sure he kept the President and his boss, John McCone in the dark. When he testified before the Church Committee, Helms was asked why he hid the plots from JFK. Helms replied with a straight face: *"Nobody wants to embarrass a President of the United States by discussing the assassination of foreign leaders in his presence"*[273].

Two men were in charge of the CIA's contacts with the Mafia: Robert Maheu, head of a private intelligence firm under contract with the CIA, and William Harvey, assassination operations and counter-espionage specialist at the CIA. David Talbot thinks Harvey was involved in Dallas. This man worked closely with Mafia don, Johnny Rosselli, who was in charge of the diplomatic relationship between the two groups. William Harvey, meanwhile, led the clique of CIA agents implicated in the assassination of Kennedy. According to Jefferson Morley,

---

[273] James W. Douglass, JFK and the Unspeakable, Why He Died and Why it Matters, A Touchstone Book, 2008

moderator of JFKfacts.gov, we will have to wait until the CIA is forced to reveal a 125-page file on Bill Harvey to show his involvement in political assassinations. To date, neither Congress nor journalists have been able to obtain access to this classified document kept in the National Archives.

In 2014, I attended the convention "JFK and the 50th anniversary of the publication of the Warren Report" organized by the Assassination Archives and Research Center in Bethesda, Maryland. Three speakers, Robert Blakey, chairman of the 1977 House Select Committee on Assassinations and two of his associates, Dan Hardway and Edwin Lopez, blamed the CIA for legal obstruction during their investigation.

Hardway and Lopez searched to find the name of the CIA person in liaison with the anti-Castro group who had communicated with Oswald during his visits to New Orleans and Mexico City. They interrogated George Joannides, the man who had made possible the liaison between the House Select Committee on Assassinations and the CIA. Joannides testified under oath before the committee saying he had done some research in vain on who could have been the CIA person liaising with the anti-Castro group and Oswald. However, the investigators eventually found out who the contact was and surprise... it was George Joannides himself! This was blatant evidence of the lies and perjury that the CIA had committed. For Blakey, the cover-up continued and American democracy was defied once again, long after the Dallas crime.

At the Bethesda conference, I learned that the House Select Committee on Assassinations found out that a CIA officer had unlawfully consulted files kept in a safe in the Committee's offices. This safe was intended for keeping sensitive documents such as physical evidence of the JFK assassination, especially photographs of JFK autopsy and x-rays. Nothing had been stolen, but it was obvious that a person unauthorized by Blakey to access to the safe, had consulted the autopsy records of the President's head wounds. The crumpled documents had obviously been very hastily put back in the safe. Through extensive investigations by the committee, the CIA finally admitted that the culprit had been identified and fired. The CIA spokesman, Herbert Hetu, minimized the incident by saying that it was only an act of curiosity and that the Agency was satisfied on this matter. When the committee asked him if it was a conscious act of espionage on the part of the CIA, Hetu exclaimed, "*My God, of course not!*"

The committee had only allowed four people to access the safe, which had to be locked every night. The committee used fingerprint experts. Some prints were found on the photographs but they failed to match those of the committee staff authorized to examine them. They actually belonged to Regis Blahut, a CIA liaison office! This incident caused great concern at the CIA because the Agency had told the committee that known mistakes and domestic espionage had been ceased for several years. Regis Blahut, compelled to take the polygraph test, admitted that they were his fingerprints on the photos but that all this was irrelevant, as he did not want to cause harm! He then made the following cryptic remarks in total incoherence: "*There are other things involved which are prejudicial to other things...*" When asked what he meant, he reminded them of his loyalty to his employer: "*I signed an oath of secrecy* [with the CIA]. *I cannot discuss it any further.*" He failed the polygraph test and when, asked if someone had ordered him to look at the photographs of the safe, he denied it. Finally the incident was dropped because the committee was too anxious to complete its investigation report in time[274].

Jefferson Morley, the founder of JFKfacts.org, had the sad and frustrating experience of suing the CIA for withholding George Joannides' documents. During years of litigation with the CIA, he was hoping to win the case demanding a full release of CIA specific documents detained by the Agency concerning George Joannides. As previously said, despite Joannides lies and the CIA's silence about the name of the anti-Castro contact, the congressional committee found out that Joannides, himself, was the CIA agent directly involved with an influential group of Cuban exiles called DRE (Directorio Revolucionario Estudiantil)

---

[274] George Lardner, File on JFK Assassination was Rifled by CIA Officer, International Herald Tribune, 1978

for which Lee Harvey Oswald was working[275]. In October 2006, Morley's case was rejected: a federal judge asserted the right of the CIA to block the publication of documents about the operations that Joannides had conducted in August 1963[276]. It is still an ongoing trial but Morley does not despair...[277]

Back in early 1961, CIA director Allan Dulles was hopeful that Castro was going to be killed by joint CIA and Mafia operations or that John Kennedy would be forced to send American military forces to retaliate for the "bogus" attack planned against the U.S. military base Guantanamo in Cuba. The Guantanamo project (coded Operation Northwoods, finally rejected) consisted of setting up a pretext by which an act perpetrated by Cuban forces hostile to the USA would look authentic.[278] After the assassination of John Kennedy, and as early as 1965, the plotters hoped, following the demise of Castro, to resume plans to invade Cuba. Priorities however changed and the Cuba plans were suspended due to the massive engagement in Vietnam. With Richard Nixon's presidential election, the anti-Castro members kept their hopes up for a possible takeover of the island. They had not forgotten that Nixon had promoted the first plan to invade Cuba when he was vice-president during Eisenhower's administration. But events turned against the anti-Castro group when the Watergate scandal erupted: 5 anti-Castro Cubans were miserably caught during the break-in of the Democratic headquarters in the Watergate building. Nixon's disgrace put an end to the hopes of the anti-Castro. Some researchers tend to speculate that the assassination of John Kennedy and the Watergate scandal, ten years later, were linked.

Howard Hunt was an undisputed master of espionage and a specialist in propaganda activities at the CIA. This diabolic character created pieces of fake writings by John Kennedy, and

---

[275] Jesse Ventura – They Killed our President – 2013. Skyhorse Publishing
[276] John Simkin, "Jefferson Morley: Biography"
[277] Jefferson Morley, "Oswald's handler? What Morley vs CIA clarified" April 2013
[278] Lamar Waldron, The Hidden History of the JFK Assassination, Counter Point Berkeley, 2013

notably bogus cables that incriminated the President for having personally ordered the assassination of Vietnamese President Diem.[279] In the 1970s, Hunt became a key member of the Watergate plotters who involved Cubans in the team. According to Politico.com, ten years earlier, Hunt had been a major player in the failed Bay of Pigs invasion

John Kennedy, who opposed his military advisers by rejecting an air raid on Cuba, attracted the wrath of the Cuban exiles who saw the President as a traitor. In 2007, Howard Hunt claimed, on his deathbed, that he knew all about the plot against JFK: that it had been organized by a few CIA agents and anti-Castro members and that he described as the "Big Event".[280] One of the most sensational White House tapes ever revealed was that of Richard Nixon's cryptic reference to the "Big Event" on June 23, 1972, just after the break-in at the Watergate building. On the tape, disclosed in August 1974, and shortly before his resignation, Nixon can be heard talking about Howard Hunt's involvement in the Watergate case: "...*Of course, this Hunt... that will uncover a lot of things. You open that scab there's a hell of a lot of things and we just feel that it would be very detrimental to have this thing go any further...This involves these Cubans, Hunt and a lot of hanky-panky....Just say (unintelligible) very bad to have this fellow Hunt, ah, he knows that? If it gets out that this is all involved, the Cuba thing would be a fiasco. It would make the CIA look bad, and it is likely to blow the whole Bay of Pigs thing which we think would be very unfortunate, both for the CIA and for the country, at this time, and for American foreign policy....*"[281]

H.R. Haldemann, Nixon's White House Chief of Staff, who was indicted for being one of the actors in the Watergate scandal, wrote the following in his memoirs, "The Ends of Power": "*In all his references to the Bay of Pigs* [in the tapes], *Nixon was actually referring to Kennedy's assassination ... After Kennedy was killed, the*

---

[279] Senate Watergate Committee Report p 126-7 & Coincidence or Conspiracy p 526

[280] http://www.politico.com/story/2015/05/why-last-of-jfk-files-could-embarrass-cia-118233

[281] Bernard Fensterwald, p 510, June 23, 1972, White House Transcript between Haldeman and Nixon.

CIA was the author of an incredible cover-up ... It literally removed any connection between Kennedy's assassination and the CIA ... In fact, CIA Counterintelligence Chief, James Angleton, called Bill Sullivan of the FBI for rehearsing the questions and answers they would provide to the Warren Commission investigators"[282].

The CIA goal was to make the American people believe that Oswald had a link with a communist country, Cuba or the Soviet Union, in order to stigmatize these countries after the assassination of John Kennedy. Behind this smoke screen, the anti-Castro, the CIA and the Mafia would then retaliate under a patriotic pretext and reconquer everything they had lost in Cuba in order to ensure American interests once again. Even if one accepts that Moscow leaders had the most malicious intentions, it is hard to see why the Soviets would want to remove from office the first American President who had finally won their trust after many years of tension during the Cold War. The Soviets understood that the perilous standoff over the Cuban missiles with potential catastrophic consequences had been finally averted by Kennedy and Khrushchev thanks to their good sense and control. The Soviets would have paid dearly such an insane act of having JFK killed.

David Atlee Phillips, a senior CIA agent, was the man behind the misinformation campaign of the Agency. He played a decisive role in the anti-Castro activities in Cuba. For many years, it was suspected, without evidence, that "Maurice Bishop" was the pseudonym of David Atlee Phillips.

He met Oswald in Dallas early September 1963 for a debriefing and to give him his future assignment: Oswald was to behave as a pro-Castro activist by distributing leaflets of the Fair Play Movement for Cuba Committee in the streets of New Orleans. The plan also included Oswald's trip to Mexico City where he was expected to make a visit to the Cuban embassy portraying him as an American dissident hoping to get a visa for Havana[283].

---

[282] H.R. Haldeman, The Ends of Power. November 1978, P 68-69
[283] Lamar Waldron, The Hidden History of the JFK Assassination, Counter Point Berkeley, 2013

Cuba or Russia was then to be incriminated for the assassination of John Kennedy, a credible scenario given Oswald's past as a defector to the Soviet Union. The U.S. intelligence created a myth by which Oswald, as a communist, had connections not only with the KGB apparatus specialized in organized assassinations but also with Castro. This ploy would help to justify airstrikes by the United States against Cuba.

The meeting between "Bishop" aka Phillips and Oswald in Dallas was unusual for two reasons. It occurred overtly in a public place, in the lobby of insurance offices located in a skyscraper in downtown Dallas. Unexpectedly, a third person attended their meeting which caught Phillips by total surprise. This individual was Antonio Veciana, a leader of the Cuban exiles, a fierce anti-Castro activist, who had the support of the CIA. The CIA was helping these Cuban exiles, under the code name Alpha 66, to carry out several assassination attempts against Fidel Castro. Veciana had been summoned by "Bishop" to also meet him, later that day, but he arrived earlier than expected. By doing so, he caught "Bishop" in the company of a young man. According to Veciana, this man was timid, silent and looked preoccupied. The three men went to a local café where the young man stayed for 10 to 15 minutes until "Bishop" dismissed him and said "OK, see you later". After he left, Phillips made no mention of the young man and Veciana did not ask any questions. After the assassination of John Kennedy, Veciana, having watched the TV and read the newspapers, recognized Oswald as the same young man he had seen with "Bishop" in Dallas. For him, there was no doubt, the man at the meeting and Oswald were the same person[284].

David Atlee Phillips appeared before the House Select Committee on Assassinations. He was suspected of having been a co-conspirator in the assassination plot of Kennedy but the committee could not prove it without a shadow of a doubt. Phillips, however, was charged with the crime of perjury before the House Select Committee on Assassinations for having denied

---

[284] Anthony Summers. Conspiracy. Who Killed President Kennedy?Gollancz,May 1980

the CIA's connection with Oswald and his role as Oswald's handler because he had been seen in his company in the lobby of a Dallas office in September 1963. With an unwavering attitude that defeated the tough attorney of the House Select Committee on Assassinations, Robert Tanenbaum, Phillips also denied that the CIA had told the American people that Oswald made phone calls to the Cuban and Soviet embassies in Mexico City. However the committee already knew that the CIA had used a "double" in order to impersonate Oswald and to ensure he would be framed as a contentious communist.

The CIA's goal was to fabricate a fake Oswald, an impostor, eager to go to Russia or Cuba; a set up to compromise the true Oswald, a leftist, so that he become a scapegoat for the JFK assassination. A man pretending to be Lee Harvey Oswald conspicuously attracted attention in public places before the assassination. This fact was confirmed by many eyewitnesses. According to the Warren Report, Lee Harvey Oswald was in Mexico City from September 27 to October 2, 1963, supposedly visiting the consulates of Cuba and the Soviet Union. From that moment, the tracking of the real Oswald in Mexico was lost while a pseudo Oswald was seen taking his place[285].

An event that occurred in Dallas at the end of September 1963 seems to confirm that an Oswald look-alike could have been planted by the CIA to impersonate the real Oswald. Silvia Odio, a Cuban immigrant, reluctantly opened the door of her house to let two Cuban exiles talk to her, late one night. These two Cubans, named Leopoldo and Angel, were accompanied by a quiet young American, somewhat lost in the conversation in Spanish, whom they introduced as "Leon Oswald", an activist very interested in the Cuban cause. They had come to talk with Silvia Odio to try to get her support for the exiles cause. Forty-eight hours later, Leopoldo telephoned Odio to ask her what she thought of Leon Oswald. She replied that she did not really have an opinion but that she found it strange that Leopoldo made some comments

---

[285] James W. Douglass, JFK and the Unspeakable, Why He Died and Why it Matters, A Touchstone Book, 2008

about the young American as if he had wanted to promote his rebellious demeanor: *"He's a former Marine and an expert marksman"* he said *"He's kind of nuts. He is disoriented, but can be secretly introduced into Cuba. He could commit anything like going underground to Cuba and killing Castro. He says we, Cubans, don't have guts because we should have killed President Kennedy after the Bay of Pigs. He thinks we should do something like that..."* Leopoldo also informed Odio that the three men were going on a road trip and that he would get in touch with her when they returned. Later, just after Kennedy's assassination, Silvia Odio would identify the "American gringo" as Lee Harvey Oswald from TV news. She testified before the Warren Commission but her testimony was ignored because the commission had already concluded that Oswald was on his way to Mexico City at the very time of Leon Oswald's visit to Odio in Dallas. Nothing is clear about this event: did Odio have a glimpse of the real Oswald? Or was it his double whom she met? The Odio's testimony certainly added a troubling fact to the other reports about a "false Oswald" (spotted at both the Soviet and Cuban embassies) made in order to compromise the real Oswald[286].

The CIA's operation to impersonate Oswald and the phone tapping of the embassies were known to the FBI. Thanks to a FBI memorandum, Tanenbaum had the evidence of it. When he asked David Atlee Phillips the whereabouts of the embassies' audio recordings, the latter insisted that they had been destroyed[287]. The Warren Commissions' investigators had no way of getting hold of the audio tapes recording of the conversations of "Oswald" inside the embassies. Neither the recording nor the transcripts were communicated to it.

According to Jefferson Morley[288] and to a sensitive CIA source, the impersonation of Oswald and the impostor's contacts at the Soviet Union embassy in Mexico City had been identified. On October 1, 1963, an individual who spoke Russian very badly

---

[286] Russell. The Man Who Knew Too Much p 309.
[287] David Talbot – Brothers, The Hidden History of the Kennedy Years - 2007
[288] Jacob. M. Carter – Before History Dies - 2015, Interview of Jefferson Morley

(whereas Oswald spoke it almost fluently) and who was probably connected to the CIA created a lot of confusion by conveying a bad image of the Soviet Union. The description of the man was given as that of an older, heavier and larger man than the real Oswald. Employees of the Soviet Embassy confirmed that the impostor was addressing to them in very poor Russian and in an excellent Spanish. Oswald spoke no Spanish[289]. The report of the House Select Committee on Assassinations confirmed that the "Oswald" who contacted the embassy of Russia spoke a Russian so bad that it was difficult for the embassy's staff to identify it as Russian. According to George De Mohrenschildt, his friend spoke Russian almost without mistakes and that his entourage was astonished by his almost perfect command of the language: *"Lee's English was also perfect, polished, and rather literary, without southern accent. He spoke like a very educated American. To know Russian, as he knew, was remarkable and to seriously appreciate* [Russian] *literature was something out of the ordinary"*[290].

We have evidence of other CIA's imposture operations using a fake Oswald, this time, at the Cuban Embassy in Mexico City.[291] Just before the visit to the Soviet embassy, on September 27, 1963, a young American named Lee Harvey Oswald had also called the Cuban Embassy to apply for a transit visa to reach first Cuba and then the Soviet Union as the final destination. As it was important that the real Oswald should not go to Cuba because he had to be framed in Dallas as a scapegoat for the murder of John Kennedy, the scheme was to use an impostor instead.

The man who pretended to be Oswald made five "fake" phone calls, all tapped by the CIA, to the Russian embassy embassies in Mexico City, while at the same time the real Oswald was in New Orleans.

---

[289] Lamar Waldron, The Hidden History of the JFK Assassination, Counter Point Berkeley, 2013
[290] HSCA, House Select Committee on Assassinations P 153-171
[291] Robert J. Groden, *The Killing of a President*, Vicking Studio Books, 1993

The pseudo Oswald continued to make a series of visits to the Cuban and the Soviet Union consulates. On each visit, this individual attracted a great deal of attention because he required travel documents that the staff of both embassies were not willing to give him in such a short time. The Cuban consul, Eusebio Azcue, and his assistant, Sylvia Duran, remembered this incident very well. After the assassination of John Kennedy, they found major physical differences between the "Oswald" whom they had seen at the embassy and the suspect arrested in Dallas on the day of the assassination and then shot by Jack Ruby. According to Azcue, they did not look like.[292] Silvia Duran, who gave a precise description of the man impersonating Oswald, asserted too that there was no physical resemblance to the man who had been killed in the Dallas jail. During the investigation of the House Select Committee on Assassinations, when a photo of Oswald was shown to him, the Consul of the Cuban Embassy said under oath: *"This individual is not the person who came to the embassy. The man who visited the embassy was blond, larger, and at least 30 years old"*[293].

The Cuban and Soviet embassies were watched by the CIA with surveillance cameras that recorded the movements of visitors, a common practice of American espionage. At first, the CIA denied the existence of a pseudo Oswald but later claimed that the recordings had "failed" and that, for each visit, no photograph of the real Oswald had been made possible. They were "routinely destroyed" by the CIA a week or more after Oswald's visit to Mexico City. Of course, the CIA could not prove Oswald's visits since an impostor had impersonated him. The agency had to invent a technical breakdown of the audio tapes and the destruction of photos. Nevertheless, much later a photograph of the man impersonating Oswald was published. It is now posted on the internet[294].

---

[292] Anthony Summers. Conspiracy. Who Killed President Kennedy, Gollancz, May 1980
[293] Robert J. Groden, The Killing of a President, Vicking Studio Books, 1993
[294] Robert J. Groden and Harrison Edward Livingstone. High Treason: The assassination of JFK. What really happened? The Conservatory Press, 1989

Thanks to *President John F. Kennedy's 1992 Assassination Records Collection Act*, and Lyndon Johnson's phone recording at the White House, we now know that Johnson was aware of the CIA's impersonation plot of Oswald. The day after the President's assassination, the FBI director, J. Edgar Hoover, called Johnson and informed him about a pseudo Oswald. "LBJ: *Have you established any more about the visit to the Soviet Embassy in Mexico in September?* HOOVER: "*No, that's one angle that's very confusing for this reason. We have up here the tape and the photograph of the man who was at the Soviet Embassy using Oswald's name. The photo and the name do not correspond to this man's voice, nor to his appearance. In other words it appears there is a second person who was at the Soviet Embassy down there*"[295].

As soon as the CIA realized that the Mexican embassy plot was about to fail and that communists' involvement in the assassination could not possibly be faked, the Mexico City CIA station backpedaled to try to hide the fraud. The CIA station first claimed that the audio tapes of the "Oswald" phone calls to the Soviet embassy had been routinely destroyed, and, as a result, no voice comparison was possible to determine who really had spoken on behalf of Oswald. It was an ironic twist because the announcement of the CIA office in Mexico City coincided with the time when Hoover and his FBI staff were listening to their own copies of the Embassy audio recordings and getting ready to report to President Johnson about the analysis results they had conducted on voice comparison![296]

On November 26, 1976, a Washington Post article entitled "*The CIA concealed details of Oswald's phone calls*" reported David Atlee Phillips' words while he was at the CIA station in Mexico City during Lee Harvey Oswald's alleged visit to the Soviet and Cuban consulates. Phillips claimed that the CIA had tapped Oswald's conversation. He himself had read the transcript of the calls and

---

[295] https://www.history-matters.com/archive/jfk/lbjlib/phone_calls/Nov_1963/html/LBJ-Nov-1963_0030a.htm

[296] James W. Douglass, JFK and the Unspeakable, Why He Died and Why it Matters, A Touchstone Book, 2008

listened to the audio recording tapes. He tried to explain the shortcomings of the CIA at the embassies: the destruction of the tapes. As to the missing photographs, Phillips pretended that there could be no photographs of Oswald taken outside the embassies because the CIA's photographic surveillance had simply missed him, the photos having been taken sporadically.

In 1978, Antonio Veciana revealed an important twist of events just after his meeting with Phillips, aka "Maurice Bishop" and Oswald in Dallas. He revealed to the investigator Anthony Summers that Phillips had urged him to contact his cousin, Guillermo Ruiz, who worked at the Cuban embassy in Mexico City with a specific request. Phillips wanted to know if Veciana's cousin would be ready, against payment, to spread the news about Lee Harvey Oswald's visit to the Cuban Embassy a few weeks before the assassination of President Kennedy. Veciana asked him if it was true that Oswald had gone to that embassy. Bishop replied that it was of little importance whether he was there or not, but the point was that his cousin, as a member of the Cuban diplomatic service, claimed that Oswald's visit had taken place. Veciana informed Phillips that perhaps he would not be able to contact his cousin immediately and that this might have to wait. However, sometime later when Veciana was about to contact his cousin, he was surprised by Phillips telling him to forget about this after all and to never mention anything or ask questions about Lee Harvey Oswald in the future[297].

Nearing the end of his life, David Atlee Phillips admitted the involvement of "rogue officers" of the CIA in the assassination of John Kennedy and stated: *"My private opinion is that JFK was done in by a conspiracy, likely including rogue American intelligence people."* [298] Phillips revealed Oswald's precise role in a written testimony found after his death: *"I was one of two case officers who handled Lee*

---

[297] Anthony Summers. Conspiracy. Who Killed President Kennedy, Gollancz, May 1980

[298] Larry Hancock – Someone Would Have Talked: The Assassination of President John F. Kennedy and the Conspiracy to Mislead History
(JFK Lancer 2006), (JFK Lancer 2010), jfkfacts.org. The Mary Ferrell Foundation.

Harvey Oswald. After working to establish his Marxist bona fides, we gave him the mission of killing Fidel Castro in Cuba. I helped him when he came to Mexico City to obtain a visa, and when he returned to Dallas to wait for it I saw him twice there. We rehearsed the plan many times: In Havana Oswald was to assassinate Castro with a sniper's rifle from the upper floor window of a building on the route where Castro often drove in an open jeep. Whether Oswald was a double agent or a psycho I'm not sure, and I don't know why he killed Kennedy. But I do know he used precisely the plan we had devised against Castro"[299].

After testifying before the House Select Committee on Assassinations, 16 years after his interview with Oswald and David Phillips, Antonio Veciana was the victim of an assassination attempt in Miami and narrowly escaped death. Professional killers ambushed him on his way home, shooting him in the head. Veciana survived his injuries but later was charged for drug trafficking and put in jail. According to him, the CIA orchestrated the plot. During an interview by the author and historian James W. Douglass, Antonio Veciana explained the circumstances of the assassination attempt. Although he had received death threats three times from the FBI, after the shooting, neither the FBI nor the Miami police did anything to investigate those people behind the assassination attempt[300].

At the *Assassination Archives and Research Center* 2014 conference on "*The Warren Report and the JFK Assassination*", in Bethesda, Antonio Veciana's spectacular intervention surprised me as a delegate. There was always a doubt about the pseudonym of David Atlee Phillips – aka Maurice Bishop - because Phillips had totally eluded the question before the *House Select Committee on Assassinations*. The conference speaker, Marie Fonzi, widow of Gaeton Fonzi who investigated the JFK assassination much of his life, asked Antonio Veciana to talk at the convention. Aged 86, although frail but lucid, Veciana removed any doubt about David Atlee Phillips' pseudonym. He revealed to the audience that

---

[299] Jefferson Morley & Michael Scott:Our Man in Mexico:Winston Scott and the Hidden History of the CIA. University Press of Kansas 2008

[300] James W. Douglass, JFK and the Unspeakable, Why He Died and Why it Matters, A Touchstone Book, 2008

Maurice Bishop was indeed David Atlee Phillips. Veciana had seen him with Oswald in September 1963 in a Dallas hotel where they both had an appointment with the CIA agent. There was no doubt in his mind: the CIA was involved in the assassination of John Kennedy and endeavored to put the blame on Castro as a ploy to make a Cuba invasion take place. Here is what Veciana signed as an official statement, on November 22, 2013, which has since been made public: *"Dear Marie Fonzi, You may publish the following statement from me: 'Maurice Bishop, my CIA agent contact was David Atlee Phillips. Phillips or Bishop was the man I saw with Lee Harvey Oswald in Dallas on September 1963 '"*.

Turning now to the FBI, its complicity in the assassination of John Kennedy is more of a cover-up of its negligence in the investigation evidence rather than an active participation in the plot. The FBI's association with the cover-up was undoubtedly intentional given the visceral hatred of the agency's director, J. Edgar Hoover, for the two Kennedy brothers. Hoover took less than 24 hours after the assassination of the President to claim that Oswald was the murderer, without providing any evidence. No one in the FBI wanted to contradict the omnipotent director. This was the beginning of the cover-up anointed by President Johnson and Edgar Hoover as historian Walt Brown puts it: *"Johnson's actions would guarantee reluctance to shed light on the assassination. The cover-up could not have been carried out by those behind the plot without the full agreement of the new president and the FBI director. They controlled everything from the moment the last firing gunshots stopped. They controlled everything but did nothing"*[301].

Hoover's henchmen did not waste time to harass the witnesses and control their evidence in such a way that the FBI could change their testimonies if they did not match with the single shooter version[302]. Some eyewitnesses were shocked to see to what extent the words in their testimony had been changed by FBI

---

[301] Walt Brown, Ph.D. "Actions Speak Much Louder than Words" What exactly did Johnson and Hoover do? JFK Deep Politics Quarterly Vol. 17 #4, July 2012
[302] Jim Marrs, Crossfire. The Plot That Killed JFK

investigators to comments they had never made[303]. A forthcoming chapter of this book will cover the most important testimonies of some eyewitnesses who, by conviction and tenacity, firmly maintained their initial statements despite the FBI intimidation... some paying with their lives.

The FBI was aware of the links between Oswald, Ruby and the intelligence agencies, as stated by Dick Russell[304] and the former governor of Minnesota, Jesse Ventura[305]. This is what Senator Richard Schweiker strongly believed when he learned about Oswald and Ruby's association. *"Why did the FBI withhold for 12 years that he'd [Ruby] informed for them on nine occasions? This wasn't national security information, so why were they so sensitive? Also I'm certain there were extenuating circumstances in Ruby's activities running guns to Cuba. We were really running a secret war against Cuba, and we know the CIA was heavily involved. Ruby had to have been at least working for someone who was working for the CIA...Oswald and Ruby had intelligence connections"*[306].

Hoover knew everything about Oswald's intelligence intrigues in Mexico City as we know from the transcript of the telephone call between the FBI director and President Johnson the day after the assassination. They both discussed the imposture of a "second" Oswald who was seen at the Soviet embassy in Mexico City impersonating Lee Harvey Oswald.[307] Hoover had doubts about the "substantial" evidence of Oswald's guilt. According to the phone call transcript on November 23, 1963, at 10:01 am, Hoover told Johnson that he was alarmed by the lack of evidence: *"The case [against Oswald], as it now stands, isn't strong enough to be able to get a conviction ... this man always denies everything. He knows nothing about anything ... "*[308]

---

[303] Sylvia Meagher; Accessories After The Fact: The Warren Commission, The Authorities and The Report (Random House 1988)

[304] Dick Russell. On the Trail of the JFK Assassins (Skyhorse Publishing: 2008)

[305] Jesse Ventura – They Killed Our President – 2013. Skyhorse Publishing

[306] https://archive.org/stream/nsia-SchweikerRichardSenator/nsia-SchweikerRichardSenator/Schweiker%20Richard%20S%20048_djvu.txt

[307] Anthony Summers, The Kennedy Conspiracy, p 386

[308] "White House Transcripts of President Lyndon B. Johnson" November 23. 1963.

Hale Boggs, member of the US Congress and also member of the Warren Commission was very critical about Edgar Hoover: *"Hoover's lies to the commission are incredible: he lied about Oswald, about Ruby, about their friends, the bullets fired, the rifle, let alone anything else ... "*[309]. The Warren Commission was under enormous pressure to write its report. While the investigation progressed, it had to wait for the FBI reports that Edgar Hoover was feeding back to the commission. The FBI director's tactic was to wait until the commission was approaching the deadline to close its investigation and then provide, at the last moment, too many files for the commission to cope with.

In 1966, New Orleans district attorney, Jim Garrison, thinking he had uncovered the evidence concealed by the CIA relating to the JFK assassination, opened an official investigation. This entirely complied with local jurisdiction. The investigation was to be conducted without obstruction of justice. After expressing serious doubts about the Warren Report's findings, Garrison launched a large-scale official investigation for which the American people were totally receptive. But his investigation was stonewalled by those who had every interest in concealing the evidence: the CIA and the FBI[310]. It was hindered in every way possible: Jim Garrison's office was wiretapped; he was victim of slander; the extradition to New Orleans that he requested for witnesses having fled to other states was blocked and his requests to subpoena eyewitnesses were dismissed by judges[311]. As for the media, they endeavored to discredit Garrison's investigations[312]. Thanks to the CIA's involvement, the jury acquitted Clay Shaw, the CIA-related businessman whom Garrison accused of having participated in the JFK assassination. Despite this verdict and the

---

[309] Bernard Fensterwald & Michael Ewing; Assassination of JFK: Coincidence or Conspiracy? (Kensington Pub Corp 1977)

[310] Jesse Ventura – They Killed Our President – 2013. Skyhorse Publishing, Inc.

[311] Joan Mellen. A Farewell to Justice: Jim Garrison, JFK's Assassination and the Case That Should Have Changed History (Potomac Books: 2005)

[312] William Davy. Let Justice Be Done: New Light on Jim Garrison Investigation (Jordan Pub: 1999)

lack of sufficient evidence to indict Clay Shaw, Jim Garrison made stunning revelations. His in-depth investigation exposed the strong association between various individuals, all "in bed" with the CIA: Jack Ruby and Oswald, Carlos Marcello, the big boss of the local Mafia, David Ferrie, Marcello's pilot for his Anti-Castro operations, Guy Banister, a former FBI agent in contact with the New Orleans Mafia mainly with Carlos Marcello.

David Ferrie followed Oswald's fate. Just before he was about to be subpoenaed by Garrison again, he was found dead at his home (the dubious circumstances of his death - suicide or murder by poison- will be covered in a next chapter).

Garrison lost the case because of insufficient evidence to charge Clay Shaw and because FBI and CIA informants, within the Garrison team, had leaked records for the benefit of Clay Shaw's defense attorneys. Although the jury considered that Clay Shaw had lied on a number of counts, a new trial for perjury could not take place due to federal authorities' obstructions.

During an audience in 1979, Richard Helms, the CIA director of secret operations in 1963, admitted under oath that Clay Shaw had indeed worked for the CIA. The *House Select Committee on Assassinations* confirmed strong evidence of Shaw's guilt. The committee revealed that Oswald, David Ferrie and Clay Shaw had met in Louisiana and that Oswald had been instructed by David Ferrie in his anti-Castro training camp. Victor Marchetti, the former assistant to the CIA director, claimed that Richard Helms had told him that David Ferrie and Clay Shaw were both CIA contract agents. Ferrie had been seen frequently in Guy Bannister's office by his secretary, Delphine Roberts. She also claimed that Oswald went there regularly. Garrison revealed that Oswald had used the exact same address of Bannister's office which was printed on the *Fair Play for Cuba Committee* propaganda that Oswald distributed in New Orleans streets. The committee proved that Bannister supervised Oswald in his role of "agent provocateur". It also revealed that Bannister had been in charge of the FBI office in Chicago and had been associated with the *Office of Naval Intelligence* (ONI). This followed a recommendation from Guy Johnson, an ONI reserve officer, who was Clay Shaw's first attorney when he was indicted by Garrison.

During the *"Passing the Torch"* Conference at Duquesne University in Pittsburgh in 2013, Professor Joan Mellen, author-historian and educator, paid tribute to Garrison's tenacity: *"Without Jim Garrison, there would not have been Oliver Stone's movie, 'JFK', and without the 'JFK' movie there would not have been the creation of the JFK Assassination Records Act. Without the JFK Records Collection at the National Archives, none of the books written about Kennedy's presidency would have been written."*

Based on Garrison's book, director Oliver Stone used the Warren Commission's inaccuracies, omissions, procedural errors, and obvious lies to make a three-hour movie. Based on 4,000 pages of declassified published reports, and on a script of more than a thousand pages, the "JFK" movie was a resounding success with the public. Like Garrison's book, the film concluded that a plot had been jointly coordinated by the CIA, the anti-Castro exiles and the Organized Crime syndicate then concealed by the high authorities of the nation. Oliver Stone partially participated in the Pittsburgh conference as a guest of honor where he evoked the Kennedy mystery as being at the very heart of the ambiguities of the American nation. By addressing the sensitive subject of the plot to assassinate Kennedy during his three-hour film, Stone chose to reveal the Machiavellian scheme of the American "Deep State", mainly the CIA complicity. Ever since his return from Vietnam, Oliver Stone, the relentless fighter against injustice, will not rest until America returns to its democratic values. Because this rebellious filmmaker brought to the screen the trilogy of disturbing films about the Vietnam War - "Platoon", "Born on the 4th of July", and "Heaven & Earth" - he was labeled as insane, a traitor and a bad American. At the Pittsburgh convention, Oliver Stone explained his motive to make his movie 'JFK". President Kennedy's death had marked him deeply: *"Kennedy was our hero. When he was murdered, it was like in 'Hamlet' ... We thought at first that it was a criminal madman who lost control. Then years later, we started to doubt and the ghost came back to haunt us. Perhaps there was a fraud with a new king on the throne ... something highly corrupt and sinister happened"*. Of course, Oliver Stone was referring to Lyndon Johnson, who "stole" the presidency of the United States on the same day John Kennedy was assassinated. It seemed obvious to the filmmaker that the new president had been involved in the cover-up in some way.

In the midst of the Cold War, it was easy for any particular individual who had a potential acquaintance with the CIA to be suspected. Several historians investigated Ruth and Michael Paine's alleged activities on behalf of the CIA. Ruth befriended Marina Oswald and temporarily hosted her when Marina and Lee Oswald's marriage floundered. Marina gave Russian lessons to Ruth Paine at home. Michael Paine's mother was very close to Allen Dulles. His father-in-law was the inventor of the Bell Helicopter and was close to the military-industrial world and he went on to have numerous future contracts for helicopters supply during the Vietnam War. Thirty years after John Kennedy's death, a CIA memorandum was declassified stating that Ruth Paine's sister, Sylvia Hyde Hoke, had been employed from 1963 by the CIA over a period of eight years. In 1968, at the Grand Jury, New Orleans District Attorney Jim Garrison received Marina Oswald's testimony concerning Ruth Paine. She was asked if she still saw Ruth Paine. Marina replied, "*No, I like her and appreciate what she did for me, but the Secret Service warned me that I should not stay in touch with her.*" Marina clarified the reason the Secret Service asked her to distance herself from Ruth Paine: "*She's a CIA sympathizer*". She was asked to elaborate. Why had the Secret Service told her about Ruth Paine's connection with the CIA? She replied: "*It seems she had a lot of friends over there* [at the CIA] *and it would hurt me if there were connections between me, Ruth and the CIA.*" To the question: "*In other words, was it clear to you that she was somehow related to the CIA?*", Marina replied "Yes"[313].

It is undeniable that the CIA worked closely with the Mafia and this fact is well documented in the next chapter. During its hearings in the mid-1970s, the Church Committee discovered that the CIA had contracts with prominent Organized Crime

---

[313] James W. Douglass, JFK and the Unspeakable, Why He Died and Why it Matters, A Touchstone Book, 2008

individuals to murder Fidel Castro. Many historians believe that the CIA-Mafia relationship may have played a role in the murder of President Kennedy.[314]

---

[314] "Alleged Assassination Plots Against Foreign Leaders". Interim report of the Select Committee to Study Governmental Operations with Respect to Intelligence Activities, The United States Senate .Final Report April 23, 1976

Chapter 8

The Vindictive Mafia

In 1979, Congressional investigations concluded that John Kennedy had been killed as a result of a probable conspiracy which had been fomented over the period of one year. They revealed that Carlos Marcello, head of the Louisiana and Texas underworld, and his associate, Santo Trafficante, the Mafia don in Florida, had the motive, the means and the opportunity to assassinate the President[315]. Robert Kennedy and many government officials who worked in the Kennedy administration shared the same conviction. Formal evidence of the CIA's alliance with the Mafia to assassinate Fidel Castro were obtained after the hearings of Santo Trafficante before the House Select Committee on Assassinations. When Trafficante was asked: *"When were you first approached by someone from the CIA?* He replied, *"It was around the end of 1960 or the beginning of 1961"*[316].

Under Fulgencio Batista's dictatorship in Cuba supported by the United States, the profits of the Organized Crime amounted to millions of dollars every day, thanks to their gambling and

---

[315] Lamar Waldron, The Hidden History of the JFK Assassination, Counter Point Berkeley, 2013

[316] Robert J. Groden and Harrison Edward Livingstone. High Treason: The assassination of JFK. What really happened? The Conservatory Press, 1989

prostitution operations. When Fidel Castro took power, the casinos were shut down and the Mafia mobsters were either imprisoned or expelled from the island. The Mafia's efforts to remove Castro and reopen the casinos at all costs were of course significantly curtailed. The Organized Crime was however convinced that an invasion of Cuba was necessary and was striving for the participation of the CIA which had also an interest in regaining its influence on the island. But the Cuban Missile Crisis in October 1962 changed the course of events. It had become difficult to militarily overthrow Castro. The Mafia found another ploy. Unbeknownst to President Kennedy and his brother, the Mafia signed a contract with the CIA to kill Fidel Castro. Four Mafia godfathers, Santos Trafficante, Carlos Marcello, Johnny Roselli and Sam Giancana (the Chicago Mafia boss active in Nevada and Hollywood), were the main co-plotters of the assassination attempts against Castro. Declassified files from the CIA revealed that the CIA-Mafia plots were fostered by Vice President Nixon, prior to John Kennedy's inauguration, and that they reached their peak in September 1960. Trafficante, in particular, and other mobsters, planned to kill Fidel Castro in the underworld's usual manner. The CIA, for its part, was determined to hit the Cuban leader by involving the Mafia and pinning on it the blame for the murder. The CIA would thus let the American people believe that it was the intervention of an entity other than the CIA or the U.S. government. But, the Mafia godfathers feared that an official and violent murder of the popular Cuban leader would directly link to their cause of regaining control of the casinos, and would immediately finger point them. Trafficante and Roselli therefore took the decision to employ low-profile assassinations attempts such as using poison[317].

All the CIA conspiracies aided by the Mafia, to kill Fidel Castro, failed miserably however. At this point, they had to find another ploy to win Cuba back .... A change of target....

---

[317] Lamar Waldron, The Hidden History of the JFK Assassination, Counter Point Berkeley, 2013

As the previous chapter described it, the CIA and the anti-Castro were hostile to John Kennedy. The Bay of Pigs fiasco and Kennedy's policy for détente towards Cuba and the Soviet Union after the Missile Crisis, had provoked the ire of the American intelligence service and the Washington "hawks". The Mafia's revenge had reached an optimal level when President Kennedy denied air cover for the invasion of Cuba at the Bay of Pigs. The Cuban anti-Castro had the support of the Mafia who sought to eliminate the Cuban dictator after the closure of casinos, the dismantling of prostitution and drug trafficking that had ended the juicy Mafia's profits on the island. A Mafia mobster said: "*Kennedy has just signed his death certificate*".[318] The hatred of the Mafia godfathers towards the President was also rooted in something more personal: to make the Kennedy brothers pay in retaliation for the war they had declared against the Mafia mobsters during their hearings before the senatorial commissions who were in charge of investigating and dismantling Organized Crime in America. Robert Kennedy, in particular, had relentlessly pursued the fight against the illegal operations of the underworld in the United States when he was Attorney General. The Mafia godfathers certainly had a motive to eliminate President Kennedy, whom they saw as a major obstacle against any attempt to destabilize the Castro regime.

The CIA-Mafia cabal deviated from its original purpose and was now aimed at John Kennedy. With JFK dead, these enemies thought that they would be able to resume their service with new operations in Cuba against Castro. After the assassination of John Kennedy, the prosecution of the main leaders of Organized Crime decreased indeed by 83%; a relief for the Mafia. After a fierce war against them, Robert Kennedy had finally capitulated, even though he was still Attorney General. It had only taken the elimination of one victim, that of his brother.

However, the Mafia godfathers, as powerful as they were, could not forge ahead with such an assassination plan without the help of U.S. intelligence agencies. Only government agencies

---

[318] Interview de David Scheim par Jacobs M.Carter – Before History Dies – 2015.

were able to plan and conceal the murder, to manipulate Lee Harvey Oswald, to label him as a scapegoat, to pin him with evidence of guilt, to disguise medical evidence and to conceal it in the safes of the National Archives. In other words, the Mafia, alone, would have been unable to enforce such a cover-up. It did not have the power[319].

According to the investigative journalist, David Talbot[320], if the Mafia had orchestrated the whole operation alone, Robert Kennedy would have destroyed it for good. He told his collaborators: *"Either the Mafia will destroy the United States, or the United States will destroy the Mafia!"* Its motive to be co-author of the assassination plot was clear. Under Robert and John Kennedy, it was about to be dismantled. Hundreds of Mafia members were either subpoenaed and charged or kept under very close surveillance which made their illegal operations impossible. The harassment of the Kennedy brothers lasted until mid-1963. Although many murders had been perpetrated by the Mafia during the Prohibition and even later, the FBI director, J. Edgar Hoover, refused to admit the very existence of Organized Crime in the United States.[321] It was blackmail. He feared that his homosexuality would be disclosed and so he was forced to turn a blind eye to the Mafia's deeds[322].

The Mafia also had also another motive to kill John Kennedy. It had significantly helped JFK to win the presidential election in 1960 by "purchasing" critical votes in Illinois; a pact that the Mafia and patriarch Joe Kennedy had signed. It felt betrayed by the Kennedy brothers who had shown no "recognition" for its support[323].

---

[319] Robert J. Groden and Harrison Edward Livingstone. High Treason: The assassination of JFK. What really happened? The Conservatory Press, 1989

[320] Jacob M. Carter – Before History Dies - 2015, Interview of David Talbot

[321] Carl Sifakis. The Mafia Encyclopedia (Facts on File: 1999)

[322] Anthony Summers. Official and Confidential: The Secret Life of J. Edgar Hoover (Ebury: 2012)

[323] Jesse Ventura – They Killed Our President – 2013. Skyhorse Publishing

The Cuban Missile Crisis had just ended. Tensions between the United States, Cuba and the Soviet Union were still palpable. In this context, members of the Mafia, Trafficante, Marcello and Roselli made the calculation that if President Kennedy was murdered in public and if it turned out that his murderer had links with Cuba and even with Russia, senior American officials would then face a real dilemma, that of the rising up of a disgusted American nation. Either government officials would retaliate against Cuba, which, counting on the commitment of the Soviet Union, would force the United States to go to war against two communist countries, or U.S. officials would temper their belligerent fervor and launch a major investigation into the murder of the President to prevent reprisals and millions of victims in what would be a Third World War. All in all, they would face two difficult options but whatever choice they would make, it would be beneficial to the underworld mobsters. Historians believe however, that national security would have prevailed and a Third World War would have been avoided. Perhaps this thinking would explain the cover-up of the JFK assassination[324].

The plots against Fidel Castro started in 1960 under Eisenhower's administration. His vice president, Richard Nixon, had a considerable influence on U.S. policy towards Cuba. At the beginning, Fidel Castro hoped that the United States would bring him financial aid after the fall of the dictator, Fulgencio Batista, but Nixon refused that help. As Fidel Castro was perceived as a dangerous ruler, Nixon enlisted the CIA who made contact with the leaders of the underworld, with the aim of killing the dictator and of protecting American interests in Cuba. Trafficante wanted Richard Nixon's personal support for the operation. The conspiracies led in September 1960 by Trafficante, Roselli and Giancana, backed by Nixon and the CIA, were concealed from the Warren Commission. Those operations would not be revealed

---

[324] Lamar Waldron, The Hidden History of the JFK Assassination, Counter Point Berkeley, 2013

until 1975, during congressional debates, a year after the Watergate scandal forced Nixon to resign. But the magnitude of these plots was neglected by historians and remained unknown to the American public until 1989.

Marcello and Trafficante were striving to secure Nixon's victory over John Kennedy in the 1960 presidential campaign when Jimmy Hoffa was under attack by the Kennedy brothers. Hoffa was the president of the Teamsters Union - the most powerful union in the United States at the time - and remained very loyal to the Mafia. The Kennedy brothers wanted to bring Hoffa to justice for malpractice and corruption within his union. In September 1960, Nixon received a bribe of $500,000 from the Mafia mobsters for his support of assassination plots against Castro. The initial payment to Nixon was a half of $1million pledge (equivalent to six million today) pending Santo Trafficante's enrollment in the conspiracy plot. Six months before the break-in of the Democratic Party in the Watergate building, President Nixon received another $1 million bribe for his support to Jimmy Hoffa, Carlos Marcello, Santo Trafficante and the New-Jersey Mafioso, Tony Provenzano. These transactions have been well documented by the FBI and Time Magazine.

The bribe to release Hoffa from jail stipulated that he should no longer serve as president of the Teamsters for at least eight years. But by the end of 1973, Hoffa, angry to see himself ousted from the Teamsters by Nixon, alerted Senate investigators on Watergate and revealed the plots that were directed against Castro by the CIA and the Mafia with Nixon and Johnny Roselli's support. The latter was subpoenaed by the commission to talk about the plots but the results of the hearings were kept secret.

Following Nixon's resignation in August 1974, leaks on assassinations plots by President Gerald Ford made the news headlines and triggered the creation of the Rockefeller Commission in January 1975. This commission was charged with investigating the CIA activities on its assassinations plots against Castro but also on the assassination of John Kennedy. These investigations were later taken over by the Church Committee. Paramount information was nevertheless concealed from the Church Committee because it would compromise important political leaders: former Warren Commission member Gerald Ford, then U.S. President, Donald Rumsfeld, his Chief of Staff, and Senior White House Adviser, Dick Cheney and even later, George Bush, the director of the CIA. These four men had taken part in the Nixon administration during the Watergate scandal that involved both Mafia-related and anti-Castro conspiracies[325].

The Mafia by itself had neither the power nor the means, let alone the opportunity to eliminate John Kennedy. It needed major support from the CIA. In his book "The Hidden History of the JFK Assassination", historian Lamar Waldrom provides many details and testimonies corroborating a Mafia-CIA collusion.[326] Both helped each other to target Cuba. The CIA needed information about the Cuban actions that the Mafia was able to provide through its introductions and its presence on the island, during the time of the casinos. The Mafia in return required that the CIA would facilitate the supply of drugs coming from Southeast Asia.

Historians Waldrom and Scheim have based their findings on numerous official sources pointing out Marcello, Trafficante and Hoffa as the key suspects in the assassination of President Kennedy. According to them, their motive was clear but their target was somewhat divergent. Jimmy Hoffa wanted to "aim" at Robert Kennedy, while Marcello and Trafficante preferred John Kennedy dead. Because of his many criminal acts associated with Marcello and Trafficante, Jimmy Hoffa, under such pressure from the Kennedy brothers, made it his primary intention to kill Robert Kennedy. In September 1962, Edward Partin, a Justice Department informant, witnessed Hoffa's bribe to Nixon. Partin offered his services by tapping Jimmy Hoffa's conversations about a plan to kill Attorney General, Robert Kennedy. The polygraph tests were conclusive on Partin's reliability. Towards the end of 1962, however, Hoffa ceased to make any threats against Robert Kennedy's life and was persuaded by Carlos

---

[325] Ibid
[326] Ibid

Marcello and Santo Trafficante that the problem was not Robert Kennedy; another solution had to be found. Despite his visceral hatred for Robert Kennedy, Marcello wanted to assassinate John Kennedy, as it would be more effective in ending the war sought by his brother against Organized Crime. This was revealed by Marcello's confident, a man who was in charge of public relations for two Las Vegas casinos. In a passionate conversation about how to eliminate Robert Kennedy, he reported the unhappy godfather's very words in Sicilian: "*Livarsi na piedra di la scarpa!* (Take the stone out of my shoe!)".

A promoter from Las Vegas, Edward Becker, who was close to Marcello, also reported Marcello's words referring to Robert Kennedy's fate: "*Don't worry about that little Bobby son of a bitch. He's going to be taken care of*" But when Becker retorted that Robert Kennedy's assassination would result in terrible reprisals from President Kennedy and a total destruction of the Mafia in America, Marcello invoked an old Italian proverb: "*If you want to kill a dog, you don't cut its tail, you cut its head.*"

The House Select Committee on Assassinations investigated Becker's affidavit and found his story credible[327]. By killing Robert Kennedy - their initial reasoning - the godfathers would run the risk of causing a destructive reaction from the President to avenge his brother's assassination by harassing Organized Crime until it was totally eradicated by force from the country. By eliminating the President instead, at the head of the "Kennedy problem", the Mafia would make sure that any attempt from Bobby Kennedy to carry out implacable reprisals would be paralyzed. Bobby Kennedy could always be taken care of later. If he managed to execute his threats against the Organized Crime, he would then be assassinated in turn. This was exactly what the Mafia did by killing him in 1968! The commissions investigating the murders of both Kennedys believed they were linked. Few Americans know that the assassination of Robert Kennedy in Los Angeles, in 1968, during his campaign for the presidential election, was just the finalization of the Mafia vendetta. Hoffa

---

[327] Ibid

finally saw it all clear and rallied to Marcello's plan: by killing Robert Kennedy, his brother would have decimated the Mafia for good after a very thorough investigation but if the President was assassinated instead, Bobby Kennedy's power could only exist within his brother's entourage and he would fall in turn.

The FBI knew that Marcello and Trafficante were involved with the CIA. The Bureau tracked them down. Telephone tapping of their conversations helped establish their complicity in the assassination of John Kennedy. Mafia informants, under cover, also provided detailed revelations of the Mafia's direct involvement in the assassination of the President[328]. FBI documents referred, more than once, to Carlos Marcello's confession about his participation[329]. FBI phone tapping revealed Santo Trafficante's role as well when he spoke about the assassination plot. According to his lawyer Frank Ragano, he also made a confession on his deathbed[330]. According to historians Waldron and Hartmann, Santo Trafficante's friend and businessman, Jose Aleman, testified under oath before the Congress that he and Trafficante had had a compelling conversation in 1963 shortly before the Kennedy assassination:
Trafficante : *"Have you seen how his brother is hitting Hoffa? Mark my words, this man Kennedy is in trouble, and he will get what is coming to him"*
Jose Aleman : *"Kennedy will be reelected"*.
Trafficante : *"You don't understand me. Kennedy's not going to make it to the election. He is going to be hit"*[331].

Trafficante's words "He is going to be hit" were ambiguous. Some suggested that it was not necessarily a murder that Trafficante was referring to and that, in the context of the 1964

---

[328] Jesse Ventura – They Killed Our President – 2013. Skyhorse Publishing, Inc.
[329] FBI Document 124-10182-10430. Bradley S. O'Leary & L.E. Seymour. Triangle of Death. Waldron &Hartmann. Ultimate Sacrifice
[330] Frank Ragano and Selwyn Raab. Mob Lawyer. Waldron and Hartmann. Ultimate Sacrifice
[331] Lamar Waldron, The Hidden History of the JFK Assassination, Counter Point Berkeley, 2013

presidential elections, the words could also mean: "He will be defeated in the election".

During a FBI phone tapping in 1975, Trafficante declared right after the murder of Sam Giancana: *"There are now only two people who know who killed Kennedy and they aren't talking."*

Carlos Marcello was a very powerful Mafia godfather. For nearly 40 years, he had unquestionable control over a vast territory including Louisiana, Texas and Mississippi. Investigators determined that his criminal empire was worth as much as General Motors, the largest American company in the 1960s. This power helped him to compromise mayors, judges, governors and even members of Congress and senators. Despite the saying posted on the exit door of his office - *"Three can keep a secret if two are dead"* - Marcello was talking too much! After the assassination of John Kennedy, he was very talkative and bragged endlessly about the JFK elimination.[332] When he referred to having helped Jimmy Hoffa get rid of John Kennedy - whose brother, Bobby, was a true nemesis for him - Marcello said to Mafia lawyer Frank Ragano: *"When you see Jimmy, you tell him he owes me big"*[333].

According to FBI document 124-10182-10430, Carlos Marcello also made these remarks when he confided in two prison inmates in December 1985: *"I had the little son-of-a-bitch killed, and I'd do it again...I wish I could have done it myself"*.

A secret FBI operation, coded CAMTEX (for CArlos Marcello TEXas), was also revealed by declassified government files in 1998. The FBI file disclosed Carlos Marcello's "confession" in 1986 about the order he had given to have John Kennedy killed[334]. For several months in 1985 and 1986, the FBI infiltrated, under cover, a FBI informant into the same prison where Carlos Marcello was

---

[332] Thomas L. Jones. "Big Daddy in the Big Easy" Crime Library.

[333] Frank Ragano & Selwyn Raab. Mob lawyer (Random House Value 1996)

[334] Lamar Waldron, The Hidden History of the JFK Assassination, Counter Point Berkeley, 2013

incarcerated. The FBI spy was Jack Van Laningham, himself detained for an attempted bank robbery. He made a deal with the FBI: he would agree to collect Marcello's confidences if, in return, due to the significant risk he was taking, his sentence was reduced. Jack Van Laningham thus set his conditions to accept this dangerous mission. The FBI committed to protect him if anything went wrong. The Bureau would transfer a modest sum of money to his prisoner bank account and, above all, Van Laningham would be freed from prison before the end of his sentence. Using a concealed tape-recorder provided by the FBI, Laningham would encourage Carlos Marcello to speak without his knowledge and would thus record several sensitive conversations in the prison cell they shared together.

Laningham was interviewed by historian, Lamar Waldron, no less than a dozen times, from August 2009 to 2012. These exclusive interviews were set not only with 20 to 30 former assistants of John and Robert Kennedy but also with the FBI, the Secret Service, the Military Intelligence and Congressional staff. The author describes the Mafioso's operation to kill John Kennedy in his book *"The Hidden History of the JFK Assassination "*. What Carlos Marcello revealed was big news. He asserted that Lee Harvey Oswald and Jack Ruby knew each other[335]. The FBI's description of Carlos Marcello's plan to kill John Kennedy was corroborated by the many statements given by those close to the godfather, by John H. Davis, historian and author of the biography of Carlos Marcello and by the House Select Committee on Assassinations.

For "political" reasons, senior government officials decided not to reveal Operation CAMTEX or Marcello's confession to Congress, the press, and the public. The decision not to make these revelations public was taken in 1986 when Operation CAMTEX ceased and lasted until 1992 when Congress passed the *JFK Assassination Records Act,* intended to make public all government documents on this crime. It took until September 1998 for the FBI to finally decide the release of hundred pages

---

[335] Ibid

about Operation CAMTEX to the members of the *Review Board* created as a result of the JFK Act. Over the next five years, the investigators found a mass of pages on the CAMTEX activity at the National Archives, some of which containing 80% of blacked out text. Finally, in 2006, the author Lamar Waldron, with the help of the National Archives' staff, managed to obtain those files that showed almost no censorship. Then, in 2008 and 2009, the press and the television publicized Marcello's confession. NBC News and The Discovery Channel produced specific programs on the event ("*Did the Mafia kill JFK?*"). Jack Van Laningham, who since his release from prison in 1989 had kept a low profile, reappeared. He was given a polygraph test which proved conclusive: he was telling the truth.

There were hundreds of hours of recording of Marcello's revelations. The Godfather boasted that he had ordered the assassination of President Kennedy whom he hated deeply. The many reasons Marcello gave for his revenge were the Kennedy brothers' legal proceedings against him, their continued harassment against the Mafia, mainly against his allies, Santo Trafficante and Jimmy Hoffa and, above all, his aggressive deportation to Guatemala. On April 4, 1961, the godfather had indeed been kidnapped and found himself in the depths of the Guatemalan jungle after a direct order had been given by the Kennedy brothers. While Carlos Marcello was on his way to the local tax collection office for a routine visit, he was arraigned then expelled by air from the United States to Guatemala. A week later, the IRS confiscated $835,000 of Marcello and his wife's assets. Seven months earlier, Marcello had given half a million dollars to the man he thought was going to be the next President of the United States, Richard Nixon, and then he found himself exiled to Guatemala.

There was much criticism of the USA-backed dictator of Guatemala by his people and the media for hosting an undesired Mafioso. The ruler of Guatemala ordered the expulsion of both Marcello and his lawyer from the country and had them escorted to the Honduran border. Far from all civilization, Marcello found himself 30 kilometers from the border in the deepest jungle of the Sierra. The most powerful man in underworld America struggled to extricate himself from the jungle roads of Honduras. According to John Davis, Marcello's biographer, Marcello, still wearing his urban clothes and his luxury shoes filled with banknotes, vowed revenge against the "kid", Robert Kennedy, who had put him in this hell. With little water and food, out of breath, he slumped three times. During a moment of total exhaustion, he told his lawyer who had remained with him: "*If I do not get out of this, tell my brother, upon your return, what Robert Kennedy has done to us and tell him to do what is necessary ...* " But the ordeal ended for both when they managed to reach a small local airport[336].

Meanwhile, Marcello's other lawyers had ruled that the extradition had been illegal[337]. Carlos Marcello resurfaced in the United States - thanks to his pilot, David Ferrie, who had fetched him from the Honduran hell. He later declared a merciless war on the Kennedy brothers. In November 1963, he appeared in a New Orleans court. Ironically, on the very day of the assassination of John Kennedy, he was acquitted! That evening, Marcello celebrated his release and drank a toast to the assassination of the President[338].

Sam Giancana, was under constant pressure from the Justice Department headed by Robert Kennedy. He and Roselli, the Mafia don in Hollywood and Las Vegas, joined efforts to assist with assassination plots. Robert Kennedy and his assistants were struggling to understand Sam Giancana's role in these plots. According to a 1975 New York Times article and two of Robert Kennedy's relatives, journalist Seymour Hersh discovered that in 1969 the CIA had lobbied for a preferential treatment towards one of the Mafia bosses because he had contributed to the assassination attempts against Fidel Castro on behalf of the U.S. government in 1959. During the hearings, Giancana declared:

---

[336] Ibid

[337] G.Robert Blakey, Chief Counsel and Staff Director, Gary T. Cornwell, Deputy Chief Counsel & Michael Ewing, Researcher. Appendices to Final Report of Select Committee on Assassinations. U.S. House of Representatives. January 2, 1979

[338] Lamar Waldron, The Hidden History of the JFK Assassination, Counter Point Berkeley, 2013

"You can't touch me. I have been given immunity". To Robert Kennedy's question: *"Who gave you immunity?"* the leader of the underworld replied with sarcasm: *"The CIA. I work for them but I cannot talk to you about it. It's top secret ..."* Later on, after his own investigation, Kennedy discovered that it was the CIA itself that had made the deal with the Mafia boss[339].

Three figures of the underworld, Marcello, Trafficante and Roselli were thus strongly suspected of being behind the assassination of John Kennedy with the help of the CIA and the anti-Castro. The plan was to kill the President during a parade in one of three cities: Chicago, the city of Roselli's influence, Tampa, the base for Trafficante and Dallas, Marcello's territory. Each plot for each city had a plan B in another city. Marcello revealed that he had used professional killers, some being sharp shooters who had entered the U.S. from Europe via Canada. The first plot in Chicago was a logical geographical location since the killer would arrive via Canada from Michigan. After the failed Chicago and Tampa plots, Dallas was chosen as the place where John Kennedy would be shot.

In their shared jail cell, Marcello revealed to Jack Van Laningham how his Mafia lieutenant, Joe Campisi Jr, a Dallas restaurant owner, became involved. The House Select Committee on Assassinations had already suspicions about Campisi. He was also Jack Ruby's close associate who was seen in his restaurant the day before the assassination of John Kennedy. Later, Campisi visited Ruby in his prison just after Oswald's murder. According to Van Laningham's covert recordings, Marcello facilitated Oswald's transportation by his pilot, David Ferrie, to meet the godfather himself. The House Select Committee on Assassinations had evidence that Oswald and Ferrie knew each other. Ferrie oversaw Oswald's activities in the Civil Air Patrol in the summer of 1963.

---

[339] Ibid

Marcello also revealed that Ruby's nightclub in Dallas, like most cabarets in the city, belonged to the mobster's organization. Ruby was only the manager. In the spring of 1963, Jack Ruby owed a small fortune to the tax department - about $160,000 today - and was desperate about the size of his debt. According to Marcello, Ruby stole the cash he needed from the strip club. As the cabaret funds were largely in the red compared to other years, it did not take long for Marcello's henchmen to find the author of the crime and the source of the financial deficit that had been used to pay Ruby's tax arrears. Marcello summoned Ruby and confronted him in his residence at Churchill Farms, an old farmhouse where, according to Jack Laningham, several bodies had disappeared in the swamps near this huge property. Ruby begged an enraged Marcello to give him another chance and promised he would do anything for him. Marcello then made an offer that Ruby could not refuse: the theft would have no consequences if Ruby, who knew the details of the plot that was waging against JFK, could arrange to have the designated scapegoat (Oswald) shot by a Dallas police officer…and failing this, Ruby would have to do it himself! Ruby understood the blackmail, that his life and that of his entire family were endangered if he did not meet the terms of Marcello's contract. When Ruby left Marcello's property, his life spared, he knew there was no way of avoiding becoming heavily involved in the assassination plot against John Kennedy.

Marcello's meetings with Ruby and Oswald are well documented in the FBI's declassified CAMTEX files and have been confirmed by independent evidence. The author Lamar Waldron is the only one to have interviewed in length both Van Laningham and his FBI boss, Thomas Kimmel, as well as the FBI agent in charge of the CAMTEX project and to have listened to all the secret tapes of Marcello's conversations with Van Laningham. Lamar Waldron and his associate, Thomas Hartmann, also interviewed Dean Rusk (Kennedy's Secretary of State), Dave Powers (JFK adviser) and Cuban exiles such as Antonio Veciana who had met Oswald and David Atlee Phillips, his CIA contact, in 1963. One of the interviewees, Richard Goodwin, Robert

Kennedy's advisor, confirmed that Bobby Kennedy had told him that "*the guy of the Mafia in New Orleans*" - Carlos Marcello - was behind the assassination of his brother. All these interviewees showed consistent statements and credibility.

Oswald's family also had acquaintances with the Mafia. Oswald spent his childhood in New Orleans where his mother knew Organized Crime members under the control of Carlos Marcello. Oswald's uncle, "Dutz" Murret, also had links to the Mafia and served as a bookmaker for Marcello[340].

The House Select Committee on Assassinations discovered Marcello's other links with Oswald. During the summer of 1963, a man close to one of Marcello's best friends bailed Oswald out of jail after the altercation occurred in New Orleans streets when an anti-Castro had been witness to Oswald distributing pro-Castro leaflets. This man, Nofio Pecora, was the same person whom Jack Ruby then called three weeks before the assassination of John Kennedy[341].

Another revelation concerning the Mafia's involvement in the assassination of John Kennedy came from the American far right. The Miami police tapped Joseph Milteer, a fierce supporter for the supremacy of the white race. On the tapes, less than two weeks before the Dallas crime, the police heard him discuss the murder of John Kennedy. Milteer was talking to an undercover police informer in Miami, William Somersett, about a "*plan to assassinate the President with a long-range rifle from the top of a building.*" On the audio recording of the police, Milteer said very openly that the authorities "*would arraign someone in the next few hours after the crime and throw him out as bait to the public.*" He added that the assassination had been planned so that "*the responsibility would fall into communists ... or Castro*". Somersett reported Milteer's words to the authorities. Milteer had also given him troubling details: "*this plot was fomented in New Orleans and probably Miami ... there was a lot of money involved in the project coming not only from the far

---

[340] Ibid
[341] Ibid

right but also from powerful contributors such as a politician from Louisiana in acquaintance with Carlos Marcello and Guy Bannister ". The Miami police gave the recordings to the Secret Service and the FBI. Milteer's words were published in 2006 thanks to credible witnesses revealing Milteer's direct relationship with Guy Banister and other associates of Carlos Marcello[342].

It was all fixed during the spring of 1963. Carlos Marcello, Santo Trafficante and Johnny Roselli had the motive and the means to assassinate President Kennedy by supporting the CIA's original plot to kill Castro. The CIA deputy director, Richard Helms, continued to conceal these plots not only from the Kennedy brothers but also from his boss, John McCone, and lied about the fact that these plots had lasted from 1960 to 1962 and subsequently cancelled. The Mafia mobsters recruited individuals involved in anti-Castro operations for the mission to kill John Kennedy. CIA agents such as Helms hid or destroyed a lot of compromising intelligence data linked to anti-Castro and Mafia operations. In 1963, senior U.S. government officials could not afford to reveal to the world their efforts to destabilize a foreign leader such as Castro, once the Cuban Missile Crisis had ended, or their association with dangerous criminals[343].

The House Select Committee on Assassinations could not directly ascertain whether Marcello and Trafficante were partners in crime and recommended that the Justice Department take over the investigation in order to prove it "without a shadow of a doubt". Marcello continued to bribe Louisiana political officials and federal judges but was eventually charged and jailed for 17 years. While serving his sentence, his younger brother continued to manage his empire[344].

Trafficante was not indicted due to lack of charges. At seventy-two, he fell seriously ill. According to his lawyer, Frank Ragano, Trafficante gave a deathbed confession. On the subject of John

---

[342] Ibid
[343] Ibid
[344] Ibid

and Robert Kennedy, he declared in Sicilian: "*Goddam Bobby. I think Carlos fucked up in getting rid of John - maybe it should have been Bobby*". Trafficante died in March 1987.

In January 1989, while Marcello's biographer, John H. Davis, was preparing the release of his book "*Mafia Kingfish: Carlos Marcello and the Assassination of John F. Kennedy*" Carlos Marcello suffered various minor strokes. His health condition deteriorated rapidly at the prison hospital. Alzheimer's disease was diagnosed. He was released from prison on October 6, 1989. The government decided not to subpoena him again. Impaired by strokes and Alzheimer's disease, he was sent back home in Louisiana where he died on March 2, 1993 at the age of eighty-three[345]. As for the other Mafia godfathers, Johnny Roselli and Sam Giancana, they would meet a death much less sweet. A later chapter will cover their assassinations.

To coincide with the 25th anniversary of the assassination of John Kennedy, Jack Anderson, a journalist of the private television channel PBS was preparing a program on the FBI's revelations about Marcello's involvement in the murder of John Kennedy. Senior Justice Department officials, under Reagan and Bush administrations, decided not to publicize Van Laningham's revelations in the FBI's recordings. Jack Anderson's TV show nevertheless went on air in November 1988 under the title "*American Exposé: Who Murdered JFK?*" The program was centered on the actions of Marcello, Trafficante and especially Roselli, the latter having falsely exposed Castro as a sponsor of the JFK assassination. The programs and articles published in November 1988 caused consternation in the United States and the public demanded the release of all the files on the assassination of the President. In January 1989, Van Laningham was released from jail. A polygraph test revealed his credibility. Van Laningham put an end to his initial intentions of contacting the media and John Davis, Marcello's biographer, and decided to keep a low profile for twenty years. In 2009, NBC News finally located Van

---

[345] Ibid

Laningham and enlisted him in a television program produced under the initiative of the investigator Lamar Waldron [346].

The first book by authors Lamar Waldron and Thom Hartmann, *Legacy of Secrecy* - the preamble to "*The Hidden History of the JFK Assassination*" about the same investigation - inspired a movie with an eponymous title. Its release was announced by the entertainment media for May 2013. Anyone can find on internet the announcement of the making of this movie starring two of the most highly acclaimed actors of the American cinema: Leonardo diCaprio and Robert de Niro, would play Jack Van Laningham and Carlo Marcello respectively. The movie is still under development, according to www.imdb.com, but no reason is given as to why it has not been released. It is more than five years since it was announced to great acclaim, that it would be released to coincide with the 50th anniversary of the JFK assassination. To date, as this book is being written, there is no more news on the internet and no explanation for the delay or indeed for any difficulties in making this movie.[347] Like the movie "*JFK*" whose success awakened the consciousness of the American people, could the movie, *Legacy of Secrecy*, once released, have a similar dramatic impact on the public because it would confirm the complicity of the Mafia in the assassination of John Kennedy?

Although Marcello was quick to eliminate his rivals or anyone for talking too much about the Mafia actions, Jack Ruby's life was spared by the Mafia mobster. But his life would soon dramatically change. His contract with Marcello would force him to kill Oswald who sooner or later was going to talk about the whole plot behind the JFK assassination.

---

[346] Ibid

[347] http://www.comingsoon.net/movie/legacy-of-secrecy-2013#EG6sYmRZ2ErKvLwu.99

Chapter 9

Jack Ruby's Contract

The history of U.S. Mafia crimes is rich in examples of impunity. This is largely due to the lawyers and judges who, corrupted by the underworld's money, succeeded in defending the Mafia mobsters and thus avoiding their indictment.

In the case of Jack Ruby, the Mafia forced him to eliminate Lee Harvey Oswald. He was cornered and had no choice but to eliminate the President's alleged killer. The Mafia let Ruby believe that he would emerge as a true hero in the eyes of the American people and that he would not be indicted but released from jail like the top Mafia mobsters who enjoyed the indulgence of corrupted judges.

Today, the critics of the conspiracy theory continue to argue that there was no evidence that Jack Ruby had any ties to the Mafia, or, should he have had any, that they were small given the very insignificant role of the minor underworld figures who were supposedly in contact with him. These skeptics simply support the Warren Commission's position but they are mistaken as was proven by the House Select Committee on Assassinations.

Historian David Talbot interviewed Frank Mankiewicz, Bobby Kennedy's press assistant for his 1968 presidential campaign[348]. Mankiewicz said that Robert Kennedy had immediately investigated Jack Ruby's role after his brother's assassination. His investigation revealed that the nightclub owner was fully involved with the Chicago and Dallas Mafia. Just before killing Oswald, Ruby's phone calls across the country were unmistakably made to the Mafia dons' names whom Robert Kennedy had summoned to appear before the racketeering committee in the 1950s. Bobby Kennedy knew perfectly well that Ruby had contacts with the Mafia.

Fingerprints of Organized Crime were all over Jack Ruby. Bobby Kennedy asked his closest ally, Walt Sheridan, to present any evidence of it. According to an FBI memorandum, dated November 24, 1963, a few hours after the murder of Oswald, Sheridan found out that a close Chicago Jimmy Hoffa's associate had paid a sum of money to Ruby. The FBI memo confirmed the results of Sheridan's investigation: Ruby "had received a lot of money from Allen M Dorfman" the chief advisor to the Teamsters' Union headed by Hoffa. The information was crosschecked by Robert Peloquin, an attorney with the Criminal Section of the Department of Justice who had been sent to Chicago to investigate the matter[349].

According to FBI sources, Ruby had grown up in the poverty of a Chicago ghetto at the time of the Prohibition. Early in life, he rubbed shoulders with small racketeers and was enlisted by Chicago bosses to later join the Dallas Mafia where he met Joseph Civello, the Mafia boss of the city. Gambling, drug trafficking, corruption of the police and prostitution, were Ruby's racketeering activities. A Mafia boss, Joseph Campisi, one of his contacts, was the first person to visit Ruby in his prison after the murder of Oswald and he had also met him the day before the assassination of John Kennedy. In 1985, four years after Carlos Marcello's confession to FBI informant Jack Van Laningham,

---

[348] Jacob M. Carter – Before History Dies - 2015, Interview of David Talbot
[349] David Talbot – Brothers, The Hidden History of the Kennedy Years - 2007

himself incarcerated in the same prison as Marcello – a fact that was hidden from the public for twenty years - John H. Davis, Marcello's biographer confirmed Ruby's contacts with Marcello's associates Joe Civello and Joe Campisi[350].

In Dallas, just as in Chicago, Ruby handled strip clubs, gambling and arms business and became involved in drug trafficking working for both the CIA and the Mafia. In 1947, he contributed to the transfer of the Mafia from Chicago to Dallas. As soon as Carlos Marcello had control of the Dallas rackets, Ruby began working for the organization there[351]. He paid visits or made phone calls to five men from Marcello's organization and knew at least two of Marcello's brothers through the business of the strip clubs and slot machines.[352] Jack Ruby had contacts in Chicago, Tampa and Dallas, the main cities of the underworld dealings. For John Kennedy's assassination attempts in Chicago and Tampa, he presumably had been given the same role that he would be assigned to play in Dallas: to eliminate the patsy who served as a bait. On October 7, 1963 - just three weeks before the assassination attempt against JFK in Chicago - Ruby met in Dallas with a Chicago businessman, Lawrence Meyers, whom David Ferrie had contacted on September 24. Meyers was also with Ruby in Dallas, the day before the JFK assassination, and was seen dining at the restaurant of Joseph Campisi, Marcello's lieutenant in Dallas. In preparation for the JFK assassination in Dallas, an associate of Jimmy Hoffa received an envelope of about $ 7,000 in October 1963. This payment was made in Chicago, a few weeks after Ruby's meeting with Rosselli in Miami[353]. Ruby's acquaintances were therefore no less than the top Mafia bosses.

Former Minnesota Governor Jesse Ventura summarizes Jack Ruby's exact links with Oswald in his book "*They Killed Our President*"[354]. According to several witnesses, Jack Ruby knew Lee

---

[350] Lamar Waldron, The Hidden History of the JFK Assassination, Counter Point Berkeley, 2013
[351] Ibid
[352] Ibid
[353] Ibid
[354] Jesse Ventura – They Killed Our President – 2013. Skyhorse Publishing

Harvey Oswald. Shortly before the assassination of John Kennedy, Melba Christine Marcades, aka "Rose Cheramie", (she was victim of a suspicious death after giving testimony), Marilyn "Delilah" Walle, Beverly Oliver and Janet "Jada" Conforto, all four strip dancers of Ruby's cabaret claimed to have seen Oswald talking to Ruby at a table in his nightclub. Jack Ruby even introduced his dancers to Oswald.[355] Two car mechanics, Bill Chesher, in charge of the maintenance of Ruby's car, and Robert Roy both testified they had seen Oswald in Ruby's car[356]. Oswald's brother, Robert, also admitted that Lee and Jack Ruby knew each other. David Ferrie, the pilot employed by the Mafia, had enlisted Oswald in the Civil Air Patrol in New Orleans. In early November 1963, Ruby opened a P.O. Box at the same post office where Oswald rented one too. Investigators argued the fact that Ruby and Oswald had a secret verbal communication between each other and it could not have been a coincidence: their respective mailboxes were located 10 feet apart but rather per design in order to facilitate discreet exchanges[357].

According to New Orleans District Attorney Jim Garrison in 1967 (the only one to have conducted a serious justice investigation until he unfortunately lost the trial to indict Clay Shaw), Ruby, Oswald and David Ferrie not only knew each other but worked together for the CIA and anti-Castro operations. In an interview in Playboy, Garrison was adamant: *"I have solid evidence indicating that Ruby, Ferrie, Oswald and others involved in this case were all paid by the CIA to perform certain functions: Ruby to smuggle arms for Cuban exile groups, Ferrie to train them and to fly counterrevolutionary secret missions to Cuba, and Oswald to establish himself so convincingly as a Marxist that he would win the trust of American left-wing groups and also have freedom to travel as a spy in Communist countries, particularly Cuba....We have evidence linking Ruby not only to anti-Castro exile activities but, as with almost*

---

[355] Richard Belzer & David Wayne, Hit List, MJF Books New York, 2013

[356] James diEugenio, "JFK: The Ruby Connection" Citizens for Truth about the Kennedy Assassination.

[357] Michael Eddowes, "Nov 22 How They Killed Kennedy", Neville Spearman (Jersey) Limited, 1976.

everyone else involved in this case, to the CIA itself. Never forget that the CIA maintains a great variety of curious alliances it feels serve its purposes. It may be hard to imagine Ruby in a trench coat, but he seems to have been as good an employee of the CIA as he was a pimp for the Dallas cops... Ruby was up to his neck with the plotters. Our investigators have broken a code Oswald used and found Ruby's private unlisted telephone number, as of 1963, written in Oswald's notebook. The same coded number was found in the address book of another prominent figure in this case....This is the fatal flaw of the Warren Report: its conclusion that the assassination of President Kennedy was the act of a temporarily deranged man, that the murder of Officer Tippit was equally meaningless and, finally, that Jack Ruby's murder of Oswald was another act of a temporarily deranged individual. It is, of course, wildly improbable that all three acts were coincidentally the aberrant acts of temporarily deranged men although it's most convenient to view them as such, because that judgment obviates the necessity of relentlessly investigating the possibility of a conspiracy...In Jack Ruby's case, his murder of Lee Oswald was the sanest act he ever committed; if Oswald had lived another day or so, he very probably would have named names, and Jack Ruby would have been convicted as a conspirator in the assassination plot. As it was, Ruby made the best of a bad situation by rubbing out Oswald in the Dallas city jail, since this act could be construed as an argument that he was "temporarily deranged"[358].

The American people and the whole world were expected to believe that Ruby, upset by the President's death, had killed Oswald in the grip of a patriotic passion, making him a hero. This fabrication continues today, making us believe that Ruby eliminated Oswald by impulse, under sudden emotion, or to prevent JFK's widow from appearing at the hearings during Oswald's trial in Dallas!

Few Americans are aware of the resounding and highly official findings of the House Select Committee on Assassinations in its final report in 1979: "*The murder of Oswald by Ruby was not a spontaneous act and it had required premeditation*". The committee

---

[358] JFK Lancer; Jim Garrison's Playboy Interview. Part three. Jfklancer.com/Garrison4.html

believed it was unlikely that Ruby could have entered the basement of the police premises without complicity. The committee was puzzled that the police station doors, those in the stairwell leading to the garage, had remained unlocked although they were usually locked and that the security guards had been "moved" from that area immediately prior to the murder of Oswald. It was also proved that the Dallas Police Department had concealed information from the Warren Commission about Ruby's access to the garage at the time when Oswald was about to be transferred to a more secure jail[359].

After the assassination and during the following weekend, Jack Ruby had been seen all over Dallas and, not just at the Dallas Police Station. On November 22, 1963, at about 1:30 pm, Seth Kantor, a White House correspondent who had accompanied the presidential parade, saw Jack Ruby at the Dallas Parkland Hospital. When White House Press Secretary Malcolm Kilduff was about to announce the death of the President, Kantor rushed upstairs to the hospital conference room. He felt a tug on the back of his jacket behind him in the stairwell and turning around he found himself facing an anxious Jack Ruby who obviously wanted to talk to him. Kantor gave a precise description of the impression that Ruby had made on him at that moment: *"He had quite a look of consternation on his face. He looked emotional. He had tears in his eyes. He said what was obvious - how horrible it was - and did I have details about the President's condition? I did not know more than he knew and I was most anxious to continue on up the stairway"*. Later, Jack Ruby denied his presence at the Parkland Hospital at that time and the Warren Commission accepted his version rather than Seth Kantor's[360].

Did Ruby have an opportunity and the means to shoot Oswald in the police station? Is it at all credible that he could just have

---

[359] HSCA Final Assassination Report, House Select Committee on Assassinations p 157-158

[360] James W. Douglass, JFK and the Unspeakable, Why He Died and Why it Matters, A Touchstone Book, 2008

arrived by coincidence to commit his crime at the time of Oswald's transfer to the county jail?

Dallas County Jail (where Oswald was about to be transferred if his life had been spared) (author's photo)

Dealey Plaza: Dallas County Jail and Elm Street (author's photo)

Ruby shot Oswald at 11:21 am on Sunday morning, November 24, 1963. Oswald's transfer had been delayed by an hour from the time originally scheduled. Ruby went to the Western Union office very near the police headquarters to pay one of his dancers by money order and left just 5 minutes before Oswald's transfer. It was cutting it fine time-wise and perhaps a coincidence but it looked as if someone had informed Ruby of the transfer delay. He must have had accomplices at the police precinct and his walking into the Western Union office could have been intended as an alibi.

The investigation of the House Select Committee on Assassinations concluded that Ruby had probably been assisted in reaching the police station. Some investigators even speculated that just before Oswald exited from the elevator to the police headquarters garage, Ruby could well have received a signal, like hearing the horn of a car just parked on the garage access ramp. The car horn is clearly audible on the televised murder scene.

It is highly likely that Ruby had planned to be near the police precinct in downtown Dallas that Sunday, shortly before Oswald's transfer. According to investigators, Ruby owed $25 to one of his strip dancers, Karen Carlin. Ruby asked her, in the presence of other eyewitnesses, to meet him at Nichols Garage near Ruby's cabaret on that Saturday and she agreed. A partner of Ruby's had warned her, the day before, that the meeting with Ruby should not to be missed: *"if you're not down here, you won't be around too long"*.

Karen Carlin did not miss the appointment and arrived at the garage well before Ruby. He had previously made a phone call to the garage attendant to ask him to lend Carlin five dollars that he would reimburse later. When Ruby arrived at the garage, he told the garage man that he had no cash on him despite the fact that he could have gotten the money easily from the safe in his cabaret nearby. According to investigators, Ruby's plan was to promise Carlin that he would send her a $25 money order the next day from a Western Union office open on Sunday, just a stone's throw away from the police precinct where Oswald's transfer to the County Jail would be organized. The next day, the Western Union stamped a receipt that would become Ruby's alibi for being very close to the police station shortly before Oswald's transfer.

It was clear that this was Ruby's device since two Western Union offices were also open that Sunday much closer to his apartment in the suburb of Oak Cliff. Ruby had no real reason to go all the way to a Western Union office in downtown Dallas near the police station, unless he intended to kill Oswald. At the Western Union office, Ruby arranged for a money order to be sent to Carlin at around 11:17 am, four minutes before Oswald's transfer. He then walked to the nearby police station.

It would appear to be rather short timing for Ruby to claim a "sudden passion" for avenging the assassination of John Kennedy, as the official version claimed. Ruby had many friends who could have signaled him to turn up at the right time in the police station basement. We also know that one minute after Ruby had left the Western Union office, his lawyer entered the police precinct and remained there until Oswald stepped out of the elevator into the basement garage. Ruby's lawyer was about to leave the police station when he made this comment to a police officer: *"That's all I wanted to see."* At 11:21am, Ruby arrived in the basement and as soon as Oswald was in sight shot him in the abdomen. After Oswald received a fatal wound and was transferred to Parkland Hospital, the police found Ruby, once arraigned, extremely agitated and repeatedly asking whether Oswald was dead or alive. Once he heard that he was declared dead at 1:07pm, he calmed down according to Carlo Marcello's biographer, John H. Davis[361].

---

[361] Lamar Waldron, The Hidden History of the JFK Assassination, Counter Point Berkeley, 2013

Access ramp to the downtown Dallas police basement where Oswald was shot by Jack Ruby (author's photo)

The previous day, Ruby was seen prowling around the police station trying to spy on Oswald with the intent to find a police officer who could silence him. Ruby's association with hundreds of police officers made this task possible. On November 22, at 6:00 pm, John Rutledge, a Dallas Morning News reporter, saw Ruby on the 3rd floor of the police station. At 7:00 pm, Ruby was talking to detective August Eberhardt in the corridor. Then, shortly before 8:00 pm, Ruby made an attempt to see Oswald by opening the door of Captain Fritz's office where Oswald was being interrogated. Two police officers stopped him, one telling him: *"You can't go in, Jack."* Some investigators believe that if Ruby had managed to enter Fritz's office, he would have done what he finally did the next day - shoot Oswald. Frustrated by his unsuccessful attempts, Ruby called the home of his friend, Gordon McLendon, owner of a radio station, who was known to be in contact with CIA agent David Atlee Phillips and Carlos Marcello.

During Oswald's interrogation, at around 10:30 pm, one of the police officers received a phone call from Ruby who offered to get them sandwiches. The police officer refused. Around 11:30 pm, Ruby was back to the police station. A police officer saw him among a horde of reporters. After midnight, a chaotic press conference at the Dallas police headquarters was organized by the Police Chief Curry and District Attorney Henry Wade concerning Oswald's custody. Ruby attended. He had the opportunity to see Oswald and to be as close as 3 feet to him. He was carrying a revolver in his right pocket, walked past Oswald but blew his chance for a possible shot. Ruby later admitted to the FBI that he had carried his firearm during the press conference. As we can see on the video archives of the conference, when an erroneous reference was given to reporters that Oswald was a member of the "Free Cuba Committee" - an *anti*-Castro group - Ruby, perched on a table at the back of the room, made the correction by shouting that Oswald was actually acting for "Fair Play for Cuba Committee", a communist *pro*-Castro group[362].

On Saturday night, Officer Billy Grammer, on duty at the police station, received an anonymous phone threat: if Oswald was transferred the next day, he would be killed.[363] A man on the phone requested that the arrangements for Oswald's transfer to the County Jail the next day be changed: "*If you transfer Oswald as you plan, we'll kill him*", said the man. Grammer recognized Ruby's voice during that call: "*Ruby was the man who had called me. He knew me and I knew him. He knew my name*". Some investigators think that Ruby was desperately trying to free himself from his contract to kill Oswald. But the transfer route was not changed. Ruby and Oswald were going to confront each other the next day. Grammer would later say: "*It was not a spontaneous act*". He was convinced that Oswald's murder had all been planned and that there was no way Ruby could get around it[364].

So to resume, despite the fact that the "Lone Nuts" claim that he had no dealings with the Mafia bosses nor any prominent role in Organized Crime, Jack Ruby knew the right people in the right places. He had worked in Dallas, a city where the Mafia was

---

[362] Ibid

[363] Robert J. Groden, The Killing of a President, Vicking Studio Books, 1993

[364] Robert J. Groden and Harrison Edward Livingstone. High Treason: The assassination of JFK. What really happened? The Conservatory Press, 1989

controlled by Carlos Marcello. In Cuba, he had met and tried to help Santo Trafficante. He had collaborated with Johnny Roselli's Mafia in Chicago. Jimmy Hoffa's son admitted that his father knew Ruby. As Ruby's phone records showed, the Mafia bosses and Jimmy Hoffa had more than a dozen associates who knew him. The number of his long distance calls, less than 10 as a monthly average, had tripled in September 1963 and reached 110 calls in November. These calls were connected with the Mafia and Hoffa's associates. Ruby also played a small role in Marcello and Trafficante's drug network. He and Oswald shared a close relationship with the CIA. They knew each other during the Cuban crisis. Last but not least, Ruby had good contacts with the Dallas police who helped to frame a "patsy" for the Dallas assassination plot and then to eliminate him. In order to enter the police station basement to shoot Oswald, Ruby had used his contacts with the police. According to government records, Ruby knew at least 700 of the 1200 Dallas police officers, most of them corrupted![365] All this does not make Jack Ruby a temporarily deranged man who acted by impulse… what the "Lone Nuts" still believe!

Much later, from his jail cell, Ruby blamed top government officials as well as President Lyndon Johnson, for being behind a cover-up in the assassination of President Kennedy. As can be seen on YouTube, here is what Ruby had to say: *"Everything pertaining to what's happening has never come to the surface. The world will never know the true facts of what occurred, my motives. The people who had so much to gain, and had such an ulterior motive for putting me in the position I'm in, will never let the true facts come above board to the world."* When asked by a reporter, *"Are these people in very high positions, Jack?"* he responded *"Yes"*[366].

In 1964, Jack Ruby was formally charged with the murder of Oswald. According to a CIA memorandum, Melvin Belli, Ruby's

---

[365] Lamar Waldron, The Hidden History of the JFK Assassination, Counter Point Berkeley, 2013

[366] Jack Ruby Press Conference, YouTube, http://www.youtube.com/watch?v=we2eucWXqjg

lawyer, had been involved in illegal drug trafficking. Instead of using a defense strategy for a "sudden impulse" crime (which, according to Texas law, could have resulted in a lenient sentence, up to two years of jail or parole), Belli used a strange defense procedure. He defended his client by stating that he had a "psychomotor dysfunction", something never seen in Texan courts. Ruby and his lawyer finally lost the case and in March 1964 Ruby was sentenced to death in Dallas[367].

The Warren commission was under pressure to close its investigation and to write its report in the very short time required by President Lyndon Johnson and FBI Director J. Edgar Hoover. The Commission hardly had time to question Ruby despite his countless requests to be heard. During the visit of two Commission members, Earl Warren and Gerald Ford, to question him in his Dallas jail, Ruby begged them to transfer him to Washington in order to testify before the highest authorities because he felt unsafe testifying in Dallas. Ruby told them that he wanted to correct his motive for Oswald's murder: his alleged act of "patriotism" was not the real motive. He asked for a polygraph test to prove that he had not told the truth when he was arrested and that he had bluffed with his version of being a "patriot". Ultimately when he was denied a transfer to Washington, Ruby expressed his deep frustration: *"Then, I won't be around for you to come and question me again…I want to tell the truth but I can't tell it here…I am used as a scapegoat…. If I am eliminated, there won't be any way of knowing… I am the only one that can bring out the truth to our President… "*. Then, resigned, he said: «*You have lost me though. You have lost me, Chief Justice Warren*»[368].

Ruby was granted another trial by a new court, but he died before the trial began. His eagerness to finally reveal the truth and to expose the plot, in a safe place, had died with him. On December 9, 1966, Ruby was admitted to Dallas Parkland Hospital for severe pneumonia. A day later, the doctors found out

---

[367] Lamar Waldron- The Hidden History of the JFK Assassination. 2013. Counterpoint
[368] Robert J. Groden, The Killing of a President, Vicking Studio Books, 1993

that he had a cancer of the liver, lungs and brain. Ruby died of a pulmonary embolism on January 3, 1967. Throughout his incarceration, Ruby, who was a non-smoker, claimed that he had been injected with cancer-inducing cells; a procedure he said was based on a secret biochemical weapon research. He believed that the occurrence of his rapidly evolving cancer had coincided with the medical doctor's visits to his jail. In the early 1960s, a top-secret program had indeed been developed to research a new kind of bio-weapon: a fast acting cancer that could be used to remove Fidel Castro. Some believe that this vaccine was later used to murder Jack Ruby[369].

End-of-life confessions, eyewitnesses' testimonies, biographers' statements and more specifically, as this chapter recalls, claims from individuals linked with Jack Ruby, if they cannot be crosschecked, can be viewed as fragile evidence. On the contrary, if evidence is based on solid and indisputable facts, without possible error or alteration, it cannot be rejected. The next chapters will highlight the evidence of an assassination plot against President Kennedy based, primarily, on the results of physical and scientific research. Because of their serious conclusions, these studies deliver a strength of conviction capable of challenging any person who doubts the existence of a conspiracy.

---

[369] Richard Belzer & David Wayne. *Hit List* MJF Books New York 2013

Chapter 10

Ballistic Evidence

As the presidential parade was ending, John Kennedy tragically fell into an ambush set by professional killers positioned in crossfire on Dealey Plaza, not so far from the place where he was to give a speech.

Most ballistics experts believe that the bullet that struck the President's head came from the front. They are adamant: gunshots came from either the "Grassy Knoll" or the nearby triple underpass. Abraham Zapruder's film gives the evidence; Kennedy was propelled violently backwards and to the left when the fatal bullet hit him.

Those who criticize this conclusion, however, present far-fetched explanations defying the laws of physics and all human logic. From what we see from his Marine records and heard from his military companions, Lee Harvey Oswald was certainly not a sharpshooter. In the Marines, at the time of Oswald's enrollment, shooters were noted as follows: the lowest score was 190, the highest was 250. Anyone who scored 190 was ranked as a "Marksman". Marines with a 250 score or slightly less were rated as "Sharpshooter ". Before Oswald left the Marines, his military record showed that his score was just one point above the minimum and he sometimes missed not only the center of the target but the whole target itself. His Russian friends also confirmed this when they went with him to shoot rabbits in the Soviet Union. He missed the rabbits most of the time! [370]. It is hard to believe that such a poor shooter, with an obsolete Second World War rifle (the Mannlicher Carcano that was found on the sixth floor of the Texas School Book Depository and allegedly attributed to Oswald) could surpass shooting champions and moreover could fire at a moving target and with a rifle sight that was skewed after each shot. During the reenactments of the assassination, shooters using the same rifle and ammunition could not achieve the feat of firing 3 gunshots in six seconds - the Warren Report's assessment of Oswald's performance.

According to Jesse Ventura[371], himself a Marine veteran, Carlos Hathcock, the best Marine fighter, confirmed that he had tried to carry out a series of gunshots in Quantico Marine Corps base under the same conditions as those Oswald was supposed to use on Dealey Plaza. Hathcock summed up the impossible task: "*Let me tell you what we did at Quantico. We reconstructed the whole thing: the angle, the range, the moving target, the time limit, the obstacles, everything ... I don't know how many times we tried it but we couldn't duplicate what the Warren Commission said Oswald did. Now, if I can't do it, how in the world could a guy who was a non-qualified on the rifle range and later only qualified as 'marksman' do it?* "[372]

Many witnesses confirmed that two gunshots were very close, a double detonation (bang - bang, bang), something impossible to achieve with this military surplus rifle of the Second World War because, after each shot, one has to rearm the weapon and aim at the moving target again. Since two gunshots were very close, another shooter must have fired. The Warren Commission's version is therefore absurd and an insult to the intelligence of the American people.

The Warren Commission was unable to explain the movement of the President's head, back and to the left, when the fatal bullet hit his head as seen on the unrigged version of the Zapruder movie. The commission eluded the question in its report to enable

---

[370] Interview of David Talbot by Jacob. M. Carter – Before History Dies – 2015.
[371] Jesse Ventura – They Killed Our President – 2013. Skyhorse Publishing, Inc.
[372] Roberts Craig–Kill Zone: A Sniper Looks at Dealey Plaza–1994. Consolidated Press

avoiding the considerable task of having to explain it. It despicably altered the facts by reversing two photos, just after frame 313 - those showing the explosion of Kennedy's skull - in order to fake a projection forward of his head. J. Edgar Hoover claimed it was "a printing error"!

Craig Roberts, war veteran and former sniper[373], claimed that the fatal blow had been caused by a high velocity bullet, a frangible missile, according to the technical process by which the impact and the hydrostatic pressure inside the President's skull produced its explosion as seen on the Zapruder film. The bullets from the Mannlicher Carcano rifle, fired by the suspect Oswald, were rather non-breakable ammunition and corresponded to an average velocity.

Howard Donahue, an expert in firearms and ballistics, testified that it was impossible for Oswald to fire all the gunshots on Dealey Plaza[374]. The official trajectory of the bullet that struck the President's head caused an entrance wound and was incompatible with a shot fired from the sixth floor window of the school book depository. Besides, the trajectory of the bullet that impacted the chrome windshield trim of the presidential limousine was too high to be that of a bullet fired from the Texas School Book Depository.

David Talbot, interviewed by Chris Matthew on MSNBC "Hardball" show on November 24, 2013, said that fifty years after the assassination, a FBI metallurgist expert who had just published his test results on bullets and fragments of bullets that were fired in Dealey Plaza claimed that *"we could no longer say that the bullets found on Dealey Plaza came from a single rifle"*[375].

There was an enormous confusion as to what was the exact model of the rifle found on the sixth floor of the Texas School Book Depository. According to the official government version, it was a Mannlicher-Carcano rifle. The Warren Commission

---

[373] Ibid
[374] Jesse Ventura – They Killed Our President – 2013. Skyhorse Publishing, Inc.
[375] http://www.nbcnews.com/id/18941406/ns/msnbc-hardball_with_chris_matthews/t/hardball-chris-matthews-may/#.Vk-9ifmrTIV

claimed it belonged to Oswald since there was "evidence" that he had purchased it by correspondence. However, several firearms experts formally described the rifle that had been found shortly after the shooting on the sixth floor, as a 7.65 millimeter Mauser, equipped with a telescopic sight.[376] Deputy Sheriff Eugene Boone, Dallas Police Officer Seymour Weitzman, Captain Will Fritz, Homicide Brigade Chief, all testified under oath that the rifle found was a Mauser, a state-of-the-art weapon, whereas the Mannlicher-Carcano was a "museum piece".[377] There was no certainty that the Mannlicher-Carcano could have been used by Oswald, but its "hideout" on the sixth floor was probably a means to frame him since he had allegedly purchased the weapon by mail-order and had supposedly used it for the assassination attempt against General Walker a few months earlier.

How can one not believe the testimony of those at the head of the homicide squad and the expertise of the criminology laboratory? The discovery of the Mauser rifle on the sixth floor could not have been a mistake; the brand name was on the rifle's tag! To add more to the confusion, the rifle was even described as a 0.303 British rifle with a telescopic sight! It is unclear why there was this entire imbroglio but one thing is absolutely certain is that the government lied about the origin of the rifle. Such inconsistencies would be unacceptable in an investigation of any ordinary manslaughter let alone in the case of the "crime of the century", the assassination of the President of the United States in the middle of the day.

Kennedy's two loyal assistants, Kenneth O'Donnell and Dave Powers, who were following the presidential limousine, knew immediately from where the gunshots came. Like dozens of witnesses on Dealey Plaza, there was no doubt for these war veterans that gunshots came from multiple directions. As soon as he heard gunshots, Powers stammered out, "*Kenny, I think the President's been shot*". Then O'Donnell recalled: *"While we both*

---

[376] Gary Savage – JFK: First Day Evidence (The Shoppe Press: 1993) p 158
[377] Jesse Ventura – They Killed Our President – 2013. Skyhorse Publishing, Inc.

stared at the President, the third shot took the side of his head off. We saw pieces of bone and brain tissue and bits of his reddish hair flying through the air. The impact lifted him and shook him limply, as if he was a rag doll, and then he dropped out of our sight, sprawled across the back seat of the car. I said to Dave, 'He's dead.' "[378]. The FBI threatened Kenneth O'Donnell to remain totally silent about what he had seen and forced him to change his version about where the gunshots came from (two of which, O'Donnell said, came from the "Grassy Knoll") because it would be "very damaging to the country ". He remained silent for many years feeling the pressure of his family who were eager to put the whole story behind them. Much later, he told Tip O'Neill, the leader of the House of Representatives, that he was forced to lie before the Warren Commission by claiming that the gunshots had come from behind. Powers, meanwhile, made a statement that he had a vague impression that the sound of gunshots seemed to come both from the front and from the back, something that the commission was not prepared to acknowledge.

In addition, Secret Service special agents on Dealey Plaza were certain that the gunshots that had hit John Kennedy had come from the front of the presidential limousine. One of these agents, Forest Sorrels, was in the car immediately preceding the president's car. When he heard the gunshots, he looked out from his car window on his right. He said, "*I turned around to look up on this terrace part there, because it sounded like it came from the back and up in that direction*"[379]. For him, the gunshots could not have been fired from behind but from his *right* at the point where he was ahead of the President's car. Two other Service Secret agents, Lem Johns[380] and Paul Landis[381], were in the car that just followed the presidential limousine. With deep conviction, based on their

---

[378] David Talbot – Brothers, The Hidden History of the Kennedy Years - 2007

[379] Forest Sorrells–Secret Service Report Special Agent in Charge–28 November 1963

[380] House Select Committee on Assassinations. Interview of Special Agent Thomas Lem Johns. 8 August 1978

[381] Paul Landis – Statement of United States Secret Service Special Agent Paul E. Landis – 27 November 1963

professional opinion, they testified that the gunshots had come from the front.

According to the Warren Commission, only three gunshots were fired at the President's car. To explain the wounds of the President and of the Governor of Texas, John Connally, who was sitting in front of Kennedy, it took the ingenuity of the Warren Commission to limit to three bullets the number of gunshots, otherwise, it would have been impossible for Oswald to rearm his rifle in the allotted time and for the commission to hide the presence of a second shooter.

Vince Palmara quotes Roy Kellerman, the White House special agent for the Secret Service, who was sitting just in front of Connally in the President's limousine. Kellerman's official testimony totally took the Warren Commission by surprise. He told them *"that the limousine was under fire from bullets coming from all sides, that a flurry of shells fell into the limousine and that they* [the commission] *were mistaken about the number of gunshots... there have got to be more than three gunshots, gentlemen"*[382]. The commission took the decision to downplay his testimony.

Once retired, Dallas Police Chief Jesse Curry, who was criticized for his failing and ineffective services during the events of November 22, 1963, took the decision to speak openly: *"I was in the lead car, right in front of the presidential limousine, and I immediately suspected that the first shot came from the front and not from the back where Oswald was. I can't say that I believe in a single shooter"*[383].

According to Jesse Ventura[384], the total number of gunshots was six. Three ejected shells were found inside the Texas School Book Depository by the sixth floor window where Oswald was supposed to be. A bullet missed the target[385]. The Warren Commission conceded. Some investigators said it was not the first

---

[382] Vince Palmara – Survivor's Guilt
[383] Anthony Summers. The Listener: 9 March 1978
[384] Jesse Ventura – They Killed Our President – 2013. Skyhorse Publishing, Inc.
[385] http://jfkfacts.org/jfk-truth-first-shot/#more-24229

shot. This bullet hit the Elm Street sidewalk curb. A passer-by, Jim Tague, was slightly injured on the cheek by one of the projections from the ground. He was standing close to one of the pillars of the triple underpass, watching the presidential limousine on the descent of Elm Street towards the bridge. Police officer, Clyde Haygood, stopped his motorcycle and approached him. He noticed a slight cut on Tague's right cheek. Both made their statements to the Warren Commission on April 9, 1964: Tague remembered: *"Something stung me on the face when I was standing down there."* The police officer who arrived at the scene told him, *"Yes, you have blood there on your cheek."* Tague moved his hand to his cheek and noticed a few drops of blood. Both decided to walk to the sidewalk. About fifteen feet away, Haywood said : *"Look here on the curb. There is a mark quite obviously that was a bullet and it was very fresh"*.

The Warren Commission was not convinced despite Tague and Haygood's testimonies, photographs showing the scratch on Tague's cheek and the fresh mark on the sidewalk also confirmed by Dallas photographers. FBI agents, who investigated the scene in July 1964, could not find the mark on the sidewalk and suggested that street cleaning might have erased it. The Warren Commission sent its own investigators to Dallas, who had no problem finding the sidewalk mark. On August 5, 1964, a piece of the sidewalk curb was removed for spectrophotometer analysis. Traces of metals were identified as lead and antimony residues. Investigators concluded that traces of lead could come from a Mannlicher Carcano bullet. A ballistic analysis also revealed that the sidewalk mark corresponded to the trajectory of a bullet that could have been shot from the Texas School Book Depository. However, a trace of metal was missing: copper residues could not been found. This was a problem because it meant that the bullet that hit the curb was not a full metal jacket bullet.

Triple underpass: the white cross shows the spot where James Tague was standing when he was slightly wounded by a lost bullet (author's photo)

Based on its trajectory, some investigators claimed this lost bullet was fired from the top of the Dal-Tex Building and not from the Texas School Book Depository because a nearby tree could have hidden the presidential car from the sixth floor window of that warehouse.

This missed shot was a huge problem for the Warren Commission since it implied that a fourth shot had been fired thus indicating the presence of at least a second shooter. These facts imposed a revision of its initial report that indicated that no more than 3 gunshots had been fired on Dealey Plaza. Since the commission wanted to stick to its version of one single gunman, it took the decision to remain determined on the number of gunshots; three and only three. All this led the Warren Commission to develop an ingenious scheme! Their revised logic was that a single bullet had passed through both Kennedy's back and Connally's body causing multiple injuries[386].

According to eyewitnesses, another bullet also missed its target but this fact is still disputed. This missed bullet was found buried in the lawn near a manhole cover on Elm Street, near the southern point of the triple underpass. On the day of the

---

[386] Sherry P. Fiester, *Enemy of the Truth*, Myths, Forensics and the Kennedy Assassination, JFK Lancer Productions & Publications. 2012

assassination, a blond-haired man in a suit was photographed bending down to pick up something on the ground, then standing up, apparently holding a small object in his hand, and then putting his hand in his pocket.[387] The hole made by the projectile in the grass was also photographed and the photo appeared in the Fort Worth-Telegram of November 23, 1963. The Fort Worth-Telegram and the Dallas Times Herald also published an article about the bullet found in the grass near the manhole cover. The blond-haired man seen picking up something could not be identified, but he can clearly be seen on the internet photos next to policeman D.J. Foster and Deputy Sheriff Buddy Walthers. According to Dallas Police Chief Jesse Curry, this man was an FBI agent. The trace in the grass was lost and the bullet was never found. It could not have been the same bullet that hit the sidewalk which fragment had slightly hurt James Tague since the distance was too great between the impact spots of the two bullets on Elm Street.

A white mark (outlined by investigators?) where a missed bullet hit the grass can still be seen on Elm Street (author's photo)

Another bullet hit the President's throat and left a very small orifice. Based on the fact that a wound has a different physical aspect whether it is caused by a bullet entering or exiting a human

---

[387] Cover-Up by J. Gary Shaw and Larry Harris, self-published 1976, p. 72-74

body, this bullet came from the front and probably passed through the windshield of the limousine. However, according to some investigators, the crack in the windshield could have been caused by another shot. Nothing is clearly said about the exit point of the bullet that crossed through the President's throat. Then, another bullet hit Kennedy's back from behind (the holes in his jacket and his shirt proved it).

The FBI report and the Warren Commission report were diametrically opposed. Two FBI agents attended JFK's autopsy. The first FBI report concluded that the bullet that hit JFK's back was not the same one that had entered his throat since it had not exited from his back. The Warren Report placed the bullet in the back much higher than the point observed by the doctors at the autopsy (about 5 inches from the collar of JFK's jacket). The Warren Report concluded that the bullet had been fired from top to bottom, had penetrated the nape of JFK's neck and exited after tearing his trachea. The Warren Report asserted that the fact the President had slumped in his seat, the collar of his jacket had raised a few inches. But his shirt, with the collar buttoned, showed only one hole which did not match with the hole in his jacket that was 5 inches lower from the collar.

Governor John Connally, in the same car as Kennedy, was also wounded. In his testimony, he was adamant that two bullets had hit him. The first bullet that hit him was not the one that hit JFK's throat, because as soon as he heard the shot he had time to turn round to his right in order to look at the President over his shoulder. Connally was then hit by *another* bullet as soon as he had turned repositioned himself facing the front of the car.

The Warren Commission, however, explained that both men had been hit by the *same* bullet and that it had first entered John Kennedy's throat - the commission maintained that it was fired from behind – and then hit Connally. This bullet was called the "Single Bullet" by the commission whereas the critics of this version ironically refer to the "Magic Bullet"! Cyril Wecht, the eminent forensic pathologist and former president of the American Academy of Forensic Sciences, testified before the House Select Committee on Assassinations and gave his pathologist expertise concerning the trajectory of the bullet. With irony, Wecht recapped the Warren Commission's absurd version and the incredible path of the projectile: this bullet hit John Kennedy behind his neck, shot across the neck without fracturing any bones, and came out of his throat, and - after changing direction in the air; a spin to the right and to the left, up and down – hit Connally's back at the right armpit and broke his fifth rib. This same bullet then came out of his chest at the right nipple, pierced his right wrist, breaking the radius, came out at the base of his hand palm and finally lodged into his left thigh just above the knee with a depth of about 3 inches into the skin. The bullet left small residues of lead when it hit his femur.

According to the Warren Commission, this one inch copper jacket bullet was fired from Oswald's Mannlicher Carcano positioned on the sixth floor of the Texas School Book Depository. The projectile would have crossed 15 obstacles, 7 layers of skin, about 15 inches of tissues, torn the knot of the President's tie, removed 4 inches from Connally's rib, pulverized his radius... only to be retrieved almost intact on a stretcher at Parkland hospital! The Warren Commission admitted that it failed to find a response to the challenge of this bullet without evidence, but made this astonishing statement: *"Although it is not necessary for the Commission's major conclusions to determine what shot had hit Governor Connally, there is a very persuasive explanation that the same bullet that went through the President's throat also caused the injuries inflicted on Governor Connally"*![388]

Technically speaking, a single bullet could not have caused all Connally's injuries. The bullet entered his body with a declining angle of 25 degrees to the far right of his chest, near the armpit whereas the bullet that hit the President from behind was fired with a slightly ascending angle. According to the report of the two pathologists, Sibert and O'Neil, who attended the President's autopsy, the opening of the wound in his back was probed by Dr. Humes with his little finger. He thus determined that the distance

---

[388] Sherry P. Fiester, *Enemy of the Truth*, Myths, Forensics and the Kennedy Assassination, JFK Lancer Productions & Publications. 2012

travelled by the bullet was short[389]. It means this bullet did not exit from Kennedy's body but lodged itself 2 inches in his back and 6 inches lower than the point of impact of another bullet that hit his neck from a direction facing the car[390].

No one in the limousine believed in the theory of the "Magic Bullet".[391] Jackie Kennedy, John Connally and his wife, all said that one bullet hit the President's neck a fraction of second before another bullet hit John Connally. Not only the theory of the "Magic Bullet" was not plausible but Zapruder's film and testimonies gave opposite views. The Warren Commission's "evidence" was an elaborate fabrication in order to maintain its single gunman theory.

One bullet could not have caused all the injuries inflicted on both men. Despite the fact that it had gone through the flesh and the bones of two people, this so-called "Single Bullet" was found on a stretcher in an almost pristine condition- without traces of blood or organic matter - at Parkland Memorial Hospital where Kennedy and Connally were treated. Chief Engineer Darrell Tomlinson spotted it near two stretchers that had been left unattended for a few minutes in the hospital lobby. His statement was crosschecked with the testimony of two hospital employees. The skeptics of the "Single Bullet" theory came to the conclusion that someone had stealthily placed it on the stretcher. About 15 minutes before the "Magic Bullet" was discovered, Jack Ruby had been seen by two reliable eyewitnesses in Parkland Hospital. One of the witnesses, journalist Seth Kantor, said he had spoken to Ruby in the hospital that day although the latter denied it. Some investigators speculated that Ruby feared that his wrongful act of placing or having someone place the bullet on the stretcher without the hospital staff's knowledge would betray him, thus

---

[389] Ibid

[390] Robert J. Groden and Harrison Edward Livingstone. High Treason: The assassination of JFK. What really happened? The Conservatory Press, 1989

[391] Interview of Jefferson Morley by Jacob. M. Carter – Before History Dies – 2015.

linking him to Oswald's rifle and to the gunshots fired at Kennedy and Connally[392].

Governor Connally's torn shirt, which could have provided leads as to the trajectory of the bullets and blood spattering, was sent back to him all washed and ironed! No more traces, no evidence left for ballistics experts to form an accurate opinion about the direction of the bullets!

Dr. Cyril Wecht, challenged the Warren Commission's findings and in particular the theory of the "Single Bullet", a bullet that could not have exited human bodies in such a pristine condition after having caused so many injuries[393]. He lamented that the President's brain had vanished from the National Archives because it would have been helpful to examine it in order to provide evidence of his assertion, by means of complementary tests. Here is what he answered when asked if it was his opinion that no bullet - especially the same bullet referenced 399 – could have caused all the wounds inflicted to both President Kennedy and Governor Connally: *"Based upon the findings in this case, it is my opinion that no bullet could have caused all these wounds, not only 399 but no other bullet that we know about or any fragment of any bullet that we know about in this case... I have raised same questions concerning the head wound and the possibility, albeit remote, of a second shot fired in synchronized fashion from the right side or the lower right rear, synchronized with the head shot that struck the President in the back of the head....Why our panel of distinguished experts with all our expertise and this staff representing a very prominent committee which, in turn, represents the House of Representatives of the United States Congress, why such tests could not be performed is beyond me. I feel constrained to say that they were not performed because people knew full well what the results would be.... That is to say the condition of a bullet having crossed all these bones. It is absolutely false. Well, I got involved back in 1965 with the American Academy of Forensic Sciences. For the past 12 or 13 years, I have repeatedly, limited to the context of the forensic pathologist, numerous times implored, beseeched, and urged, in writing, orally, privately, collectively, my colleagues; to come up with*

---

[392] Lamar Waldron- The Hidden History of the JFK Assassination. 2013. Counterpoint
[393] Cyrilwecht.com/journal/archives/jfk/index.php.

one bullet that has done this. I am not talking about 50 percent of the time plus one, 5 percent or 1 percent--just one bullet that have done this. Not a single colleague of mine has demonstrated that a bullet having broken two bones in some human being could be found in an almost pristine condition... The panel, to the best of my recollection, was in unanimous agreement that there was a slight upward trajectory of the bullet through President John F. Kennedy. How in the world, under the single bullet theory, can a bullet be fired from the sixth floor window, strike the President in the back, and yet have a slightly upward direction? There was nothing there to cause it to change its course. And then with the slightly upward direction, outside the President's neck, that bullet then embarked upon a rollercoaster ride with a major dip, because it then proceeded; under the single bullet theory, through Gov. John Connally at a 25 degree angle of declination" [394].

The photographic evidence - Zapruder's film - fully confirmed that President Kennedy and Governor Connally were hit with a time interval of 1 to 1.5 second between gunshots. The film shows that when John Kennedy is hit, the governor does not respond to the impact of the same bullet: he still holds his hat in his right hand. According to the "Single Bullet" theory, Connally's wrist has just been hit (the bone broken and the radial nerve have been completely severed) by this same bullet but no trace of blood can be detected on the cuff of his shirt on the Zapruder's film photo capturing the very moment Kennedy is hit[395].

The cynicism of the government and specifically that of Gerald Ford, a member of the Warren Commission (then President of the United States) has been concealed from the American people. Indeed, he secretly passed confidential information from the commission's investigation to the FBI. He was caught having obnoxiously lied. Investigators revealed a document concerning the position of the bullet that had created an entry wound in the President's back. This file had been concealed in a safe for about thirty years. The Associated Press published the facts in 1997. This official document showed Gerald Ford's handwritten correction

---

[394] Robert J. Groden and Harrison Edward Livingstone. High Treason: The assassination of JFK. What really happened? The Conservatory Press, 1989
[395] Ibid

with his initials to place the entry of the bullet in JFK's back a few inches higher. His correction implied that it was the same bullet that had hit JFK in the back and in the neck in such a way supporting the "Single Bullet" theory! Without Ford's correction, the commission could never have put forward the theory that the same bullet fired from behind the limousine could have hit Kennedy in the back and passed through Connally's body[396]!

O'Neil and James Sibert, who were present during the autopsy at Bethesda Hospital, testified that measurements of bullet holes in Kennedy's jacket and shirt indicated that they were about six inches below the top of the shirt collar and much lower than the neck. Sibert declared: *"There is no way that the bullet could have gone that low then rise up and come out the front of the neck, zigzag and hit Connally and then end up pristine on a stretcher over there in Dallas"*[397].

Since more and more testimonies were received to support the origin of the bullet that hit the President's throat - from a point facing the limousine - the Warren Commission had trouble explaining that it would have come from behind! They gave a preposterous explanation: they changed their position by conceding that the neck wound was indeed caused by an entry bullet ... but they still insisted that it came from behind and not from the front of the car! So, in a manner of speaking they "dodged the bullet"! They asserted that the President had just turned his body round towards someone in the crowd who had waved to him and that, as a result, his throat had been exposed to the line of fire corresponding to the Texas School Book Depository where the sniper pulled the trigger. Of course, the frame of Zapruder's film at this very moment showed no such contortion of Kennedy's body when he moved his hands to his neck!

The slow-motion Zapruder film confirmed that a second bullet had hit Connally. After being struck by the first bullet, he was still holding his Stetson with his left hand, proof that his left wrist had not yet been wounded. The doctors found many bullet fragments

---

[396] Mike Feinsilber. "Gerald Ford forced to admit the Warren Report fictionalized" July 2, 1997. Associated Press.

[397] Lamar Waldron, The Hidden History of the JFK Assassination, Counter Point Berkeley, 2013

in Connally's body proving that one single bullet (as the Warren Commission continued to argue) could not have resulted in so much bullet fragmentation. They extracted from his wrist and his thigh a total weight that surpassed by far the weight of fragments missing from the "Single Bullet"! Of course, it defies all logic that the weight of a bullet could increase between the moment it leaves the rifle barrel and reaches its target! According to Dr. Milton Helpern, Chief Medical Examiner of New York City, "*The original, pristine weight of this bullet before it was fired was approximately 160 to 161 grains. The weight of the bullet recovered on the stretcher in Parkland Hospital was reported by the Commission as 158.6 grains. This bullet wasn't distorted in any way. I cannot accept the premise that this bullet thrashed around in all that bony tissue and lost only 1.4 to 2.4 grains of its original weight. I cannot believe, either, that this bullet is going to emerge miraculously unscathed, without any deformity, and with its lands and grooves intact.*"[398] These observations clearly showed that another bullet had passed through Connally's body and left fragments there.

In November 1970, John N Mitchell, the Attorney General under the Nixon administration, ordered that the Justice Department should not reveal ballistic evidence in the Kennedy case. There was an attempt to hide specific data concerning the FBI's spectrographic analysis of bullets or fragments of bullets recovered from the shooting site and in particular those found in Connally's body that would not match those in JFK's body nor the "Magic Bullet" conclusions. This cover-up was a response to the lawsuit brought by investigator Harold Weisberg who searched for medical evidence in the JFK case.[399] Mitchell ordered the Justice Department to block the disclosure of pivotal ballistic evidence on Kennedy's assassination, claiming that "*national security should prevail, that the publication would have created a dangerous precedent and seriously interfered with the effective FBI operation.*" The lawsuit filed by Weisberg was consequently

---

[398] Robert J. Groden, The Killing of a President, Vicking Studio Books, 1993
[399] https://ratical.org/ratville/JFK/PG/PGchp3.html

nullified and the report on ballistic analysis vanished from the National Archives[400].

The tape recording of the telephone conversation between President Johnson and Senator Richard Russel, himself a member of the Warren Commission, is enlightening. The senator, who was opposed to the commission's opinion, spoke about his dilemma in these terms: *"They're trying to prove that the same bullet that hit Kennedy first was the one that hit Connally, went through him and through his hand, his bone, and into his leg...The commission believes that the same bullet that hit Kennedy hit Connally. Well, I don't believe it."* Johnson replied: *"I don't either"* [401].

Then there was the fatal bullet that hit John Kennedy's head. The origin of this shot came from a point facing the car. It penetrated into his right temple and caused a massive gush of brain matter from the back of his skull causing his body to be violently hurtled backwards and to the left. The next day, a young medical student, William Allen Harper, found a piece of cranial bone, 2 by 3 inches large on Dealey Plaza. It was later determined that this bone fragment had been ejected about 300 feet to the left behind the President's car, with an axis directly aligned with a probable shot fired from the "Grassy Knoll" facing the limousine. The piece of skull, identified as occipital, called the "Harper Fragment", was given to the head of the pathology department of the Dallas Parkland Hospital for analysis. A lead deposit was found suggesting the impact of a bullet. The identification and the origin of this cranial fragment created a critical problem for the government cover-up. Nine years after the assassination, a student in physics at UCLA University, David Lifton, compared the fragment of the occipital bone to the government's official x-rays of the President's skull. Lifton and pathologists Dr. A. B. Cairns and Dr. Gerard Noteboom came to the conclusion that the

---

[400] Robert J. Groden and Harrison Edward Livingstone. High Treason: The assassination of JFK. What really happened? The Conservatory Press, 1989

[401] White House tapes of September 18, 1964 at 7.54 pm cited in Donald E. Wilkes, Jr. Professor Law in "JFK Killer Not Alone".

autopsy x-rays could not be authentic because they showed the posterior part of the skull practically intact. They deduced that the autopsy x-rays had been doctored in order to conceal a bullet exit wound and therefore removing evidence of a shot fired from the front[402]. Evidence of this distortion will be widely covered in a next chapter.

Some experts, such as Cyril Wecht, still think that two bullets possibly hit the President's head almost simultaneously; one bullet fired from behind and the other one from the front of the limousine: as can be seen on Zapruder's film, a very brief movement *forward* was immediately followed by a sudden thrust of the body *backwards* and to the left. An image-by-image analysis of Zapruder's film, between gunshots 312 and 313, reveals that President Kennedy's head moves slightly forward but that immediately afterwards his head and shoulders violently moved backward in response to a bullet impact. The House Select Committee on Assassination's report indicated however that the shot that struck Kennedy's head came from behind. Its conclusion was fiercely challenged by medical experts like Dr. Cyril Wecht. Despite the fact that he accepted a slight move of the President's body forward, Wecht was convinced that it was immediately followed by the kick of his head and shoulders violently towards the rear, caused by a second shot which burst the right side of JFK's forehead.

Other explanations to support that a bullet had been fired from the back and not from the front of the car but still causing JFK's head movement *backward* were advanced. Based on dynamic physics studies, some supporters only saw a "propulsive jet effect" as the reason, a propulsive force created by the blood flushing out of Kennedy's *forehead* at the impact of a bullet hitting the *back* of his skull. The explanation of the jet effect was not viable because the fluid mechanics application tests were found to be deficient. Others believe that the impact of the bullet at the back of the head would have created neuromuscular spasms capable

---

[402] James W. Douglass, JFK and the Unspeakable, Why He Died and Why it Matters, A Touchstone Book, 2008

of causing backward head movement. This explanation was also invalidated: the position of Kennedy's body - seated and crouched as Zapruder's images showed it when the fatal bullet hit his skull - had no comparison with what is observed with victims of head trauma injuries reacting to atypical spastic hypertonia.

Based on a close look at frames 312 and 313 of Zapruder's film in another study by Josiah Thompson, a private investigator[403], the slight head movement forward could have been a reaction from Abraham Zapruder himself who had jolted his camera forward when he realized a shot had hit Kennedy, thus causing a photo blur showing a forward head movement. But this last theory was dismissed and video film experts asserted that JFK's head movement forward could not have been caused by camera movement.

Although some experts believe that it was very unlikely that two bullets (one shot from behind and the other one from the front), hit Kennedy's skull almost simultaneously, current forensic research favors the explanation of a single shot from the front. Experts (Karger in 2008, Radford in 2009 and Coupland in 2011) proved that the initial transfer of energy could have caused the target, in a fraction of second, to move in the opposite direction of the line of fire[404].

In 2014, I met Sherry P. Fiester, Crime Scene Investigator, Ballistics and Blood Spatter Expert at the Assassination Archives and Research Center convention "JFK and the Warren Report" in Bethesda, Maryland. Thanks to her impressive work, compiled in a book she graciously autographed for me, an extremely detailed reconstruction of the crime on Dealey Plaza was made possible which concluded that *"the wound on President Kennedy's head was caused by a shot fired from the front"*[405]. Since the orientation of blood

---

[403] Josiah Thompson, Six Seconds in Dallas: A Micro-Study of the Kennedy Assassination. 1967

[404] Sherry P. Fiester, *Enemy of the Truth*, Myths, Forensics and the Kennedy Assassination, JFK Lancer Productions & Publications. 2012

[405] Ibid

spatter from a victim can determine the bullet trajectory from a firearm - as explained in the famous American series "Dexter" - Sherry Fiester proved, in the case of the orientation of the blood jets from John Kennedy's head that the shot had come from the front. Fiester's expertise was also confirmed by the testimony of two police bikers, Bobby Hargis and B.J. Martin, who escorted the limousine in a slightly recessed position. Both of them and particularly Bobby Hargis who was riding on the left rear, and their windshields, were splashed with the President's blood and brain matter.

Fiester explains that the blood projections, following the major impact of a bullet in the human body, are of two types: in relation to the trajectory of the projectile, the blood spurts that escape towards the front of the body are called *forward spatters* and those coming out from the rear of the body are called *back spatters*. Forward spatters are blood projections that are ejected from the *exit* wound and that spread in the same direction of the bullet. Back spatters correspond to blood projections from the *entrance* wound and are dispersed in the opposite direction of the line of fire, that is to say, in the direction from where the shooter stands. When a projectile hits a human head, a small entrance hole is created. The force of the bullet hitting a skull creates fractures that propagate in the opposite direction to the point of impact. These fractures, called radial fractures, occur until the bullet exits the skull. Then, the velocity of the bullet decreases and the kinetic energy moves away from the point of impact. The pressure increases as a temporary cavity is created while the projectile passes through tissues. A stream of blood and of other fluids then flows backward, squeezing around the bullet in the opposite direction to its trajectory. To release the pressure, back spatters can only exit from the orifice where the bullet entered and through the fractures caused by the impact. This occurs within three to five milliseconds after impact. When the bullet exits from the skull, it creates a typical irregular shaped exit hole, usually of a larger diameter than that of the entrance wound. Blood and brain matter then find a way out through the exit hole of the skull in the same direction as the movement of the bullet until the skull explodes under the accumulated pressure, creating a wider exit wound with irregular contour. Brain matter and blood are ejected through all the possible apertures at the front and at the back of the human skull in a conical form. Back spatters tend to move sideways thus creating a large cone while the forward spatters are dispersed further towards the front with the slower formation of a cone due to increased velocity, wider discharge and increased blood volume.

In the late 1980s, newspapers and scientific literature explained that the maximum of projected blood from Kennedy's head, as seen on Zapruder's film, represented a back spatter configuration. Therefore, the only possible conclusion was that the configuration of the blood projections and brain matter towards the back of Kennedy's skull proved that he had undeniably been hit by a frontal shot[406]. As for the exact position of the gunman, some experts are not convinced that the fatal bullet, shot at the President's head from a firing point facing the limousine, had come from the "Grassy Knoll". Based on the photos taken on Dealey Plaza and Zapruder's film and given the position of JFK's body and head at the time the bullet hit him, it was possible to calculate precisely the line of fire along the President's axis of vision. Based on Zapruder's film, these experts restored on computer the orientation of Kennedy's head when the fatal shot hit him and determined that it corresponded to an angle of 115 degrees. They also took into account the exact location where Zapruder himself stood and the limousine movement. They crosschecked all the parameters with the precise geographic coordinates of the crime scene obtained from the photographs. By measuring the angle with a simple protractor, the experts came to the conclusion that the firing direction along the President's line of sight had less correlation with the north or east of the "Grassy Knoll" but more with the south knoll, that is to say at the opposite point of Dealey Plaza where the gunman would have been positioned. According to Sherry Fiester, based on recent shot trajectory reconstruction tests, it was possible to determine the possible directional angle of the bullet that hit the President's

---

[406] Ibid

head. Using these well-known standard techniques, the results revealed that a gunman was likely positioned near the south side of the triple underpass or in the adjacent car park. However, against any logic, these tests did not include mathematical evidence for a shot from the "Grassy Knoll".[407]

Picket fence near the "Grassy Knoll" adjacent to the triple underpass: according to a ballistic study a gunman might have been positioned there (enlargement) (author's photos)

---

[407] Ibid

Sherry Fiester sums up the debate perfectly: "*When scientific methods prove that a theory is true, then it becomes a fact. When they prove that a theory is false, it becomes a myth. If the 'Single Bullet' theory is correct, the bullet trajectory must be no more than a straight line between the exit point of the rifle barrel and the entry point into Connally's body. The trajectory must then be reproducible and confirmed by medical evidence. In order for one and only one same bullet to cause wounds in the bodies of both Kennedy and Connally, as the Warren Report asserted, the possibility of aligning the end of the gun barrel of a sniper positioned at the sixth floor window of the Texas School Book Depository has not been proven since it is impossible to show evidence. The theory of the 'Single Bullet', because it is impossible to prove it scientifically, therefore remains a myth*"[408].

In May 2016, the 84-year-old Secret Service agent Clint Hill wrote a new book titled *Five Presidents*. Hill was responsible for the protection of President Kennedy and the First Lady in 1963 and also, subsequently, of four other Presidents from Eisenhower to Ford. In his memoirs, he describes the drama on Dealey Plaza while he was on duty to protect the occupants of the limousine. Having realized that President Kennedy was being shot at, he bravely left the running board of his vehicle immediately behind and to jump onto the back of the presidential limousine as a desperately late response to protect the President and his wife[409].

He wrote in his book: "*I am satisfied with the conclusion of the [Warren] Commission that Oswald acted alone, and to this day, I think that it is the case - there has never been factual evidence to the contrary*". Well, if this is the official version Hill believes in, why not. I respect his opinion but do not share it especially because he then adds contradictory remarks: "*The conclusion that I do not support is the 'Magic Bullet Theory' - the notion that the first shot went through President Kennedy's throat then entered Governor Connally's body. As

---

[408] Ibid
[409] Clint J. Hill, Five Presidents My Extraordinary Journey with Eisenhower, Kennedy, Johnson, Nixon and Ford, Gallery Nooks, New-York, 2016, p.178

close eyewitnesses, the Governor, Mrs. Connally, and I were all of the same opinion that the Governor's wounds were caused by a second shot that did not hit President Kennedy." Hill's comments are conflicting: either there was the "Magic Bullet", hence a single gunman, or, since he does not believe in a single bullet, there were therefore a least two shooters and not Oswald *"having acted alone"* as Hill asserts. As explained above, a first bullet missed its target – a fact that the Warren report admitted - and two other separate bullets hit the President one in the back and another one in the throat. Then, two successive gunshots hit Connally and a fatal bullet hit JFK's head; a total of five bullets hitting both men – but some investigators count more. These facts indisputably back up the scenario of two gunmen at least and therefore a conspiracy.

Clint Hill's opinion in his 2016 book is somewhat surprising because back in 1963 the way he described the horrific nature of John Kennedy's head wounds could let think that a second gunman other than Oswald had possibly fired. According to Robert Groden,[410] Hill had jumped onto the trunk of the presidential limousine where Jackie Kennedy was trying to reach for something she would later say was her husband's brain or skull fragment. Hill testified later: *"I saw that the right **back** side of the President's head had gone and that he was bleeding profusely... I saw part of his skull with his hair on the seat"*. He also told the Warren Commission that *"the portion of the **back** right side of the President's head was missing. While he laid in the back seat of the car, his brain was exposed."* Clearly, 50 years earlier, doctors and ballistic experts had already explained that the nature of the terrible wounds inflicted at JFK's head was the result of a bullet fired from the front of the limousine because an entrance bullet hitting the back of his head would not have caused such a dramatic skull destruction – what Hill described to the Warren Commission. Although Hill did not make a direct reference to the origin of the fatal bullet, his testimony seemed to imply that a gaping wound in the back of JFK's skull had likely been caused by a bullet shot

---

[410] Robert J. Groden and Harrison Edward Livingstone. High Treason: The assassination of JFK. What really happened? The Conservatory Press, 1989

from the front thus indicating that another gunman could have been on Dealey Plaza and therefore a conspiracy had been fomented.

According to experts, the minimum number of bullets was four. I see a lot more. According to my research and to what has been said above, my count is seven bullets: two bullets missed their targets (a bullet hit Elm Street curb with a blast that slightly wounded Tague and a bullet that an official agent most probably picked up near a manhole), three other bullets hit Kennedy's body (back, neck and head) and two separate bullets wounded Connally. So many more bullets were shot on Dealey Plaza than the number of three gunshots that the Warren Commission defended in order to indict one single shooter, Lee Harvey Oswald.

The violent movement of Kennedy's body, back and to the left, when a bullet hit his head and the direction of blood spatters and brain matter are evidence that a gunshot had been fired from the front. The combination of gunshots fired both from the front and from the back of the limousine path proved that at least two shooters were on Dealey Plaza and that there was a plot to kill the young U.S. President who was ambushed in the middle of crossfire. The official government version should have collapsed like a house of cards because of decades of overwhelming evidence of the existence of at least a second gunman on Dealey Plaza. But the cover-up endures so long as the defenders of the Warren Report struggle to manipulate the opinion of the American people.

When Sherry Fiester says the trajectory of the shot that hit John Kennedy's head must be reproducible and crosschecked by medical evidence so that the theory becomes a fact, we take the full measure of the importance of properly correlating physical and medical expertise; which is the subject of the next chapter.

Chapter 11

The Medical Evidence

According to the ballistic tests reenactment on Dealey Plaza, we are almost certain that at least one shot was fired from a location facing the limousine during the presidential motorcade in Dallas. Can the medical evidence regarding JFK's wounds necessarily confirm this fact without any ambiguity? Were the throat and head injuries entrance or exit wounds?

Immediately after the shooting, as the injured President was rushed to Dallas Parkland Hospital, 22 witnesses claimed that they had seen a massive head injury, at the right rear of his skull, evidence for them that the fatal bullet had been shot from a location facing the limousine. During a press conference, Dr. Malcolm Perry, the first surgeon to provide intensive care on John Kennedy, repeatedly insisted that a bullet had entered his throat, providing a key testimony that there had been a second gunman facing the limousine. Once the President's body had been transferred from Dallas to Bethesda Naval Hospital that late Friday night, the hospital's commander-in-chief, Admiral Calvin Galloway, ordered that the doctors attending the autopsy should not to meddle with the throat wound.

Medical experts and investigators examined the official autopsy photographs and x-rays of the head injury, once they became public. These revealed an incredible forgery: the rear part of Kennedy's skull appeared intact on the x-rays despite the fact that a large fragment of the occipital section (the "Harper Fragment" that had been ejected from the cranial cavity and found on Dealey Plaza after the shooting) should have been missing. This crucial observation proved that the x-rays had been tampered with in order to hide the massive exit wound at the rear of John Kennedy's head[411].

Dr. Robert McClelland, the 34-year-old surgeon at Dallas Parkland Hospital, was in the hospital's trauma room on November 22, 1963. He positioned himself for many long minutes directly behind the head of the President while his colleagues provided intensive care and tried to do what it was humanly possible to do to save his life. Fifty years later, during the Pittsburgh conference, "Passing the Torch," Dr. McClelland, by live video interview, confirmed, with great dignity, his conviction that the fatal bullet to the President's head could only have come from a position facing the limousine since what he had seen from his position at the rear of the President's head was, without a shadow of a doubt, a bullet exit injury.

In a recent interview with Jacob Carter, McClelland came back on what he had seen: "*a frightful vision of the President lying on his back, a spot light directed towards the rear of his bloody head*". He confirmed that he was standing at the end of the gurney for many long minutes, looking at the head wound that seemed to him to be fatal "*because the entire back right part of his head and brain was gone*"[412]. Yet some skeptics rejected his testimony at the time, claiming he was mistaken, that there was no real injury to the back of Kennedy's head. But Dr. McClelland was adamant: "*Someone who stayed behind the gurney, as I was, watching the back of the President's head for a dozen minutes, 18 inches away from a massive hole, 4 to 6 inches in diameter, could not be wrong.*" When half a century later Carter asked him if he had a single doubt in his

---

[411] James W. Douglass, JFK and the Unspeakable, Why He Died and Why it Matters, A Touchstone Book, 2008

[412] Interview of Robert McClelland by Jacob. M. Carter – Before History Dies – 2015.

mind, he answered: *"No more doubt than I know the sun rises every day."*

According to the former governor of Minnesota, Jesse Ventura[413], other doctors, after making sure that it was safe for them to testify, confirmed the fact that Kennedy's lethal wound was an entrance wound, caused by a bullet fired from the front of the car that created a gaping hole in the back of the skull. Dr. Malcolm Perry, Dr. Charles Crenshaw, Dr. Charles J. Carrico, Dr. Richard Dulaney, Dr. Ronald Jones, Dr. Robert McClelland, Dr. Paul Peters and Dr. Kenneth E. Salyer, no less than eight physicians, all of them with recognized experience in treatment of gunshot wounds, surrounded the President at Parkland Hospital, and all certified that the cranial explosion corresponded to an exit wound[414]. Their testimonies can be found on YouTube. Their body language is eloquent: when they claimed that the gaping wound in JFK's head was an exit wound, all doctors touched the *back* of their heads.

The expertise of these doctors was based on the principle largely developed in the previous chapter and recalled by Sherry Fiester, a ballistics expert. The injury caused by a bullet entering a human body is small, more or less equal in size to the circumference of the bullet itself, and has a smooth appearance whereas an exit wound is much wider than the bullet circumference given the fact that the "explosion" of the bullet that leaves the body creates a ragged and irregular cavity. It is, therefore, hard to comprehend that one would doubt the words of these doctors who had the medical expertise, the opportunity and the time to examine the President's terrible injuries. How could they possibly not have a flawless visual memory of the wounds inflicted to the then most powerful man in the Free World?

The exit wound in the back of Kennedy's skull was also confirmed by observers and officials very close to the President:

---

[413] Jesse Ventura – They Killed Our President – 2013. Skyhorse Publishing
[414] Aguilar, Gary L., M.D. John F. Kennedy's Fatal Wounds: The Witnesses and the Interpretations, From 1963 to the Present. August 1994, Electronic Assassinations Newsletter

Frank O'Neal (FBI Special Agent), Clint Hill (Special Secret Service Agent), Audrey Bell (ER nurse at Parkland Hospital), Jerrol Custer (radiologist), Fyod Riebe and Paul O'Connor (autopsy technicians)[415].

New evidence on John Kennedy's autopsy photographs was revealed by the Assassination Records Review Board in the 1990s and published by professional journalists such as Deb Reichman of the Associated Press and George Lardner of The Washington Post. The medical technicians who took photographs during the autopsy declared under oath that the official photographs from the National Archives did not match those that they had developed[416].

The President's autopsy was carried out in troubling circumstances. It was under the control of two Navy admirals, one Army general and U.S. military officers who did even not have medical qualifications![417] The autopsy was assigned to two pathologists who had never performed autopsies on bodies with wounds caused by gun bullets. These doctors not only lacked experience but they acted with deliberate negligence. They allowed the destruction of the original films taken during the autopsy! John Kennedy's clothes did not receive the proper examination. Prior to the Bethesda autopsy, there was no consultation with the Dallas Parkland Hospital physicians who had provided life-saving care to JFK. The wounds were not probed or dissected as any autopsy protocol would have required. According to eyewitnesses' statement under oath, one injury had not been examined although it was reported that it had been done in the falsified autopsy file. The autopsy report was not dated. Original notes and drafts were burned. The microscopic slides that had been used to sample the President's wounds and brain just disappeared. The autopsy was simply botched for the purpose of a cover-up. Although Admiral Burkley, the President's physician, described in the autopsy report that a

---

[415] Jesse Ventura – They Killed Our President – 2013. Skyhorse Publishing
[416] http://jfkfacts.org/faith-overwhelms-facts-aps-un-journalism-on-jfks-assassination
[417] David Talbot – Brothers, The Hidden History of the Kennedy Years - 2007

wound was located at JFK's back, Gerald Ford, one of the Warren Commission members, manually corrected the report to show that the wound was in fact at the neck level. Photographs of the inner cavity of John Kennedy's chest, which would have helped to locate the back injury, also disappeared. The military doctors who performed the autopsy were simply intimidated and threatened with court martial if they deviated from the commanders' instructions.

Let us keep in mind that in 1963, the murder of a President of the United States fell within the legal authority of the state where the crime had been committed. Under Texas law, the Dallas jurisdiction had the legal right to hold the President's body for a local autopsy. Despite the fact that John Kennedy's autopsy should have been performed in Texas because it was not a federal crime, there was a violent altercation at Dallas Parkland Hospital that ended with the President's body being "kidnapped" in order to enforce an autopsy in Washington D.C.! The Secret Service men managed to repatriate the body on Air Force One to the capital after a muscular intervention, gun drawn, against the medical examiner of the Dallas hospital who, in compliance with the law of Texas, had insisted on performing the autopsy. It was the same Secret Service that Robert Kennedy had fought with concerning the safety of his brother. He had had doubts about the performances of the Secret Service and had preferred to entrust the protection of his brother to the Department of Justice. After his brother's death, he speculated that maybe some of the Secret Service men could have been "influenced" thus enabling indirectly the assassination's plan to roll ahead and therefore explaining as to why they had failed miserably to protect the President.

The autopsy was performed and headed by Medical Commander James J. Humes at the Bethesda Military Hospital, near Washington D.C. At the end of the autopsy, he made an incredible decision: he simply burnt his notes! This was undoubtedly the most important autopsy of his career, but he found nothing better to do than to destroy his observations!

Despite the fact that the autopsy photographs showed the occipital part of Kennedy's head complete, Dr. McClelland persisted: there was no doubt for him: a portion of the back of the skull, 4 to 6 inches in diameter, was missing. He felt comforted in his conviction that the shot had indeed been fired from a spot facing the vehicle when he saw Abraham Zapruder's film in which the President's body thrown violently backwards and to the left by the shot in the head[418].

President Kennedy's personal physician, Dr. George Burkley, who was removed from the Bethesda morgue by military doctors, was strangely never called to testify before the Warren Commission, the Secret Service, nor the FBI. The President's death certificate, which Dr. Burkley signed while rejecting the government claim that the throat injury had been caused by a shot from behind, was not even included in the official documents. After many years of silence, Burkley decided to give his own opinion about what he believed had happened to the President. In 1982, he stated, without further elaboration, to the assassination investigator, Henry Hurt, that John Kennedy had been the target of a conspiracy. His opinion as a medical expert was confirmed by Dr. Malcolm Perry, who told a press conference at Parkland Hospital that he had noted an entrance wound at the base of the President's throat.

Dr. Charles Crenshaw was another doctor who confirmed the origin of the bullet wounds at JFK's throat and head. Crenshaw had assisted the other doctors in the Parkland Hospital emergency trauma room. He was standing by the President's waist when he noticed "*a small opening in the middle of his neck. It was small, the size of the end of my little finger. It was a bullet entry wound. There was no doubt in my mind. I was used to seeing dozens in the ER.*" Dr. Crenshaw then positioned himself behind JFK's head. He was dismayed by what he saw: "*the right part of his brain was no longer there. It looked like a crater, an empty cavity. All that was visible was crushed bloody tissue. Looking at such a damage, there was no doubt in my mind that the bullet had penetrated the President's head from the front.*"[419]

---

[418] Interview of Robert McClelland by Jacob. M. Carter – Before History Dies – 2015.

[419] James W. Douglass, JFK and the Unspeakable, Why He Died and Why it Matters, A Touchstone Book, 2008

According to the official version, the wound in the President's back was caused by the "Single Bullet", that was found almost in a pristine condition on a stretcher at Parkland Hospital. Dr. Albert Osborne, the Deputy Surgeon General, however told congressional investigators that he saw "*a practically intact bullet rolling from the autopsy table at Bethesda Hospital when the President's body was removed from his coffin*". He testified that he "*had that bullet in his hand and was looking at it*", that it "*appeared to him reasonably clean and undamaged and which the Secret Service seized.*" Osborne's testimony was corroborated by Jerrol Custer, an x-ray technician. The bullet that was found almost intact on a stretcher of Parkland Hospital could not have been the same bullet, since it had already been sent to the FBI laboratory well before the discovery of the bullet in the President's back at the Bethesda morgue[420].

Parkland Hospital doctors were formal: 20-25% of President Kennedy's brain was no longer in his cranial cavity when they treated him, whereas at Bethesda Hospital, there was almost no brain, probably because it had been removed in its entirety and was never found again... There is speculation that it had been secured in the National Archives or that it had been buried with the President at Arlington Cemetery according to the wishes of the Kennedy family. Dr. Cyril Wecht regrets that no micro-sections were performed and scanned on the President's brain to determine the origin of the head injuries. In a television program, Dr. Wecht gave his opinion as to why the brain had not been sectioned or closely studied according to autopsy official procedure and had disappeared: "*I am very suspicious. I believe there was something sinister conducted at a very high level to hide the post-assassination evidence and to make sure that the brain would not be examined. We could not visualize the inside* [of the brain]. *It's as if it never existed*"[421].

---

[420] Lamar Waldron, The Hidden History of the JFK Assassination, Counter Point Berkeley, 2013

[421] Robert J. Groden and Harrison Edward Livingstone. High Treason: The assassination of JFK. What really happened? The Conservatory Press, 1989

It is preposterous that the Warren Commission never saw John Kennedy's autopsy photographs or x-rays. The author and former governor of Minnesota, Jesse Ventura, a navy veteran specialist in firearms, reports that experts who studied the President's x-rays certified that bullet fragments were lodged in his head. The bullet type undoubtedly corresponded to that of an explosive ammunition[422]. In other words the Mannlicher Carcano rifle allegedly linked to Lee Harvey Oswald could not have fired the bullet that hit John Kennedy's head because this obsolete World War II rifle could only fire military copper jacketed bullets without fragmentation at impact. Various mixed bullet fragments from standard ammunition and frangible bullets were found inside the presidential car. Bullet velocity was another indicator: "Oswald's rifle" fired low-velocity bullets (about 2000 feet per second) whereas high velocity bullets (2600 feet per second and above) had killed the President according to the death certificate, the autopsy report and the Warren Commission report.

Whether it was incompetence or a cover-up, it is likely that the Warren Commission drafted the conclusions of its report in such a way that members would be confused about the evidence presented. They were therefore obliged to defend a position of "plausible deniability". In response to criticism of the Warren Report's findings, Commissioner Gerald Ford, a member of the commission, made the following comments "*I believe that you should read very attentively what the Warren Commission said and what I said as a commission member who attended and participated to the draft report...We said that the commission did not find any evidence of foreign or domestic conspiracy. These words were written carefully...The commission was right when it gave its position. It said it precisely at least on this very point and I want to stress it again based on the evidence that we had*"[423].

Let us keep in mind the context of the early 1960s. The research, the methodology and the resources of crime laboratories

---

[422] Jesse Ventura – They Killed Our President – 2013. Skyhorse Publishing

[423] Robert J. Groden and Harrison Edward Livingstone. High Treason: The assassination of JFK. What really happened? The Conservatory Press, 1989

were far from being those used by the scientific crime investigations methods today (such as can be seen in the popular TV series "CIS"). Oswald's guilt would certainly have been very difficult to prove in court if the criminal police had presented findings based on present-day investigative methods!

In 1988, several eyewitnesses who attended President Kennedy's autopsy at Bethesda Naval Hospital made the decision to speak publicly on a television channel, KRON-TV in San Francisco. What they declared had a resounding effect. Their testimony confirmed the investigators' own revelations of the House Select Commission on Assassinations namely that the autopsy photographs and x-rays posed a problem of authenticity. Both the coffin and the bag wrapping the President's body, when they arrived at Bethesda Naval hospital, were not the same as those used in Dallas Parkland Hospital, despite these conditions having been apparently secured by the Secret Service at the time of transfer[424][425]. During the KRON program, Paul O'Connor, the Bethesda Naval Hospital morgue technician who assisted doctors Joseph Humes, Thornton Boswell and Pierre Finck in conducting President Kennedy's autopsy, certified that his body was received in a mortuary bag upon arrival in Bethesda. There was no way that it could be confused with the rubber sheet in which JFK's body had been wrapped when it had left Dallas. O'Connor was also adamant that the body had arrived at the Bethesda Naval Hospital, in a simple shipment coffin, 15 to 20 minutes before Jacqueline Kennedy's separate arrival at the hospital in an ambulance with JFK's casket!

When Air Force One from Dallas landed at Andrews Air Force Base with Jacqueline Kennedy on board, Robert Kennedy joined his sister-in law on the tarmac and together they travelled in the ambulance with a bronze coffin. Another military assistant in charge of receiving Kennedy's body in Bethesda, Dennis David, confirmed that the body had arrived earlier in a black ambulance, resembling a hearse. Inside, there was no bronze casket but a gray

---

[424] Ibid

[425] http://jamesfetzer.blogspot.fr/2012/03/what-happened-to-jfks-body-cover-up-on.html

metal box, the type normally used for shipping bodies.... David made it clear that he and his colleagues were ordered not to talk to anyone and were threatened with court martial if they did. They therefore kept their mouths shut for fear for their lives as they were well aware that "embarrassing" eyewitnesses could be easily got rid of.

Nevertheless KRON television interviewed some eyewitnesses, such as Ambulance Assistant Aubrey Rike, who confirmed what O'Connor and David had said. Rike and his colleague, Dennis McHuire, both certified that they had wrapped the President's body in a rubber sheet at Parkland Hospital and not in a body bag and that the casket they had placed it in, when it left Dallas, was a top bronze model with no similarity to any shipment casket. According to the morgue technicians, most of John Kennedy's brain was no longer in his cranial cavity when the body arrived at Bethesda.

All these anomalies generated the wildest speculations. According to one theory, the body had been taken by force by the Service Secret who arranged for the casket to be switched between the moment the presidential plane landed in Washington from Dallas and the moment John Kennedy's body arrived at Bethesda Naval Hospital for the autopsy. The body switch during transportation would have enabled a better assessment of what measures to take to conceal the evidence of the presence of more than one shooter, for example by restoring the occipital part of the President's skull that showed a gaping hole related to a bullet exit wound. O'Connor, who was also present at the autopsy, claimed that the photographs he was shown afterwards *"looked nothing like what he had seen ... that is to say a much worse wound over the whole back of the head'*. According to another theory, John Kennedy's body could have been moved from the original bronze coffin on the plane itself during the return flight to Washington. But many people on board the plane, including JFK's wife, were formal that the coffin had not been left unattended during the entire flight from Dallas to Washington. Some investigators believe instead that the body had been removed in Dallas from the original casket provided at Parkland Hospital and replaced in another one before taking the body back to Washington. Firearms had been pointed at the Dallas hospital officials who opposed the transfer of the body. Investigators believe that the fight and the intimidation of the Secret Service agents at Parkland Hospital was a ploy to take control of the coffin in order to manage the autopsy as they wished. The body would have been immediately transferred to another coffin, unbeknownst to Jackie Kennedy and the Dallas hospital staff. Some researchers even put forward the theory that the bronze coffin placed on board Air Force One to Washington was actually empty!

The rigged autopsy photographs that showed no missing section of the back of the skull have been widely published and can be seen on internet. Twenty-five years after the assassination, a U.S. national television program tried to understand the controversy between the medical evidence of the entrance wound and the probable doctored photographs of the occipital portion of Kennedy's skull. During the TV show, Dr. Robert McClelland said, "*Someone is covering up the entire plot. There was someone on the Grassy Knoll who fired a fatal shot to the President's head. I am sure that* [television] *programs, such as those broadcasted in France and in England on the 25th anniversary of John Kennedy's death, under no control unlike here, would be a source of concern to anyone in the United States and would provoke a public outcry. Anyone who is highly ranked would think that such suspicions could not be tolerated. So I'm afraid we're stuck with the Warren Report again and I think it's all nonsense*" [426].

Several doctors, including Dr. McClelland, insisted on specific medical evidence: when a bullet fired from a rifle exits a human skull, it forces large bone pieces along its path and seriously damages the scalp that fragments itself. A clear and well-delimited removal of the scalp at the bullet exit point does not occur under these conditions. The forensic expert, Dr. Cyril Wecht, confirmed it: "*In this case, the scalp explodes in large pieces. It is lacerated due to the explosive effect of the missile and the fracture of*

---

[426] Robert J. Groden and Harrison Edward Livingstone. High Treason: The assassination of JFK. What really happened? The Conservatory Press, 1989

the underlying skull. The [allegedly rigged] *photographs of the back of the President's head showed no laceration of the scalp. The lacerations should be absolutely visible."* But these photographs show no such damage. The scalp is completely intact, except for a very small hole. Then Dr. Wecht continues: "*X-rays of the President's head showed no large bone defects in its posterior section ... It's totally absurd. You cannot falsify wounds. You do not know what you're going to face to... you cannot rebuild the structure of a skull if it has broken bones. If you are trying to collect the broken pieces and replace the scalp over them to hide them, you may be able to do it and take pictures once the scalp is superimposed, but x-rays will still reveal the fracture lines. By trying to bring dislocated pieces together, there is no way to opacify the fracture lines*" [427].

According to the testimony of x-rays technician, Jerrol Custer, before the Assassinations Records Review Board on October 28, 1997, Kennedy's x-rays taken during the autopsy showed radial fractures originating from the forehead bone. Most of the concentric fractures were located near the President's forehead. These radial fractures had spread from the front to the back of the skull because small fragments near the point where the bullet hit the forehead widened as they progressed toward the exit wound. As research revealed that the configuration of Kennedy's cranial fractures corresponded to an entry injury on the forehead bone, it was clear that a bullet had been fired from a direction facing the limousine[428].

From 1993 to 1995, Dr. David W. Mantik, a specialist in radiation oncology and a doctor in physics, examined the x-rays of John Kennedy's skull taken during the autopsy and those kept at the National Archives in order to check their authenticity. He used an optical density meter to measure the brightness levels corresponding to different parts of the official x-rays. In this process, the denser body parts naturally produce whiter images and the cavities produce darker images. Mantik was surprised by the striking contrast between the front and the back of Kennedy's

---

[427] Ibid

[428] Sherry P. Fiester, *Enemy of the Truth*, Myths, Forensics and the Kennedy Assassination, JFK Lancer Productions & Publications. 2012

skull, as shown on the "official" x-rays, something that was even visible to the naked eye. By taking measurements of the optical density of these x-rays, he made an astonishing discovery. The posterior white part of the skull transmitted nearly a thousand times more light than the dark part. There was far too much bone density visible in the posterior part compared with the anterior part. He concluded that the "official" x-rays could only be the result of a composition of images. The results of the optical density tests revealed a fraud: a patch had been placed on the original x-rays to cover the posterior part of the skull, corresponding to the gap left by the ejection of a skull fragment, the "Harper Fragment" that was discovered on Dealey Plaza. Mantik had thus highlighted the fraud, the patch up of a bullet exit wound. Dr. Mantik's results are well documented in the National Archives and are available on internet to anyone (just type the words "twenty conclusions after nine visits").

The reference to the "official" x-rays in the Warren Report was just a decoy to deceive the American people. Decades after the assassination, the discovery of the "Harper Fragment" and of Dr. Mantik's results, would reveal the government's cover-up[429].

---

[429] James W. Douglass, JFK and the Unspeakable, Why He Died and Why it Matters, A Touchstone Book, 2008

Chapter 12

The Photographic Evidence

As the presidential motorcade made its way into Elm Street, John Kennedy's reactions to the impact of gunshots, to his throat and to his head, were captured on Abraham Zapruder's camera, thus providing the most famous historical film of the assassination. The film shows the President's body being thrown violently backwards and to the left at the moment a bullet hit the right part of his skull where the forehead meets the scalp. As we saw in the previous chapter, the location of the fatal bullet wound was confirmed under oath by several Dallas Parkland Hospital doctors. Zapruder's film is on YouTube and makes disturbing viewing[430].

Zapruder's film rights were purchased by Time-Life Inc. and the original was sequestrated in 1963. In March 1975, Robert Groden, a photographer and expert on visual documents concerning the JFK assassination, got hold of an unaltered version of the Zapruder's film. He and a reporter, Geraldo Rivera, decided to make it public. Both believed it was about time the American people saw the entire film and decided for themselves what really happened in 1963 during the motorcade on Dealey Plaza: the horrific 313 frame showing the fatal blow and the President's body violent push backwards and to the left.

---

[430] Youtube.com/watch?v=jWHdEeHNbXY

ABC was the first television channel to broadcast the program on Good Night America. The ABC program set a watershed for the investigation of the Dallas assassination. It generated a renewal of public interest and the creation of four congressional investigations on a probable conspiracy. A controversy started to fuel many debates that would last more than half a century after the event[431]. The ABC program also inspired movie director, Oliver Stone to make his movie "JFK". Stone's pivotal argument was that JFK's lethal wound on his forehead was an entrance wound, a bullet having been fired by another gunman from a direction facing the limousine. For the filmmaker, all this showed the fingerprints of a conspiracy and the Zapruder's film was the keystone on which his conviction rested. Stone also asked Robert Groden to be an advisor for his movie and to make short appearances in "JFK".

Back in 1964, in order to better match a preconceived investigation in its report, the Warren Commission interchanged some frames of the Zapruder's film in such a way that the President's body would appear to be propelled forward by the deadly shot. The commission wanted us to believe the shot came from behind, from the Texas School Book Depository 6th floor window where a "convenient" scapegoat, Lee Harvey Oswald, was positioned[432]. The embarrassed government then found a preposterous "medical" explanation: the deadly bullet came from behind and hit the occipital part of Kennedy's skull. Because the President was sitting upright (his corset was worn for extra back support), it had thus created a force that resulted in an explosion of brain matter from the back of his skull. This argument was quickly invalidated by military experts and war veterans who were quite familiar with injuries inflicted during sniper combat[433].

---

[431] Robert Hennelly and Jerry Policoff - JFK: how the media assassinated the real story. 2002. http://www.assassinationresearch.com/v1n2/mediaassassination.htm

[432] Robert J. Groden, The Killing of a President, Vicking Studio Books, 1993

[433] Jesse Ventura – They Killed Our President – 2013. Skyhorse Publishing

Time Magazine altered Zapruder's film by eliminating frames 208 to 211. William Bader of the Senate Intelligence Committee said: *"There were CIA people at the Time Magazine management level"*.[434] The FBI, the Secret Service, the Dallas police and the Warren Commission, all were formal: no gunshot could have been fired by Oswald before frame 210 because a tree masked the view from the sixth floor window of the Texas School Book Depository. It was therefore necessary, for the cover-up, to eliminate some frames of the Zapruder's film.

An eyewitness, Phillip Willis, was taking pictures of the motorcade from the opposite side of Elm Street to where Zapruder was filming. Willis took a photo when the President was hit for the first time. The frames of Zapruder's film, corresponding to this very moment, had to be removed. Without such a manipulation, evidence would have been clear that the first shot that hit the President had occurred despite the Warren Commission's assertion that Oswald could not have fired at that moment! According to Groden, the shot that hit the President's throat came from the front as evidenced on frames 189 to 191 of Zapruder's film. On frame 220, John Kennedy put his hand to his throat where the bullet hit him. On frame 226, he is hit again, this time from behind, and his body is projected forward. This was the shot that Arlen Specter and Gerald Ford chose to build the theory of the "Magic Bullet" on which supposedly would have hit both Kennedy and Governor Connally simultaneously. Evidence, beyond a shadow of a doubt, would later show that Connally had been hit at frame 237 and not before. There was another inconsistency based on the synchronization of the film. It was impossible that two consecutive gunshots, allegedly fired from Oswald's rifle, could be set off within a time interval of 1.6 second. Oswald, in the event he fired, could not have rearmed his rifle then aimed at his target and fired again in less than 2.5 seconds. The tests of the most experienced sharpshooters have proved it. It would have taken at least two gunmen to fire both gunshots 1.6 seconds apart on Dealey Plaza.

---

[434] Carl Bernstein, The CIA and The Media, The Rolling Stone

In the 1990s, the Zapruder family agreed that the original film and its authenticated copies for which they held the copyright, could be placed in the National Archives. It was a decision by the government to prevent the historical film from falling into the hands of the public. This was a curious arbitration procedure which resulted in the payment to the Zapruder family of 16 million dollars (equivalent to 23 million today) for a 26-second film! This film is perhaps the most important historical film of our time. With several thousand views on YouTube, it is considered the most viewed movie in the world[435].

An Associated Press photographer, Ike Atgens, took one picture during the parade on Elm Street. According to Atgens and Groden, when the photo was published it had been cropped. The cars behind the presidential limousine could not be seen, which meant that the reaction to the first gun shot from the Secret Service agents in the fourth car was not visible. Without having been cropped, the photos would have revealed that the President, when hit by the first gunshot, was hidden by a large tree from the window of the sixth floor where the alleged sniper was[436]. In other words it could not have been Oswald who fired that shot.

Another film was shot by Orville Nix, who was on the opposite side of the street from where Zapruder was, when the bullet hit President Kennedy's head. The Zapruder film was believed to be the only one at the time and the American people were unaware of the existence of Nix's film. Several photos and films, taken that day on Dealey Plaza, were temporarily seized and only some returned. A copy of Nix's film showed very clearly that the President was hit by a shot fired from the front that propelled him violently backwards, just as several eyewitnesses saw a cloud of smoke rising above the "Grassy Knoll".

---

[435] Edward Kosner, The Curse of the Zapruders, The Wall Street Journal, November 12-13, 2016

[436] Robert J. for Groden and Harrison Edward Livingstone. High Treason: The assassination of JFK. What really happened? The Conservatory Press, 1989

I have met Robert Groden on several occasions at conferences and the first time I met him was in Dallas on Dealey Plaza. Hardly a weekend goes by without Groden setting up his sales booth, near the "Grassy Knoll", and relentlessly selling his books and DVDs that present the photographs (some are graphic) of the bullets impact on John Kennedy in a cross fire ambush on Dealey Plaza. The city of Dallas has made various attempts in vain to prevent him from doing this. Based on the Zapruder film and the photos taken by eyewitnesses at the precise moment of the assassination, Groden had the idea, although somewhat sinister, to have two crosses painted in white on the road surface, in the middle of Elm Street, at the very spot where the presidential limousine was riding when the president's throat and head were hit. For me and no doubt for many others, the crime site should remain a revered historic place. So on this topic of photographs, let me add a personal note. I find it sad to see so many "tourists" who absolutely have to cross Elm Street in order to pose smiling for a selfie photo on the exact spot where President Kennedy died. Out of curiosity and simply to immortalize the present moment by standing in the middle of the street by the cross to take photos shows a lack of respect, quite apart from it being a dangerous location. The motorists coming from the crossing of the top of Elm Street and those taking the left fork of Houston Street, when they leave the traffic light, often reach high speeds as they descend to the triple underpass. Because of the terrain's decline, these motorists cannot see these tourists in the middle of the road and are forced to brake hard. They use their horns not only to warn them that they are actually risking their lives but also to signal them that they show no reverence for this place. Their photos are just a vacation souvenir for them.

The arrow shows the 2nd white cross painted on Elm Street marking the location of the presidential limousine when the fatal shot hit JFK (author's photo)

To return to that fateful day, Dallas Morning News photographer, Tom Dillard, who was riding eight cars behind the presidential limousine, took a picture of the outside of the entire sixth floor of the Texas School Book Depository a few seconds after the shooting. This photo, before being widely published after the assassination, had been cropped on the far left, truncating the window of the south-west corner of the sixth floor. Robert Groden managed to get the original unaltered photo. Despite the coarse grain of the picture, a person can be seen: the outline of the head, the forehead, the eye sockets, the cheeks and the shoulders[437]. The presence of another person in addition to Oswald allegedly there on this floor just after the shooting is paramount: the entire sixth floor is just one very large room, without walls or partitions, with just structural pillars! To this day, the floor layout has not changed and visitors to the Texas School Book Depository Museum can still walk around this entire floor, undivided by walls. This just means that, on the day of the assassination, anyone who was on the south-west corner of the

---

[437] Robert J. Groden, The Killing of a President, Vicking Studio Books, 1993

same floor would have been able to see perfectly well a sniper at the opposite corner window and vice versa.

The SW corner window on the 6th floor of the TSBD (left) where another gunman might have been positioned according to Groden. Oswald allegedly fired from the opposite corner window (right) (author's photo)

As it was stated in the chapter on medical evidence, the inconsistencies between the published autopsy photographs and the x-rays of the President's head suggest that they were falsified by "experts". We have seen that they do not match the descriptions of the eyewitnesses - doctors and lawyers - in Dallas or Bethesda hospitals, who were formal that the gaping portion at the right rear of John Kennedy's skull was caused by an exit bullet[438]. Although unquestionable answers could have been provided to put an end to the medical contradictions and to reveal the forgery on the autopsy photographs, the House Select Committee on Assassinations did not find it useful to exhume the

---

[438] Kent Heiner. Without Smoking Gun: Was the Death of Lieutenant Commander William Pitzer Part of the JFK Assassination Cover-up Conspiracy.

President's remains. On the "official" autopsy photographs, no exit bullet injuries are noticeable at the back of the skull.

This means that either the photographs were falsified (the wounds were patched up) or all the doctors and other eyewitnesses in the Dallas emergency room lied or were confused. Given their high level of skill and professionalism, it is highly unlikely that these doctors would have lied or made up stories. It was therefore concluded that the exit wound at the back of the head had been "pasted" back. James Sibert, the FBI Special Agent, had the following comments after the autopsy: *"...They showed the pictures at that deposition that were neat in appearance, and boy, I don't remember anything like that...but my recollection of the way the head looked is nothing that would appear as this photograph shows. This photograph is too neat. Right back here is where you would have had that massive wound, right in here, and you see that's neat. My thought was that that was probably taken after reconstruction was done... there was a big cavity there. I mean that you could look into. The skull wasn't intact, the bones weren't in place...there definitely was a large cavity. It was just that apparent that there was so much skull missing"*[439].

When the official version of the autopsy photos was shown to those who had seen the President's body in Dallas or Bethesda with the head wounds, all said, *"It's not the wounds that I saw"*.[440] Douglas Horne, Chief Analyst of the Military Records Team for the Assassination Records Review Board, compiled, in a massive 1,800-page work, data of medical and scientific evidence and of abnormalities of photographs and x-rays observed after the autopsy. He wrote: *"There is something seriously wrong with the autopsy photographs of the body of President Kennedy. It definitely is President Kennedy in the photographs, but the images showing the damage to the President's head do not show the pattern of damage observed by either the medical professionals at Parkland hospital in Dallas or by numerous witnesses at the military autopsy at Bethesda Naval hospital. These disparities are real and are significant, but the*

---

[439] Parker. First on the Scene: Interviews with Parkland Doctors.
[440] Horne, Inside the Assassinations Records Review Board.

reasons remain unclear"[441]. According to the Washington Post, the documents released by the Assassination Record Review Board in 1998, revealed that doctors who performed the autopsy of President Kennedy could have examined two different brains. [442] [443] They claimed that archived photographs of the brain were not those of Kennedy because they revealed far fewer injuries than those that the President have suffered in the head. Doctors at Parkland Hospital told the media that the fatal shot, which blew up Kennedy's skull, came from the front and not from the rear (as the Warren Commission wanted us to believe) and that the head injury was the size of a large egg. Douglas Horne, who was 90 to 95% convinced that the brain was not Kennedy's, concluded in a 32-page memorandum that this could only mean one thing: a cover-up of medical evidence had been engineered because archived brain photographs revealed injuries that were caused by a shot from behind. According to the testimony of the former FBI agent, Francis X. O'Neill Jr, present at the autopsy at Bethesda Naval Hospital on November 22, 1963, very little of Kennedy's brain remained in his cranial cavity - about less than half - and he did not remember that the size of the brain was as important as what the archived photographs showed it; a more or less complete brain. Additional photographs taken by Navy photographer John Stringer during another brain scan, presumably on the morning of November 25, revealed an almost complete brain. According to Stringer's testimony, the "official" photographs preserved at the National Archives did not correspond to those he had taken, citing divergences such as the viewing angles and the type of film used.

The eminent Dr. Mantik examined the official documents. As we have seen in a previous chapter, he provided the details of these anomalies in his online presentation. He summarized his

---

[441] Lamar Waldron, The Hidden History of the JFK Assassination, Counter Point Berkeley, 2013

[442] George Lardner Jr., Archive Photos Not of JFK's Brain, Concludes Aide to Review Board. Washington Post. November 10, 1998

[443] Deb Riechmann, Newly Released JFK Documents Raise Questions About Medical Evidence, Washington Post, November 9, 1998

analysis in these words: *"The official x-rays do not show the condition of the skull or the brain as seen at Parkland Hospital"*[444].

These experts are formal: on the official autopsy photographs and x-rays, the wounds were physically concealed to remove the massive exit wound on the back of John Kennedy's skull in order to prove that the bullet had been shot from the rear of the limousine path. According to Brian Rooney, a clandestine surgery was performed at Bethesda Hospital during the autopsy. It consisted of widening JFK's forehead injury to create a temporal-parietal exit hole by incising it in order to remove the evidence of a bullet entrance wound. The back of the skull was covered-up to eliminate the location and the size of the "explosion" at the occipital part and then a "lesion" was created in order to simulate a small entrance bullet hole.[445] As incredible and unacceptable as it may seem, it was at the Bethesda morgue that this illicit surgery was practiced on the President's body in order to fit in with the official version supporting that only one gunman triggered the fatal shot behind the presidential limousine.

A U.S. Navy senior officer, Lieutenant Commander William B. Pitzer, in charge of the audio-visual department at the Bethesda Military Hospital, decided to publicly unveil the fabrication of the autopsy photographs. He did not achieve his ends. He "committed suicide"; many believing he was in fact "got rid of". The case of this very disturbing murder will be mentioned in a next chapter "Embarrassing Witnesses. Mysterious disappearances ".

---

[444] David W. Mantik, M.D, Ph. D."The JFK Autopsy MaterialsTwenty Conclusions after Nine Visits". Nov 20-23,2003: assassinationresearch.com/v2n2/Pittsburgh.pdf

[445] Brian Rooney. "Burying The Truth. Book Review of Doug Horne's Epic Effort. April 2010. JFK: Deep Politics Quarterly.

Chapter 13

The Acoustic Evidence

In 1978, fifteen years after the assassination, the House Select Committee on Assassinations' investigation revealed that more than three gunshots had been fired on Dealey Plaza. This was in contradiction with the 1964 version of the U.S. government which had found only three. Thanks to the scientific analysis of the acoustic tests carried out on the radio soundtrack of a motorcycle police officer riding closely behind the presidential limousine, the number of gunshots was found to be greater than three. The police officer had mistakenly left his communication radio on, which enabled all the noises on Dealey Plaza, including the gunshots, to be recorded.

The scientific analysis of the recording soundtrack (known as the Dictabelt) revealed that six impulses had different origins (from behind the limousine and from the front) and corresponded to more than three gunshots. According to witnesses and to the acoustic analysis of the Dictabelt, the gunshots came from at least three different locations on Dealey Plaza.[446]

The analysis of the motorcycle police officer's radio soundtrack revealed far too many gunshots, each one spaced from the other

---

[446] Robert J. Groden and Harrison Edward Livingstone. High Treason: The assassination of JFK. What really happened? The Conservatory Press, 1989

by a time lapse too short for Lee Harvey Oswald to have fired them all. This was because the origin of one of the gunshots was the "Grassy Knoll", not the Texas School Book Depository.

One impulse corresponded to a gunshot that came from the "Grassy Knoll" and was followed by another impulse less than a second later. For four of the six impulses recorded, there was strong evidence that snipers were positioned facing the presidential limousine at the corner of the railway bridge and the wooden picket fence. The study also revealed the likelihood that at least one gunman was positioned on the second floor of the Dal-Tex Building behind the limousine path and adjacent to the Texas School Book Depository. For the two remaining impulses, it was not possible to determine their origin[447].

In the sequence of the four shots, the first bullet and the second were fired from the Texas School Book Depository, 1.6 second apart. The third shot seemed to come from the "Grassy Knoll", 5.9 seconds later. Finally, the last shot seemed to have been fired from the Texas School Book Depository in the half-second that followed.[448]

This indicated the high probability of the presence of a third or even fourth gunman. For the "Grassy Knoll" impulses, the tests indicated that a gunman was most probably positioned behind the picket fence not far from the location where some bystanders were watching the motorcade. The analysis of the echo profile revealed that the sound must have originated in a precise point behind the wooden fence and that could not have corresponded to the misfires of motorcycles riding next to the limousine. By calculating the time it took for sound to travel to and from an obstacle, it was possible to calculate the distance between a shooter and the target. It could even reveal that a shooter was firing from an elevated position because the blast noise bounces off the ground.

---

[447] Ibid
[448] George Lardner Jr. House to Re-Explore Evidence of Kennedy Death Conspiracy. International Herald Tribune, Dec 22, 1978

Firing a rifle causes a supersonic sound wave, a shock wave that precedes the speed of sound. In other words, the firing of a rifle has its own signature: the echoes that the firing produces are the signature of bullets shots from a high power rifle and are preceded by a shock wave. All six pulses produced decibels higher than any other noise detected on the soundtrack and could only be from gunshots.

The company in charge of the scientific analysis of the Dictabelt also made the recommendation to the House Select Committee on Assassinations to make an acoustic reconstruction of the sounds profiles during a re-enactment on Dealey Plaza. The purpose of the HSCA study was to determine whether, among the impulses recorded on the motorcycle police officer's radio soundtrack, there were some that could match the sounds of gunshots fired from the Texas School Book Depository or the "Grassy Knoll ". The HSCA re-enactment in 1978 consisted of firing gunshots from the Texas School Book Depository and from the "Grassy Knoll" on specific targets and of recording the sounds using multiple microphones on Dealey Plaza.

For the re-enactment of firing tests, using the best computer techniques at the time, scientists were able to isolate the echoes specific to the gunshots recorded on the Dictablet on 22 November 1963. The results showed that the first and the second gunshot sounds came from behind the path of the presidential limousine. The third shot sound came from the front and from the right, presumably from the "Grassy Knoll". The fourth came from behind. Between each of the first two shots and of the last two shots, the time lapse for firing was too short to have been from "Oswald's rifle". The sound recordings seem to confirm that the fatal head shot did not come from the Texas School Book Depository but from the "Grassy Knoll".

The best evidence that supported the sound recordings analysis on Dealey Plaza was presented by Robert Groden, Dr. Mark Weiss and Dr. Ernest Aschkenasy to the House Select Committee on Assassinations. After working for very long hours at the Library of Congress, all three experts submitted a precise study consisting in synchronizing the sounds emitted by the gunshots on the Dictabelt with the images of Zapruder's film. They selected the sounds of the last two gunshots and checked whether these could be possibly synchronized with the film capturing the fatal shot at the President's head.

All three experts came to the same conclusion. As said above, the analysis of the Dictabelt revealed a minimum of four gunshots (scientifically proven as coming from firearms) and at least two additional impulses; an extremely high probability of a crossfire scenario. For their tests, they only took into account the sixth floor window of the Texas School Books Depository and the wooden fence on the "Grassy Knoll" as points of origin of the suspicious gunshots and disregarded 16 other possible places on Dealey Plaza.

Whether Oswald was suspected of shooting at the President or not, someone else fired the third shot that killed the President. Robert Groden, Dr. Mark Weiss and Dr. Ernest Aschkenasy proved it. When they tried to synchronize the fourth shot with the shot to the head none of the other three gunshots could be matched properly with the film footage but as soon as they synchronized the third shot with the fatal shot seen on the film, all the other impulses perfectly fit with the unfolding actions of the film. The "Grassy Knoll" shot was therefore the third and not the final shot in the four-shot sequence for the specific places of origin studied. In addition, the acoustic study of gunshots sounds synchronized with Zapruder's film revealed that President Kennedy had been hit by the first bullet well before it could have been fired by the sniper at the sixth floor window of the Texas School Book Depository.

According to Groden, Professor Blakey, head of the House Select Committee on Assassinations, took him aside and ordered him not to present to the committee the conclusions of the synchronization work of the soundtrack with the film. Instead, Congress and the American people were surprisingly told that the fatal shot came only from behind and that it was the fourth shot. However, some Congressmen, anxious to know the full details of the study, expressed some doubts and considered that it was the third gunshot which came from the front that matched the frame of the film corresponding to the fatal shot. Blakey told them that they were wrong and that the third shot had actually missed the target[449].

The House Select Committee on Assassinations concluded that the scientific acoustic evidence established a high probability that at least two gunmen fired at President Kennedy[450]. Here is the precise wording in the conclusion of the House Select Committee on Assassinations' investigation: *"On the basis of the evidence available to it, President John F. Kennedy was probably assassinated as a result of a conspiracy... The Committee was unable to identify the other gunman or the extent of the conspiracy"*[451].

Few American citizens are aware today that the conspiracy around the assassination of their 35th President was already acknowledged by a congressional investigation some 40 years ago. They continue to hear the same official version supporting one single gunman. The media continue to carry this message today and do not oppose it in any way to the conclusions of the 1979 U.S. Congressional investigation which they prefer to ignore[452].

In order to negate the conclusion of the Congress about a probable conspiracy, the "Lone Nuts" reached out to experts who "proved" that the gunshots did not come from two different places or even affirmed that there had been no police motorcycle with a live microphone "stuck" on that day on Dealey Plaza. A batch of tests, counter-expertise and counter-counter expertise were performed. In 2010, however, a serious study by William E. Kelly validated the acoustic evidence resulting from the 1979

---

[449] Robert J. Groden and Harrison Edward Livingstone. High Treason: The assassination of JFK. What really happened? The Conservatory Press, 1989

[450] US House of Representatives, "Report of the Select Committee on Assassinations, Ninety-fifth Congress, second session" 1979

[451] Ibid

[452] Jesse Ventura – They Killed Our President – 2013. Skyhorse Publishing

investigation and put an end to the doubts created by the "Lone Nuts". This study can be viewed on the internet[453].

The FBI flatly rejected the acoustic study without having even conducted tests at their end and, more likely, did not know how to analyze the 1979 scientific data that was presented as evidence[454]. The House Select Committee on Assassinations Chief Advisor, Robert Blakey, finally conceded defeat:
"They just want this thing to die. They want to cloud it with enough uncertainty and questions that it will not continue to be a matter that is of concern to people...There was a conspiracy to kill my president, and yours, and for some reason that entirely escapes me, people don't want to investigate it further"[455].

Four years ago, in Bethesda, Maryland, I had the opportunity to listen to Robert Blakey, at the Assassinations Archives and Research Center (AARC) during the conference on the "Warren Report and Assassination of JFK ". In his presentation, I saw that his frustration over the decades had not faded. The lack of cooperation from the CIA at the time of the investigation conducted by the House Select Committee on Assassinations, which Blakey then chaired, was, in his view, a recurring problem that went far beyond the investigation of the murder of President Kennedy: the US Senate Committee had also revealed in 1975 other CIA's sinister activities. His presentation can be found on the internet[456].

All in all, despite the "Lone Nuts"' skepticism, let us keep the facts in mind: the soundtrack of the motorcycle police officer's radio contained indisputable evidence that more than 3 gunshots had been fired and that the sound impulses could not have been

---

[453] William E Kelly, "Dealey Plaza Echo Analysis-Acoustical Forensics 101," November 22, 2010:   jfkcountercoup.blogspot.com/2010/11/dealey-plaza-echos.html
[454] Robert J. Groden and Harrison Edward Livingstone. High Treason: The assassination of JFK. What really happened? The Conservatory Press, 1989
[455] William E Kelly, "Dealey Plaza Echo Analysis-Acoustical Forensics 101," November 22, 2010:   jfkcountercoup.blogspot.com/2010/11/dealey-plaza-echos.html
[456] Prof. G. Robert Blakey – The HSCA and the CIA: The View from the Trenches and the View from the Top. http://aarclibrary.org/aarc-2014-conference-videos/

motorcycles misfires. These sound effects were precisely and scientifically duplicated by the House Select Committee on Assassinations on Dealey Plaza. In addition, studies of the synchronization of the gunshots sounds with the images of Zapruder's film confirmed that there were more than three gunshots indicating that at least another gunman facing the limousine path had fired. The congressional investigation had given evidence of an ambush in a crossfire on Dealey Plaza hence there was a very high probability of a conspiracy.

These scientific studies also confirmed the testimonies of eyewitnesses who had been affected by the horrendous crime on Dealey Plaza on November 22, 1963. Their senses had not betrayed them: they had heard gunshots fired from a spot facing the limousine path. They claimed to have seen smoke above the picket fence on the "Grassy Knoll" from where they thought the gunshots had been fired. Just at the time the gunshots were fired, they had smelled gunpowder that did not come from the Texas School Book Depository. Everything matched. At least one other assassin was waiting for Kennedy when his limousine headed towards him on Dealey Plaza.

Chapter 14

Embarrassing Witnesses

Mysterious Disappearances

Some of the JFK assassination witnesses on Dealey Plaza were shocked that their initial testimonies had been altered and that they were also intimidated by the government. They took the decision therefore, by resignation, to keep a low profile and not speak out for fear of serious consequences. In contrast, other witnesses would not remain silent and took the courageous decision to defend their original statement. Those were the less fortunate. Because they were resolutely determined to reveal the truth about the plot and the cover-up, they represented an intolerable threat and their lives were cut short, often under brutal and suspicious circumstances. There were a significant number of men and women, some caught up with the assassination of John Kennedy or some just witnesses, who were considered "inconvenient" individuals. These individuals met with violent deaths in mysterious conditions during and even beyond the first few months after the Dallas events of November 1963.

As a result, some investigators started to look into specific and suspicious unnatural deaths related to the Dallas crime and came to the conclusion that it was impossible for these casualties to have been mere coincidences. These witnesses had to know "something sinister" in order to have been eliminated so ruthlessly. More than 100 key witnesses of the assassination scene received death threats and indeed many suffered mysterious deaths after having been put under huge pressure to change their statements. Over the years, the "Conspiracy Nuts" exploited the statistical interpretation of these "convenient" deaths but the "Lone Nuts" considered it a mere myth endeavoring to prove its inconsistency while government commentators did their best to destroy the study.

Two American authors, Richard Bletzer and David Wayne, have done impressive work of compiling facts, fiction and myths around these suspicious deaths following the assassination of John Kennedy[457]. From some 50 most disturbing cases described by the authors, I will select only those that seem credible enough to conceive there was a sinister scheme giving rise to their disappearances. It is hard to fully comprehend the eyewitnesses' deaths or "suicides" that are strongly correlated to the Dallas plot in so much that there is an inconsistency of facts and a certain lack of logic.

It is important first to take a look at the statistical interpretation surrounding these suspicious deaths. Experts in probability and statistics analysis have examined the high number of eyewitnesses and investigators who met unexplained violent deaths in the years following the JFK assassination. Although these experts are reminded that "as time passes men and women die", they have nevertheless demonstrated that there was an extremely high and surprisingly violent death rate among these witnesses during the period of the JFK assassination study compared to the statistically proven *normal* death rate.

Richard Charnin, author and Applied Mathematics expert, published an intensive study on this very topic in the London Sunday Times[458]. During the fall of 2013, he also published a convincing update on the same subject in his blog: "*JFK Witness*

---

[457] Richard Belzer and David Wayne; Hit List, An in-Depth Investigation into the Mysterious Deaths of Witnesses to the JFK Assassination. Fine Communications 2013

[458] Richard Charnin, "JFK Assassination; A probability Analysis of Unnatural Witness Deaths". 18 May 2012

Deaths: Graphical Proof of a Conspiracy "[459]. Based on statistical rates of annual mortality resulting from major causes, out of 1,400 key witnesses related to the JFK assassination, Charnin first estimated that 214 deaths would be "normally" expected during the period 1964 to 1978 (196 natural and 18 unnatural deaths). However, the reality for that period was quite different: he counted 85 unnatural deaths (50 homicides, 8 suicides, 24 accidents and 3 unknowns), about five times as many, which occurred among the JFK assassination witness population. Using the Poisson probability law, Charnin calculated the probability of these unnatural deaths and found a probability of E-73 (one in a trillion trillion trillion trillion trillion trillion. In the American system - short scale - one trillion is 1,000,000,000,000 or 10 to the power 12).

The probability would still tend to zero (E-61) with 78 official unnatural deaths instead of 85. Charnin's study is critical due to the fact that he could cross-check the suspicious deaths with the circumstances under which the victims were connected to the JFK assassination. In other words, he could demonstrate that the connection was well established in the case of the key and sensitive witnesses who had testified during the four investigations into the JFK assassination (Warren Commission, District Attorney Jim Garrison's trial, Church Senate Intelligence Committee, House Select Committee on Assassinations).

In his blog, Richard Charnin summarizes his conviction: "*The probability analysis is straightforward; it is not a theoretical exercise. It is mathematical proof of conspiracy based on factual statistical data of historical witnesses' mortality... I have proved mathematically what many have long suspected: The scores of convenient JFK unnatural witness deaths cannot be coincidental.*"

The murder of police officer Tippitt, in dubious circumstances, the killing of Lee Harvey Oswald, a commissioned execution, and Jack Ruby's death are part of these statistics. Oswald's death, two days after the JFK assassination, was certainly convenient in the

---

[459] https://richardcharnin.wordpress.com/2013/10/14/jfk-witness-deaths-graphical-proof-of-a-conspiracy/

absence of eyewitnesses to his alleged murder against the President and of a court trial. Not long after Oswald was shot by Jack Ruby in the police headquarters, the American people and the world began to strongly suspect that he had been eliminated in order to make sure he would not reveal anything that would point a finger at those who used him as a patsy.

Suspects of Organized Crime would have an identical fate. Johnny Roselli, an influential Mafia don- as we saw in a previous chapter - was a major player in the project to assassinate Castro, a plot that would turn against John Kennedy. After Roselli's disappearance, Jack Anderson, a reporter of a national union, who knew him well, reported Roselli's remarks about Oswald's murder in a publication: *"When Oswald was picked up, the underworld conspirators feared he would crack and disclose information that might lead to them. This almost certainly would have brought a massive U.S. crackdown on the Mafia. So Jack Ruby was ordered to eliminate Oswald making it appear as an act of reprisal against the President's killer"*[460].

Near the end of his life, Frank Sheeran, another informant who was well introduced to mobsters, gave a kind of "deathbed confession" in a book about Oswald's execution: *"Jack Ruby's cops were supposed to take care of Oswald, but Ruby bungled it. That's why he had to go in and finish the job on Oswald. If he didn't take care of Oswald, what do you think they would have done to him? Put Ruby on a meat hook. Don't kid yourself. Santo, Carlos and Giancana and some of their element, they were all in on Kennedy"*[461].

As we saw in the previous chapters, Oswald and Ruby knew each other. The Attorney General Robert Kennedy was himself very surprised to see how Ruby was involved with the big mafia bosses. When he was shown the list of the phone calls that Ruby

---

[460] Jack Anderson & Les Whitten; Behind John F. Kennedy's Murder, September 7, 1976. The Washington Post.

[461] Charles Brandt; "I heard You Paint Houses". Frank "The Irishman" Sheeran and the Inside Story of the Mafia, the Teamsters and the Last Ride of Jimmy Hoffa. Steerforth Press: 2005.

had made to the Mafia, immediately after the assassination of his brother, he said it reminded him of the list of Organized Crime bosses who had been subpoenaed before the court: *"When I saw Ruby's phone records, the list was almost a duplicate of the people I called before the [Senate] Rackets Committee"*[462].

Gerald Ford, a Warren Commission member, however gave a different opinion: *"The Commission found no evidence that Lee Harvey Oswald or Jack Ruby participated in any plot whatsoever, domestic or foreign, to assassinate President Kennedy "*[463]. The U.S. Congress rejected Gerald Ford's remarks and the Warren Report's findings. Its position was clear: *"The murder of Oswald by Ruby was not a spontaneous act but required a minimum of premeditation."* The Congress also confirmed the fact that Ruby had easily entered into the Dallas police precinct with the help of his police friends: there was also evidence that the Dallas Police Department withheld relevant information from the Warren Commission concerning Ruby's entry to the scene of the Oswald transfer[464]. The assassin of the alleged assassin himself confirmed it: *"I was framed to kill Oswald"*[465].

William B. Pitzer, United States Navy officer, Chief of the Educational Television Division at the Bethesda Military Hospital knew too much[466]. He had been called to the autopsy room to run the photo proofs of JFK's autopsy[467]. During the week following the assassination, a fellow naval officer found him working on a 16 mm film that he had secretly taken during the autopsy. Pfizer noticed a small bullet entrance wound at the right side of the

---

[462] David Talbot; Brothers, The Hidden History of the Kennedy Years , 2007 p 21
[463] President Gerald R. Ford; President John F. Kennedy: Assassination Report of the Warren Commission. Flatsigned Press: 2005
[464] House Select Committee on Assassinations, "HSCA Final Assassinations Report" p 157-158
[465] Don Freed, Jim Cookson & Jeff Cohen; *Jack Ruby: I was framed to kill Oswald*! May 1975
[466] Washington Post. Cmdr William B.Pitzer, Head of Navy TV Unit" November 2, 1966
[467] John Simkin. "William Pitzer: Biography" Spartacus International

President's forehead and a much wider hole at the lower rear of his skull. Pitzer was determined to prove that Kennedy had been hit by a bullet that came from the front of the limousine and therefore from a different direction in contradiction with the official findings of the autopsy[468]. Just before his retirement, he was about to publicly reveal the falsified autopsy photographs but he was prevented from doing so. On October 29, 1966, Pitzer was found in a pool of blood in his television studio office at Bethesda Hospital. For the official version, it was a suicide, a voluntary act with a firearm during a moment of depression. But more than thirty years after the assassination of the President, U.S. Army Special Forces Lieutenant-Colonel Daniel Marvin found out that Pitzer had been murdered. There was no doubt in Marvin's mind: the murder had been sponsored by the CIA[469].

There was plenty of evidence that the suicide version was bogus[470]. For example, paraffin tests performed by the FBI on Pitzer's hands revealed no trace of gunpowder which would have indicated that he had used a firearm against himself.[471] The FBI also revealed that the traces of powder found on the head wound came from a revolver that had been fired not at close range but at one meter from the victim's body. Pitzer's entourage formally dispelled any doubt that he had shown signs of depression or that he was planning a suicide. Quite on the contrary, his relatives argued that his state of mind was rather that of a cheerful and very active man during the last days of his life.

While New Orleans District Attorney Jim Garrison was about to subpoena key witnesses in court for his investigation on the JFK assassination, a significant number of these witnesses met a suspicious and tragic death, for some, just hours before their appearance in court. *David Ferrie*, who was suspected of

---

[468] Richard Belzer & David Wayne, Hit List, MJF Books New York, 2013 p 153-154

[469] Dan Marvin. "Bits and Pieces: A Green Beret on the Periphery of the JFK Assassination" May 1995.

[470] Heiner. Without Smoking Gun

[471] Allan R.J. Eaglesham & R. Robin Palmer. The Untimely Death of Lieutenant Commander William B. Pitzer: The Physical Evidence. January 1998.

complicity in the assassination of John Kennedy, was one of them. As an experienced pilot, he was employed for the transportation of Mafia mobsters and weapons to Cuba. He was close to Carlos Marcello, the Mafia boss in Texas and Louisiana. Ferrie knew Oswald and they had been seen together: Oswald, as a teenager, had been enlisted in David Ferrie's Civil Air Patrol Unit in New Orleans. At least one photo proves there were both together during practice. Stalked by Garrison's team, David Ferrie said that he was in great danger. He spoke to Garrison's deputy in these terms: *"You know what this news story does to me? Don't you? I'm a dead man. From here on, believe me, I'm a dead man"*[472].

Ferrie died on February 22, 1967, a week after Garrison's investigation began. The coroner concluded that Ferrie had died of a natural death, a cerebral aneurysm. Ferrie had left two typed notes announcing his "suicide" in his apartment. Both notes, unsigned and undated, can be viewed on the internet. Empty pillboxes, were also found, one of which contained Proloid, an overdose of which would cause a cerebral hemorrhage. The autopsy report revealed that there were bruises around Ferrie's mouth, perhaps as a result of heavy pressure to his mouth to force him to swallow tablets.

The same day, *Eladio del Valle*, an anti-Castro exile, was another key witness who had been subpoenaed by Garrison. Del Valle had connections with the CIA and the Mafia for their joint project to kill Fidel Castro. He was brutally murdered in Miami. A bullet was lodged in his heart and his skull was smashed by a machete[473].

The most disturbing case is perhaps Dorothy Kilgallen's death. In 1964, this popular reporter was the first to privately interview Jack Ruby in prison. She died after she announced she had very important news to reveal about the assassination of John Kennedy[474]. The circumstances of her death were totally

---

[472] Garrison. On the Trial of the Assassins, 138.
[473] Richard Belzer & David Wayne, Hit List, MJF Books New York, 2013 p 153-154
[474] Heiner. Without Smoking Gun. P 113

incomprehensible. She was the government's nightmare: she claimed that the JFK assassination was a conspiracy, that she would not let a cover-up go unnoticed and that she had collected tangible evidence. She announced that everything would be revealed in a book which would be "the biggest scoop of the century"[475].

According to the official report, Kilgallen was found dead on November 8, 1965 in her bed in her Manhattan apartment. The report concluded a suicide or an accidental overdose after 15 to 20 tablets of a cocktail of three different sleeping pills and alcohol were found in her body. When her relatives saw her for the last time, sometime earlier, she seemed lucid and coherent. They found her happy without any sign of depression and were surprised that she could have taken so many sleeping pills. The most suspicious part of this case was the almost "clinical" state of the room where she was found: there was no vomiting and the room was not in shambles[476].

Whoever set the "suicide" scene made monumental mistakes! Dorothy Kilgallen was found in a room that was not her usual bedroom and in a double bed that her relatives knew she never used. By her side, an opened book laid on the bed. According to her relatives, it was a book she had already read and recently discussed with her friends and, for them, all this was staged to show that she was reading when "the accident" occurred. She could not read without glasses but no reading glasses were found. She was not wearing nightwear and, again according to her family, she would not have worn clothes other than her usual pajama in bed.[477] She was still wearing makeup and false eyelashes. Although she never slept with air conditioning, it was still on when the authorities accessed her room. Only traces of a single barbiturate were identified in the glass from which she was supposed to have drunk whereas the autopsy revealed the presence of three different barbiturates in her blood. The notes

---

[475] David Talbot – Brothers, The Hidden History of the Kennedy Years - 2007
[476] Jesse Ventura – They Killed Our President – 2013. Skyhorse Publishing
[477] Sara Jordan. Who Killed Dorothy Kilgallen? October 21, 2007. Midwest Today

she had written about the JFK assassination were not found in her apartment. She had however previously handed over a copy to Flo Pritchet, a journalist she trusted. Two days later, Pritchet was also found dead and Kilgallen's back up notes were gone forever!

Lee Bowers, as noted earlier, was one of the main eyewitnesses to claim that several shots were fired from the "Grassy Knoll" during the presidential parade. Bowers had an excellent vantage point from his workstation on that day: the top of the railroad depot tower that stood behind the "Grassy Knoll" and the wooden picket fence. According to his testimony, the railway man noticed suspicious movements of cars in the parking lot shortly before the passage of the presidential limousine. He also saw a flash of light and smoke near the palisade where two men were stationed.

From that moment on, Bowers became overcautious and confided to his friends that he had decided to stop making public statements, for fear of losing his life. Unfortunately, it was too late and he had already said too much. On August 9, 1966, Bower was killed. His car was found on a straight Texas road crashed against a wall. Eyewitnesses and a Texas traffic patrol officer stated having seen another car that had forced Bower's vehicle off the road[478][479].

Mary Pinchot Meyer, a brilliant and seductive woman, had a serious affair with President Kennedy. She told her friends that, having known people at the CIA, she was convinced of a plot to assassinate Kennedy and that she was determined to prove it.

Before her death, she shared her views that the CIA, assisted by the Mafia and Cuban exiles, was behind the assassination[480]. On October 12, 1964, she was found dead along the Georgetown Canal in Washington D.C., her jogging spot every morning. She was hit by two bullets fired point-blank, one in the back of her head and the other in her heart. The local police quickly

---

[478] Robert J. Groden and Harrison Edward Livingstone. High Treason: The assassination of JFK and the Case for Conspiracy (Carroll & Graf: 1998).
[479] John Simkin. "Lee E. Bowers: Biography". Spartacus Educational
[480] Peter Janney's. Mary's Mosaic. 2012

concluded it was a homicide, probably as a result of a sexual assault. The police arrested an Afro-American who had been walking along the canal at the time of the crime and who was charged with murder. However, this middle-class man found a good defense lawyer who exculpated him totally. The investigation of this crime has since remained obscure and no conclusion has ever been reached.

Former CIA repentant killers, who had been under contract to eliminate embarrassing individuals, revealed that the murder of Meyer had looked like a typical CIA elimination scenario because "*she knew too much* "[481]. They went as far as naming the CIA killer under the false name of William L. Mitchell.

The sudden deaths of Sam Giancana and Johnny Roselli prompted Congress to create an official commission to reopen the investigation into the assassination of the President.

Sam Giancana, the Chicago Mafia boss, was involved in assassination attempts against Fidel Castro instigated by the CIA. He had been linked with the racketeering of Nevada casinos, Miami Beach hotels and Hollywood mafia business. After the assassination of JFK, he fled to Mexico where he lived under a false name in a beautiful castle. The Senate Church Committee took the decision to have him extradited. One morning, at dawn, FBI agents flanked by Mexican police officers surrounded Giancana's residence. Pulled from his bed, still in pajamas, Giancana was pushed into a car and was put on a plane for the United States. At the age of 67, he was threatened with spending the rest of his life in jail. The Senate Church Committee, despite determination to bring him to court, chose to offer him conditional immunity: in return for his testimony, he would be offered freedom, a new identity and $100,000 provided that he confirm his involvement in the failed CIA projects to kill Castro and also his connection with Jack Ruby, Carlos Marcello and Trafficante for the assassination of JFK. Worried that he too would be killed, Giancana protected himself by making his house

---

[481] Richard Belzer & David Wayne, Hit List, MJF Books New York, 2013 p 151

a real fortress under constant surveillance by the FBI. Even the Feds followed him around the golf course[482].

The night before being subpoenaed in Washington, he was found murdered at his home, in his kitchen, as he was preparing a Sicilian specialty presumably intended for a guest. According to the police and his relatives, only a person of trust, very well known to him, could have been invited by him that night and let in. A plausible explanation was given for the crime: while he was leaning over the stove, turning his back on his attacker, Giancana was shot in the back of his head[483]. He was found with five bullet holes around his mouth, a very clear message in Mafia language: the fate reserved for anyone who would dare to speak.

In June 1975, *Johnny Roselli* was subpoenaed before the Church Committee on Capitol Hill to testify about the CIA's pact with the Mafia in the plot to assassinate JFK. He was invited to cooperate. He had been first threatened with expulsion out of the country unless he would agree to speak. The committee was ready to give him a new identity, a secret hideout, an important protection and $100,000.

Resigned, fearing extradition, finally at the age of seventy, although he knew that by testifying he would sign his death certificate, he took the decision to reveal his secrets. During an intense interrogation, Roselli gave the name of Santo Trafficante as his contact involved in the assassination of John Kennedy. According to historian Richard Mahoney, Roselli also confided to his lawyer, Tom Wadden, that he had a role in the plot to assassinate the President. Roselli's confession was later confirmed by Wadden to former Mafia prosecutor William Hundley[484].

A year later, as he was about to testify again, Roselli's decomposed body was found in the waters of Miami Bay with a

---

[482] Sam Giancana; Biography.

[483] Craig Roberts & John Armstrong. JFK: The Dead Witnesses (Cumberland Press International: 1994), p 105

[484] Lamar Waldron, The Hidden History of the JFK Assassination, Counter Point Berkeley, 2013

bullet in his head. He had been garroted, stabbed and his arms and feet had been sawn off. The remains of his body were retrieved from a barrel of oil that had lost its ballast. One of the members of the Church Committee, Gary Hart, commented on the massacre: "*Roselli was killed in every possible way to kill.*" Clearly, former Roselli henchmen had done everything they could to prevent Senate investigators from shedding light on the actions of the Mafia.

The Church Committee investigators concluded that Roselli's execution and Giancana's killing had been sponsored by Florida Mafia godfather, Santo Trafficante, who was also suspected of helping to plot to assassinate John Kennedy[485].

Chuck Nicoletti, another key Mafia mobster was closely linked to the Chicago underworld and to Sam Giancana. On March 29, 1977, Nicoletti was in turn assassinated, soon after the decision taken by the House Select Committee on Assassinations to subpoena him. He was in Dallas on the day of the JFK assassination[486].

On the very day of Nicoletti's assassination, *George de Mohrenschildt* was shot in the face three hours after he had revealed Oswald's connection with the CIA before the House Select Committee on Assassinations. The authorities concluded that he had committed suicide by firing a .20 caliber gun in his mouth. Evidence was found that he had contacts with the CIA and that he had befriended Lee Harvey Oswald. According to James Southwood, a military intelligence veteran, who was instructed to track Oswald, said: "*All the information I had about Oswald came from George de Mohrenschildt who supplied it to the 112th Military Intelligence Unit*"[487].

The House Select Committee on Assassinations Deputy Counsel, Robert Tanenbaum, took the decision to send the

---

[485] David Talbot – Brothers, The Hidden History of the Kennedy Years - 2007
[486] Hughes Giancana, DM Oxon. *JFK and Sam*
[487] Dick Russell. The Man Who Knew Too Much. P 456.

investigator, Gaeton Fonzi, to interview George de Mohrenschildt about Oswald and about his own reporting to U.S. intelligence concerning his protégé and friend. But George de Mohrenschildt was found dead before the investigator arrived at his villa in Florida. The local authorities concluded that he had killed himself.

The precise hour of de Mohrenschildt's death by a gunshot wound was determined thanks to an audio recording of a television show that the house cleaner had programmed that night. From the house cleaner's TV recording, the facts of the "suicide" were able to be investigated by lawyer Mark Lane who revealed the trickery: *"They claimed that it was a suicide. But if you listen carefully to the soundtrack of the* [external] *recording, you will hear 'beep...beep...beep' followed by the sound of a gunshot. The beeps sounded like the security system of the main house door that was set on intermediate mode (without triggering the alarm but signaling the opening of the door). Someone had indeed entered the house"*[488]. The soundtrack also recorded the sound of footsteps, the opening and closing of a door, a silence then a detonation. George de Mohrenschildt had not left a note to his daughter nor wished to spare her from the shock of finding him in a pool of blood[489]. All this did not look like a suicide.

The year before his death, de Mohrenschildt had complained that FBI agents were tracking and harassing him and had said that he feared for his life. On September 5, 1976, de Mohrenschildt wrote a polite letter which was tainted with panic to his old friend, George H. W. Bush, the CIA director at the time. In his letter, he asked Bush to intervene so that the FBI program monitoring him could be removed:

"You will excuse this hand-written letter. Maybe you will be able to bring a solution into the hopeless situation I find myself in. My wife and I find ourselves surrounded by some vigilantes; our phone bugged; and we are being followed everywhere. Either FBI is involved in this or they do not want to accept my complaints. We are driven to insanity by the situation. I have been behaving like a damn fool ever since my daughter

---

[488] Mark Lane. G de Mohrenschidt. The Security Alarm.
[489] Jesse Ventura – They Killed Our President – 2013. Skyhorse Publishing

Nadya died over three years ago. I tried to write, stupidly and unsuccessfully, about Lee H Oswald and must have angered a lot of people I do not know. But to punish an elderly man like myself and my highly nervous and sick wife is really too much. Could you do something to remove the net around us? This will be my last request for help and I will not annoy you anymore. Good luck in your important job. Thank you so much" [490]. To this letter, Bush's response to de Mohrenschildt was vague and stereotyped. He wrote back that he did not really know what he was trying to tell him...

Witnesses disappear but writings remain. De Mohrenschildt had been very wise to have written a manuscript in which he described Oswald and their friendly relationship. The House Select Committee on Assassinations published it in its entirety. Among other things, he wrote: "*...For me Lee is innocent of Kennedy's assassination. I cannot prove it but the later events, which will be discussed, tend to prove Lee's innocence. I did not know Lee to be a dangerous man, a man who would kill like a maniac without any reason...and we proved that he was rather an admirer of Kennedy*" [491].

Less known but equally mysterious were the sudden deaths of people whose testimonies revealed the U.S. government cover-up. Some investigators have speculated on the case of *Carlos Prio*, the former President of Cuba, who was shot dead one week after George de Mohrenschildt. He, too, was on the HSCA list of witnesses for its hearing sessions.

Similarly, the death of *William Whaley*, the taxi driver who claimed to have transported Oswald after leaving the Texas School Books Depository, was sudden and mysterious. He died in 1965 of a car accident. If it was true that Oswald was in his taxi, Whaley might have been privy to Oswald's behavior and comments about the assassination on Dealey Plaza.

There was also the disappearance of *Thomas Hale Howard*, a friend of Jack Ruby, who was with his friends in his apartment on

---

[490] Russ Baker, Family of Secrets. The Bush Dynasty, America's Invisible Government, and the Hidden History of the Last Fifty Years. 2008.
[491] HSCA, House Select Committee on Assassinations P186, 132

the night of Oswald's murder. He was the first lawyer chosen by Ruby. He died of an alleged heart attack in early 1964.

Equally doubtful is the case of *Karyn Kupcinet*, the daughter of one of Ruby's friends in Chicago, who was killed five days after the assassination of John Kennedy. She said she had heard that the assassination was being planned. A telephone operator claimed to have heard Kupcinet discuss the assassination on line.

More credible is the death of *Melba Christine Marcades* (aka Rose Cheramie), one of Jack Ruby's cabaret strippers. Her death still appears today like a sponsored murder because she knew too much. On November 21, 1963, the day before John Kennedy's trip to Dallas, Cheramie was found with severe injuries by the side of a Louisiana road. She had been ejected by force from a car driven by two men who worked for Jack Ruby. That was what she explained to the hospital staff.

The hospital caregivers could hardly understand what she was saying, why she was so agitated, and nearly hysterical. They finally understood what she was trying to tell them. She was saying repeatedly that she was aware of a forthcoming plot to assassinate President John Kennedy. She also stated that Jack Ruby and Lee Harvey Oswald knew each other (this was on the eve of the President's visit to Dallas, and neither the circumstances of the JFK assassination nor the name of his alleged killer were known at the time!).

The hospital doctor who was assigned to her case reported that *"Cheramie was absolutely certain Kennedy would be murdered in Dallas the next day"*, that *"Organized Crime in New-Orleans had given the order to execute the contract against JFK"*. Other doctors and nurses at her bedside found themselves with the same quandary[492]. But Cheramie's dramatic warning was not taken seriously and was considered as purely rumors and nonsense because she was known for her addiction to drugs. She had been part of a small circle that was connected to the heroin traffic managed by

---

[492] Lamar Waldron, The Hidden History of the JFK Assassination, Counter Point Berkeley, 2013

Marcello, Trafficante and the French Connection and she had facilitated heroin dealings on behalf of Ruby.

Once she recovered from her injuries, she was released from the hospital but her fate was sealed in 1965. She was found dead by a roadside after having been hit by a car.

In the space of less than three years, congressional inquiries were hampered by the death of at least nine of their key active or potential witnesses: the sensational murders of Roselli, Giancana, Hoffa and the questionable deaths of Morales, Artime and de Mohrenschildt, all before they could testify[493].

The president of the Teamsters Union, *Jimmy Hoffa*, Robert Kennedy's nemesis, who was closely linked to the Mafia, also disappeared. His body was never found. His death was only acknowledged in June 30, 1975 after seven years of research. The case still remains open ... His assassination had all the fingerprints of a Mafia contract. He had held sensitive and highly relevant information about the JFK assassination. He had come to a point in his life when he was too talkative and enjoyed the publicity around him[494].

Manuel Artime died of a devastating cancer on November 18, 1977. He had been subpoenaed before a congressional committee for his exactions as double agent on behalf of Cuban Intelligence. The investigators connected Artime's death to those of David Ferrie and Dr. Mary Sherman because their deaths had common disease characteristics such as an aggressive and very fast developing cancer.

Mary Sherman was found dead at her home on July 21, 1964; officially an unsolved murder. Ferrie and Dr. Sherman both had done researches on the practical induction of rapid cancer in individuals as a basis of developing an assassination technique aimed at Fidel Castro. Ferrie's notes describing the methods of

---

[493] Ibid

[494] Charles Brandt; "I heard You Paint Houses". Frank "The Irishman" Sheeran and the Inside Story of the Mafia, the Teamsters and the Last Ride of Jimmy Hoffa. Steerforth Press: 2005.

cancer induction were found in his apartment, when his "suicide" by drug absorption was declared by local authorities[495].

The government's program of research on cancer induction in humans is well explained in Belzer & Wayne's book, "Hit List"[496]. Methods for induction of rapidly developing carcinomas in rats from human malignant tumors have been described in American publications such as the 1965 publication of the *American Association for Cancer Research* [497] or the more recent one in *World Journal of Surgical Oncology* [498]. These scientific studies of metastatic induction by injection in animals have fueled theories launched by some people who saw a possible extrapolation in humans!

Even though the incidence of the unexplained deaths of all these victims connected to the JFK assassination is considered by skeptics as just a coincidence or a far-fetched theory, there is nevertheless substantial evidence for a statistical occurrence of a brutal and highly suspicious death for these "inconvenient" witnesses involved in the Dallas event.

Even if "natural" deaths (for example cardiac arrest or death following a fast developing cancer) are excluded, the suspicious cases still remain strong and are well documented. We cannot totally rule out that these "natural" deaths might have been induced by techniques used by the CIA for targeting assassinations as was discussed in 1975 during the Church Committee's hearings.

---

[495] Edward T. Haslam, Dr Mary's Monkey, 2014
[496] Richard Belzer & David Wayne, Hit List, MJF Books New York, 2013
[497] http://cancerres.aacrjournals.org/content/25/4_Part_1/565.short
[498] https://www.ncbi.nlm.nih.gov/pmc/articles/PMC1266403/

Chapter 15

Can the Media's Apathy be Justified?

Now that we have covered the facts leading to the irrefutable evidence of a coup d'état, let us go back to the media's role in this historical moment for truth, a critical professional duty that they overlooked.

Why did the American mainstream media fail to seriously question the conclusions of the official version of the JFK assassination instead of endorsing it, as it still is the case today? Should they not remain loyal to the true vocation of investigative journalism? Shouldn't the revelation of irrefutable evidence have helped to shed light on the Dallas crime, putting aside manipulation and thus closing the case forever more?

To serve their masters is rather their watchword. Faced with embarrassment for holding files on Oswald, the CIA and the FBI, at the highest command level, took the decision to quickly destroy them after the assassination of President Kennedy in order to eliminate compromising evidence of their long time connection with Oswald. They did it successfully, notably during the Warren Commission's investigation because they never informed the commission of this relationship[499].

The files about Oswald should have given the CIA a legitimate reason to prevent the assassination of the President. For this reason, the agency made the decision to conceal a coup at all costs, a huge governmental cover-up of what had caused the disappearance of the most powerful man of the Free World. A sinister secret operation was behind the assassination of John Kennedy and the manipulation of Oswald. More than fifty years after the tragic event, such behavior is practically impossible for the agency to admit and to reveal to the American people.

According to journalist Jefferson Morley, Richard Helms, the CIA deputy director and James Angleton, the CIA head of counterintelligence, were both the main actors behind the cover up. Hiding the evidence of the conspiracy from the American people remains a duty for the CIA today; otherwise, the official version of a lone nut assassin without an accomplice would crumble. Historian Anthony Summers confirms it: *"We can no longer deny it. Documents are now available that confirm what the CIA and the FBI have hidden for too long, what they knew about Oswald before the assassination of President Kennedy"*[500].

Morley believes that the plot against John Kennedy is far from trivial with regards to the abuse of power of today. Looking at the current National Security Agency's control, we can better understand the impact of the JFK assassination. The mass surveillance of American citizens under the Patriot Act is very real and goes against constitutional law. How did we arrive at this situation? After the Second World War, these control agencies gained their full power, especially during the Cold War. The JFK assassination came at a pivotal moment. It was still possible to reveal their illegal practices but nothing was done to that effect. The coup of November 1963 must confront us today because it was at that precise time that the CIA and the NSA illegally consolidated and extended their power. Consider for a

---

[499] Interview of Jefferson Morley by Jacob M. Carter – Before History Dies. 2015.
[500] Anthony Summers. The Kennedy Conspiracy. P 376

minute: with the JFK assassination, a change of government was made possible without the recourse to democratic elections, without the will of the people. The American people deserve all the answers about this coup d'état otherwise, those who seek to be above the law will continue their abuse of power... These agencies will continue to believe that they have neither to be accountable to the nation, nor to respect the law and that they can do it with impunity in an authoritarian system. The assassination of John Kennedy is not just a passage of history. What happened on November 22, 1963, remains with us because we are still waiting for the U.S. government to admit its responsibility for its lack of transparency in this matter. Even today, the JFK assassination remains, for the American people, a symbol because the Dallas crime marked the beginning of a period of mistrust towards their own government. This sentiment remains: the emergence of a political revolution against the "Establishment" and the interventionism of the Washington government was illustrated around the 2016 U.S. presidential elections.

The "Conspiracy Realists" keep reminding us that if the media tried to justify the immoral and unethical practices of intelligence agencies by an absent coverage or by a distortion of the facts on the JFK assassination, it was under the pretext that it was intended to "spare the Kennedy family".

Robert Hennelly, an investigative reporter, and Jerry Policoff, a senior editor, analyzed the motives of the inability of the American press to objectively cover the murder of the President: *"It was Vietnam all over again: the war was good for the country, so don't report how badly it was going; a conspiracy to kill the President would be demoralizing at home and humiliating abroad, so sweep under the rug any evidence pointing in that direction. And then of course there was the national security issue"*[501].

There is also another media's evasion, a feeble excuse in the eyes of historians: the national press had largely covered President

---

[501] Robert Hennelly and Jerry Policoff - JFK:how the media assassinated the real story 2002. http://www.assassinationresearch.com/v1n2/mediaassassination.

Kennedy's charisma and intelligence, as well as the great saga of his family, which had always fascinated and seduced all Americans. If the whole Kennedy myth was to end abruptly, for the sake of the memories of the Kennedy family, it would be "better" that the public believe the assassination was the act of a lone nut assassin rather than that backed by a huge plot.

The editors of the national press who covered the Dallas assassination were, for the most part, of the generation who lived through the Second World War. Perhaps, for patriotic reasons, they would give the CIA and the FBI the benefit of the doubt rather than reveal the truth because it was, above all, the country that mattered.

Hennelly and Policoff believe that if the media had been more willing to cover the JFK assassination, they could have exposed the state of America's security system long before the Vietnam War and long before the shameful government practices of Watergate and Iran-Contra.

The reasons for such a media silence are possibly multiple: blind patriotism, institutional paternalism and a determination to keep face and not to admit mistakes. Once they jointly supported the Warren Report, editorial writers and journalists felt united in their coverage of the assassination. Any whisper supporting a conspiracy would have meant a form of infidelity. Those who sought to feed the "rumors" could only be traitors and hysterics.

However, as soon as Oliver Stone's movie, "JFK" was released by the end of 1991, it caused a media outcry. CBS, the New York Times, Newsweek, Time, and the Washington Post all condemned the movie with a "sincere" desire to safeguard American memory and to ensure that sacred history could not be revisited by charlatans or those who were "enlightened". The virulent attacks on Oliver Stone, about the "absurdities" of the movie and the liberties that the filmmaker took to tell the story, showed how much the press was constantly defending the opposite views and how inappropriate it was to report the truth about the Dallas murder. One wonders why the official publication of the facts about the assassination was not systematically on all the Washington media agendas. If the

Congress made the decision to reopen the investigation by creating the "JFK Records Act" in 1992 (leading to the founding of the Assassination Archives and Research Center), it was, without a doubt, less the action of CBS, the Washington Post or the New York Times but rather thanks to Oliver Stone.

Progressive journalist David Talbot measures the impact of JFK's assassination today in these terms: *"This case is not just dead history. This is live history and it's something that continues to weigh heavy on the American people because if you can't solve a mystery like this, then you can't protect your own democracy. So, going back to that day, unless we get to the bottom of this case, we really have no control over the truth that our government sells us. If we have no control of our past, then we have no control over our future… Our democracy can't survive the reign of secrecy and lies"*[502]. … *Most of the press lords and pundits in the 1960s who allowed themselves to be convinced that the Warren Report was the correct version of what happened in Dallas - whether because they genuinely believed it or because they thought it was for the good of the country - are now dead or retired. But after buying the official version for so long, it seems the elite media institutions have too much invested in the Warren Report to change their minds now, even if they're under new editorial leadership"* [503].

For Russ Baker and Milicent Cranor : *"There may be elements in the government whose job is to 'keep people calm' through efforts to perpetuate reassuring fairy tales… It is a deal with the devil, apparently one without adverse consequences – except for those of us who would prefer the truth to comforting lies"*[504].

Personally I was very sensitive to the analysis made at the 2013 Pittsburgh conference, "Passing the Torch", as to the reasons behind the media's apathy to accept there was a conspiracy. During a panel discussion, Jefferson Morley, David Talbot, Russ

---

[502] Interview of David Talbot by Jacob M. Carter – Before History Dies. 2015, p35-36.

[503] David Talbot, The Mother of All Cover-Ups, http://www.salon.com/2004/09/15/warren/

[504] Russ Baker & Milicent Cranor – The Mystery of the Constant Flow of JFK Disinformation – November 24, 2013

Baker, Lisa Pease and Jeff Policoff and filmmaker Oliver Stone all debated the role of the press in the JFK case and tried to explain why editors and journalists, to this day, are reluctant to discuss the conspiracy theory. Some of these panel journalists had worked with the media and bravely published the results of their own investigations into the assassination, knowing well that their claims (such as the involvement of the CIA in the death of John Kennedy) would be unpopular.

In Pittsburgh, David Talbot said : *"There were leaks all over the place from the beginning of the Kennedy assassination and yet, the whispers behind closed doors in Washington weren't getting to the press or weren't getting reported."*

Lisa Pease, a chief archivist of RealHistoryArchives.com, criticized the media *"that has never addressed the idea that operatives in the CIA carried out the assassination of the president. If the press had looked seriously at the JFK assassination they would have found conspiracy."* She put it this way: "*They do not dispute, they repeat what they are told to say: They are Repeaters, not Reporters*".

In Pittsburgh, these historians who condemned the persistent media neglect of today were convinced that the media was perpetuating the idea that Lee Harvey Oswald was the killer in order to help American citizens recover quickly from the devastating tragedy.

Oliver Stone philosophized: *"The idea is that evil comes out of the murkiness and kills the good. It's easy"*.

Jerry Policoff, a writer for The New York Times and The Village Voice, saw it as "*a case of microcosm of everything that's wrong with the media.*" One year later at the Bethesda convention, he recalled the words of the New York Times reporter, Tom Kicker, who had covered the events in Dallas: "*It would have taken me too long to research. I had a deadline to hold ...*"

Russ Baker, founder of the site WhoWhatWhy.com, rebelled: "*In almost all cases, journalists stay with the pack. This is not just about the JFK assassination. These stories are happening all the time"*[505]. He

---

[505] Pittsburgh City Paper,
 Don't call them conspiracy theorists: JFK assassination experts come to Pittsburgh, Rebecca Nuttall, Oct. 18, 2013

considered that the assassination of President Kennedy was a watershed for America, the end of democracy and the emergence of new events that continue to threaten democracy.

Jefferson Morley, moderator of jfkfacts.org, confided his own experience. After fifteen years at the Washington Post, he decided to leave after his management refused to publish several of his articles concerning new revelations about the assassination of John Kennedy. Morley learned quickly. *"The press is uncomfortable when this topic is discussed,"* he said in Pittsburgh, *"It does not want to take any chances. Since Oliver Stone's 'JFK' movie, which had impacted public opinion, the media apathy on this subject is notable. The press does not want to be associated with far-fetched conspiracies. Because they don't want to take part in the debate, they take refuge behind a weak argument: the Americans are not interested in this assassination case! It is an enormity to act like this: it ignores the resounding success of Oliver Stone's film and the public interest in its release, with its $200 million in global revenue!"* Morley, however, remained confident: *"The relay for research on what really happened in Dallas, the symbolic force of 'Passing the Torch to a new Generation' to quote JFK, will now be provided by the Internet and social networks that will raise awareness for millions of people, able in turn to let the truth be known and to demand the opening of new governmental or private investigations by signing petitions".*

Already, thanks to web sites such as JFKfacts.org, which Morley moderates with objectivity and factual rigor, or MaryFerrell.org, most historical data on the assassination of John Kennedy is available to anyone, anywhere. The citizenship of the world has just unreservedly started to feed in the facts about this historical crime. These websites, which are excellent sources of information and forums, have already reduced the power of the print media over the JFK assassination. The information has become that of a civil society that wants to be well informed, to understand and to act so that "the torch passes to a new generation".

This new quest for the truth now drives history students to highlight the actions of the U.S. government and the intelligence agencies who failed and still fail to respect the law with full impunity. The journalistic profession is getting younger and experiences a resurgence thanks to the social networks that are taking over the functions of traditional journalism and of old reporters contemporaneous to the 1963 Dallas event who have retired or have been ousted.

It is still too early and difficult to measure today the impact that these investigators of the new generation will have if they get serious about the task. David Talbot believes that the collusion of the press with the power has been such that there is still a strong consensus to put this story behind, to move on, in order to avoid collapse of democracy in the U.S.A.

Therefore, the media was and still is afraid to take part in the debate. CBS journalist Dan Hewitt openly disclosed in private his opinion about the JFK assassination; precisely that the CIA and the Mafia had sponsored him. When asked why he was not trying to investigate the case, he admitted his failure.

Washington Post critic, Hank Stuever, encourages a respite position; the whole thing becomes tedious and any new debate must stop: *"Nothing to see here folks, just move along," as police at a crime scene typically say"*.[506].

To illustrate this media indifference, Talbot refers to Ben Bradlee, the Washington Post's editor-in-chief, known for his "CIA culture." Despite being a close friend of John Kennedy, Bradlee tried to explain the reasons for his refusal to cover the murder. In 2004, at the age of 83, he told Talbot that he had feared that his investigation would hurt his career. *"People would have criticized my obsession with covering this tragedy. Well, I thought it would ruin my career and did not want to take chances"*[507].

One year after the Pittsburgh Convention, Russ Baker came to the Bethesda Conference on the 50th anniversary of the Warren Report to talk again about the apathy of the American media today, especially around the JFK assassination. He said that

---

[506] Andrew Kreig Self-Censorship In JFK TV Treatments Duplicates Corporate Print Media's Apathy, Cowardice.

[507] David Talbot – Brothers, The Hidden History of the Kennedy Years - 2007

journalists were – and still are - afraid that their careers would be destroyed, that their jobs and their salaries would be lost and they would be unable to support their families. The press must quickly move on to justify their position and secure their pecuniary means so important for them. They are often ignorant of the facts about the JFK assassination because of lack of time to do historical research. The JFK assassination event is too complex and can be disconcerting. These journalists avoid going deep into their interviews, asking disturbing questions, being trapped in the debate over the plot scandal because, let us face it, this story still remains sensitive today. The press does not want to analyze the documents that have been released, nor do they want to ask the right questions and make strong arguments that would have allowed closing the case. Due to lack of time, the media coverage is often superficial...

In Bethesda, Jefferson Morley admitted that there was for sure much media indifference on the JFK assassination but he tried to understand the root cause. It is true, he said, that the reporters have neglected to cover the facts supporting a highly probable conspiracy but it must also be recognized that the topic is extremely demanding in terms of research time and that these journalists must quickly move on in order to prepare and release a new edition each day. New and relevant information about the assassination tend to destabilize Liberal leaders who control the news organizations and the television networks in America and, as such, will contribute to journalistic evasion. Editors and reporters, especially in Washington and New York City work, are under intense stress and victims of continual criticism in the current political context[508].

Only professional, well-experienced liberal-minded journalists could conceive that most Americans continue to believe that Kennedy's political enemies eliminated him with impunity. However, they furtively covered the 50th anniversary of the Warren Report's publication with minimal analysis. How could

---

[508] http://jfkfacts.org/cognitive-dissonance-overpowers-the-50th-anniversary-of-the-warren-commission/

these open-minded journalists fail to ignore that occult powers exist in America, outside the reach of laws, the Congress and media organizations and that, in the case of the Dallas assassination, democratic institutions had failed to control and unmask them? The 50th anniversary of the Warren Report's publication should have been a reminder that many Americans no longer trust the efficiency and the integrity of their government to tell them the exact circumstances of their President's death.

Cyril Wecht, the forensic pathologist, believes that the CIA is still very powerful and continues to influence the press today. The journalists would rather not debate the conspiracy theory by "patriotism"...but by cowardice too. They are afraid to say: "*No, I do not believe in the Warren Report*". They fear to damage their reputation.

Unfortunately, this is the sad reality of the media communication nowadays, especially on the TV channels. They switch too quickly to another matter without taking the time through thorough journalistic investigation to return to this or that aspect of major events taking place in our society. These words of the French hero, Marquis de Lafayette, engraved on the pedestal of a statue near my American home come to my mind:

I read. I study. I examine. I listen and I reflect. I try to get an idea of all this in the most meaningful way possible

Marquis de Lafayette

Journalists would do well to heed the advice of this French hero and firm believer in the American cause during the Revolutionary War!

Let us play the devil's advocate for a moment: could we possibly understand the cover-up, the concealment of the plot because it was committed in an America shaken by extreme tensions with Cuba and the Soviet Union? Let us think that the plot was fomented by the Soviet Union or by Cuba, that Kennedy could have been victim of a Soviet plot (as the CIA told President Johnson)[509]. To avoid a nuclear clash with Russia, Johnson's administration would have taken the decision to hide the truth to the American people and press instead charges against Oswald in order to quash the affair. Even though this explanation is often accepted by historians as plausible, how, half a century later, once the passions of a shocked American nation have been cleared, can we explain the persistence in concealing the truth?

Andrew Krieg, an investigative lawyer and journalist, believes that self-censorship is self-powered because television producers need the backing of the corporates that run the finance of their programs. At multiple stages of news reporting, there is a conflict between gaining TV audience and the realities of the corporate world and there is also federal control over parent companies and their affiliates[510].

In the end, Andrew Krieg's own website says it all. In the United States, the term "conspiracy theorist" seems to have become an insult, a "dirty word" since 1967. Establishment journalists want to protect their sources and their self-esteem by denigrating any research from anyone who promotes the idea that a crime could have ever been committed by government officials of law enforcement, military or intelligence. Some journalists use the term "conspiracy theorists" in a derogative way in order to humiliate them and to abolish any recourse to the examination of evidence. By looking at it more closely, it usually turns out that these journalists have little knowledge of the exact facts, for example in the case of the hasty condemnation of Oswald. More generally, these establishment journalists encourage smear campaigns. Their goal is to discourage the analysis of evidence of any sensitive topic that private

---

[509] David Talbot. "The Mother of all Cover-ups"

[510] Andrew Kreig
http://www.justice-integrity.org/index.php?option=com_content&view=article&id=584:self-censorship-in-jfk-tv-treatments-duplicates-corporate-print-media-s-apathy-cowardice&catid=21&Itemid=114%20

investigators, historians and every citizen have the responsibility to make[511].

---

[511] Andrew Kreig: https://www.popularresistance.org/who-are-the-puppets-that-control-the-media-and-politicians/

Chapter 16

Yes, we do want to know!

Is there a glimmer of hope for historians and investigators who, for some, have spent a great deal of their life ever since that fateful day searching for the truth about the JFK assassination?

The National Archives and Records Association (NARA) developed an ambitious program for the release of many classified files on the assassination of John Kennedy. October 26, 2017 was set as the date for the public release.

Why this date? The JFK Assassination Records Collection Act was created in response to the enactment of the JFK Assassination Records Act, signed on October 26, 1992 by George H. W. Bush. This law stipulates that no document relating to the assassination of John Kennedy should remain "classified" beyond the 25 years following its enactment, that is, beyond October 26, 2017.

Following this decision, an independent agency, the Assassination Records Review Board was created to ensure the identification of all documents and to schedule their publication (a massive job that took five years from 1993 to 1998).

Bill Clinton, running at the time for the presidential election campaign in 1992, admitted that he believed in a conspiracy to assassinate John Kennedy but retracted as soon as he took office.

Once in office, however, he did not oppose the continuation of the "Assassination Records Review Board" project.

During the 2016 U.S. presidential election campaign, since the release date of the JFK files was to fall during the new presidential term, each candidate was asked for an opinion on the project. Some candidates eluded the question (we can understand there are issues in the country which have more priority). Others replied that they would not oppose the release... with the caveat: "unless the information would harm the national security".

Investigative journalist, Russ Baker made the following comment: "*Release of the remaining documents, under the President John F. Kennedy Assassination Records Collection Act of 1992, can be postponed until October 26, 2017. Not so bad, you say? Actually, the Act further states that even in 2017, the president may decide to drag this on further, by withholding records indefinitely*"[512].

Investigator William Kelly notes that the JFK files remain, in the eyes of senior U.S. government officials, a matter of national security and that thousands of historical documents are so sensitive that they will not make them public, even half a century later: "*We know that files have been intentionally destroyed, others have disappeared completely or are kept secret without opposition and with total contempt for the law* "[513].

All files concerning the assassination of President Kennedy have been transferred from various government agencies to NARA. The collection is made up of more than 5 million pages. These are documents, photographs, sound recordings and various artifacts that total an approximate volume of 56 cubic meters. Since 2014, NARA has been responsible for archiving the files, employing 4 archivists and 3 technicians to scan them. After indexing and digitalization, the collection was to be made public on the website www.archives.gov. Specifically, tens of thousands of JFK files that had still not been made public were to be legally released on October 26, 2017, in accordance with the JFK Assassination Records Collection Act.

---

[512] Russ Baker, "Is The Government Holding Back Crucial Documents?" May 30, 2012

[513] William Kelly, "Playing Politics with History – The Still Secret JFK Assassination Records 20 years after the JFK Act".

This law was however designed with the provisions that any JFK files released be subject to a possible veto from the President of the United States and could therefore be postponed. Even today, this means that government agencies, mainly the CIA and the FBI that generated many files on the JFK assassination, can appeal to the President of the United States as a last resort in order to maintain their secrecy. *"Each assassination record should be publicly disclosed in full, and be available in the Collection no later than the date that is 25 years after the date of enactment of this Act, unless the President certifies that: (1) continued postponement is made necessary by an identifiable harm to the military defense, intelligence operations, law enforcement, or conduct of foreign relations; and (2) the identifiable harm is of such gravity that it outweighs the public interest in disclosure"* [514].

An article from Politico.com entitled "Why the last JFK files could embarrass the CIA?" recalls that roughly 3,600 documents in the National Archives about the JFK assassination were classified in total secrecy and have therefore never been consulted by the American people. These are essentially very sensitive files containing information about the privacy of individuals, their tax status, or the identity of a confidential source[515]. NARA's inventory and the reliable source Maryferrell.org (probably the largest independent JFK assassination research database), indexed 3,600 secret documents related to the assassination that are kept secret, 1,300 of which come from the FBI and 1,100 from the CIA (about 50,000 pages according to JFKfacts.org). The remaining documents include testimony from the Warren Commission, the House Select Committee on Assassinations, reports from the National Security Agency and U.S. Department of Defense offices, as well as tax returns from key figures[516].

The CIA documents include references to mysterious and highly controversial individuals in the history of American espionage, including those involved in worldwide assassination plots. Unfortunately and unsurprisingly, having failed to comply

---

[514] https://www.congress.gov/bill/102nd-congress/senate-bill/3006
[515] http://www.politico.com/story/2015/05/why-last-of-jfk-files-could-embarrass-cia-118233
[516] http://www.maryferrell.org/pages/Featured_Mark_the_Date.html

with the 1992 JFK Assassination Records Act and with the will of the U.S. Congress, the CIA is reluctant to agree to the publication. According to NARA, there are more than 3,000 pages of unpublished documents related to the covert actions of 7 individuals in connection with the JFK assassination. The National Archives give with extreme precision the references of these documents in which the content is classified. Here is the list of the relevant files about the following individuals: they are primarily CIA agents such as E Howard Hunt (332 pages), William King Harvey (123 pages), David Atlee Phillips (606 pages), Anne Goodpasture (286 pages), David Sanchez Morales (61 pages), George Joannides (50 documents) but also Yuri Nosenko, an officer of the Soviet KGB who was suspected by the CIA for his surveillance of Oswald when he was in Russia (2,224 pages). All died during the period of between 7 and 40 years following the JFK assassination.[517] Journalist Jefferson Morley has run in-depth investigations of the CIA's actions. According to him, the Agency is reluctant to open this dark page of its history to the eyes of the world due to the fact that a dozen of CIA agents conducted intelligence operations on Oswald prior to the JFK assassination and that they might have participated in the 1963 plot[518].

Unfortunately, the date of October 26, 2017 did not mark the turning point for the epilogue of this case! The declassification of the files was eagerly awaited for in the United States. Even though the American and foreign press had given it much coverage, expectations were that not everything however would be revealed or that we might not even see anything at all! It was still possible that compromising reports could have been destroyed by the CIA and the FBI. If that were the case, it would be a criminal action, because it is a crime in the United States to destroy any federal record without a supreme authorization. Among all the confidential documents concerning the JFK

---

[517] Gary Fannin, The Innocence of Oswald, 2015
[518] Jefferson Morley, CIA & JFK: The Secret Assassinations Files, Kindle edition.

assassination, we also suspect that some files were rewritten after their initial development. It is known from the past declassified files that some entire paragraphs were blacked out (sometimes more than 80% of the page), thus making them illegible or completely impossible to analyze!

So what happened on October 26, 2017? The bottom line is that the release of these final JFK files was far from complete. It was announced that some more documents were due for release later, in April 2018, but the whole publication did not happen then. In the end, President Trump decided to allow the CIA and the FBI to withhold more than 15,000 JFK files until October 26, 2021 before public release as material that "*must remain classified for national security reasons*".

And so, it was not the great transparency promised. It was more of a travesty and the few documents released showed redactions with blacked out areas. Rex Bradford who is president of maryferrell.org, commented with irony. "*In at least one case, the very same document has been available in fully non-redacted form at the National Archives for more than 10 years* [available on Mary Ferrell Foundation (MFF)]...*By comparing the newly released version and the MFF on line version, these are two different copies of the same document held by different agencies, so perhaps one being redacted and the other not is just an accident. But why are there any redactions at all in the new copy? It is as yet unclear why so many redactions appear in what are supposed to be fully released records*"[519].

Among the files that have however been released, which is the most revealing one? What have we learned? According to Jefferson Morley, "*The new JFK files shed more light on how the CIA monitored Oswald's travels, his politics and his personal life for four years before JFK's assassination. The files show how the CIA ought to hide the details of pre-assassination interest in Oswald from the public*

---

[519] https://www.maryferrell.org/pages/Featured_What_Happened_Thursday.html

and investigators, lending credence to the notion that the JFK investigation was controlled, not botched"[520].

From the documents released on October 26, 2017, one particular document is troubling and could fuel more credibility about an assassination plot with Oswald used as a CIA asset. It contains details of former CIA director Richard Helms being interrogated by the Rockefeller Commission in the mid-1970s. David Belin, an attorney for the Commission which looked into whether the CIA was involved in Kennedy's killing, asked Helms: "Well, now, the final area of my investigation relates to charges that the CIA was in some way conspiratorially involved with the assassination of President Kennedy... Is there any information involved with the assassination of President Kennedy which in any way shows that Lee Harvey Oswald was in some way a CIA agent or agent..." The released page is cut off in mid-sentence! Helms' answer is missing from the document released in October 2017. There are no further pages included! Why is a page missing which concerns the answer to the crucial question of Oswald's possible involvement with the CIA[521]?

The U.S. National Archives do not work for the CIA. They work for the American people with respect to the 1992 JFK Records Act. Twenty-five years after the enactment of this law, the fact that the CIA has failed firstly in its obligation to respect the law, by invoking a lack of "Time and Resources", and secondly to tell the truth about the murder of a sitting president, shows not only the Agency's clear disdain for JFK's memory but also its shameful intent to circumvent the law. The National Archives must therefore be honored for putting the CIA and other government agencies on notice in order to enforce the law. Unfortunately, we have witnessed the CIA's persistence to extend the publication period even longer. Clearly, if public awareness weakens, the Agency will continue exonerating itself from its legal duty.

---

[520] https://www.salon.com/2018/01/01/the-new-jfk-files-reveal-how-the-cia-tracked-oswald_partner/
[521] https://www.maryferrell.org/showDoc.html?docId=1386#relPageId=20&tab=page

Why then is the release of the classified JFK assassination files still rejected? Is it because they are deemed too sensitive? It is deeply disturbing to hear from the American government, more than five decades after the Dallas tragedy, that it cannot release certain files under the pretext that they would affect national security.

Is this really a state secret? We can only speculate. Is the U.S. government waiting for the death of Fidel Castro's brother, Raúl, for a sensational revelation of the involvement of Cuba? Could remaining classified CIA documents contain testimonies incriminating the Agency for the numerous assassination plots against Fidel Castro in the 1960s? Don't we already know that from the Church Committee hearings? As for speculative Russian accountability, many years have passed since the fall of the Iron Curtain and the disintegration of the Soviet Union. What could really be the impact today of the hypothetical revelation of a Soviets' plot to assassinate John Kennedy? Can we truly imagine a disastrous American-Russian confrontation resulting from such a revelation and that, in order to keep the world safe, maintaining secrecy could be so critical? The JFK assassination researchers however are watching. They continue to raise disturbing questions as to why the government defends "national security" arguments and criticizes the debate over the conspiracy that it sees prejudicial to U.S. institutions.

If one day all the classified JFK files are all released and if government agencies are not found to be compromised in any way, the conspiracy theorists will accept the verdict and end their crusade. But as long as the secrecy remains, they see no reason to lower their guard and they continue to maintain that there is evidence of foul play, something sinister about the JFK assassination and its cover-up.

With the rise of current global terrorism and the fear of attacks against the United States and elsewhere, the citizens of the world expect vigilance from their governments. At a crucial moment when all the U.S. efforts are needed to fight against terrorists and to dismantle their cells that pose a threat to the country, it is my opinion that it could possibly be counter-productive for the CIA and the FBI to reveal to the American people now the role played by their government agencies in the cover-up of the JFK assassination. It might not be an opportune time for the American people to know the truth of what happened to their President because there would certainly be a strong reaction and a sense of betrayal resulting in a loss of confidence in their government. During this critical moment of national unity against terrorism, they would deeply distrust their security agencies whose reputation would be tainted. This is perhaps why the secrecy is maintained as there is priority given to protecting the American people and keeping their trust. I therefore doubt that a strong desire for transparency on the JFK assassination could outweigh the destabilizing and confusing impact that a spectacular revelation would create. It is therefore not inconceivable that the cover-up will continue.

Even if the U.S. government is finally willing to come clean about its involvement in the assassination of one of his most popular presidents in the U.S. history, it is highly probable that we will never know the whole truth. How can we be sure that no documents have been previously redacted or that evidence has not been destroyed? The JFK researchers fear this scenario. They are realistic and do not expect much of a scoop, or that a "smoking gun" could still be found. After all these years, it is no doubt too late to identify guilt beyond a shadow of doubt. The investigation trails have been well blurred before, during and after the assassination of John Kennedy. Even if some government agencies admit their share of responsibility, bad faith could prevail since they would tend to minimize the scale and the consequences of their cover-up. Although the Agency director and other senior officials admitted having withheld information from investigators about the JFK assassination, they nevertheless considered that it was a "benign" cover-up! This is what the Daily Mail, the British Conservative newspaper, wrote in its article of October 14, 2015 about CIA declassified files. The facts however still show that the evidence of a conspiracy have been removed and that false testimonies to support the lone assassin theory have been encouraged. To hide the truth about the elimination of a great politician is certainly not an insignificant act, nor a benign crime!

At the twentieth annual JFK Lancer conference in November 2015, to my question "Will we ever know the truth?" a resident of Dallas, another activist and delegate like me, replied: "*But we already know the truth! You only have to open your eyes and study the case well. We just now need our voice to be heard!*"

Shortly after the assassination, a journalist asked the Warren Commission Chairman if all the files would be made public. His reply was cynical: "*Yes, there will come a time. But it might not be in your lifetime*". May this day come quickly so democracy is truly respected!

David Talbot[522], certainly a better observer of the current U.S. political context than I, sees little chance that an inquiry into the JFK assassination be resumed by a new commission given the Congress' priorities today. The Kennedy assassination is not the only unsolved case in the history of the United States. The investigations into the murders of Martin Luther King Jr. and Robert Kennedy in 1968, still unresolved today, about which the press coverage has been very quiet, deserved to be reopened too.

Robert G. Blakey, the Chief Counsel of the House Select Committee on Assassinations, who was interviewed by Talbot in 2003, remained deeply pessimistic: "*The Kennedys are not part of this generation. I teach this generation. It* [The assassination] *is not a big deal for them. They grew up in a different world*"[523].

Talbot proposes the following action which has the merit of laying the foundations for a real strategy to shed light on the murders of JFK, RFK and MLK all of which have changed the course of the American history. A survey should be quickly conducted by an independent commission, composed of legal experts, using both the work of a large number of historians and on testimonies received by those observers and actors of the time who are still alive. Talbot believes it is time for the CIA to be urged to reveal the travel and telephone conversation details of

---

[522] Interview of David Talbot by Jacob M. Carter – Before History Dies. 2015.
[523] David Talbot – Brothers, The Hidden History of the Kennedy Years - 2007

its agents who are suspected of having been involved in the JFK assassination. Washington should also officially request that the Cuban and the Mexican governments reveal all their secret files on this case.

Perhaps it might also be necessary to grant - with reluctance but with pragmatism – some sort of conditional amnesty to any repentant conspirators still alive whose role was minor, provided that they are willing to provide relevant and verifiable testimonies.

Today state-of-the-art technology should be used in order to put an end to the ambiguities and the arguments of experts especially concerning the ballistic and acoustic tests performed on Dealey Plaza a few decades ago. If public lobbying could be added to this action, Congress, with all its power, would then be able to support these investigations and force the CIA to respect the 1992 law. Despite the fact that the majority of Americans are unaware of this law, some understand the scope of the "JFK Records Act" and know that keeping classified files in the National Archives on this case is completely illegal.

We can only hope that the JFK files which are still classified will one day shed light on the actions of a government that have repeatedly stonewalled the investigation into the JFK assassination. What we are waiting for is that a cover-up by the authorities, at the highest level, be officially and publicly recognized; that the botched autopsy of the President or that the many witnesses' deaths related to the assassination disguised as suicides be admitted.

The JFK files might also reveal that the FBI, under the leadership of President Lyndon Johnson and of FBI Director J. Edgar Hoover, obstructed the investigation of the assassination. Some members of the Warren Commission were skeptical and frustrated. The final report was made public under pressure in order to keep President Johnson's deadline, but troubling questions had been raised by the commission at the last minute and time ran out for further investigation.

Let us not totally despair. There was a recent example that showed that the principle of transparency in American democracy can work remarkably well and can be done in a short time. In April 2016, under the pressure from the families of the 9-11 victims and from lawmakers, President Obama agreed to publish the "classified" pages of the U.S. Congressional inquiry into the terrorist attacks on that fateful day. In July 2016, 28 pages of the commission's investigation report into the role of Saudi Arabia in the execution of 9-11 attacks on U.S. soil were finally made public. At first sight, these pages revealed what U.S. officials suspected, but could not prove then: that senior officials in the Saudi kingdom had given support to the plane hijackers, most of them Saudi nationals. Similarly, despite the American intelligence agencies' opposition but due to possible public lobbying, it is not unthinkable that the veil on the JFK assassination files could be lifted one day.

Besides the 9-11 terrorist attacks, America has experienced few tragedies of this magnitude on its soil since Pearl Harbor. In 1963, the assassination of President Kennedy was undoubtedly felt as the worst U.S. tragedy since that day in December 1941. Every American and, to a certain extent, every citizen of the Free World, was affected by the Dallas tragedy which changed the future of the world and kept the Cold War for 26 more years. Every person alive that day, all over the world, remembers what he or she was doing when the news of President Kennedy's death broke.

With John Kennedy in charge of the all-powerful country, the hope for a better and peaceful world should have prevailed but instead everything was brutally destroyed by the gunshots of fanatics. His disappearance affected not only those who were contemporaries of the President's political epic but also to a certain extent those who were yet to be born not just in the U.S.A. but all over the world. In the light of the mediocrity of the politicians today, it is all the more poignant to have lost such a leader.

Some historians dwelled on JFK's imperfections, but it was his humanity, his compassion, his intelligence, his charisma and his sense of humor that made him an exceptional leader. Since the assassination of Abraham Lincoln, no other death of an American president marked the country as much as that of President

Kennedy. On the night of his death, a deep affliction was felt all over the world: in London, the Westminster Abbey bell sounded the death knell for an hour; 300,000 people marched through the streets of Berlin; all radio programs were canceled in Ireland; all the stores in Paris were closed and the Champs-Elysees was totally deserted on that Friday night. He was the President of all people.

The government's scheme in covering up the evidence of a conspiracy is no doubt as bad as the despicable Dallas crime itself. The American people reacted to the assassination of their President with stupor, anger and disbelief and quickly realized that they were lied to about a secret implication and a highly probable conspiracy. It is not a theory, it is an indisputable fact. After more than five decades of lies, the U.S. government is under pressure to present a credible explanation for the assassination of John Kennedy. Fortunately, there are many documents about the JFK assassination that are now available on the internet. Because we now have access to reliable sources of information that cannot be censured, we are able to analyze the facts – certainly not fake news - of this historical crime. Even today, there is not a single year nor even a few months that go by without there being new and relevant articles on-line containing new revelations or testimonies that shed more light on the case.

At the Pittsburg convention for the 50th anniversary of Kennedy's death, Mark Lane, a civil rights activist and the posthumous lawyer for Lee Harvey Oswald, made a surprising comment and comparison. He referred to the French people's apathy during the Dreyfus affair, a similarity to the U.S. lassitude towards the historic coup d'état in Dallas and to the far-fetched conclusion about a man, presumed innocent, who was accused of assassination. Mark Lane said that the courage of France that, in the end, proved Dreyfus was innocent should be an example in the United States after half a century of denial of the truth about the Dallas crime: to defy guilt by finally rehabilitating an innocent man (Lane's position), in full knowledge of the facts.

During the darkest moments of American government policy, from Dallas to Vietnam, from Watergate to the invasion of Iraq, the truth has too often been ignored and charges for crimes have frequently been neglected. On November 22, 1963, the message from Dallas was clear: if a President could be gunned down with impunity, any foul play could then be possible. Whoever killed John Kennedy made every effort to hide the evidence and ignore key eyewitnesses. Let us imagine for a moment how the people of an all-powerful country, claiming true democracy, would react today to the announcement of the assassination of its president, in broad daylight, in the streets of one of its big cities; an internal coup d'état that would be suspected but that would be covered-up by its government with lies and false accusations? What would be the recourse for the people of this nation? There would certainly be a media outcry and a vast journalistic enquiry, a strong involvement from people all over the world on social media, evidence provided from cellular phone recordings etc. All people with any moral sense would rally globally for the search of the truth.

In the absence of an honest inquiry, the American people, who have still not heard the truth about the assassination of their President, have become skeptical about the political power of their country. Awareness of this despicable crime stays with them and has ripple effects. It is not a simple story, long gone.

So, is it really relevant with today's world challenges to know who was behind the assassination of John Kennedy and how the cover-up was made possible? Certainly, these questions bother us, especially those researchers of the truth who have been working for decades. One day, we may have to face the fact that the individuals who were directly involved in the assassination plot and in its cover-up will never be charged even after definite results of new investigations and with proof of their guilt. But it is nevertheless of paramount importance that the truth be officially acknowledged. Vigilance is essential. By exposing the past, we analyze the present. A careful examination of the historical facts is our responsibility in order to take the necessary steps to avoid repeating the mistakes of the past.

If obstruction of justice to solve the JFK assassination endures, then the American people will have no choice other than to make the decision to be their own "jury". After all, more than 60% of Americans today think that there was a conspiracy. This fact is much more reassuring than any shortcomings from the media. Ultimately, the real assassins may be charged in a "trial" that was impossible at the time. It is a safe bet to say that this "jury" will come to its senses and take action. So let us stay confident.

This is precisely what has happened very recently! An action for the search of the truth has been surprisingly launched when despair was gaining ground. On January 21, 2019, a petition was sent to the U.S. Congress calling for the reopening of the investigations into the four political assassinations of President John F. Kennedy, Malcolm X, Martin Luther King, Jr. and Senator Robert F. Kennedy. A group of over 60 prominent citizens (including family members of the victims, lawyers, doctors, Hollywood entertainers, legal experts, activists, scholars and journalists) have all had the determination to stand against apathy. By aiming to convene an American Truth and Reconciliation Committee, they are determined to bring out the facts concerning the four major assassinations that still haunt America and changed the course of this nation and the world. All we can hope for now is that this action will not be in vain !

President Kennedy's brain was never found after the autopsy. It is still unknown today where it is or if it was destroyed. It is a whole symbol to steal the brain of an exceptional man like John Kennedy! If the plotters feared that his brain would reveal the origin of gunshots (a certainty according to forensic pathologist Cyril Wecht), they however failed to confiscate his heart, his soul and above all his quality features left in our collective memory.

In 1962, for the 20th anniversary of the Voice of America, President Kennedy made a statement that today, more than half a century later, takes on a premonitory meaning in the current context of the search for the truth about his assassination: *"We are not afraid to entrust the American people with unpleasant facts, foreign ideas, alien philosophies, and competitive values. For a nation that is afraid to let its people judge the truth and falsehood in an open market is a nation that is afraid of its people."*

May the strength of John Fitgerald Kennedy's message always resonate and be heard throughout the world. To honor this President who, in his short life, strived for peace, truth and justice, we owe it to his memory that one day the full light will be finally shed on the circumstances surrounding his assassination.

Evidence of a Plot to kill JFK and of a Cover-Up

Supporting Facts	Evidence/References	Factual Sources	Witnesses' Claims (Credibility?)
Oswald's *motive, means* and *opportunity* to commit the crime could not be demonstrated.	Different ID for the rifle (Mauser instead of Mannlicher-Carcano) that was immediately found on the crime scene.	Various firearms experts' testimonies.	
	No eyewitness could locate Oswald at the crime scene with a weapon. There is no evidence that he was seen firing the shots on Dealey Plaza.	Testimonies of Chief Dallas Police, Jeff Curry (Dallas Morning News Nov. 6, 1969) and of several eyewitnesses.	
	JFK's head was hit by a high velocity frangible bullet. The bullets of Oswald's alleged rifle were non frangible and of medium velocity.	Firearms and ballistic experts.	
	Oswald claimed his innocence and that he was a patsy. He repeatedly said that he bore no grudge against JFK but that he rather admired him and that he had no reason to kill him.	TV Interview of Oswald. De Mohrenschildt's testimonial.	Journalists and police officers' testimonies during Oswald's arrest.
More than 3 bullets were fired on Dealey Plaza => Oswald could not have been the lone gunman.	The timing of 5.6 seconds for the 3 shots to be fired (Warren Report) could not be matched by the best U.S. Marine *snipers* with the same obsolete rifle, the same munitions and the same constraints.	Published shooting results. Video reconstitution.	
	Two shots were real close. The Mannlicher Carcano scope that Oswald allegedly used was faulty.	Eyewitnesses. Sharpshooters' expertise. Secret Service agents' testimonies	
	Minimum 6 bullets, perhaps 7 were fired: 1 or 2 were lost, 3 hit JFK, 2 Connally.	Testimonies from Kellerman, Connally, Tague. Zapruder film.	
	The scientific sound analysis of the Dictabelt revealed that more than 3 shots had been fired and that they came from 2 different locations.	Acoustic analysis. *House Select Committee on Assassinations* (HSCA) Report.	
Some shots came from a location at the front of the limousine => at least a second gunman was	A large number of eyewitnesses on Dealey Plaza rushed towards the "Grassy Knoll"/palisade.	Video films, Witnesses' testimonies.	
	Exit wound at the back of JFK's skull: consensus of 8 medical doctors and 6 eyewitnesses (FBI, Secret Service, Health care providers).	Medical sources. Official reports. Vidéos	

posted in the "*Grassy Knoll*"/Triple pass area.	The Zapruder film shows that the fatal shot hit the temporal section of JFK's skull and violently propelled him back and to the left.	Photographic sources. Zapruder film.	
	Secret Service agents certify that the shots came from a location facing the limousine	Interviews/Official reports.	
Two other assassination plots against JFK were planned in November 1963, in Chicago and in Tampa, but were foiled at the last minute. The plans had a modus operandi identical to that in Dallas.	The U.S. Secret Service had been informed as well as the Congress and JFK.	U.S. Congress investigators. Declassified files from the CIA and the Warren Commission.	
The Secret Service changed the motorcade formation at the last minute. The motorcycle police officers were moved behind the limousine and were unable to give effective protection to the President.	The infringement to the strict security rules was confirmed by the Secret Service and the *House Select Committee on Assassinations*	Photographs of the presidential car: the motorcade formation was different in Dallas and was not the usual one used in other cities	
Two Secret Service agents were ordered to keep off the running boards of the presidential limousine.		YouTube, Zapruder film.	
The morning of Nov 22, Oswald could not possibly carry a dismantled and wrapped rifle under his armpit as he walked to the *Texas School Book Depository*.	The Mannlicher Carcano rifle could not be totally dismantled. Its length would have exceeded the size of the parcel which was found by the Warren Commission investigators.		Buell Frazier's testimony (Oswald's colleague).
There are no scientific evidence that Oswald used the Mannlicher-Carcano rifle to shoot at the President.	There is no serious correlation between the partial hand prints found on the rifle and Oswald's finger prints. The paraffin tests were negative for traces of nitrates on Oswald's face.	FBI Scientific tests.	
Oswald was most probably an Intelligence Service agent.	Oswald was sent to the Soviet Union as part of a CIA and ONI program to fill the role of a false defector.		Testimonies/confessions from former CIA agents and anti-Castro members
	Oswald had most likely a double. The fake Oswald could have been created by the US Intelligence Service as an impostor to impersonate the real Oswald. Scars on Oswald's body at the morgue did not match those described in Oswald's military records.	FBI director, J Edgar Hoover informed his colleagues about this possibility by memo 3 years before the Dallas crime!	Testimonies of medical doctors and undertaker.
2 photos of Oswald holding the "crime weapon" before the JFK	Technical impossibility: the shadows do not match. The back ground		Oswald's statements. Testimonies of his wife

assassination are a montage. Based on the photos, the Warren Commission concluded that the rifle was linked to Oswald.	of the 2 photos is strictly identical with two difference positions of Oswald's body. Oswald's head seems to be superposed on a body.		and photography experts.
There is no evidence that Oswald killed police officer Tippit despite the charge. This crime, 45 minutes after JFK assassination remains unsolved.	Oswald did not have the motive, the opportunity, nor the means. The chronology of precise facts exonerates Oswald.		Eyewitnesses on the crime scene. Prosecutor Jim Garrison's investigation
The murder of Oswald by Jack Ruby was a premeditated act to eliminate an embarrassing witness.	Jack Ruby was given the contract by the Mafia.	Robert Kennedy's position after he ordered a private investigation. HSCA investigation	Mafia informants. Jack Ruby's confession
Jack Ruby knew Lee Harvey Oswald and was connected to Mafia Godfathers.	Not only Ruby and Oswald knew each other but they also worked together on behalf of the CIA for anti-Castro operations.	Robert Kennedy's opinion after he ordered a private investigation.	Eyewitnesses in Ruby's cabaret. Prosecutor Jim Garrison's investigation
Although a critical crime scene, the presidential limousine was taken away from investigators.	The vehicle was sent to Ford factory in Detroit, and was totally refurbished 3 days after the JFK assassination	Photographic evidence: a bullet hit the windshield that was then replaced in Detroit	Testimony of a senior executive of Ford Motor Company
Government recommendation to the national press (guidelines against the critics of the official lone gunman position): start of the Cover-up.	3 days after the assassination, the new Attorney General under Lyndon Johnson outlined the communication strategy that would prevail: Oswald did it alone without assistance.	Katzenbach's memo of November 25, 1963	
Illegal takeover of JFK's body in Dallas and immediate transportation to Washington D.C. by the Service Secret.	The autopsy should have been performed in Dallas according to the law. It was executed and controlled by military staff at Bethesda Naval Hospital.	Official files from Dallas Parkland Hospital and Bethesda Naval Hospital	
FBI Director, J. Edgar Hoover, fueled the cover-up	Less than 24 hours after the JFK assassination, the FBI charged Oswald despite the lack of evidence.	Transcript of Hoover's phone call to President Johnson	
The x-rays of JFK's skull revealed the presence of explosive bullets fragments whereas Oswald's alleged rifle could only fire medium to low velocity and non-frangible bullets.	Two types of bullets were fired from different weapons based on the x-rays and the bullets fragments found in the presidential car.	Autopsy and x-rays reports.	
The official photographs of the autopsy were doctored.	The occipital part of JFK's skull was "reconstructed" in order to remove the evidence of an exit bullet wound.	Photographs made public and testimonies of medical experts.	
	Lt Commandant William Pitzer (eyewitness attending the autopsy), who was about to disclose this		His relatives' claims and testimony of an officer of the U.S. Army Special Forces.

		forgery, was assassinated.		
The theory of the "Magic Bullet" proved to be a fabrication of the Warren Commission.	In order to cause so many injuries, the "Magic Bullet" or "Single Bullet" had to go through the bodies of JFK and Governor Connally. It was found in a near pristine condition.	Forensic experts. Photograph of the "Single Bullet".		
The U.S. government stone walled the official investigation from District Attorney, Jim Garrison, who sought a connection between key accomplices who plotted the JFK assassination	Obstruction of justice by the CIA and the FBI	Phone tapping. Slanders. Judge's rejection to subpoena witnesses. Discredit by medias.		
Highly doubtful suicide of key witness, David Ferrie, just before being subpoenaed by the Louisiana District Attorney.	David Ferrie was connected to the CIA, the Mafia and Lee Harvey Oswald.	Type written notes of the "suicide" were left on the crime scene with no correlation with Ferrie's death.		
Assassination of the star reporter, Dorothy Kilgallen. Her "suicide" had all the fingerprints of an assassination.	She was the only journalist to have interviewed Jack Ruby in his jail. She claimed that she would reveal tangible evidence of a conspiracy in the JFK assassination in an upcoming book.		Her suicide was staged. It was full of gross negligence from the murderer as reported by her relatives.	
Probable assassination of Lee Bowers.	He was a key eyewitness: from his control tower, just before the shots, the railway worker saw two gunmen ambushed behind the picket fence on Dealey Plaza. The Warren Commission disregarded his testimony but Bowers held firm on what he saw.		Eyewitnesses and a Texas highway police officer stated that they saw a car pushing Bowers' vehicle off the road.	
Assassination of Mary Pinchot Meyer	After the JFK assassination, she claimed that she would soon reveal the CIA-Mafia-Anti Castro plot against the President		CIA killers (under contract and known for their job to eliminate embarrassing individuals) revealed that her murder had all the fingerprints of a CIA operation.	
Assassination of Sam Giancana	The Chicago Mafia godfather was connected to the assassination attempts against Castro and JFK. He was about to be subpoenaed before a Senate commission.		The Chicago Tribune reported the alleged assassination of Sam Giancana by the CIA.	
Assassination of Johnny Roselli.	The Mafia don, with connection to the CIA, was about to testify before a commission charged to investigate his dealings in the assassination attempts	Media reports.		

	against Castro and JFK's murder.		
"Suicide" of George de Mohrenschildt	Key witness with connection to the CIA. He was about to be subpoenaed before the HSCA for his "babysitter" role with Oswald and for the information about him that he regularly provided to the Agency.	Media reports. Investigations.	
The Warren Commission concealed ballistic, medical, photographic evidence and lied to the American people marking the start of the cover-up.	The commission led an investigation in reverse. It finger-pointed a culprit (Oswald) right away and then contrived to have all the clues and evidence match with a preconceived result.	Zapruder's film. Testimonies. In 1997, the Associated Press revealed Gerald Ford's hand written forgery on the Warren Commission report concerning the location of the president's injuries.	
Even today, the U.S. media keep supporting the conclusions of the Warren Report	The CIA endeavored to ignore the evidence of the plot and to control the media.	The control began with a CIA document dated April 1967 and stamped "Destroy after reading". The document gave the media instructions to foil any critics against the Warren report.	
The Role of the Mafia	Carlos Marcello, Santos Trafficante [and Jimmy Hoffa] were all key suspects in the assassination of the President.	Phone tapping by the FBI and FBI documents.	Testimonies, Marcello and Trafficante's "death bed" confessions.
The Role of the CIA and anti-Castro	Enraged by JFK's politics of détente towards Cuba after the failed Bay of Pigs invasion and the Crisis of Cuban Missiles, the CIA turned the plot against the U.S. President in order to blame Cuba for the Dallas assassination thus justifying reprisals.	Investigation of District Attorney Jim Garrison. Memorandum from the U.S. embassy in Mexico City. Robert Kennedy's opinion	
Oil tycoons' financial support (H.L. Hunt)	The oil Texan millionaires were hostile to John Kennedy and it is highly probable that they paid for his assassination.		Testimonies concerning the links between H.L. Hunt and the Mafia.
Collusion with the military-industrial complex	JFK's military advisers strongly opposed his politics of détente towards Cuba and the Soviet Union and his announced withdrawal from Vietnam (a long-lasting war would generate a financial windfall).	The JFK administration meetings were recorded. Communication through letters between JFK and Khrushchev. JFK's confidences.	
The true facts concerning the JFK assassination have not yet been fully published.	The CIA, the FBI and other U.S. government agencies still hold secret	Obstruction to the *Assassination Records Collection Act* issued by	

| | | thousands of classified documents. | the American Congress in 1992. | |

Main Actors

Angleton, James Jesus : head of the CIA counter intelligence from 1954 to 1975.

Attwood, William : JFK presidential campaign aid.

Ball, George : Under Secretary of State during the JFK administration.

Banister, Guy : FBI agent linked to New Orleans Organized Crime.

Batista, Fulgencio : Cuban dictator, evicted from power by Fidel Castro.

Blakey, Robert : American lawyer. House Select Committee on Assassination Chief Counsel.

Castro, Fidel : First Secretary of the Cuban Communist Party.

Church, Frank : Senator who created a sub-committee to investigate the JFK assassination.

Connally, John : Governor of Texas, seriously wounded in the presidential limousine.

Daniel, Jean : French journalist. JFK emissary to Cuba to interview Fidel Castro.

De Mohrenschildt, George : businessman, CIA pseudo agent. He befriended Lee Harvey Oswald.

Dulles, Allen: CIA Director during the administrations of Presidents Eisenhower and Kennedy. Member of the Warren Commission.

Dulles, John Foster : Secretary of State during Dwight Eisenhower's administration.

Ferrie, David : paramilitary officer. As a pilot, he ensured the transportation of people for anti-Castro and Mafia operations.

Ford, Gerald : Member of the Warren Commission then 38th President of the United States.

Garrison, Jim : New Orleans District Attorney who investigated the JFK assassination.

Giancana, Sam : Mafia godfather in Chicago.

Greer, William : Service Secret Agent during the JFK presidency. Driver of the presidential limousine in Dallas.

Harvey, William : CIA Counter Intelligence Specialist.

Helms, Richard : CIA Assistant Director during the JFK administration.

Hill, Clint J. : Service Secret Agent who jumped on the back of the presidential limousine after the gunshots.

Hoffa, Jimmy : Labor Union Leader (Teamsters) who had connection with the Mafia.

Hoover, J. Edgar: FBI Director from 1935 to 1972.

Hunt, Haroldson Lafayette : Texan oil tycoon suspected of having provided financial support for the JFK assassination plot.

Hunt, Howard: CIA Agent. Undisputed master of espionage. He was later involved in the Watergate scandal.

Joannides, George: CIA Agent involved with an influential group of Cuban exiles.

Johnson, Lyndon B. : Vice-President during the Kennedy administration who became the 36th President of the United States of America immediately following JFK's assassination.

Katzenbach, Nicholas: Attorney General during the Johnson administration.

Kennedy, John Fitzgerald (JFK): 35th President of the United States of America.

Kennedy, Robert Francis (RFK): JFK's brother and Attorney General during his presidency. He was assassinated in 1968.

Kilduff, Malcolm : Deputy Press Attaché during the Kennedy Presidency.

Khrouchtchev, Nikita : First Secretary of the Communist Party of the Soviet Union from 1953 to 1964.

McClelland, Robert Dr. : Medical Doctor who attended to President Kennedy at Dallas Parkland Hospital.

McNamara, Robert : Ministry of Defense during the Kennedy Presidency.

McCloy, John : member of the Warren Commission.

McCone, John : CIA Director after the dismissal of Allen Dulles by JFK.

Mankiewicz, Frank : Press Assistant for Robert Kennedy's presidential campaign in 1968.

Marcello, Carlo : Godfather of the Organized Crime in Louisiana and Texas.

O'Donnell, Kenneth : President Kennedy's adviser.

Oswald, Lee Harvey (LHO) : alleged assassin of President Kennedy and of police officer Tippit.

Phillips, David Atlee : CIA Senior Agent. He orchestrated the disinformation campaign during the investigation of the JFK assassination.

Powers, David : President Kennedy's adviser.

Roselli, John : Member of the Organized Crime in Hollywood and Las Vegas.

Ruby, Jack (Rubinstein) : assassin of Lee Harvey Oswald.

Salinger, Pierre : John Kennedy's Press Secretary.

Schlesinger, Arthur : American historian. JFK's friend and adviser.

Schweiker, Richard : Senator of Pennsylvania. He co-chaired the Senate Sub-Committee in charge of investigating the assassination of John Kennedy.

Stevenson, Adlai : Ambassador of the United States at the

United Nations during JFK presidency.

Sprague, Richard : American investigator and author. He first chaired the House Select Committee on Assassinations.

Tannenbaum, Robert : Prosecutor. House Select Committee on Assassinations Deputy Advisor.

Tippit J.D. : Dallas police officer killed within an hour of the JFK assassination. Oswald was arrested by the police allegedly for his murder.

Trafficante, Santo : Mafia godfather in Florida.

Truman, Harry : 33rd President of the United States.

Van Laningham, Jack : FBI agent. He was placed under cover in Marcello's jail cell in order to record the godfather's confidences on his complicity in the JFK assassination plot.

Veciana, Antonio : Anti-Castro activist. He had the CIA support for his activities with Cuban exiles.

Warren, Earl : Judge of the U.S. Supreme Court. Chairman of the Warren Commission.

Yarborough, Ralph : Democratic Senator. Eyewitness of the JFK assassination in Dallas.

Zapruder, Abraham : Dallas tailor who filmed the scene of the JFK assassination on Dealey Plaza.

Timeline

October 1959 : Lee Harvey Oswald leaves the Marine Corps for the Soviet Union.

June 1960: J. Edgar Hoover, the FBI director, is informed of the existence of a "double" Oswald who is seen at the same time in the U.S.A. and in Russia.

September 1960: The Mafia assassination plots against Fidel Castro, with the CIA support, before John Kennedy's presidential inauguration, are reaching full force.

January 1961: John F. Kennedy becomes the 35th President of the United States of America.

April 4, 1961: the two Kennedy brothers order the Mafia Godfather, Carlos Marcello, to be extradited to Guatemala.

April 15-19, 1961: Invasion of the Bay of Pigs in Cuba by Cuban exiles.

August 13, 1961: Berlin Crisis. The Berlin wall is built.

September 1961: start of a private and confidential correspondence through letters between Kennedy and Khrushchev.

May 1962: JFK asks his generals to plan a withdrawal of U.S. military personnel from Vietnam.

June 1962: Oswald leaves the Soviet Union to return to the United States with his Russian wife, Marina.

October 1962: Cuban Missile Crisis

April 21, 1963: Fidel Castro accepts an interview, in Havana, in front of American cameras. He says he is ready to open a dialogue with JFK.

May 6, 1963: JFK drafts a treaty between the U.S.S.R. and the U.S.A. to ban all nuclear tests.

June 10, 1963: JFK delivers a speech on peace during a graduation ceremony at the American University.

August 1963: Oswald distributes procommunist leaflets in the streets of New Orleans for the Fair Play for Cuba Committee.

Beginning of September 1963: CIA agent David Atlee Phillips, aka Maurice Bishop, meets Oswald in Dallas.

September 20, 1963: JFK delivers a speech at the United Nations. He reiterates his vision of pursuing a peace strategy.

September 26, 1963: Oswald travels to South Texas and Mexico.

From September 27, 1963: an American, with no physical resemblance to Oswald but impersonating him, makes several visits to the Cuban embassy in Mexico City. He applies for a transit visa in order to reach the Soviet Union from Cuba.

October 1, 1963: A pseudo Oswald visits the Embassy of the Soviet Union in Mexico City. The embassy staff describes the man without any physical resemblance to the real Oswald.

October 11, 1963: JFK signs a National Security Action Memorandum planning the return of 1,000 military advisers from Vietnam by the end of 1963.

October 16, 1963: Oswald starts his employment at the Texas School Book Depository.

October 24, 1963: JFK emissary, the French journalist Jean Daniel, interviews him at the White House before meeting Fidel Castro: JFK wants to start a dialogue with Fidel Castro and a normalization of the relations between the United States and Cuba.

Beginning of November 1963: Oswald hands over his handwritten note to the Dallas FBI office, whose contents will be kept secret forever. The note is destroyed by the FBI, 2 days after the JFK assassination and a few hours after the murder of Oswald.

November 2, 1963: assassination attempt against JFK in Chicago.

November 18, 1963:
- authorities discover another serious threat to assassinate JFK during his visit to Tampa, Florida.
- JFK delivers a speech at the Inter-American Press Association in Miami. He sets the conditions for a sincere, lasting but conditional rapprochement with Cuba.
- the Soviet embassy in Washington receives a badly typed letter, signed "Lee H. Oswald". This forged document, revealed in 1999, was designed to incriminate the Soviet Union for its alleged connection to Oswald.

November 22, 1963:
- John F. Kennedy is assassinated in Dallas, Texas, at 12:30 p.m. local time.
- Fidel Castro learns the news in his Varadero Beach residence in the company of JFK's emissary for peace, Jean Daniel.
- Lee Harvey Oswald is arrested at 1:50 p.m. at the Texas Theater in the suburbs of Dallas.
- Seth Kantor, a White House correspondent, sees Jack Ruby at the Dallas Parkland Hospital when JFK's death is announced.
- After being subpoenaed in a New Orleans court, Mafia godfather, Carlo Marcello, is acquitted.
- JFK autopsy at Bethesda Naval Hospital, Maryland.

November 23, 1963: Hoover, the FBI director, calls Lyndon Johnson, the new President: He is alarmed by the lack of evidence for Oswald's guilt.

November 24, 1963: at 11:21 am in the Dallas police headquarters, Jack Ruby, a cabaret owner, shoots Oswald, who will die shortly after.

November 26, 1963: President Johnson cancels JFK's initiative to withdraw from Vietnam and orders a massive US military engagement.

December 22, 1963: former President Harry Truman publishes an article in the Washington Post warning the American people of the danger represented by the CIA.

March 1964: Jack Ruby loses his case and is sentenced to death.

September 18, 1964: In a telephone conversation with President Johnson, Senator Russell, a member of the Warren Commission, voices his doubts about some conclusions of the investigation.

September 24, 1964: The Warren Commission submits its report on the investigation of the JFK assassination: Lee Harvey Oswald is the lone killer, without accomplice.

January 3, 1967: Jack Ruby dies of a pulmonary embolism following a fast evolving cancer.

1969: the investigation by New Orleans prosecutor Jim Garrison leads to the trial of Clay Shaw, a CIA-linked businessman, allegedly guilty in the plot to murder JFK. He is nevertheless acquitted.

Beginning of 1975:
- creation of the Rockefeller Commission in charge of investigating the CIA's activities for its assassination plots against Fidel Castro and John Kennedy.
- creation of the US Senate Committee, the Church Committee to investigate the JFK assassination.

March 1975: Abraham Zapruder's film is shown on American television for the first time.

June 1975: Mafia don Johnny Roselli testifies before the Church Committee about the CIA's dealings with Organized Crime and the JFK assassination.

1977-1978: hearings of the House Select Committee on Assassinations, the last U.S. government investigation into the JFK assassination. In 1979, its report concludes a probable conspiracy. The committee is however not able to identify the participants (other than Oswald) nor the extent of the conspiracy.

1991: release of Oliver Stone's "JFK" movie about the JFK assassination plot. Its success awakens the conscience of Americans.

1992:
- The President John F. Kennedy's Assassination Records Act - or JFK Records Act - is passed by the U.S. Congress.
- an independent agency, the Assassination Records Review Board (ARRB) is charged of identifying secret files relating to the JFK assassination and of taking decisions on their publication.

September 1998: the FBI secret operation, coded CAMTEX, started in 1986 (confession of Carlos Marcello that he gave order to kill John Kennedy) is made public.

October 26, 2017: in accordance with the JFK Records Act and with the help of the U.S. National Archives, only a fraction of the classified material about the JFK assassination is published.

Appreciations

To my precious family without which this book could not have been written. Warm thanks to my wife for her encouragement and guidance. Special recognition to my friends for their interest in this project and for their support.

SOURCES AND REFERENCES

John Kennedy's political legacy

BUCHANAN Thomas G., Who Killed Kennedy?, 1964

CARTER Jacob M. – Before History Dies - 2015. World Crafts Press

CARTER Jacob M. – Before History Dies - 2015, Interview of David Scheim

DOUGLASS James W., JFK and the Unspeakable, Why He Died and Why it Matters, A Touchstone Book, 2008

KHRUSHCHEV Sergei N., Nikita Khrushchev and the Creation of a Superpower (University Park, Pa.: Pennsylvania State University Press, 2000).

TALBOT David – Brothers, The Hidden History of the Kennedy Years – 2007

WALDRON Lamar, The Hidden History of the JFK Assassination Counter Point Berkeley, 2013

The "Lone Nuts" against the "Conspiracy Nuts"

CARTER Jacob M. – Before History Dies -2015, Interview of Dan Hardway

HILL Clint J., Five Presidents, My Extraordinary Journey with Eisenhower, Kennedy, Johnson, Nixon and Ford, Gallery Nooks, New-York, 2016, p.178

Report of the President's Commission on the Assassination of President Kennedy – September 24, 1964

TALBOT David, The Mother of All Cover-Ups,

http://www.salon.com/2004/09/15/warren/

https://www.youtube.com/watch?v=No0JSg7wp0Q

The Coup d'État and the Cover-Up

ANDERSON Kevin. "Revelations and gaps on Nixon tapes" March 1, 2002. BBC News.

BUNDY McGeorge, Danger and Survival, 354; Dean Rusk, As I Saw It 246-247

BROWN Walt, Ph. D. – The Warren Omission

CARTER Jacob M. – Before History Dies – 2015, Interview of Jefferson Morley

CARTER Jacob M. – Before History Dies - 2015, Interview of Dan Hardway

CARTER Jacob M. – Before History Dies - 2015, Interview of David Talbot

DOUGLASS James W., JFK and the Unspeakable: Why he died and why it matters. Touchstone 2010.

ESCALANTE Fabian. Cuban Officials and JFK Historians Conference. 7 December 1995

FETZER Ph.D. "Smoking Guns" in the Death of JFK and "Murder in Dealey Plaza"
Findings of the Select Committee on Assassinations in the Assassination of President John F. Kennedy in Dallas, Tex., November 22, 1963, Section C

GRIFFITH Michael T.: Suspects in the JFK Assassination. December 9, 2002

GRODEN Robert J. and LINGSTONE Harrison Edward. High Treason: The assassination of JFK. What really happened? The Conservatory Press, 1989

GRODEN Robert J., The Killing of a President, Vicking Studio Books, 1993

HORNE Douglas P., referencing Doug Weldon. "Photographic Evidence of Bullet Hole in JFK Limousine Windshield Hiding in Plain Sight. June 2012

JOESTEN Joachim. How Kennedy Was Killed (Dawnay, Tandem; 1968)

KELLY William. "November 21, 1963. The Cabana Motor Hotel, Dallas, Texas". October 27, 1998

MORLEY Jefferson – Charles Briggs, retired CIA officer who assisted JFK museum, was accused of deception by a federal judge. JFKfacts.org, 7 November 2015.
MORROW Robert D. First Hand Knowledge: How I Participated in the CIA-Mafia Murder of President Kennedy (S.P.I. Books: 1992)

PALAMARA Vince, Survivor's Guilt, The United States Secret Service: conspiracy to assassinate a President, Carrier

PALAMARA Vince: kennedydetailkennedydetailkennedy.blogspot.com/2012/08/updated-jfk-did-not-order-agents-off.html

RUSSELL Dick. The Man Who Knew Too Much.

SORRELLS Forest – Secret Service Report Special Agent in Charge – 28 November 1963

TALBOT David, The Mother of All Cover-Ups, http://www.salon.com/2004/09/15/warren/

TALBOT David – Brothers, The Hidden History of the Kennedy Years - 2007

VENTURA Jesse – They Killed Our President – 2013. Skyhorse Publishing, Inc.

WALDRON Lamar and HARTMANN Thom–Ultimate Sacrifice– (New York: Carroll & Graf, 2005)

WALDRON Lamar - The Hidden History of the JFK Assassination. 2013. Counterpoint

WASHINGTON Post, January 19, 1970.

WIDNER Ted. JFK's Secret White House Recordings Unveiled" September 5, 2012

http://22november1963.org.uk/richard-russell-warren-report

https://www.youtube.com/watch?v=XY02Qkuc_f8

http://mcadams.posc.mu.edu/route.htm

The Witnesses' reactions on Dealey Plaza

CURRY Jesse E., Retired Dallas Police Chief, Jesse Curry, reveals his personal JFK Assassination File (self-published 1969)

DOUGLASS James W., JFK and the Unspeakable, Why He Died and Why it Matters, A Touchstone Book, 2008

FIESTER Sherry P. – Enemy of the Truth, Myths, Forensics and the Kennedy Assassination –
JFK Lancer Productions & Publications, Inc. 2012

GRODEN Robert J. and LIVINGSTONE Harrison Edward. High Treason: The assassination of JFK. What really happened? The Conservatory Press, 1989

GALANOR Stewart, "The Art and Science of Misrepresenting Evidence: How the Warren Commission and the House Select Committee on Assassinations manipulated evidence to dismiss witness accounts of the assassination," retrieved 14 April 2013: historymatters.com/analysis/Witness/artScience.htm

HAYGOOD Clyde, "Testimony of Clyde A. Haygood to the President's Commission (Warren Commission) 9 April 1964. Jfkassassination.net/russ/testimony/haygood.htm

JFKfacts.org

TAGUE James, "Eyewitness Statement of James Tague," retrieved 14 April 2013:karws.gso.uri.edu/jfk/History/The deed/Sneed/Tague.html

WALDRON Lamar, The Hidden History of the JFK Assassination, Counter Point Berkeley, 2013

http://mcadams.posc.mu.edu/rambler.txt

The Fourth Estate under Control

BAKER Russ & CRANOR Milicent – The Mystery of the Constant Flow of JFK Disinformation – November 24, 2013

BERNSTEIN Carl, The CIA and the Media

CARTER Jacob M. – Before History Dies - 2015, Interview of David Talbot

CIA Document # 1035-960. "RE; Concerning Criticism of the Warren Report". 1 April 1967.

Citizens for Truth about the Kennedy Assassination, "The MSM and RFK Jr: only 45 Years Late this Time" February 3, 2013: ctka.net/2013/The_MSM_and_RFKJr.html

DOUGLASS James W., JFK and the Unspeakable, Why He Died and Why it Matters, A Touchstone Book, 2008

FANNIN Gary, The Innocence of Oswald, 2015

FETZER Ph.D. "Smoking Guns" in the Death of JFK et "Murder in Dealey Plaza"

FIESTER Sherry P. – Enemy of the Truth, Myths, Forensics and the Kennedy Assassination – JFK Lancer Productions

& Publications, Inc. 2012 gaylenixjackson.com/Research/CIA-Memo-Warren-Commission.pdf

GRODEN Robert J. and LIVINGSTONE Harrison Edward. High Treason: The assassination of JFK. What really happened? The Conservatory Press, 1989

GRODEN Robert J., The Killing of a President, Vicking Studio Books, 1993

HENNELLY Robert and POLICOFF Jerry - JFK: how the media assassinated the real story. 2002.

KOSNER Edward, The Curse of the Zapruders, The Wall Street Journal, November 12-13, 2016

LOUISE Mary, "Operation Mockingbird: CIA Media Manipulation". 2003

POLICOFF Jerry, "The Media and the Murder of John Kennedy". August 8, 1975

TALBOT David – Brothers, The Hidden History of the Kennedy Years - 2007

TALBOT David, The Mother of All Cover-Ups, http://www.salon.com/2004/09/15/warren/

The American Media – The 2nd Assassination of President John F. KennedyUnited States Senate. Final Report, Select Committee to Study Governmental Operations with Respect to Intelligence Activities. April 1976.

VENTURA Jesse – They Killed Our President – 2013. Skyhorse Publishing, Inc.

VENTURA and RUSSELL. American Conspiracy, p 38

WALDRON Lamar,The Hidden History of the JFK Assassination Counter Point Berkeley, 2013

Who Owns the Media? Free Press.
www.freepress.net/ownership/chart

WOODWORTH Elizabeth, "JFK, MLK, RFK, 50 Years of Suppressed History: New Evidence on Assassination of John F. Kennedy, Martin Luther King and Robert F. Kennedy"
April 5, 2013

http://triblive.com/opinion/qanda/3292514-74/commission-kennedy-warren#ixzz2MjNJAkPy

http://us.cnn.com/2013/11/14/us/jfk-assassination-5-things/index.html

http://www.nbcnews.com/id/18941406/ns/msnbc-hardball_with_chris_matthews/t/hardball-chris-matthews-may/#.Vk-9ifmrTIV

http://www.accesshollywood.com/videos/chris-matthews-talks-jfk-assassination-conspiracies-44633/

http://articles.latimes.com/2013/nov/22/entertainment/la-et-st-chris-matthews-jfk-50-years-assassination-20131122

http://www.mediaite.com/tv/a-guide-to-all-the-jfk-specials-that-will-air-on-tv-this-month/

https://www.youtube.com/watch?v=kwMCIe2AGW8

http://www.carlbernstein.com/magazine_cia_and_media.php

https://www.maryferrell.org/showDoc.html?docId=62268#=29&tab=page

https://consortiumnews.com/2016/04/22/how-cbs-news-aided-the-jfk-cover-up/

http://www.jfklancer.com/CIA.html

http://www.justice-integrity.org/index.php?option=com_content&view=article&id=618:june-news-reports-2012&catid=93:june-2012&Itemid=10

http://www.justice-integrity.org/index.php?option=com_content&view=article&id=599:jfk-s-murder-the-cia-8-things-every-american-should-know&catid=21:myblog&itemid=114

http://www.justice-integrity.org/index.php?option=com_content&view=article&id=636:investigative-reporter-implicates-wikipedia-in-smear-campaign&catid=21&Itemid=114%20%20%20

http://www.bbc.com/news/technology-28481876

http://www.boilingfrogspost.com/2014/01/10/bfp-exclusive-interview-with-andrew-kreig-the-cia-global-empire-the-u-s-presidency/

http://www.justice-integrity.org/index.php?option=com_content&view=article&id=584:self-censorship-in-jfk-tv-treatments-duplicates-corporate-print-media-s-apathy-cowardice&catid=21&Itemid=114%20

http://www.justice-integrity.org/faq/896-beware-of-wrong-conclusions-from-new-cia-disclosure-on-Oswald

https://freedomhouse.org/report/freedom-press/2015/united-states

http://ap-gfkpoll.com/featured/five-decades-after-jfks-assassination-the-lucrative-conspiracy-theory-industry-hums-along

http://whowhatwhy.org/2012/02/23/the-jfk-factor-bill-oreilly-on-the-assassination-then-and-now/

https://whowhatwhy.org/2017/02/16/dr-cyril-wecht-jfks-murder-coup-detat-america/

The Enigmatic Lee Harvey Oswald

ARMSTRONG John, Harvey and Lee: How the CIA Framed Oswald (Quasar: 2003)

ARMSTRONG John – Harvey and Lee: "The Magic Tonsillectomy, Vanishing Scars" mindserpent.com

BAKER Judyth Vary. "Oswald Framed: Convenient Lies and Cover-Ups" June 29, 2011.

BELZER Richard & WAYNE David, Hit List, MJF Books New York, 2013, p 8

BELZER Richard & WAYNE David, Dead Wrong.

BRUSSELL Mae, The Last Words of Lee Harvey Oswald

CARTER Jacob M. – Before History Dies - 2015

CARTER Jacob M. – Before History Dies - 2015, Interview of Jefferson Morley

CARTER Jacob M. – Before History Dies - 2015, Interview of David Talbot

DiEUGENIO James & PEASE Lisa – The Assassinations: Probe Magazine on JFK, MLK, RFK & Malcolm X (Feral House 2003, p 131
DOUGLASS James W., JFK and the Unspeakable, Why He Died

and Why it Matters, A Touchstone Book, 2008

FANNIN Gary, The Innocence of Oswald, 2015

GARRISON Jim; On the Trail of the Assassin: My Investigation and Prosecution of the Murder of President Kennedy (Sheridan square 1988).

GRIFFITH Michael T. – Was Oswald's Palm Print Planted on the Alleged Murder Weapon? 2012

GRIFFITH Michael T.; "Did Oswald Shoot Tippit?" A review of Dale Myer's book "With Malice: Lee Harvey Oswald and the Murder of Officer J.D.Tippit" 2002.

GRODEN Robert J. and LIVINGSTONE Harrison Edward. High Treason: The assassination of JFK. What really happened? The Conservatory Press, 1989

GRODEN Robert J., The Killing of a President, Vicking Studio Books, 1993

GRODEN Robert J. – The search for Lee Harvey Oswald

HANCOCK Larry. Someone Would Have Talked (JFK Lancer 2010), jfkfacts.org. The Mary Ferrell Foundation

KREIG Andrew
http://www.justice-integrity.org/index.php?option=com_content&view=article&id=599:jfk-s-murder-the-cia-8-things-every-american-should-know&catid=21:myblog&itemid=114

LEWIS Anthony - Warren Commission Finds Oswald Guilty and Says Assassin and Ruby Acted Alone. The New York Times 27 September 1964.

LIVINGSTONE Harrison; High Treason 2 (Carroll & Graf: 1992)

MARRS Jim – Crossfire: The Plot that Killed Kennedy (Carroll & Graf: 1989), citing Dallas Morning News, Nov. 6, 1969

MAY Hoke. "Simple Enciphering System Used to Encode Oswald Notebook – DA. New Orleans States-Item, 13 May 1967.

O'TOOLE George; The Assassination Tapes: An electronic probe into the Murder of John F. Kennedy and the Dallas Cover-up (Penhouse Press, 1975).

PATOSKI Joe Nick; 'The Witnesses: What They Saw Then, Who They Are Now". Texas Monthly. November 1998

PLUMLEE William Robert, interview with author Jesse Ventura, 12 June 2006

PROUTY Colonel L. Fletcher. "The Col. L. Fletcher Prouty Reference Site" retrieved 23 April 2013: prouty.org/

SAVAGE Gary, JFK: The First Day Evidence (The Shoppe Press: 1993) p 105-106

SIMKIN John; Acquilla Clemons: Biography. Spartacus Educational, 30 Sept 2012

SUMMERS Anthony, "Interview with Victor Marchetti" in John Simkin, "Lee Harvey Oswald: Biography, "Spartacus Educational, retrieved 22 April 2013.

SUMMERS Anthony.Conspiracy.Who Killed President Kennedy Gollancz, May 1980

SUMMERS Anthony & SWANN Robyn;The Arrogance of Power (Penguin Books: 2001)

SUMMERS Anthony - The Kennedy Conspiracy? (Sphere Books: 2007), 64

TALBOT David , Brothers, The Hidden History of the Kennedy Years – 2007 p 381

VENTURA Jesse – They Killed Our President – 2013. Skyhorse Publishing

WALDRON Lamar,The Hidden History of the JFK Assassination, Counter Point Berkeley, 2013

Warren Report, New York Times ed. p 367; p 613-14

www.dealey.org/updown.pdf

http://www.wnd.com/2013/10/girl-on-the-stairs-refutes-pc-jfk-narrative/

http://22november1963.org.uk/lee-oswald-speech-in-alabama

http://reopenkennedycase.forumotion.net/t1382-caster-and-the-two-rifles

The Murky Role of the CIA, the FBI and the anti-Castro

Alleged Assassination Plots Against Foreign Leaders". Interim report of the Select Committee to Study Governmental Operations with Respect to Intelligence Activities, The United States Senate .Final Report April 23, 1976

BROWN Walt, Ph.D. "Actions Speak Much Louder Than Words" What exactly did Johnson and Hoover do? JFK Deep Politics Quarterly Vol. 17 #4, July 2012

CARTER Jacob M. – Before History Dies - 2015, Interview of David Talbot

CARTER Jacob M. – Before History Dies - 2015, Interview of Jefferson Morley

CONWAY Debra, "US-Cuba Relations: Castro Assassinations Plots" November 2007

DAVY William. Let Justice Be Done: New Light on Jim Garrison Investigation (Jordan Pub: 1999)

DOUGLASS James W., JFK and the Unspeakable, Why He Died and Why it Matters, A Touchstone Book, 2008

FENSTERWALD Bernard, p 510, June 23, 1972, White House Transcript between Haldeman and Nixon.

FERNSTERWALD Bernard & EWING Michael; Assassination of JFK: Coincidence or Conspiracy? (Kensington Pub Corp 1977)

GRODEN Robert J. and LIVINGSTONE Harrison Edward. High Treason: The assassination of JFK. What really happened? The Conservatory Press, 1989

GRODEN Robert J., The Killing of a President, Vicking Studio Books, 1993

HALDEMAN H.R., The Ends of Power. November 1978 P 68-69

HANCOCK Larry. Someone Would Have Talked (JFK Lancer 2010), jfkfacts.org. The Mary Ferrell Foundation

HANCOCK Larry – Someone Would Have Talked: The Assassination of President John F. Kennedy and the Conspiracy to Mislead History (JFK Lancer 2006), (JFK Lancer 2010), jfkfacts.org. The Mary Ferrell Foundation.

HSCA, House Select Committee on Assassinations P 153-171

KREIG Andrew. http://www.justice-integrity.org/index.php?option=com_content&view=article&id=599:jfk-s-murder-the-cia-8-things-every-american-should-know&catid=21:myblog&itemid=114

LARDNER George, File on JFK Assassination was Rifled by CIA Officer, International Herald Tribune, 1978

MAHONEY Richard. The Kennedy Brothers: The Rise and the Fall of Jack and Bobby (Skyhorse Publishing): 2011

MARRS Jim, Crossfire. The Plot That Killed JFK

MEAGHER Sylvia; Accessories After The Fact: The Warren Commission, The Authorities and The Report (Random House 1988)

MELLEN Joan. A Farewell to Justice: Jim Garrison, JFK's Assassination and the Case That Should Have Changed History (Potomac Books: 2005)

MORLEY Jefferson, "Oswald's handler? What Morley vs CIA clarified" April 2013

MORLEY, Jefferson http://jfkfacts.org/tag/washington-post/

MORLEY and SCOTT: Our Man in Mexico: Winston Scott and the Hidden History of the CIA

RUSSELL Dick. On the Trail of the JFK Assassins (Skyhorse Publishing: 2008)

RUSSELL. The Man Who Knew Too Much p 309.

SCOTT: The CIA, the Drug Traffic and Oswald in Mexico. 1999. Senate Watergate Committee Report p 126-7 & Coincidence or Conspiracy p 526

SIMKIN John, "Jefferson Morley: Biography"

SUMMERS Anthony, The Kennedy Conspiracy?, p 386

SUMMERS Anthony. Conspiracy. Who Killed President

Kennedy, Gollancz, May 1980

TALBOT David – Brothers, The Hidden History of the Kennedy Years - 2007

TALBOT David. "Case Closed? A new book about the JFK assassination claims to finally solve the mystery" December 2005

VENTURA Jesse – They Killed Our President – 2013. Skyhorse Publishing

WALDRON Lamar & HARTMANN Thom. Ultimate Sacrifice

WALDRON Lamar, The Hidden History of the JFK Assassination, Counter Point Berkeley, 2013

White House Transcripts of President Lyndon B. Johnson" November 23. 1963.

WILKES Donald E. Jr, Professor of Law. "Destiny Betrayed: the CIA, Oswald and the JFK Assassination. December 7, 2005

http://jfkfacts.org/tag/washington-post/

http://jfkfacts.org/faith-overwhelms-facts-aps-un-journalism-on-jfks-assassination/

http://www.politico.com/story/2015/05/why-last-of-jfk-files-could-embarrass-cia-118233

http://www.maryferrell.org/showDoc.html?docId=1565#relPageId=2&tab=page

https://www.history-matters.com/archive/jfk/lbjlib/phone_calls/Nov_1963/html/LBJ-Nov-1963_0030a.htm

https://archive.org/stream/nsia-SchweikerRichardSenator

/nsia- SchweikerRichardSenator/Schweiker%20Richard%20S%20048_djvu.txt

The Vindictive Mafia

BLAKEY G. Robert, Chief Counsel and Staff Director, Gary T. Cornwell, Deputy Chief Counsel & Michael Ewing, Researcher. Appendices to Final Report of Select Committee on Assassinations. U.S. House of Representatives. January 2, 1979

CARTER Jacob M. – Before History Dies - 2015, Interview of David Talbot

CARTER Jacob M. – Before History Dies - 2015, Interview of David Scheim

FBI Document 124-10182-10430. Bradley S. O'Leary & L.E. Seymour. Triangle of Death. Waldron &Hartmann. Ultimate Sacrifice

GRODEN Robert J. and LIVINGSTONE Harrison Edward. High Treason: The assassination of JFK. What really happened? The Conservatory Press, 1989

JONES Thomas L. "Big Daddy in the Big Easy" Crime Library.

RAGANO Frank and RAAB Selwyn. Mob Lawyer. Waldron and Hartmann. Ultimate Sacrifice

RAGANO Frank & RAAB Selwyn. Mob lawyer (Random House Value 1996)

SIFAKIS Carl. The Mafia Encyclopedia (Facts on File: 1999)

SUMMERS Anthony. Official and Confidential: The Secret Life of J. Edgar Hoover (Ebury: 2012)

VENTURA Jesse – They Killed Our President – 2013. Skyhorse Publishing, Inc.

WALDRON Lamar, The Hidden History of the JFK Assassination, Counter Point Berkeley, 2013

http://www.comingsoon.net/movie/legacy-of-secrecy-2013#EG6sYmRZ2ErKvLwu.99

Jack Ruby's Contract

BELZER Richard & WAYNE David, Hit List, MJF Books New York, 2013

CARTER Jacob M. – Before History Dies - 2015, Interview of David Talbot

DiEugenio James, "JFK: The Ruby Connection" Citizens for Truth about the Kennedy Assassination.

DOUGLASS James W., JFK and the Unspeakable, Why He Died and Why it Matters, A Touchstone Book, 2008

EDDOWES Michael, "Nov 22. How They Killed Kennedy", Neville Spearman (Jersey) Limited, 1976.

GRODEN Robert J., The Killing of a President, Vicking Studio Books, 1993

GRODEN Robert J. and LIVINGSTONE Harrison Edward. High Treason: The assassination of JFK. What really happened?
The Conservatory Press, 1989
HSCA Final Assassination Report, House Select Committee on Assassinations p 157-158

JFK Lancer; Jim Garrison's Playboy Interview. Part three. Jfklancer.com/Garrison4.html

RUBY Jack Press Conference, YouTube, http://www.youtube.com/watch?v=we2eucWXqjg

TALBOT David – Brothers, The Hidden History of the Kennedy Years – 2007

VENTURA Jesse – They Killed Our President – 2013. Skyhorse Publishing

WALDRON Lamar, The Hidden History of the JFK Assassination, Counter Point Berkeley, 2013

The Ballistic Evidence

CARTER Jacob M. – Before History Dies - 2015, Interview of Jefferson Morley

CARTER Jacob M. Interview of David Talbot – Before History Dies – 2015.

Cyrilwecht.com/journal/archives/jfk/index.php.

DOUGLASS James W., JFK and the Unspeakable, Why He Died and Why it Matters, A Touchstone Book, 2008

FEINSILBER Mike. "Gerald Ford forced to admit the Warren Report fictionalized" July 2, 1997. Associated Press.

FIESTER Sherry P., Enemy of the Truth, Myths, Forensics and the Kennedy Assassination, JFK Lancer Productions & Publications. 2012

GRODEN Robert J., The Killing of a President, Vicking Studio

Books, 1993

GRODEN Robert J. and LIVINGSTONE Harrison Edward.High Treason:The assassination of JFK. What really happened? The Conservatory Press, 1989

HILL Clint J., Five Presidents; My Extraordinary Journey with Eisenhower, Kennedy, Johnson, Nixon and Ford, Gallery Nooks New-York, 2016, p.178

House Select Committee on Assassinations. Interview of Special Agent Thomas Lem Johns. 8 August 1978

jfkfacts.org/jfk-truth-first-shot/#more-24229

LANDIS Paul – Statement of United States Secret Service Special Agent Paul E. Landis – 27 November 1963

PALAMARA Vince, Survivor's Guilt

ROBERTS Craig – Kill Zone: A Sniper Looks at Dealey Plaza. – 1994. Consolidated Press

SAVAGE Gary – JFK: First Day Evidence (The Shoppe Press: 1993) p 158

SHAW Gary and HARRIS Larry, Cover-Up, self-published 1976 p. 72-74

SORRELLS Forest – Secret Service Report Special Agent in Charge – 28 November 1963

SUMMERS Anthony. The Listener: 9 March 1978
TALBOT David – Brothers, The Hidden History of the Kennedy Years – 2007

THOMPSON Josiah, Six Seconds in Dallas: A Micro-Study of the Kennedy Assassination. 1967

VENTURA Jesse – They Killed Our President – 2013. Skyhorse Publishing

WALDRON Lamar - The Hidden History of the JFK Assassination. 2013. Counterpoint

White House tapes of September 18, 1964 at 7.54 pm cited in Donald E. Wilkes, Jr. Professor Law in "JFK Killer Not Alone".

https://ratical.org/ratville/JFK/PG/PGchp3.html

http://www.nbcnews.com/id/18941406/ns/msnbc-hardball_with_chris_matthews/t/hardball-chris-matthews-may/#.Vk-9ifmrTIV

The Medical Evidence

AGUILAR Gary L., M.D. John F. Kennedy's Fatal Wounds: The Witnesses and the Interpretations From 1963 to the Present/. August 1994, Electronic Assassinations Newsletter.

CARTER Jacob M. – Before History Dies - 2015, Interview of Robert McClelland

DOUGLASS James W., JFK and the Unspeakable, Why He Died and Why it Matters, A Touchstone Book, 2008

FIESTER Sherry P. – Enemy of the Truth, Myths, Forensics and the Kennedy Assassination – JFK Lancer Productions & Publications, Inc. 2012

GRODEN Robert J. and LIVINGSTONE Harrison Edward. High Treason: The assassination of JFK. What really happened? The Conservatory Press, 1989

KOSNER Edward, The Curse of the Zapruders, The Wall Street Journal, November 12-13, 2016

TALBOT David, – Brothers, The Hidden History of the Kennedy Years – 2007

VENTURA Jesse – They Killed Our President – 2013. Skyhorse Publishing

WALDRON Lamar, The Hidden History of the JFK Assassination, Counter Point Berkeley, 2013

http://jfkfacts.org/faith-overwhelms-facts-aps-un-journalism-on-jfks-assassination/

http://jamesfetzer.blogspot.fr/2012/03/what-happened-to-jfks-body-cover-up-on.html

The Photographic Evidence

BERNSTEIN Carl, The CIA and The Media, The Rolling Stone

GRODEN Robert J., The Killing of a President, Vicking Studio Books, 1993

GRODEN Robert J. and LIVINGSTONE Harrison Edward. High Treason: The assassination of JFK. What really happened? The Conservatory Press, 1989
HEINER Kent. Without Smoking Gun: Was the Death of Lieutenant Commander William Pitzer Part of the JFK Assassination Cover-up Conspiracy?

HENNELLY Robert and POLICOFF Jerry - JFK: how the media assassinated the real story. 2002.

http://www.assassinationresearch.com/v1n2/mediaassassination.html

HORNE, Inside the Assassinations Records Review Board.

LARDNER George Jr., Archive Photos Not of JFK's Brain, Concludes Aide to Review Board. Washington Post. November 10, 1998

MANTIK David W., M.D, Ph. D." The JFK Autopsy Materials: Twenty Conclusions after Nine Visits". November 20-23, 2003:assassinationresearch.com/v2n2/Pittsburgh.pdf

PARKER. First on the Scene: Interviews with Parkland Doctors.

RIECHMANN Deb, Newly Released JFK Documents Raise Questions About Medical Evidence,Washington Post,November 9, 1998

ROONEY Brian. Burying the Truth. Book Review of Doug Horne's Epic Effort. April 2010. JFK: Deep Politics Quarterly.

VENTURA Jesse – They Killed Our President – 2013. Skyhorse Publishing

WALDRON Lamar, The Hidden History of the JFK Assassination, Counter Point Berkeley, 2013

Youtube.com/watch?v=jWHdEeHNbXY

The Acoustic Evidence

BLAKEY Prof. G. Robert – The HSCA and the CIA: The View from the Trenches and the View from the Top.
http://aarclibrary.org/aarc-2014-conference-videos/

GRODEN Robert J. and LIVINGSTONE Harrison Edward. High Treason: The assassination of JFK. What really happened? The Conservatory Press, 1989

KELLY William E, "Dealey Plaza Echo Analysis-Acoustical Forensics 101," November 22, 2010: jfkcountercoup.blogspot.com/2010/11/dealey-plaza-echos.html

LARDNER George Jr., House to Re-Explore Evidence of Kennedy Death Conspiracy. International Herald Tribune, Dec 22, 1978

US House of Representatives, "Report of the Select Committee on Assassinations, Ninety-fifth Congress, second session" 1979

VENTURA Jesse – They Killed Our President – 2013. Skyhorse Publishing

Inconvenient Witnesses. Mysterious Disappearances

ANDERSON Jack & WHITTEN Les; Behind John F. Kennedy's Murder, September 7, 1976. The Washington Post

BAKER Russ, Family of Secrets. The Bush Dynasty, America's Invisible Government, and the Hidden History of the Last Fifty Years. 2008.

BELZER Richard and WAYNE David; Hit List, An in-Depth Investigation into the Mysterious Deaths of Witnesses to the JFK Assassination. Fine Communications 2013.

BRANDT Charles; "I heard You Paint Houses". Frank "The Irishman" Sheeran and the Inside Story of the Mafia, the

Teamsters and the Last Ride of Jimmy Hoffa. Steer forth Press: 2005.

CHARNIN Richard, "JFK Assassination; A probability Analysis of Unnatural Witness Deaths". 18 May 2012

EAGLESHAM Allan R.J. & PALMER R. Robin. The Untimely Death of Lieutenant Commander William B. Pitzer: The Physical Evidence. January 1998.

FORD President Gerald R.; President John F. Kennedy: Assassination Report of the Warren Commission. Flat signed Press: 2005

FREED Don, COOKSON Jim & COHEN Jeff; Jack Ruby: I was framed to kill Oswald! May 1975

GARISSON Jim. On the Trial of the Assassins, 138.

GIANCANA Sam; Biography.

GIANCANA Hughes, DM Oxon. *JFK and Sam*

GRODEN Robert J. and LIVINGSTONE Harrison Edward. High Treason: The assassination of JFK and the Case for Conspiracy (Carroll & Graf: 1998).

HASLAM Edward T., Dr Mary's Monkey, 2014

HEINER. Without Smoking Gun
House Select Committee on Assassinations, "HSCA Final Assassinations Report" p 157-158
HSCA, House Select Committee on Assassinations P186, 132

JANNEY'S Peter. Mary's Mosaic. 2012

JORDAN Sara. Who Killed Dorothy Kilgallen? October 21, 2007. Midwest Today

LANE Mark., G de Mohrenschidt. The Security Alarm.

MARVIN Dan. "Bits and Pieces: A Green Beret on the Periphery of the JFK Assassination" May 1995.

ROBERTS Craig & ARMSTRONG John.JFK:The Dead Witnesses (Cumberland Press International: 1994), p 105

RUSSEL Dick. The Man Who Knew Too Much. P 456

SIMKIN John. "Lee E. Bowers: Biography". Spartacus Educational

SIMKIN John. "William Pitzer: Biography" Spartacus International

SUMMERS Anthony. The Kennedy conspiracy.

TALBOT David, – Brothers, The Hidden History of the Kennedy Years – 2007

VENTURA Jesse – They Killed Our President – 2013. Skyhorse Publishing

WALDRON Lamar, The Hidden History of the JFK Assassination, Counter Point Berkeley, 2013

Washington Post. Cmdr William B. Pitzer, Head of Navy TV Unit" November 2, 1966

https://richardcharnin.wordpress.com/2013/10/14/jfk-witness-deaths-graphical-proof-of-a-conspiracy/

http://cancerres.aacrjournals.org/content/25/4_Part_1/565.short

https://www.ncbi.nlm.nih.gov/pmc/articles/PMC1266403/

Can the Media's Apathy be justified?

BAKER Russ & CRANOR Milicent – The Mystery of the Constant Flow of JFK Disinformation – November 24, 2013

CARTER Jacob M. – Before History Dies - 2015, Interview of Jefferson Morley

HENNELLY Robert and POLICOFF Jerry - JFK: how the media assassinated the real story. 2002.

http://www.assassinationresearch.com/v1n2/mediaassassination.html

Interview of David Talbot by Jacob M. Carter – Before History Dies. 2015, p35-36.

KREIG Andrew
http://www.justice-integrity.org/index.php?option=com_content&view=article&id=584:self-censorship-in-jfk-tv-treatments-duplicates-corporate-print-media-s-apathy-cowardice&catid=21&Itemid=114%20

KREIG Andrew, Self-Censorship in JFK TV Treatments Duplicates Corporate Print Media's Apathy, Cowardice.

KREIG Andrew: Who Are The Puppet Masters That Control The Media And Politicians?
https://www.popularresistance.org/who-are-the-puppets-that-control-the-media-and-politicians/

Pittsburgh City Paper, Don't call them conspiracy theorists: JFK assassination experts come to Pittsburgh, Rebecca Nuttall, Oct. 18, 2013

SUMMERS Anthony. The Kennedy Conspiracy. P 376

TALBOT David, The Mother of All Cover-Ups, http://www.salon.com/2004/09/15/warren/

TALBOT David – Brothers, The Hidden History of the Kennedy Years – 2007

http://jfkfacts.org/cognitive-dissonance-overpowers-the-50th-anniversary-of-the-warren-commission/

Yes, we do want to know!

BAKER Russ, "Is The Government Holding Back Crucial Documents?" May 30, 2012

CARTER Jacob M. – Before History Dies - 2015, Interview of David Talbot

FANNIN Gary, The Innocence of Oswald, 2015

KELLY William, "Playing Politics with History – The Still Secret JFK Assassination Records 20 years after the JFK Act".

MORLEY Jefferson, CIA & JFK: The Secret Assassinations Files, Kindle edition.

TALBOT David – Brothers, The Hidden History of the Kennedy Years - 2007

http://www.maryferrell.org/pages/Featured_Mark_the_Date.html

https://www.maryferrell.org/pages/Featured_What_Happened_Thursday.html

https://www.maryferrell.org/showDoc.html?docId=1386#relPageId=20&tab=page

http://www.politico.com/story/2015/05/why-last-of-jfk-files-could-embarrass-cia-118233

https://www.congress.gov/bill/102nd-congress/senate-bill/3006

https://www.salon.com/2018/01/01/the-new-jfk-files-reveal-how-the-cia-tracked-oswald_partner/

Printed in Great Britain
by Amazon